FROM PURITANISM TO PLATONISM
IN SEVENTEENTH CENTURY
ENGLAND

by

JAMES DEOTIS ROBERTS, Sr.

MARTINUS NIJHOFF / THE HAGUE / 1968

PRINTED IN THE NETHERLANDS

To My Parents; Inspirers of Faith

FOREWORD

The research of Professor J. D. Roberts has interested me for several years. It has interested me because he has been working in a really rich area of intellectual history. Even before Professor Whitehead taught us to speak of the seventeenth century as the "century of genius," many of us looked with wonder on the creativity of the men who produced religious and philosophical literature in that period of controversy and of power. It was, in a most unusual way, a flowering time of the human spirit.

The present volume is devoted to one fascinating chapter in the history of ideas. We know now, far better than we knew a generation ago, how incendiary Puritan ideas really were. They had tremendous consequences, many of which continue to this day, in spite of the absurd caricature of Puritanism, which is popularly accepted. The best of Milton's contemporaries were great thinkers as well as great doers. Some of them were Puritans and Platonists at the same time, exhibiting a wonderful union of mind and heart, which men of later generations might well envy and seek to emulate. Since we do not know enough about these intellectual giants, we are naturally grateful to any scholar who increases our acquaintance and understanding of them. If honest men were able to be both Christians and Platonists at the same time, we want to know how the combination was achieved. It has been the purpose of Professor Roberts, in his painstaking research, to give a rational answer to this and to related questions.

I welcome the present volume and solicit for it a careful scrutiny.

D. ELTON TRUEBLOOD

TABLE OF CONTENTS

FOREWORD by Professor D. ELTON TRUEBLOOD   VII

PREFACE   XIII

LIST OF ABBREVIATIONS   XVII

I. BENJAMIN WHICHCOTE: A MAN OF GOOD-NATURE   I
His Childhood. Life as a Student. Ordination and Campus Ministry.
Tutor at Emmanuel College. Parish Ministry at Somersetshire. Pro-
vost of King's College. The Collin's Incident and the Covenant. Which-
cote Meets Anthony Tuckney. Ministry at Milton. Vice-Chancellor at
Cambridge University. Whichote and Cromwell. Town and Gown
During Civil Strife. The Whichcote-Fleetwood Incident. Whichcote
and Lord Lauderdale. Whichcote's Dismissal from the University.
Ministry in London. At St. Anne's Blackfriars. Whichcote and Bishop
Wilkins of Chester. At St. Lawrence Jewry. Whichcote's Death. Tillotson's Eulogy.

II. FROM ATHENS TO CAMBRIDGE   17
The Insights of Socrates and Plato. Aristotle as The Philosopher.
Cicero the Stoic (Tully). The Philonic Synthesis. The Christian Plato-
nists of Alexandria. His Use of Plotinus. The Augustinian Metaphysic
of Light. Renaissance Platonism. Ficino and Whichcote. English
Humanism. Colet and Erasmus. The Socinian and Arminian Reaction
to the Reformation. Oxford Rational Theologians. Tuckney as Vice-
Chancellor of Cambridge University. Hooker and Whichcote. Bacon's
Novum Organum. Hobbes. Locke. Descartes. Chillingworth. Jeremy
Taylor and Edward Stillingfleet.

III. CONTROVERSY WITH A PURITAN   42
Puritanism as a Politico-Theological Force. The Revolt of the Masses
and the Westminister Divines. Emmanuel College as the Cradle of
Puritanism. Whichcote Rejects the Calvinism of Puritanism. Pro-
nouncements of the Westminister Assembly. On Scripture. On the
Light of Nature. Tuckney as a Westminister Divine. The Whichcote-
Tuckney Controversy Begins. Whichcote Presents the Germ of Cam-
bridge Platonism. Tuckney Criticizes Whichcote's Proposals. The

Issues Set Forth. The Problem of Religious Authority. Christian
Tolerance. The Doctrine of Reconciliation. Agreement to Differ. Divergence from Puritanism.

IV. RELIGION OF FIRST-INSCRIPTION – THE CANDLE
    OF THE LORD (i)   66
Natural Religion. The Intellectual Search for God. Natural Truth.
Cudworth's Commentary. The Light of Nature and the Universal
Logos. From Natural to Revealed Truth. Concerning Atheism. The
Self-Evident Nature of Theism. The *Via Negativa* of Platonism. From
Natural Phenomena to a Primal Cause. Supra-rational Knowledge and
Divine Illumination. The Perfections of God. God in Creation and
Providence. The God – Man Encounter. Self – Fulfillment and Divine
Communion.

V. RELIGION OF FIRST-INSCRIPTION –
   NATURAL ETHICS (ii)   91
Eternal and Immutable Morality. Truth and Goodness as Things – In-
Themselves. Natural Principles and Moral Duties. The Context of
Decision. The Growth of Conscience. Of Ends and Goals. Knowledge
and Goodness. The Voice of God. The Nature of Moral Evil. Evil and
God. Evil, Finite Rationality and Freedom. The Meaning of Vir-
tue. Cardinal Virtues. On Sobriety, Justice and Piety. Social Respon-
sibility. Morality and Religion. *Summum Bonum* and Beatitude.

VI. RELIGION OF AFTER-REVELATION – SAVING KNOW-
    LEDGE (i)   116
On Natural and Revealed Theology. Reason Divinely Illuminated.
The Logic of Belief. The Authority of Scripture. Implicit Faith. Reve-
lation. Man as *Imago Dei*. The Fall. Guilt. Temptation. A Concept of
Sin. Social Sin. Incarnation as Atonement. Goodness as *Agape* in God.
The Mediatorial Office of Christ. From Middle Power to Middle
Person. The Cruciality of the Cross. The Author of Nature as the
Giver of Grace. Knowledge of Christ as Saving Wisdom. The Christian
Experience of Forgiveness. Faith Seeking Knowledge. Conversion.
Regeneration. Justification. Christ's Righteousness and Ours.

VII. RELIGION OF AFTER-REVELATION – CHRISTIAN
     MORALS (ii)   147
The Christian Faith and Social Action. On Righteousness. Equity.
Piety. In Defense of Christian Morality. The Inner Reformation. Love
of Self and Love of God. Christian Graces as Fruits of the Spirit. The
Love of Mercy as Neighbor-Love. The Divine Example. Purity as
Holiness. The Stewardship of Wealth. The Spirit of God as a Living
Law. Christian Morals and Last Things. Heaven Moral as Heaven
Local. Hell Moral as Inward Torture. Eternal Life as Participation in
the Divine Nature. Life against the Background of Eternity. God as
Governor of the Moral Order. The Death of Socrates and *Christus
Victor*. Christ brings Life and Immortality. The Resurrection and
Christian Hope.

VIII. RELIGION OF AFTER-REVELATION – THE
UNIVERSAL CHURCH (iii)   171

Against Romanism. On Transubstantiation. Against an Infallible
Pope. The Reformed Church. Whichcote and the Liberals. His Doctrine of the Ministry. The Intellect and Devotion. The Meaning of
Prayer. Faith and the Sacraments. Tolerance in Religion. Mono-episco-
pacy as the *Bene Esse* rather than the *Esse* of the Church. The Centrality of Scripture to Church Theology.

IX. THE FATHER OF THE CHRISTIAN PLATONISTS OF
CAMBRIDGE   201

Whichcote as a Platonist. As Founder of Cambridge Platonism. Joseph
Mead and Whichcote. The Fellowship of Kindred Minds. John Smith.
Ralph Cudworth. Henry More. A Critical Comparison.

X. WHICHCOTE AND THE INTELLECTUAL TRADITION   225

The Latitudinarians and the Cambridge Platonists. Stillingfleet and
Tillotson. Whichcote and the Friends. John Locke and the Lights of
Reason and Faith. John Toland and the New Rationalism. Samuel
Clarke. The Third Earl Of Shaftesbury. Bishop Butler's *Analogy*. John
Norris. S. T. Coleridge. F. D. Maurice. Bishop Westcott. Archbishop
William Temple. Dean Inge. Whichcote and British Modernism.
Canon C. E. Raven.

XI. EPILEGOMENA   257

Whichcote's Lasting Contribution to Theology. The Province of
Christian Philosophy. Whichcote on Faith and Philosophy. An Inade-
quate Intellectualism. The Rationality of Faith. Faith and Ethics.The
Rational Basis of the Union of Religion and Morality. Johannine
Ethics. Eternal Life as a Quality of Existence. Christian Tolerance.
Anticipating Christian Unity. A Concluding Word.

APPENDIX   267

SELECTED BIBLIOGRAPHY   275

PREFACE

During the middle of the seventeenth century, Humanism came to full flower in England in the Christian Platonists of Cambridge University. The founder of this movement was Benjamin Whichcote whose thought is being given comprehensive treatment, perhaps for the first time, in the present work. Whichcote has been treated briefly here and there in relation to the movement as a whole. But as the movement is being given more attention in the history of religious thought; it is now appropriate to examine thoroughly the thought of Whichcote, the father of the Cambridge Platonists.

The background to Whichcote's thought is the context in which the philosophy of the more perceptive thinkers of the movement must be understood. His thought is seminal and suggestive of what Cudworth and More present with more brilliance and erudition. Whichcote's impact upon the men of this movement is due mainly to the attractiveness of his personality and the persuasiveness of his character. He is a sincere common sense thinker who is existentially involved in a historical stream of thought which reaches back at least to Socrates and forward to Canon C. E. Raven and others in our time. Thus the life and thought of Whichcote is presented here in the framework of the intellectual history of Christian Platonism.

The present study does not attempt a thorough treatment of Cambridge Platonism. Our concern for the associates of Whichcote is secondary. Their contributions to the movement will be considered only to the extent that they shed light upon Whichcote's thought.

We are limited; therefore, to the intimate circle of Cambridge men who were directly influenced by Whichcote. Only Ralph Cudworth, Henry More and John Smith are thus honored in view of our purpose. Cudworth and More have been given special attention in recent scholarly publications. Whichcote and Smith have been generally neglected. They have been given only casual attention. This work attempts to overcome to some extent this omission.

There is a two fold task indicated in bringing to the scholarly public the value of Cambridge Platonists to subsequent religious thought. First, there is a need to re-produce new editions of their major works. And, second, there is a need to make an intense study of the thought of each of the Cambridge Platonist.

This study was first done as the research requirement for the Doctor of Philosophy degree at the University of Edinburgh and was completed in 1957. Though my mind has changed on some matters, the original research and conclusions have not been altered to any great degree. There have been some valuable publications in more recent years on Cudworth and More in English and German as well as intellectual studies of the general period of our interest which have contributed to the present statement. In addition there has been one other comprehensive research project on the life and thought of Whichcote. In 1964, Jay Gomer Williams wrote a thesis for his Doctor of Philosophy degree at Columbia University entitled: "The Life and Thought of Benjamin Whichcote." It was Prof. John Macquarrie of Union Theological Seminary who brought this to my attention. As a result of his help, I have both corresponded with Prof. Williams and examined his findings at the Columbia University Library.

The work is valuable, but does not alter my conclusions. There are some points of dissimilarity which are so crucial that they deserve attention. Since these came to my attention after the manuscript was completed, I present them here for the sake of critical scholarship.

First, Williams considers Henry More as the co-founder of the movement. He reasons that Whichcote is a Platonist of Puritanism and thus in line with Ramus, Preston and, by implication, Jonathan Edwards; while More, Smith and Cudworth belong to the neo-Platonism of the Renaissance (p. 288). Second, it follows that the dependence relationship he sees between Whichcote and others differs from my own. Williams finds it necessary to consider Culverwell and Worthington in his treatment. Third, Williams did not clearly see the role of Whichcote as the founder of the movement and, therefore, could not present his discussion in this light. This imposes a great limitation, I believe, upon his findings. And, fourth, he has imposed a modern theological structure on Whichcote's thought; while I have thought it best to retain more of Whichcote's own manner of expression. The reader's attention is called to chapters two and nine for my reaction to these differences.

It was through the encouragement of the late Principal of New College, University of Edinburgh who was also Professor of Divinity and Principal C. S. Duthie, formerly of the Scottish Congregational College and presently of New College, University of London, that my research on this subject began. Principal Duthie as Visiting Lecturer in Theology and Prof. J. S. McEwen, of the University of Edinburgh guided my research. For their patience and encouragement, I am grateful.

I wish to thank Professor Norman Sykes of Cambridge University for his helpful suggestions. I am grateful to Professor John Baillie and Professor H. H. Farmer, Professor Emeritus of Divinity of the University of Cambridge for improving my theological insights.

I wish to acknowledge my indebtedness to those who have personally assisted me in collecting important data for this study. They are: Principal R. D. Whitehorn of Westminster College, Cambridge; Rev. J. M. Plumley, Rector of Milton (near Cambridge); Rev. T. H. Pyke, Rector of North Cadbury; Rev. J. F. D. Trimington, Minister, St. Lawrence Jewry, London; and Mrs. R. H. Harrison, Secretary, St. Anne's Blackfrairs, London. My gratitude goes to the librarians and staff members of Emmanuel, King's and Westminister Colleges and the University Library, Cambridge University; The British Museum, Guildhall Library, London; The National Library of Scotland and the libraries of New College and the main library of the University of Edinburgh; The Library of Congress, Washington, D.C. and Weidner and Divinity Libraries, Harvard University, Cambridge, Massachusetts.

In addition to Principal C. S. Duthie, there are two other persons to whom I owe a debt which cannot be put into words. Canon C. E. Raven, late Regius Professor Emeritus of Divinity at the University of Cambridge, a Christian Platonist himself in the tradition of Whichcote, read most of the manuscript as it was in preparation and made many valuable suggestions. In addition, Canon Raven added his personal interest, seasoned judgment and critical scholarship to my endeavor. More recently, Professor Elton Trueblood of Earlham College has examined the manuscript and assured me of the need for bringing my findings to the scholarly public.

I am grateful to him for inspiring me to revise this work which has been an experience of personal growth. I am pleased that the book should be launched with a foreword from his fruitful pen.

Last but, most of all, I am grateful for an understanding wife and children who through their interest and affection have inspired me at every stage of the preparation of this manuscript.

Cambridge, Mass., 1965.

ABBREVIATIONS

A.C.	*Alumni Cantabrigienses*
A.T.R.	*Anglican Theological Review*
B.M.	British Museum
C.C.	*Christian Century*
C.E.	*Catholic Encyclopaedia*
C.H.E.L.	*Cambridge History of English Literature*
C.M.H.	*Cambridge Modern History*
C.R.	*Contemporary Review*
D.E.C.H.	*A Dictionary of English Church History*
D.N.B.	*Dictionary of National Biography*
E.R.E.	*Encyclopaedia of Religion and Ethics*
F.Q.E.	*Friends' Quarterly Examiner*
Gh.L.	Guildhall Library, (London)
G.O.T.R.	*The Greek Orthodox Theological Review*
H.J.	*Heytrop Journal*
H.T.R.	*Harvard Theological Review*
I.J.E.	*International Journal of Ethics*
J.C.S.	*Journal of Church and State*
J.H.I.	*Journal of the History of Ideas*
J.R.T.	*Journal of Religious Thought*
L.P.	*Lauderdale Papers*
L.Q.R.	*The London Quarterly Review*
M.P.	*Modern Philology*
P.L.	Milton's *Paradise Lost*
P.R.	*Philosophical Review*
S.J.T.	*Scottish Journal of Theology*
W.F.	*World Faiths*
Y.R.	*Yale Review*

CHAPTER ONE

BENJAMIN WHICHCOTE: A MAN OF GOOD NATURE

Benjamin Whichcote was born on May 4, 1609,[1] into an "ancient and honourable family." [2] His father was Christopher Whichcote, probably a "Squire," and his mother Elizabeth, daughter of Edward Fox of Greet in the county of Salop. He came from a very large family of five girls and seven boys.[3] Unfortunately, nothing is known of our author before he was seventeen.[4]

[1] Basic sources of Whichcote's biography are: (1) D.N.B. XXI, 1–2; (2) Benjamin Whichcote and Anthony Tuckney, *Eight Letters*, ed. Samuel Salter (London, 1753) from the *Preface*; (3) John Tillotson, *A Sermon Preached at the Funeral of Dr. Benjamin Whichcot* (London, 1698); (4) J. E. B. Mayor, *Cambridge in the Reign of Queen Anne* (Cambridge, 1911); A. C., Vol. IV, pt. i, p. 382; and (6) Gilbert Burnet, *History of My Own Time*, Vol. I, ed. Dean Swift 2nd ed. (Oxford, 1833). Burnet should be regarded as a memoir writer rather than an accurate historian. See Richard Lodge, *The History of England* (London, 1910), VIII, 477. In the seventeenth century, funeral sermons were considered as valuable biographical documents; hence our frequent use of Tillotson's sermon. See C. F. Richardson, *English Preachers and Preaching, 1640–1670* (London, 1928), p. 96. The material concerning Whichcote's life is not abundant. See S. H. Kenwood, *The Emmanuel Platonists* (Giggleswick, 1916), p. iii. Whichcote's name is spelt in various ways, i.e. Whichcot, Whichcott, Whichcote, Whitchcote, etc. See James Heywood and Thomas Wright, *Cambridge Transactions During the Puritan Controversies* (London, 1854), II, 563–564, 593–594, 619. cf. St. Lawrence, *Minutes of Vestry, 1669–1720* in (G.H.L.), folios 115, 122, 129 and 156. The present writer prefers the "Whichcote" spelling. There is disagreement on his date of birth. March 11, 1609 is held by Slater in his preface to Whichcote and Tuckney, *Ibid.* p. xvi and Tillotson, *Ibid.* p. 21; while May 4, 1609 is held by Mullinger, *Ibid.* p. 1 and A. C., *Ibid.* The present writer accepts May 4, 1609 as the more historically reliable.

[2] Whichcote and Tuckney, *Ibid.*, p. xvi. Hereafter referred to as Whichcote, *Letters*.

[3] Owen and Blakeway, *Shrewsbury*, II, 436; I, 408 (Note 7). Whichcote's brother, Sir Jeremy, baronet of Hendon, Middlesex, barrister-at-law, and solicitor-general to the Elector Palatine, was the author's youngest brother. His brother Christopher was a Spanish merchant, residing in London. His brother Samuel and his sisters Anne and Catherine all made "good marriages." In 1637, his niece Mary was married to Dr. Worthington by Whichcote and Cudworth attended the wedding. Cf. Worthington, *Diary* (Crossley's note), I, 87, 274. In addition to what has been said concerning Sir Jeremy, he was Justice of Peace, Deputy Lieutenant and Colonel of the militia for the County of Middlesex, and held the wardenship of the Fleet during the reign of Charles II. H. Owen and J. B. Blakeway, *A History of Shrewsbury* (London, 1825), II, 436; I, 408 (n. 7). John Worthington, *Diary and Correspondence*, ed. James Crossley (Manchester, 1847), I, 87–89, 274.

[4] F. J. Powicke, *The Cambridge Platonists* (London, 1926), p. 51. Cf. John Tulloch, *Rational Theology and Christian Philosophy in England in the Seventeenth Century* (Edinburgh, 1872), II, 47.

On October 25, 1626, he was admitted pensioner at Emanuel College, Cambridge, on which occasion his name in the entry in the register is spelt "Whitchcote." [1] His college tutor was Anthony Tuckney, a divine whose career was subsequently interwoven with his own. Says Tuckney, "From your first coming to Cambridge I loved you: as finding you studious and pious, and very loving and observant of me." [2] In 1629–30 he graduated B.A. and in 1633 he became M.A., in which year he was elected fellow of his college. When his tutor Thomas Hill left the University the following year, Whichcote became tutor. The Cambridge tutors acted as guide, philosopher and friend to their pupils and had special influence over their religious opinions. Such an office Whichcote magnified.[3] He was an excellent tutor and instructor of youth; a great encourager and kind director of young divines; "a candid hearer of sermons and his judgment was highly reverenced, though there was no fear of his censure," as a "critic he was humble and kind." [4] Among his students who afterwards attained distinction were John Smith, John Worthington, John Wallis and Samuel Cradock.[5] John Smith is said to have "lived on Whichcote." This phrase has financial as well as mental and spiritual implications, as is apparent when one reads the *Discourses* of Smith, who became a student at Emmanuel College, Cambridge, in 1636 while Whichcote was a fellow and tutor of the same college.[6]

Whichcote was ordained by John Williams, bishop of Lincoln, on March 5, 1636, "both deacon and priest," "which irregularity," says Salter, "I know not how to account for in a prelate so obnoxious to the ruling power both in Church and State." [7] In the same year he was appointed Sunday afternoon lecturer at Trinity Church, Cambridge, where he served for nearly twenty years. About this time he was appointed one of the University preachers and in 1640 he became Bachelor of Divinity. In 1641 his candidature for the divinity chair at Gresham College was defeated by Thomas Horton. In 1643 the Master and Fellows of Emmanuel presented him with the living of North Cadbury in Somersetshire. There he married Rebecca, widow of Mat-

---

[1] *D.N.B.*, XXI, 1.

[2] Whichcote, *Ibid.*, p. 36.

[3] E. A. George, *Seventeenth Century Man of Latitude* (London, 1909), p. 70–71.

[4] Tillotson, *Ibid.*, pp. 22, 33; Cf. Whichcote, *Ibid.*, p. xvii; E. S. Shuchburgh, *Emmanuel College* (London, 1904), p. 81.

[5] Whichcote, *Ibid.*

[6] John Smith, *Select Discourses*, ed. H. G. Williams, 4th ed. (Cambridge, 1859), pp. vi, xv–xvi.

[7] Whichcote, *Ibid.*, p. xviii.

thew Cradock, governor of Massachusetts, and retired to Cadbury.[1] Nothing is known of the influence of his wife upon his career.

In 1644, Whichcote was summoned back to Cambridge by the Earl of Manchester and the Parliamentary Commissioners, as Provost of King's.[2] This post had been held for many years by Dr. Samuel Collins, the Regius Professor of Divinity, whom Whichcote respected greatly, and Whichcote was reluctant to accept the position from which Collins had been dismissed. It was only after careful thought and considerable pressure that he consented to do so, and he provided for Collins a portion of the stipend of the provostship. The arguments *pro* and *con* by which he ultimately arrived at the conclusion that he should accept the post were written down. His acceptance was out of a sense of duty and was fortunate not only for King's, but for the University and the Church of England.[3] Someone else with Whichcote's standing would have been difficult to find.

... One, whose Capacity should have been so indisputable, his Reputation for Piety Learning Prudence and Temper so established, his Interest and Credit with those in Authority so very considerable, and his Fortune so independent: by all which in conjunction our Author was enabled to do so much more Service than any other man; without stooping to anything unworthy of his Character.[4]

Mullinger agrees as he says:

In the midst of all the bitterness of feeling and deep depression, the influence of Whichcote stands out in bright relief.[5]

---

[1] *D.N.B.*, XXI, 2; Cf. Whichcote, *Ibid.*, p. xviii. Salter in his preface assumes Whichcote's marriage, but does not know to whom. The account of his marriage to Rebecca Glover of St. Swithins, widow, 26th April, 1649, in A.C., *Ibid.*, is dubious both as to date and marriage partner. Tulloch in the first part of his work, *Ibid.*, II, accepts Salter's agnostic view, but later in the same volume (p. 431) refers to a letter from H. A. Miles, which gives definite information on this subject. Whichcote married Rebecca, widow of Matthew Cradock, a wealthy London merchant and first governor of Massachusetts Bay.

In 1650 Whichcote petitioned the general court of Massachusetts for the payment of a sum of money due to her former husband. The court voted that one thousand acres of land be given Dr. Whichcote and his wife Rebecca.

[2] Thomas Fuller, *The History of the University of Cambridge*, pp. 233–235. Cf. Christopher Hill, *Puritanism and Revolution* (London, 1958). The entire work is a worthy treatment of the relation between Puritanism and the upheavals of mid-seventeenth England.

[3] Whichcote, *Ibid.*, pp. xviii f. Cf. James Heywood and Thomas Wright, *The Ancient Laws of the Fifteenth Century for King's College* (London, 1850), p. 290. See "Harley" (MS), 7045, p. 474 in (BM) for *pros* and *cons* of his decision. Concerning his appointment, see Shuchburgh, *Ibid.*, p. 81. For a character sketch of Collins, see David Masson, *The Life of John Milton* (London, 1873), I, 92–93. Cf. "Harley" (MS), 7034, p. 229 and 7038, pp. 17, 213.

[4] Whichcote, *Ibid.*, p. xix.

[5] J. B. Mullinger, *The University of Cambridge* (Cambridge, 1911), III, 296.

The tendering of the Covenant had a marked effect upon the University.[1] A Committee was appointed for the purpose of expelling those who refused the Covenant, and a subsequent Committee instructed to enforce its acceptance upon those who should be elected to fill the vacancies. The newcomers were required to sign a certificate pledging their loyalty before admission. It attests to the profound respect which his character inspired that Whichcote appears to have been admitted to his post without taking the Covenant. On the other hand, an example of the detrimental effects of this action may be seen in the experience of Collins. But Whichcote's generosity, combined with the slender stipend Collins continued to receive as Regius Professor of Divinity, enabled him to pass the remainder of his life in comfort. The influence of Whichcote may be discerned in the fact that at King's only five fellows were ejected and only one sequestration was made, besides that of Collins' books. Whichcote also came to the rescue of Robert

---

[1] The Civil War began in August 1642 when Charles raised his standard at Nottingham. It was at once a religious and political struggle. On one side were ranged the King and Anglicanism (represented by episcopacy and the Prayer Book), but also Autocracy and despotism; whereas on the other side stood Parliament and Puritanism (whether Presbyterian or Independent).

As soon as the war began, Parliament made plans for enlisting the support of the Scots. Having first abolished episcopacy, a meeting of Puritan leaders was held in London, known as the Westminster Assembly, which proceeded to draw upon a religious agreement which might serve as a basis for an alliance with Presbyterian Scotland. Scotland had declared its faith in the Covenant of 1638, and it was an amended form of this document which was discussed by the Westminster Assembly in 1643. The result was the publication of the Solemn League and Covenant which was imposed on all Englishmen over the age of eighteen. This declares that they have entered into a mutual and solemn league and covenant for the extirpation of popery, prelacy, superstition, heresy, schism and whatever is found to be contrary to sound doctrine and godliness. It also sought to preserve the rights and privileges of Parliament.

When the Covenant became law in 1964 it meant the end of the Church of England wherever Parliament could make its will obeyed. Many of the clergy were Puritan at heart, and these signed the Covenant gladly and continued in their benefices as Presbyterian ministers rather than as priests of the Church of England. Almost all those, however, who could not consciously subscribe to the Covenant were ejected from their livings, local committees being formed to examine, on matters of politics, religion and morals, any waverers. A few went abroad into exile, some were committed to prison, some became tutors or chaplains to such as could afford to support them.

Parliament allowed a pension up to one-fifth of the usual salary to be set aside for the wife and children of the evicted incumbent, but this was seldom paid. The result was great hardship and widespread misery.

Against this background one can appreciate the stature of Whichcote, who never took the Covenant and yet was retained in distinguished positions at the University and in the Church. He remained a priest of the Church of England throughout this turbulent period. In addition, we can now understand more completely the extent of his concern for Dr. Collins who out of conviction refused to take the Covenant and was therefore evicted from the Provostship of King's College. J. R. H. Moorman, *A History of The Church of England* (New York, 1954), pp. 237–239. Cf. Fuller, *Ibid.*, pp. 233–234 and G. M. Trevelyan, *England Under the Stuarts* (New York, 1914), pp. 225–271.

Heath, whose sequestered property was restored after his ejection in 1644.[1]

When Whichcote became Provost, Tuckney was made Master of Emmanuel, Arrowsmith of St. John's and Hill of Trinity. These four were friends and all but Whichcote had met at the Westminster Assembly. Among this group Whichcote was the only one to refuse the Covenant. The youngest of this group, he had broken away from the narrow and dogmatic principles of his education. His advocacy of freer and more liberal opinions led to some disagreement between Whichcote and his three friends which finally broke out in a frank discussion between Whichcote and Tuckney.[2]

Among the above mentioned friends of Whichcote, Tuckney is the one most closely associated with an understanding of his life and thought. Tuckney was born in 1599 at Kirton in Lincolnshire. At fourteen he entered Emmanuel College, Cambridge. He took his first degree at seventeen, and became fellow three years later. He proceeded to M.A. in 1620 and was for a time in the Earl of Manchester's family before he came back to live in the college, where he became an eminent tutor. He continued as tutor until receiving his B.D. in 1627. He went to Boston as an assistant to John Cotton, Vicar of the town. Cotton, a resolute Nonconformist, soon left for New England, and Tuckney, who was now married, became Vicar and remained in this position until the Restoration. When Parliament convened an Assembly of Divines, he was nominated from the county of Lincoln. Tuckney took his family with him and never returned to Boston to live. He was "highly considered" by the Assembly and obtained a London parish. Manchester appointed him as Master of Emmanuel in 1645, but he did not reside in Cambridge until three years later when he became Vice-Chancellor of the University. He served in that office with credit and received the D.D. degree the next year, as did Arrowsmith and Whichcote. Later, Tuckney became Master of St. John's and Regius Professor of Divinity. However, he was "civilly turn'd out" of both latter positions for his nonconformity at the Restoration.[3]

---

[1] *Ibid.*, pp. 296–297, 288; Cf. Tillotson, *Ibid.*, pp. 22–24. A good example of Whichcote's moderation is seen in his support of Barrow for Greek Professor. Barrow was a Royalist, refused both the Covenant and Engagement and was suspected of Arminianism; Dyer suggests that Whichcote most probably took the Covenant. This I reject for lack of evidence. See George Dyer, *History of the University and Colleges of Cambridge* (Cambridge, 1814), II, 196, 355.

[2] Whichcote, *Ibid.*, pp. xx–xxi.

[3] *Ibid.*, pp. i–vi; Edmund Calamy, *The Nonconformist's Memorial*, ed. Samuel Palmer, 2nd and abridged ed. (London, 1802), I, 264–265. Dyer, *Ibid.*, 354–355; Shuchburgh, *Ibid.*, p. 79.

In 1649 Whichcote resigned his Somerset living which was presented in 1650 to Ralph Cudworth, now Master of Clare Hall. Whichcote was soon afterwards presented by King's to the living of Milton at Cambridgeshire, which he held for the remainder of his life. There were some difficulties at the restoration concerning his Milton charge which will be discussed later in this chapter. In November, 1650, he was elected Vice-Chancellor of the University. He sought to preserve a spirit of "sober piety" and "rational religion" in the University and town of Cambridge; in opposition to the "fanatic enthusiasm" then prevalent. This seems to have been the motive for his Sunday afternoon lectures at Trinity Church. Another course of lectures was given on Wednesdays at the same church and was served by the very best preachers, fellows of various colleges and others, all probably friends of Whichcote.

His efforts and influence resulted in the "great talents and excellent performances of many eminent divines after the Restoration," most of whom were educated at Cambridge and were "formed if not actually brought up by him." As an official of the University, he maintained a truly Christian temper and made worthy use of the influence he had with those in authority, while Tuckney, Arrowsmith and others were apprehensive of a total destruction threatening the seats of learning. His generosity to Collins and other ejected members of the society increased his influence. He had "too noble and great a spirit to serve a party and was never so attached to any as not to see, own and wish to serve real merit; wherever it was to be found." In spite of his differences with Tuckney, he contributed his vote to "raise" Tuckney to the Divinity Chair.[1]

In 1654, on the occasion of peace with Holland, Whichcote contributed to the volume of verses, *Oliva Pacis,* composed by members of the University to celebrate the event and dedicated to Cromwell. In December, 1655, he was invited by Cromwell to advise him, in conjunction with Cudworth, Tuckney and others, on the question of toleration for the Jews. In 1658 he wrote a copy of Latin verses upon the death of Oliver Cromwell. In 1659 together with Cudworth, Tuckney and other Cambridge divines, he supported Matthew Poole's scheme for the maintaining of students of "choice ability at the University and principally in order to the ministry." [2]

---

[1] *Ibid.*, pp. xxiv–xxv; Cf. George, *Ibid.* According to George, the fears of the other University officials were well founded.

[2] *D.N.B.*, XXI, 2–3. For an account of Cromwell's Conference concerning the Jews, see

The University of Cambridge shared in the political and religious conflicts of the period leading up to the Restoration. There was the abrupt dismissal of scores of fellows and masters by first Puritan and then Royalist officers from 1644–1660; the military situation at Cambridge during the Civil War; the occasional wanton destruction of college property; and the inevitable relaxation of both rules and routine.[1] Following on all this, a further blow fell upon the University and especially upon some of its officials at the Restoration. In 1660, a message was sent from the King to the Vice-Chancellor of the University of Cambridge as follows:

> To observe all the directions given by his father and grandfather especially obedience to the governors and restraint of all letters in Cambridge without due order, also to call in all licences granted since 1643 and have the persons licenced put to the vote of the present University and choose others in the place of those rejected.[2]

In the same spirit a royal letter was sent to the Vice-Provost and Fellows of King's College, affecting Whichcote directly:

> ... Whereas, the provost of our colledge called King's Colledge, became void by the death of Dr. Collins ... we have appointed for the supply thereof ... Dr. James Fleetwood, one of our chaplains in ordinary ....'' [3]

On the basis of the King's letter, Fleetwood petitioned the King for the appointment in July, 1660.[4] The King's letter was written the previous month, June 22, 1660. Fleetwood ignored Whichcote as Provost, thus his letter was followed by a protest from Whichcote and supporters. The request of the latter was that Whichcote "be confirmed in the place of Provost." The response of the King was that Whichcote continue as Provost until further orders, "notwithstanding his previous letter to elect Fleetwood, which they could not do statutably, there being no voidance fifteen days previous." Barlow, the Vice-Provost, and twenty-two Fellows signed a statement in favour of Whichcote's retention.[5]

Worthington, *Ibid.* (Crossley's note), I, 78. Whichcote's poem at the death of Cromwell is found in his *Works* (Aberdeen, 1751), I, iii. Concerning his support of Poole's education scheme see Matthew Robinson, *Autobiography*, ed. J. E. B. Mayor (Cambridge, 1856), pp. 191–193. The reader is referred to the following reference for a comprehensive coverage of Cromwell's life and thought: R. S. Paul, *The Lord Protector* (London, 1955).

[1] M. P. (1929–30), XXVII, 35; C. H. Cooper, *Annals of Cambridge* (Cambridge, 1845), III, 423.

[2] Cooper, *Ibid.*, p. 431.

[3] Haywood and Wright, *Ancient Laws*, p. 293; Cf. "Harley" (MS) 7045, p. 473.

[4] Cooper, *Ibid.*; Cf. Mullinger, *Ibid.*, p. 567–569.

[5] *Ibid.*, p. 432.

Whichcote sought the aid of Lord Lauderdale to intercede for him before the King, which Lauderdale did. The King heard the appeal "graciously" and afterwards spoke to the Lord Chamberlain, Chancellor of the University, about Whichcote's "concerns." Thus, Lauderdale, together with the Lord Chamberlain, were of the opinion that Whichcote's position was secure. Lauderdale concludes that "there is no need to make a particular application," and promises that "I shall not faile to watch all opportunities to serve you." [1]

Whichcote's position was not secure, for Fleetwood was determined to be Provost of King's. Fleetwood requested that the Vice-Provost and Fellows of King's accept him as Provost. He based his request upon the King's original letter and considered himself as duly elected. He had taken the oath of office, received the statute book, seals and keys of office, but had been opposed by the "pretended" Provost and a few younger Fellows. He insisted that the King be informed that "Dr. Whichcote is incapable by statute of the Provostship of King's College having never been a Fellow, that of the seventy Fellows of King's College, only thirty, twenty-two of whom are juniors, signed his certificate, and the others refused and resolved against him, Dr. Whichcote having never been elected, but put upon them by a private committee...." [2]

Whichcote urged that the appointment be left with the King and remarked that others who were not fellows of King's had held this office, further pointing out that he had accepted it unwillingly and had given up a valuable living to do so. [3] One senior Fellow, Dr. William Godman, highly commended Whichcote's life and work at King's. Although admitting that Whichcote was statutably incapable of the appointment, he insisted that Whichcote's "great learning, prudence and civility" made him worthy. Godman added that Whichcote had been an "encourager of learning and virtue and had never persecuted any upon difference of opinion." [4] There was another letter from Dr. Richard Love, Master of Corpus Christi College, Cambridge,

---

[1] Haywood and Wright, *Ibid.*, p. 287–288. "Harley" (MS), *Ibid.* For Whichcote's letter to Lauderdale, see "Lauderdale Papers" (MS) in (BM), May-December, 1660, II, folio 9. Date of letter is June 12, 1660. Cf. A. Austen-Leigh, *King's College* (London, 1899), p. 137.

[2] Cooper, *Ibid.*

[3] Haywood and Wright, *Ibid.*, pp. 288–290. Cf. "Harley" *Ibid.* pp. 473–474. Here are recorded various reasons why Whichcote's party felt he should be confirmed as Provost, together with Whichcote's own reasons for accepting and holding the post from the time of his appointment.

[4] Haywood and Wright, *Ibid.*, pp. 292–293. Cf. "Harley," *Ibid.*, pl 475. Godman was Dean of Divinity at King's.

attesting to the life and work of Whichcote. Love wrote:

"By these I testify that Benjamin Whichcote, who for fifteen years hath been the Provost of King's College in Cambridge, is a worthy and learned person, of exemplary sobriety and gravity, prudent in government, and hath been carefull of the good of the college sundry ways, as well in regard to revenues thereof, as of persons belonging thereto. So that the College hath always thrived under his government above former ages. I further testify that the said Dr. hath as head of the University, been exceedingly usefull and helpfull to the management of our public affairs, for the safety of the whole body in times of greatest danger. Lastly, I testify that he hath always been highly ready and industrious to relieve all such deserving persons as were either in trouble or danger for their duty and loyalty to the King's Majesty, many particulars in which I am able to alledge out of my experiences.[1]

On July 11, 1660, Fleetwood with Fellows, Scholars and servants of King's College went to the Provost's lodgings. They found some of Whichcote's servants there who refused them entrance. Once again, Fleetwood asserted that he was Provost by "royal command." He insisted that Whichcote's "contempt" should be punished. Further he accused Whichcote of turning Collins out of the same office and of failing to observe the College Statutes, by not filling the "singing men and choristers' places, etc." Thus, on July 16, 1660, Fleetwood wrote the King's secretary, Nicholas, that "he was received at King's College but shut out of the Provost lodgings by order of Whichcote, whom he allowed to continue there as a matter of convenience." He urged the King to rule on this matter.[2]

Neither the merits of Whichcote's life and work, nor the intercession of Lauderdale could save him from ejection.[3] In the opinion of Charles II, his were all negative virtues. Fleetwood, on the other hand, was an army chaplain exerting considerable influence upon the soldiery. Further, the King's personal feeling was that Whichcote's conduct seemed to have been designed to vindicate the legality of his position rather than to maintain himself in office. Whichcote now saw clearly the situation which faced him. There was no necessity for further intervention from without. His protest made, he retired from his post at King's.[4]

As we observe this struggle between Whichcote and Fleetwood, it is worthwhile to make certain observations. First, Whichcote and Fleetwood were arguing at cross-purposes. Whichcote held that his

---

[1] *Ibid.*, p. 291.
[2] Cooper, *Ibid.*
[3] Austen-Leigh, *Ibid.*, p. 137.
[4] Mullinger, *Ibid.*, pp. 567; Cf. Masson, *Ibid.*, VI, 306–307.

position was official, while Fleetwood completely ignored his authority. Second, there is the possibility that many who supported Fleetwood were misguided by his appeal to the statutes and "group-loyalty." Godman's statement is a good example. It is obvious that Fleetwood's real motive is primarily selfish. Third, without the pressure from Fleetwood, it is a reasonable probability that Whichcote would have been confirmed in office. Fourth, however much we may admire the "sweet-temper" or "good-nature" of Whichcote, we cannot but wonder if his final stand at the Provost's lodge was not an indication of a callousness in his nature. Finally, we must remember that the available evidence is not sufficiently conclusive to condemn either man, especially in view of the "evil days" in which they lived. The controversy also brings out a valuable summary of Whichcote's contribution to the life of the University.

As far as his ejection is concerned, Whichcote merely shared the fate of most University officials appointed by the Puritans, but by the testimonials of influential friends, by the recommendation of his own life and work, and by his conformity to the Act of Uniformity, he was restored to "court favour." Thus his eminence as a city pastor and preacher was yet to come.[1]

Whichcote's connection with Cambridge, however, did not end with his ejection from the Provostship of King's. His successor, Fleetwood, and Fellows agreed that Whichcote should retain the Rectorship of Milton. The question arises as to whether this "preferment" can be attributed to the generosity of Fleetwood or to the many Fellows of King's who loved Whichcote and desired that he should be provided for and who had consented to his ejection only out of loyalty to the statutes of the founder of the College.[2] The latter reason seems to be most probable. Accordingly a letter was sent to Whichcote promising re-appointment to the living of Milton if he would resign. From this letter, it appears that it was necessary for Whichcote to resign and be re-appointed by the College that the College might retain the right to present this rectory. We may summarize the matter as follows:

(1) To make the presentation official under the new administration of State and University, he was presented by Matthew, Bishop of Ely, for the College, on November 13, 1660;

---

[1] *D.N.B.*, XXI, 3. For a description of the Act of Uniformity, see Heywood and Wright, *Cambridge Transactions*, II, 555.

[2] Here Whichcote states that many of the fellows preferred him to Fleetwood, but they wished to follow the statutes, viz. that a Kingsman must always be Provost, although in the history of the College this rule had not always been followed. "Lauderdale Papers," *Ibid.*

(2) Since the "cure" had lapsed for the King, on December 10, 1660, he was also presented by Matthew for the Crown; and,

(3) Upon his resignation by the request of the College (November 20, 1661), he was finally instituted Rector of Milton, November 20, 1661 by King's College.[1] Though Whichcote's future was more distinguished by his London ministry, yet it is to be remembered that he remained Rector of Milton until his death.[2]

On November 8, 1662, he became minister of St. Anne's Blackfriars, London.[3] Concerning this appointment, Salter says:

> Though removed, he was not disgraced or frowned upon .... He was on the contrary only called up from the comparative obscurity of a University life to a higher and more conspicuous station; from a place where he had done much service to one where there was still much to be done; by men like him.[4]

When St. Anne's burned down in the Great Fire of 1666, he retired to Milton and resided there for several years. There "he preached constantly, and relieved the poor, and had children taught to reade at his own charge; and made up differences among neighbours." [5]

In 1668, Whichcote's friend Wilkins was appointed Bishop of Chester, thereby vacating the vicarage of St. Lawrence Jewry, to which by the interest of Wilkins, Whichcote was appointed.[6] This church, however, had to be rebuilt, and during the work, which occupied some seven years, he preached regularly to the Corporation at Guildhall Chapel.[7] Tillotson says:

---

[1] Haywood and Wright, *Ancient Laws*, p. 294–295, Cf. "Harley," 7045, p. 476.

[2] I received the following information from a list of incumbents and a brief history on the wall by the main entrance to All Saints Church, Milton. The history of this church goes back to about 970 A.D. when it was perhaps connected to the Monastery of Ely. The church is in the Diocese of Ely.
The Parish had from its early beginnings a Rector, who received the greater tithes and had to keep the Chancel in repair, and also Vicars. In some parishes a monastery owned the tithes and appointed a deputy or vicar to act as Parish Priest. In these parishes the clergyman is still called vicar. But in Milton, the Rector as well as the Vicar was clergyman and often lived in the parish, sometimes only one of them. The altar rails were given by a Provost of King's College together with Fellows. Collins served as Rector from 1638 until his death and Whichcote was his successor. The historical value of this account is slight, but we are introduced to the rectory of Milton and Whichcote's ability to carry on work elsewhere in the meantime is explained. A list of the vicars serving with Whichcote is also given.

[3] St. Anne's is now joined with St. Andrew-by-the-Wardrobe. The building was destroyed by fire bombs in World War II.

[4] In Whichcote, *Letters*, p. xxv–xxvi.

[5] Tillotson, *Ibid.*, p. 25. Cf. "Cole" (MS), 5810, p. 182. For an account of the Great Fire, see Richard Baxter, *Autobiography*, abridged, ed. J. M. L. Thomas (London, 1931) pp. 198–99.

[6] *D.N.B.*, *Ibid.*

[7] Tillotson, *Ibid.* Again St. Lawrence has been destroyed by fire, by fire bombs in World War II. Fortunately, the records of St. Anne's and St. Lawrence are safe in the Guildhall Library. We have made use of the following: St. Anne's *Marriage Register*, 1562–1726, *Burial Register*, 1566–1700 and *Baptism Register*, 1560–1700; St. Lawrence, *Ibid.* There is little

... During the building of it upon the invitation of the Court of Aldermen in the mayoralty of Sir William Turner, he preached before the Honourable Auditory at Guild Hall every Sunday in the afternoon, with great acceptance and approbation for about the space of seven years.

And when St. Lawrence was rebuilt,

he bestowed his pains here twice a week, where he had the general love and respect of his Parish; and very considerable and judicious Auditory, though not very numerous, by reason of the weakness of his voice in his declining Age.[1]

In a letter to Sancroft, December, 1670, Whichcote gives an account of his services both to literature and to the Church. In 1674, along with Tillotson and Stillingfleet, he co-operated with certain non-conformists in furthering Thomas Gouge's efforts to extend education in Wales. Whichcote's work at St. Lawrence Jewry continued until his death.[2]

Whichcote died in Cambridge in 1683, when he had gone to visit Cudworth. Like Socrates, he seemed pleased to leave the body for "that happy state to which I am going." He was calm and serene during his illness. Following prayers for the "visitation of the sick" and Holy Communion, his last words were: "The Lord fulfil all his declarations and promises and pardon all my weaknesses and imperfections."[3] Tillotson adds:

He disclaimed all merit in himself; and declared that whatever he was, he was through the grace and goodness of God in Jesus Christ. He expressed likewise great dislike of the Principles of Separation: and said he was the more desirous to receive the Sacrament that he might declare his full Communion with the Church of Christ all the world over. He disclaimed Popery as well as things of near affinity with it, superstition and the usurpation upon the consciences of men. He thanked God that he had no pain in his body, nor disquiet in his spirit.[4]

He was interred in St. Lawrence Jewry, where his funeral sermon was preached by Tillotson on May 24, 1673. He left bequests to the University Library and also to King's and Emmanuel Colleges, at which last society he had founded before his death, scholarships to the value of one thousand pounds "bearing the name of William Larkins, who making him his executor entrusted him with the said summe to dispose

---

valuable information in these records. They do attest to the period of Whichcote's tenure as minister and of course his official signature is affixed to the important transactions of these parishes.

[1] Tillotson, *Ibid.*
[2] *D.N.B., Ibid.*
[3] Tillotson, *Ibid.*, pp. 28–29.
[4] *Ibid.*, Cf. Whichcote, *Aphorisms*, ed. Samuel Salter (London, 1753), 293, 198, 939.

of to pious users at his own discretion." He left no children; his executors were his two nephews, the sons of Sir Jeremy Whichcote.[1]

According to Shuchburgh, it was by preaching and by personal intercourse with pupils and friends that Whichcote's great work was done and his extraordinary influence at Cambridge, and in the Church, was exercised.[2] He was a thinker rather than a scholar, a teacher not through books only, but by personal experience. By his example, the University and especially its younger members were deeply impressed.[3] All that we know of Whichcote's life goes to show that his practice did not fall short of his principles. Even those who differed from him loved and trusted him.[4] Within his own College, he encouraged classical studies.[5] Burnet says:

... He set his young students much on the reading of the ancient philosophers, chiefly Plato, Tully and Plotin, and in considering the Christian doctrine sent from God, both to elevate and sweeten nature, in which he was a great example, as well as a wise and kind instructor.[6]

What of his effectiveness as a preacher? Locke in a letter to Richard King, highly commended his preaching.[7] While I am aware that a philosopher even of Locke's standing is not necessarily an able judge of preaching, it appears that he is in the position to estimate the "thought-value" of a sermon. A similar estimation of his sermons is made by Shaftesbury who describes Whichcote as a "preacher of good-nature." There seems to be no doubt that his sermons challenged the minds of his hearers: for though he preached without full notes, he did not preach "without study." [8] There appears to be no doubt that the great instrument of Whichcote's influence was the pulpit, both in Cambridge and in London; for he possessed remarkable power as a

---

[1] D.N.B., Ibid. Cf. St. Lawrence, Ibid. In the minutes of May, 1683, an account of his death is given. There are portraits of Whichcote in the Provost's Lodge at King's and in a Chapel window at Emmanuel. In my opinion the better of the two portraits is at Emmanuel. Westcott considered the latter most "characteristic." D.N.B., Ibid. Cf. Shuchburgh, Ibid., p. 81. His epitaph is recorded in "Harley" (MS), 7034, p. 332. A detailed account of the charitable bestowal of his wealth at his death is recorded by Tillotson, Ibid., pp. 26–27. His benevolent spirit was reflected by his relations, of "blood" and "intellectual" kinship. The present rector of Milton informed me that he left several acres of "charitable land" to be cultivated by the poor.

[2] Shuchburgh, Ibid., p. 81–82.

[3] C. E. Raven, John Ray, Naturalist, His Life and Works (Cambridge, 1942), p. 37.

[4] Austen-Leigh, Ibid., p. 137. A. H. Thompson, Cambridge and Its Colleges (London, 1908), p. 114.

[5] Ibid., pp. 134–135. Whichcote, Letters, pp. 38–40.

[6] Burnet, Ibid., p. 340. Cf. Manson, Ibid., III, 75.

[7] Whichcote, Ibid., p. xxxiv.

[8] W. F. Mitchell, English Pulpit Oratory From Andrews to Tillotson (London, 1932), p. 23.

preacher.[1] He was the great University preacher of the Common-wealth; and to his Sunday afternoon sermons, probably more than to any single means of influence, is the progress of the new movement which he founded to be attributed. Both by his own language and that of his opponents, it is clear that he aimed by his sermons to give a new tone to contemporary thought – to turn men's minds away from po-lemical argumentation to the great moral and spiritual realities lying at the basis of all religion.[2] It seems appropriate to conclude that in Whichcote as a preacher we find a strong personality, a capable and learned person, but also one who is the very incarnation of his message – a real "communication of truth through personality." Perhaps, then the dynamic personality of the preacher coupled with the thoughtful-ness of his message will serve as a partial explanation of Whichcote's amazing power as a preacher. Thus, Tillotson says:

> ... Besides his care of the college, he had a very great influence upon the University in general. Every Lord's day in the afternoon, for almost twenty years together, he preached at Trinity Church, where he had a great number not only of the young scholars, but those of great standing and best repute for learning in the University his constant and attentive auditors. And in those wild and unsettled times contributed more to the forming of the Students of the University to a sober sense of Religion than any man in that Age.[3]

Finally, we consider the secret of his personal influence. We must recognize the remarkable influence of Whichcote as a teacher, thinker and preacher. He was also a good pastor and University administrator. He combined considerable social influence with personal popularity. He had a "reputation for sound judgment and a discernment unrivalled in the University." [4] He was a man whose work was his life. Whichcote echoed and answered the *cogito ergo sum* of Descartes by the words, "I act, therefore I am." [5]

The question now arises as to why Whichcote is scarcely known in the history of English thought. Little is understood either of his character or writings; yet he was among the most influential preachers and theologians of his age. He was held in high esteem by eminent statesmen of his day and he, probably more than any other Cambridge teacher, impressed his mode of thought upon his colleagues and upon

---

[1] Tulloch, *Ibid.*, II, 84.
[2] *Ibid.*, p. 85; Cf. Whichcote, *Letters*, p. 108.
[3] Tillotson, *Ibid.*, p. 24. Cf. Mullinger, *Ibid.*, p. 590; Whichcote, *Works*, III, ix.
[4] Mullinger, *Ibid.*, p. 289–290.
[5] B. F. Westcott, *Essays in the History of Religious Thought In the West* (London, 1891,) pp. 362–366. Cf. Whichcote, *Ibid.*, II, 61, 94.

the rising generation of students. In a true sense he may be said to have founded the new school of philosophical theology known as Cambridge Platonism, although it is chiefly known through the more elaborate writings of others. The influence of his mind and personality exceeded his own literary productiveness. Even Tuckney felt that Whichcote had a party behind him and that his teaching was representative. He spoke not merely for himself, but for others of whom he was the reputed leader.[1]

It is difficult to say what gives a man a position of leadership in such a learned circle as a University. The greatest ability and the most profound learning may not suffice. Distinction as a writer has often no effect. Whichcote had "a certain attractiveness and glow of feeling, a persuasive enthusiasm, an aptness to teach, that goes right to the heart of the young." This constitutes a power more effective than mere literary and intellectual capacity. Thus in Whichcote, it is easy to see from elements, at once, of "intellectual strength and moral beauty," what gave him the role of "leader of minds" and such unusual influence at Cambridge. He was "well-born" and appears to have been wealthy throughout his life, and this, no doubt, helped his influence.[2] Perhaps his ability to see good in men and hope for their recovery drew many to him, as did the dignity and impressive nature of his "bearing and conversation." [3] There appear to have been few in Whichcote's time of greater celebrity than our author.[4] He is presented by his contemporaries as a man of exceptionally "sweet temper and restrained judgment" and one who exerted great influence upon the religious thought of his time.[5]

To sum up our estimation of Whichcote's influence, let us observe that he maintained his independence and position under Puritan domination, and was sympathetic and helpful to the persecuted. He was above partisanship, and untouched by changing fortunes. For almost half a century, under three evil regimes, he preached without molestation. He was silenced neither by the Puritans and the Army in the day of their power, nor by the Anglicans and King in the day of theirs, "his light shone steady, while others were flickering and snuffed." [6]

---

[1] Tulloch, *Ibid.*, pp. 45–46, 83.

[2] *Ibid.*, pp. 83–83, 92–93.

[3] William Whewell, *Lectures on the History of Moral Philosophy in England*, new edition (Cambridge, 1862) p. 69.

[4] Dyer, *Ibid.*, p. 355.

[5] Florence Highams, *Faith of Our Fathers* (London, 1939) pp.188–189.

[6] George, *Ibid.*, pp. 73–75.

Burnet has well said:

> Whichcote was a man of rare temper, very mild and obliging. He had credit with some that had been eminent in the late times, but made all the use he could of it to protect good men of all persuasions. He was much for liberty of conscience and being disgusted with the dry and systematical way of those times, he studied to raise those who conversed with him to a nobler set of thoughts, and to consider religion as a seed of deiform nature.[1]

It is hoped that this study of the life and work of Whichcote will enable the reader to view his thought with greater appreciation. Tulloch's observation appropriately closes this chapter:

> It is strange that he should have been so little known and studied; but the obscurity which has overtaken him is not without some relation to his very greatness, and the silent way in which he passed out of sight after the Restoration after he had done his work at Cambridge. ... He was careless of his own name... He possessed the highest magnanimity of all – a magnanimity extremely rare – of forgetting himself in the cause which he loved, and rejoicing that others entered into the results for which he laboured. It is all the more necessary, therefore, that we should endeavour to do some degree of justice to his name and opinions – to bring before us as complete an image as we can of the man and his academic and theological activity. Standing as he does at the fountainhead of our school of thinkers, it is especially important to catch the spirit of his teaching, and to present it in its historical and intellectual relations.[2]

---

[1] Burnet, *Ibid.*, p. 349. Cf. Tillotson, *Ibid.*, pp. 31–33; Westcott, *Ibid.*, pp. 375–376.

[2] Tulloch, *Ibid.*, II, 46. The section on Whichcote's writings which appeared as Chap. I, Pt. ii, pp. 24–38 of the original MS has been moved to the Appendix of the present work.

CHAPTER TWO

FROM ATHENS TO CAMBRIDGE

The thought of Plato is closely allied at some points with that of his predecessors. It was Socrates who, so far as can be seen, created the conception of the soul which has ever since dominated European thinking. The idea that man has a soul, the seat of his normal waking intelligence and moral character stems from Socrates. This soul is either identical with him or the most important thing about him. A. E. Taylor argues that this idea did appear in the generation immediately subsequent to Socrates (in the literature of Isocrates, Plato and Xenophon) but was absent from the literature of earlier times. Thus he reasons that it must have originated in Socrates' own generation and in that period there was no thinker to attribute it to others than Socrates himself. According to Taylor the fact that the idea of the soul was common ground for Isocrates, Plato and Xenophon means that it cannot be the discovery of any one of them.

This Socratic doctrine of the soul is neither psychology in our sense of the word, nor psycho-physics. It does not specifically define the soul, except as "that in us, whatever it is, in virtue of which we are denominated wise and foolish, good and evil," and that it is something which cannot be seen or apprehended by any of the senses. It is not a doctrine which treats either the faculties or the substance of the soul. According to Socrates, the work or function of this divine constituent in man is just to apprehend things as they really are, and consequently, in particular, to know good and evil, and to direct or govern a man's acts so that they lead to a life in which evil is avoided and good achieved. What Socrates is concerned with, therefore, is neither speculative nor empirical psychology, but a common principle of epistemology and ethics.[1]

---

[1] A. E. Taylor, *Socrates* (Boston, 1951), pp. 139–147. Cf. Taylor's account of Socratic ethics, *Ibid.*, pp. 148–162.

Though Whichcote was impressed by the thought of Socrates, especially his views on the nature and destiny of the human soul, it was the personal example of the man that moved him most.[1] From Plato himself and from Aristotle's commentary, the influence of other predecessors can be seen: Heraclitus, the Eleatics, Protagoras and other Sophists, and later by Anaxagoras, the Pythagoreans, and others.[2] While Socrates, being a Sophist, had mainly concerned himself with man, his moral and religious life, Plato was concerned with all Reality. In Plato Greek philosophy reached its highest expression up to this time, and his main addition to Greek speculation was his doctrine of Ideas whereby he sought to comprehend "all time and all existence."

Ideas are for Plato the Genii of the general notions, exempt from all space limitation, incapable of motion, possessed of life and intelligence. They are eternal realities belonging to the world of real being, but the Ideas are not all on the same level. They have their various ranks, the highest being the Idea of the Good.[3] The Idea is not the essence immanent in the various similar individual objects as such, but rather the essence conceived as perfect in its kind, immutable, unique and independent. To express the relation of individuals to their corresponding ideas, Plato employs the term "participation" and "imitation." He wavers between these two terms without making his position clear. It is obvious, however, that Plato is asserting that an Idea, though existing independently, has also a certain community with other Ideas and is in some sense present in them. But the specific nature of this community Plato has neglected to define precisely.[4] Perhaps this dependent-independent-relationship may best be described as one of interdependence. It is interesting that when Which-

---

[1] Whichcote, *Works*, II, 110–111, 122, 353; III, 255. The relation of Whichcote to his followers is remarkably similar to that of Socrates to Plato and others. In both cases the personal element is most important; for though neither man published anything, yet their thought survives through their successors, by virtue of the force of their personal example. The self-control of each through life and their calmness in the face of death, are similar. See Plato, *Apology*. Cf. Tillotson, *Funeral Sermon*, pp. 28–29. Particulars of classical sources used in this study will be found in the bibliography. English translations were used in all cases except where critical examination appeared necessary.

[2] Cf. Plato, *Cratylus*, 402 A; Aristotle, *Meta.*, 987a. The following works are suggested for a fuller analysis of the thought of Plato's predecessors: J. B. Crozier, *History of Intellectual Development*, 2nd and revised ed. (London, 1902), I, 49–51; R. G. Collingwood, *The Idea of Nature* (Oxford, 1945), pp. 29–40; Frankford, H. and H. A.; Wilson, J. A.; Jacobson, Thorkild and Irwin, W. A.; *The Intellectual Adventure of Ancient Man* (Chicago, 1948), p. 377. Paul Friedlander, *Platon: Seinwahrheit und Lebenswirklichkeit*, 2nd ed. (Berlin, 1954), Chs. 1, 2, and 6. W. W. Jaeger's, *The Theology of the Early Greek Philosophers* (New York, 1947) is basic reading.

[3] Plato, *Rep.* vi, 508c.

[4] Plato, *Tim.* 27C–29D. Cf. F. M. Cornford, *Plato's Cosmology* (New York, 1957) pp. 2–33.

cote appropriates the Platonic terms "participation" and "imitation" in his description of the divine life, he does so in the same obscure manner as Plato.

The highest Idea, the Good, is the cause of being and cognition. Good is exalted above Being, thus making clear the ethical character of his doctrine of Ideas. The Good may be considered as an Idea quite as universal as Being, since everything in so far as it is existent is necessarily good. The highest Good is not pleasure or knowledge alone but the greatest possible likeness to God, as the absolutely good.[1] The universe in which we live falls short of the perfections of the world of Ideas. It has been created by a good God in order to express his goodness, but fashioned as it is out of indeterminate matter, it does not adequately fulfil that purpose. The universe is pervaded by soul, the soul of the universe and of the individual forms a link between the world of phenomena and Ideas. Because the Creator is incapable of imperfection, he creates the lesser deities and points out to them the need of mortal creatures. They proceed to create the bodies, while he creates the souls which are to be assigned to mortal bodies as needed. The soul, therefore, is divine in origin and nature: it exists before the body as well as after it.[2] Whichcote's general indebtedness to Plato appears obvious.

Aristotle is valuable to our purpose not only for his transmission of Plato's thought with his modifications and his contribution to Neo-Platonism through Plotinus and others, but mainly because of his direct influence upon Whichcote. Our author quotes more frequently from Aristotle than from Plato in a direct sense, though his indebtedness to Platonism is greater. However, Whichcote is obviously impressed by Aristotle's moral theology and has great admiration for the man himself as shown by his frequent use of the appellation "the Philosopher" or "the great Philosopher" as he refers to Aristotle.[3] Whichcote appears to have Aristotle in mind when he speaks of God as a "superior and intelligent Agent";[4] of "necessities and impossi-

---

[1] Plato, *Theaetetus*, 176a, b. Cf. Friedrich Solmsen, *Plato's Theology* (Ithaca, 1942), pp. 149–174. His identification of good with God in Plato is not justified by evidence. See also, I. M. Crombie, *An Examination of Plato's Doctrines* (New York, 1962), Vol. I, Chs. 1, 2, 6, 7 and 8. Armstrong holds that Plato's *Timaeus* had more influence on early Christian writing than any other single Greek philosophical writing. See A. H. Armstrong and R. A. Markus, *Christian Faith and Greek Philosophy* (London, 1960) pp. 2–3.

[2] *Tim.* 29D; Cf. *Rep.* X, 617E; *Phaedo*, 78–79, 105D; *Laws* X.

[3] Whichcote, *Ibid.*, I, 334 *passim*.

[4] Whichcote, *Ibid.*, III, 187; Cf. *Meta*, ii, 8.

bilities"; [1] of the self-improvement of "powers and faculties"; [2] of personal virtue and integrity; [3] of "prudence" as the orienting virtue; [4] of intrinsic and instrumental good; [5] of equity as the truest justice; [6] and the superiority of practical knowledge to mere speculative knowledge. [7] It appears safe to say that Whichcote was further influenced by Aristotle as interpreted by the Neo-Platonists and the Schoolmen. [8]

Stoicism made its impact upon Whichcote mainly through Cicero usually referred to by Whichcote as Tully. Cicero asserts that in order to be able to judge between conflicting opinions, man must already have a yardstick on which to base his judgment, and in this the most important factors are the inner, immediate certainty, the natural consciousness of truth and innate knowledge. The consciousness of right is planted in man by nature; not until later a desire for evil, is formed which has darkened this original consciousness of right. Not only the moral characteristic but the moral, basic terms themselves are innate, even if they must be developed by ourselves. Together with reason man has in him that which drives him into moral unity with others, and into the search for truth. On account of the divinely related nature of the soul, the consciousness of God is immediately given with self-consciousness. Man has only to remember his own origin to be led to his Creator. Nature itself teaches us God's existence, because that to which all agree must always be valid as an expression of nature. The conception of the immorality of the soul and the freedom of the will are also innate. [9] When Whichcote speaks of piety; [10] of the existence of God; [11] of the immortality of the soul; [12] of man as fallen; [13] of goodness

---

[1] *Ibid.*, I, 334; Cf. Aristotle, *Rhet.* i, 4.

[2] *Ibid.*, pp. 314–315; Cf. *Rhet.*, i, 9.

[3] *Ibid.*, II, 141; Cf. Aristotle, *Eth.* i, 1; *Rhet.* iii, 11.

[4] *Ibid.*, p. 51; Cf. *Ibid.*, IV, 297; *Eth.* vi, 13.

[5] *Ibid.*, p. 391; Cf. *Rhet.* i, 6.

[6] *Ibid.*, IV, 18.

[7] *Ibid.*, pp. 288–289; Cf. *Ibid.*, I, 178, 304; IV, 72 *passim.*

[8] W. C. De Pauley, *The Candle of the Lord: Studies in the Cambridge Platonists* (London, 1937), pp. 35–36.

[9] Leif Egg-Olofsson, *The Conception of the Inner Light in Robert Barclay's Theology* (London, 1954) pp. 22–24.

[10] Whichcote, *Ibid.*, II, 52; Cf. *Ibid.*, IV, 299.

[11] *Ibid.*, III, 143; Cf. Cicero, *De Natura Deorum*, ii, 6, 7. Cicero held that right knowledge is implanted in the soul by God and is innate within it. The rational part of the soul is, therefore, a consubstantial emanation from the divine World-reason. Right reason is a kind of divine revelation in man. See W. Windelband, *A History of Philosophy*, tr. J. H. Tufts (New York, 1893) p. 223. Cf. Markus in Armstrong and Markus, *Ibid.*, pp. 100–101.

[12] *Ibid.*, II, 122.

[13] *Ibid.*, 159; Cf. Cicero, *Letters to Atticus*, ii, Ep. 1.

as natural for man;[1] of the Right and the Just as determined by Nature and Reason;[2] of the agreement of God's power with His goodness,[3] he is repeating much he has derived from Cicero. It is little wonder that Whichcote describes Tully as "a better divine than some who pretend to be Christians and yet deny reason." [4]

There was a new stream of speculation which had begun to exercise a considerable influence upon the general current of men's thought at this point in history. The Alexandrian Jews entered readily into the intellectual life of Alexandria. They welcomed Greek philosophy as a further revelation in the light of which the records of the Old Testament received a deeper meaning. In particular the personifications of the Word and Wisdom of God, which had been described with gradually increasing clarity by the writers of some of the later books of the Old Testament, now found a counterpart in the conceptions of Plato and the other Greek philosophers. Jewish writers added to the purely ethical monotheism of their own religion these new ideas, and this gave rise to the Jewish-Alexandrian school, of which Philo was the most distinguished representative.[5] However, it is my view that Whichcote is more indebted to Jewish wisdom literature directly and to the Johannine and Pauline syntheses of Jewish, Hellenic (Platonic-Stoic), and primitive Christian strands than to the Philonic synthesis.[6] This position will be pursued further in Chapter Nine, but it is important to remember that Whichcote's favourite text which became the

[1] *Ibid.*, p. 64; Cf. *Ibid.*, III, 259. According to Whichcote, Aristotle observes that man is a "mild and gentle creature." See I, 168. Cf. Aristotle, *Eth.* ii, 7, 10; iv, 5.

[2] *Ibid.*, IV, 10.

[3] *Ibid.*, p. 426; Cf. *Ibid.*, II, 159 *passim.*

[4] *Ibid.*, III, 167. Whichcote observes that Seneca speaks of man's soul as a "blast of God's mouth." See II, 43. Cf. Seneca, *Ep.* 31 and 93. Whichcote refers to Seneca elsewhere. Cf. IV, 18, 312. *passim.*

[5] Charles Elsee, *Neo-Platonism in Relation to Christianity*, (Cambridge, 1908) pp. 32–34. Though the tendency to compare Plato and Moses, Socrates and Christ, is native to Neo-Platonism in Christian history (even among the Cambridge Platonists, i.e. More and Cudworth), Whichcote is cautious at this point. Therefore, it appears unnecessary to go deeply into Philo's system which contributed much to this "allegorizing" tendency in Christianity. Cf. Charles Bigg, *The Christian Platonists of Alexandria* (Oxford, 1913) p. 32; Karl Bormann, *Die Ideen und Logoslehre Philons von Alexandrien*, (Monheim, 1955) and H. A. Wolfson, *Philo* (Cambridge, Mass., 1947), chs. 4–6. For an account of the influence of Greek ideas on Judaism between the first century B.C.E. and the fourth century C.E. in Palestine, see Saul Liebermann, *Hellenism in Jewish Palestine* (New York, 1962).

[6] See C. K. Barrett, *The Gospel According to John* (London, 1935), p. 129. Concerning syncretistic tendencies in early Christianity, see the following: F. C. Grant, *Hellenistic Religions* (New York, 1953) pp. 152–196; W. L. Knox, *Some Hellenistic Elements in Primitive Christianity* (London, 1942), pp. 1–2; Johannes Weis, *The History of Primitive Christianity*, ed. F. C. Grant (New York, 1937), I, 440–441; Hans Jonas, *The Gnostic Religion* (Boston, 1958), p. 25. Rudolf Bultmann, *Das Urchristentum* (Munich, 1962), pp. 117–118; Werner Jaeger, *Early Christianity and Greek Paideia* (Cambridge, Mass., 1961).

maxim of Cambridge Platonism is from the Book of Proverbs.[1] Whichcote seems to support our view by his insistence that John did not derive his views from the Platonists but from another source.[2]

Whichcote was obviously influenced by the Christian Platonists of Alexandria. To make this assertion is not to ignore the contribution of Justin Martyr and others like him, who reacted against the Gnostic heresy, and sought a truer union of Christianity and philosophy.[3] The most outstanding exponents of the Christian Alexandrian school were Clement and Origen, and of the two, Origen is the most representative.[4] Origen's treatment of such subjects as God, the world and rational creatures in his chief work, *On First Principles,* points toward Whichcote's treatment of the same subjects.[5] Further, his views concerning Christian tolerance; [6] the role of reason in the comprehension of religious knowledge;[7] "divine likeness" as a prerequisite for revelation;[8] punishment for sin as remedial and the present as a "probation-state";[9] and the authority of Scripture,[10] are remarkably simi-

---

[1] Prov. xx, 27.

[2] Whichcote, *Ibid.,* II, 173.

[3] Fridrich Ueberweg, *A History of Philosophy,* tr. G. S. Morris, 2nd ed. (London, 1875), I, 313. It is Ueberweg's opinion that the influence of Plato upon the Church Fathers is often overrated. Of much greater consequence, he insists, was the direct influence which Platonism (and Stoicism), in their Jewish Alexandrian form, and in their combination and blending with Jewish ideas, exerted in shaping the doctrine contained in the New Testament writings of Paul and the Fourth Gospel, and so, in consequence of the canonical importance of these writings, in determining the creed of all Christendom. Subsequently, the ideas thus introduced into Christianity, having become common Christian property, served as points of union and departure for further studies. Etienne Gilson, *The History of Christian Philosophy in the Middle Ages* (London, 1955), pp. 93–94. W. R. Inge, *The Philosophy of Plotinus* (London, 1918), II, 227. When Whichcote attempts to distinguish between eternal rights and lesser of changeable rights, he quotes from Justin Martyr. See, IV, 108. Our author opposed the Gnostic tendency in his day just as vigorously as Martyr did in his with similar weapons. Cf. II, 319; III, 126; IV, 344–345. Hans Jonas, *Ibid.* and Prof. Gilles Quispel, visiting Professor of Church History at Harvard Divinity School during the academic year, 1964–65, describe Gnosticism as a religion in its own right. The present writer has not been convinced, however, that Gnosticism is not primarily a Christian "heresy."

[4] Elsee, *Ibid.,* pp. 41–43; Cf. Bigg, *Ibid.,* pp. 11–14; Inge, *Ibid.,* I, 99. Clement held the Platonic maxim, that "nothing is to be believed which is unworthy of God." This maxim makes reason the judge of revelation. Cf. Bigg, *Ibid.* pp. 76–126; Inge, *Ibid.* p. 101; Egg-Olofson gives a valuable account of Clement's views of Law and Philosophy as preparatory to the "perfect revelation in the Incarnate Word." Further, Clement's contribution to the notion of the relation of the Logos to human reason as well as the means whereby man is led to moral perfection by the Logos is set forth. See, *Inner Light,* pp. 37–39. Cf. Whichcote, *Ibid.,* II, 316.

[5] Origen, *De Princ.* i, 3, 8, ii, 9, 6; iii, 6, 1.

[6] *Ibid.* iii, 10–15; Cf. Whichcote, *Ibid.,* II, 25.

[7] *C. Cels.* vii, 43.

[8] *Ibid.* iv, 30; v. 43; vi. 2.

[9] *De Princ.* ii, 1, 2, 10; Cf. *C. Cels.* iv. 99; Whichcote *Ibid.,* IV, 15–16.

[10] B. F. Westcott, *Essays in the History of Religious Thought in the West* (London, 1891), p. 236.

lar to Whichcote's views on the same subjects. Thus to Origen the end of philosophy is truth in all spheres; truth apprehended in its highest unity. The name of Christianity is truth and Christianity is the fulfilment of philosophy. Human wisdom is the school of the soul, while Divine Wisdom is the end. Faith, Knowledge, Wisdom – that is the order of spiritual growth.[1] From this brief sketch the relation of the Christian Platonists of Alexandria to those at Cambridge seems unmistakeable.

Neo-Platonism is in full bloom in the philosophy of Plotinus. A representative sketch of his massive system seems necessary in view of his impact upon all Neo-Platonism from his time and in view of the charge that Whichcote and his disciples made no distinction between Plato and Plotinus. We observe that Plotinus agrees with Plato in the doctrine of "sensibles" and "intelligibles" and physical natures. But he differs with Plato radically when he teaches that the One, which with Plato was the highest of Ideas, is elevated above the sphere of Ideas. Ideas, to which Plato conceived independent existence, are conceived by Plotinus as emanations from the One, the Sensibles being the last in the series of emanations. He differs from Plato, further, in teaching that the Ideas are in the Nous, while Plato in the *Timaeus*, wavering between the tendency to poetic personification and dogmatic doctrinalism, styles the highest Idea the Idea of the Good.[2] It is easier to say what Ideas meant to Plotinus than to Plato. To Plotinus all the thoughts of spirit are ideas. Spirit embraces all Ideas, as the whole its parts. Each idea is spirit, and Spirit is the totality of Ideas. The Kingdom of Ideas is the true reality.[3] Though Whichcote mentions Plotinus only once by name together with Trismegistus, this reference is of the utmost importance.[4] Plotinus here witnesses to Whichcote's concept of God creating man as a middle-being between divine and mortal nature, with the freedom to move up or down. By motion downwards we lose ourselves, but by motion upwards we find our fulfilment and true happiness. In speaking of natural and revealed truths, Whichcote refers to them as the first and second "emanation," respectively, and even his conception of the mediation of Christ is cast in the mould of Plotinian metaphysics.[5]

[1] *C. Cels.* vi. 13.

[2] Ueberweg, *Ibid.*, pp. 240; Cf. Philip Merlan, *From Platonism to Neoplatonism*, 2nd ed., revised (The Hague, 1960) pp. 221–231.

[3] *Enneads*, vi. 5, 6; Inge, *Ibid.*, I. 49, 56; Windelband, *Ibid.* p. 370.

[4] Whichcote, *Ibid.*, II, 160.

[5] See *Infra*, chs. IV, VI. When Whichcote refers to the Platonists, it is logical to suppose

Hereafter we shall be directly concerned with the parallel development of Platonism and Christianity. It is to this tradition that Whichcote belongs rather than to any purely philosophical tradition. When
we think of the Christian-Platonic tradition as it existed in the Middle
Ages we recall such noteworthy names as Gregory of Nyssa,[1] Augustine, Dionysius,[2] Erigena,[3] Anselm,[4] Cusa,[5] and others.[6] Of this
group, Augustine is the most valuable for our purpose. The religious
philosophy to which he was converted was the Platonism of Plotinus
with the Incarnation added.[7]

Augustines' doctrine of knowledge is interwoven with the metaphysics of light. The symbolism of light is already used in the possibility
and truth of the knowledge of the senses, in that he postulates two kinds
of light, a bodily one that our eyes observe, and a light with the

that he includes in this general appellation Plotinus and Neo-Platonism since his time as
well as the similar trend of thought from Plato's time. Cf. Whichcote, *Ibid.* II, 127; 177, 187,
300, III, 103; 120; IV, 70, 319 *passim.*

[1] Gilson, *Ibid.* pp. 57–59. Cf. Jean Daniélou, *Platonism Et Théologie Mystique: Essai Sur
La Doctrine Spirituelle De Saint Grégoire De Nysse* (Paris, 1944), pp. 50–65, 119–121.

[2] Westcott, *Ibid.* pp. 156–191. Cf. Pseudo-Dents L'Aréopagite, *Oeuvres Complètes,* traduction par Maurice de Gandillac (Paris, 1953), pp. 140–146, 99–100. Boethius deserves
mentioning as an exponent of the same tradition, see Gilson, *Ibid.* pp. 101–103.

[3] A. C. McGiffert, *A History of Christian Thought,* (London, 1933), II, 172, 178–179. See also
Aristotle *Meta.,* xii. 7. Augustine, *De Civ. Dei* v. 9;

[4] Anselm, *Cur Deus Homo?,* esp. bk. II. There appears to be an affinity between Anselm's
theory of atonement and Whichcote's, but this will be examined later. See *Infra,* ch. VI. It is
valuable to compare Anselm's thought with Augustine's to see how they are related. Cf.
Anselm, *Monol.* i, 17, 18–20. 29–31, 67–77 with Augustine, *De Civ. Dei,* xii. 25.

[5] Cassirer, *The Platonic Renaissance in England,* tr. Pettegrove (New York, 1953), pp.
13–15, 32, 103–104. Cassirer does not hesitate to use the others, of the same school. For a
brief synopsis of Cusa's thought see Gilson, *Ibid.,* pp. 534–536.

[6] Gilson, *Ibid.* pp. 139–140, 150–152. Here our attention is called to a Platonic movement
whose centre was the school of Chartes in the 12th century under a leader by the name of
Chartes. This school is known mainly through John of Salisbury. See also, *Ibid.* pp. 431–37,
where the same author speaks of what he calls "philosophical Augustinianism" kept intact
by Albert the Great and his favorite pupil, Ulrich of Strasburg. Cf. Proclus, *The Elements of
Theology,* ed. E. R. Dodds, 2nd ed. (Oxford, 1963). Dodds considers this as one of the chief
links between ancient and medieval thought and as the one genuinely systematic exposition
of neoplatonic metaphysic which has come down to us (p. ix). He asserts that the thought
of Proclus flowed into Christian history through the writings of Dionysius the Areopagite
(pp. xxvi–xxvii). Cf. Raymond Klibansky, *The Continuity of the Platonic Tradition During
the Middle Ages* (London, 1939), pp. 13–37.

[7] Augustine, *Conf.* vii, 9; Cf. Whichcote *Ibid.* III, 25. Here Whichcote asserts that
Augustine found the beginning of the first chapter of John among the Platonists. However,
this is but a half-truth since he fails to tell us what Augustine certainly did not find, viz., the
all-important doctrines of Incarnation and Atonement. Cf. Aug. *De Div. Dei,* viii, 4, 5, 12;
ix–xii. See also, Erich Przywara, *An Augustine Synthesis* (New York, 1958), pp. 58, 175, 185.
H. A. Wolfson, *The Philosophy of the Church Fathers,* 2nd ed., revised (Cambridge, Mass.,
1964), pp. 257–286. Wolfson deals with the relation between the *Logos* and the Platonic Ideas
in Justin Martyr, Clement, Origen, Augustine and other Church Fathers. He thus provides
a conprehensive coverage of the subject. Cf. Ernst Hoffman, *Platonismus und Christliche
Philosophie* (Zurich, 1960), pp. 230–311.

assistance of which our eyes gaze upon the physical light. The one is an object perceived, the other a means of knowledge. The ability to perceive is thus a light of purely spiritual nature, derived from the soul. All ideas are already to be found in the soul. Augustine's doctrine of knowledge culminates in his theory of illumination. Since men are capable of comprehending eternal, necessary and unchangeable truths, although they themselves are temporal, accidental and changeable, and since God alone is eternal, necessary and unchangeable, so do we comprehend such truths in immediate contact with God. In Augustine the Platonic Ideas become God's thoughts and man acquires knowledge of them through the Augustinian reminiscence, the deepening of the conscience in which reason becomes conscious of God's presence.[1] This illumination doctrine of Augustine has never disappeared from the Christian tradition.

To Augustine the Incarnation is central. The Logos in Augustine corresponds to Nous in Plotinus. The Logos is eternal as God, is His son, born of God, of the same being, itself God, participating in God's unchangeableness. The world has been created through the Logos which, also, as a life-giving principle sustains the world even if the latter has not accepted it. The Logos is the light of men, for men's souls are not the light itself.[2] Accordingly, Augustine sees as the greatest mistake in Neo-Platonism, its ignorance of the Incarnation, of "logos debasement" through which men are saved by humility and faith.[3] Even Augustine's doctrine of illumination is bound up with his concept of the Son as the Logos.

...When anything concerning wisdom is declared or narrated in the Scriptures, whether as itself speaking, or where anything is said of it, the Son chiefly is intimated to us. And by the example of Him who is the image of God, let us also not depart from God since we also are the image of God; not indeed that which is equal to Him, since we are made so by the Father through the son and not born of the Father, as that is. And we are so, because we are enlightened with light; but that is so, because it is the light that enlightens; and which, therefore being without pattern, is to us a pattern.[4]

---

[1] Augustine, *Trin.* viii. 2, 3, 4, 6, 8, 9; ix., xiii–xv.

[2] *Ibid.*, vii. 3.

[3] Augustine, *De Civ. Dei.* xi–xiv.

[4] Augustine, *Trin.* vii. 3, 5. Whichcote quotes Augustine a number of times. See his *Works*, I, 175–176 where he refers to Augustine (*Ep.* 50, 68 and 159); Whichcote, *Ibid.*, I, 178 concerning the interpretation of scripture; *Ibid.* II, 396 regarding Augustine's conversion (*Conf.* viii. 12); *Ibid.* III, 420 where Augustine is referred to as a "great father" (Cf. *Ibid.* IV–423), and *Ibid.*, II, 350 concerning Augustine's assertion that if we take away the grace and goodness of God we render Him impotent to do us good, and we remove human freedom as well as God's power to command. Whichcote's concept of happiness is from Augustine (Cf. *Conf.* i.i. with *Works*, IV, 31).

Augustine's teaching was perpetuated by a long series of followers, and it was not until the thirteenth century that Aristotelianism as interpreted by Aquinas, became the official system of the Church and displaced its rivals. Even so, the Neo-Platonic tradition lingered in the schools of Europe, and especially Italy, to emerge once more in full life, in the fifteenth century.[1] Thus, the tribute of Windelband to Augustine is significant.

> The two great streams of theosophy which burst forth from Alexandria, on the one hand, into Christian theology, on the other, into Neo-Platonism, were not long separate from each other. Although Neo-Platonism was destroyed by scholasticism, it sent its thought through a thousand channels into the orthodox as well as the heterodox development of Christian thought after Origen. Both systems of thought found their perfect reconciliation in an original thinker, who was the philosopher of Christianity – Augustine. The doctrine of Augustine ... was much more than a receptacle for the confluent streams of Hellenic-Roman philosophy. It was rather a living fountain of the thought of the future. His was an initiating rather than a consummating work, and therefore he does not belong to the history of ancient philosophy.[2]

It appears more appropriate to speak of the "Neo-Platonism" of the Italian Renaissance than of its "Platonism." Neo-Platonism is less misleading when applied to the teaching of the Platonic Academy of Florence in the latter part of the fifteenth century. For the earlier Italian humanists Plato was more venerated than understood. Petrarch and his immediate successors knew little or no Greek, so that their ideas of Platonism were pieced together from Latin authors and from dialogues then existing in Latin. Only three of Plato's works were available, *Timaeus, Meno* and *Phaedo* in translations. As the fifteenth century advanced Greek scholarship advanced. However, it was not easy for scholars at this time to form a clear estimate of Greek thought in view of their many preconceptions. At first their interest in Plato was mainly literary, and there was no commanding philosophic intellect among them. In spite of this, many treatises on moral philosophy during

[1] Robb, *Neo- Platonism of the Italian Renaissance*, (London, 1935) pp. 17–18.

[2] W. Windelband, *History of Ancient Philosophy*, tr. by H. E. Cushman, (London, 1900), p. 383. While the present writer is aware that another great contribution of Augustine, viz., his doctrine of Predestination, has had tremendous consequences in the history of religious thought, it has been omitted here.

The reason seems to be a logical one, viz., the positive, direct and constructive contribution of Augustine to Whichcote's thought appears to be his Christian Platonic synthesis. However, the Predestination doctrine of Augustine, culminating in Puritanism in 17th century England, is a definite negative influence upon Whichcote. But it seems sufficient to consider this latter influence of Augustine when we come to an examination of Whichcote's reaction to Puritanism; for it is the Puritan version of Augustine's doctrine of Predestination, rather than the doctrine directly, that affects Whichcote. See *Infra*, ch. III.

this first period of humanism reveal, if not a deep understanding of Plato, a distinct Platonic colour.[1]

Plato becomes for Petrarch and his followers a "symbol and rallying cry." Others of the same tradition with original suggestions before Ficino were: Coluccio, Salutati, Valla, Alberti, Bessarion, Pletho, Isidore of Salonika, and George of Trebizond. Picod ella Mirandola was one of Ficino's most notable disciples. However, the main representative in the Italian Renaissance of Platonism was Ficino himself.[2]

Ficino merits our attention for various reasons. As a translator and commentator of Plato he represents one of the most important epochs in the history of Platonism: as leader of the Platonic Academy in Florence, he occupies a central position in the history of Renaissance civilisation. Continuing the work of earlier humanists, he was the first who gave the work a philosophical significance. Absorbing a vast body of ideas from ancient, early Christian and mediaeval sources, he was able to incorporate them into a comprehensive system of Christian Platonism which displays many original and important characteristics of its own. Both as an original thinker and as a transmitter of earlier ideas, he exercised a widespread and powerful influence on subsequent generations, and traces of his influence are found in many philosophers, theologians, moralists, poets and artists of the later Renaissance in many European countries.[3]

According to Ficino, God transcends our faculties, but He is none the less part of them, the part by which the identification of the human mind with the divine is accomplished. The Absolute is within us, and God became man in order that man might become God.[4] Ficino is torn between the idea of the Absolute as utterly unknowable, and that of the Absolute latent in every soul and created in it anew with each increase of spirituality and true knowledge. This uncertainty has given rise to most of the contradictions that have been noted in his work; and it is mainly in an attempt to resolve it that he elaborated his theory of love by which the human soul gives itself to God, and becomes assimilated

---

[1] Robb, Ibid., pp. 11–12.

[2] Ibid., pp. 12, 18–20; 35, 41, 46–52, 60–63. Cf. Kristeller, The Philosophy of Marsilio Ficino, tr. by Virginia Conant (New York, 1943), p. 7.

[3] Kristeller, Ibid. p. viii. Elsewhere Kristeller states that through his translations and commentaries, Ficino did for Plato, Plotinus and other ancient philosophers what the humanists did for the ancient Greek orators, poets and historians. Ibid. p. 11. Cf. Robb, Ibid. pp. 85–86. Kristeller adds that Ficino combines mediaeval Aristotelianism and the Christian-Platonism of the Church Fathers and Augustine. Ficino is also in direct contact with Plato and the ancient Neo-Platonists. Ibid. pp. 3–16, 23, 28; Cf. Jean Festugière, La Philosophie de l'Amour de Marsilo Ficin pp. 63–65, (Paris, 1941).

[4] Robb, Ibid. p. 67.

to Him. Man can give himself in love to God, because God created him out of love and loved him first. The affection of God and man is mutual and reciprocal like that of parent and child. Man's love is spontaneous and voluntary, and yet it is a response to something that is at once the utmost goal of desire and a presence at the root of his being, deeper than all conscious life.[1]

Since the natural appetite, *Appetitus Naturalis*, toward God, infused in us by God, cannot be in vain, the minds of men are eternal so that some time they may reach the eternal and divine good by nature. The rational soul is placed on the borderline between temporal and eternal things. Thus being placed midway, it has rational forces and actions ascending toward the eternal and also descending toward the temporal.[2]

Wherefore by a natural instinct he [man] ascends to things above, and descends to those beneath. And while he ascends he discards not the lower, and while he descends he discards not the higher. For if he relinquish either he will lapse to the opposite extreme, neither will he be the true bond of the eternal world.[3]

However, the mind of man seeks God always and in everything, and cannot be satisfied till it finds Him. It is natural for man to desire perfect goodness and felicity or a god-like life. Man has not only the desire but the capacity to know and possess the forms of all things including the *Summum Bonum*. His mind cannot be satisfied with the finite because it contains a ray of the divine light.

When our mind is illuminated by the ray of God, it thinks in Him the concepts of all things whose source is God and which are God, Himself, and therefore [the mind] thinks through the light of God and knows only the divine light itself. But it seems to know different Ideas and concepts of things emanating from there.[4]

He continues:

[God] illuminates each man who enters this world in such a way that anybody thinks in God and through Him whatever he thinks, though dark minds may not comprehend Him, because they do not recognize that they see all things through Him.[5]

Unity, truth and goodness form a single stable reality that underlies this unstable and inconsistent world and all knowledge is a return toward a single source.

[1] *Ibid.*, pp. 68–70. Festugière, *Ibid.*, pp. 24–26.

[2] Kristeller, *Ibid.*, pp. 178, 197–198. 305; Cf. Cassirer, Kristeller, Randall, et al., *The Renaissance Philosophy of Man*, (Chicago, 1945), ch. III.

[3] Robb, *Ibid.*, p. 87 (from Ficino, *Theologia Platonica*, II, ii). Cf. Pico, "The very Elegant Speech on the Dignity of Man," tr. by C. G. Wallis (Annapolis, Md., 1940).

[4] Kristeller, *Ibid.*, p. 253.

[5] *Ibid.*, Cf. (Jn. 1, :9); Augustine, *Trin.* vii, 3.5.

If therefore in the one living body of the world there is everywhere a single life ... much more is there a single good which is present everywhere, even beyond the world.[1]

Grace is the pervading expression of the divine in the world; therefore, all religions contain some good, though Christianity which alone is founded on the sole virtue of God is supreme among others.[2]

The doctrine of the place of the soul in the Universe provides Ficino with an opportunity to justify the Christian dogma of the Incarnation in a new and special manner. In his opinion Christ is not only the Mediator between God and men but also the Mediator between the Creator and the creation as a whole. Because of this universal connection the Word of God was forced to choose man himself for His instrument as the universal link between all things. Ficino asserts that the work of God is perfect in every way, therefore the created Being had to be at some time connected with the Creator. Thus in Christ the union of God and man, Creator and creation, Infinite and finite, is accomplished; in Him may be sought the unity and harmony that the world of appearance seems to deny.[3]

With Ficino there is no radical distinction between rational and religious activity.[4] The relationship he indicates between Platonism and Christianity is most valuable for our purpose. Ficino's view was that though Platonic philosophy has its own authority and tradition, it is in no way opposed to the Christian doctrine and tradition. More than any other system, it is able to give Christian doctrine a philosophical confirmation. The Platonic doctrine is a religious philosophy. It guarantees the accord between philosophy and religion, and may therefore be called "theology" as the title of his chief work the *Theologia Platonica* indicates. As to the intimate affinity of Platonism with the Mosaic and Christian doctrines, Ficino quotes Numenius and Augustine again and again, even writing small tracts to prove the agreement between the Socratic and the Christian conduct of life, and between the Mosaic and Platonic doctrines. He considers "religious philosophers" such as Pythagoras, Socrates, and Plato precursors of Christianity and allows them a share in eternal salvation, along with the prophets in the Old Testament. He assigns to Platonic philosophy the task of furthering religion and bringing men back to Christian faith.[5]

---

[1] Robb, *Ibid.* p. 86 (from Ficino, *Ibid.* II, iv, 91).
[2] Robb, *Ibid.* pp. 63–74. Cf. F. S. Ferré, *The Finality of Faith and Christianity Among the World Religions* (New York, 1963), p. 90.
[3] Kristeller, *Ibid.* pp. 405–406.
[4] Robb, *Ibid.*, p. 63.
[5] Kristeller, *Ibid.*, pp. 28–29, 322–323.

We must not think (he writes to Johannes Pannonius) that the subtle and philosophical minds of men can ever be gradually enticed and led to the perfect religion by any lure other than a philosophical one. For subtle minds trust themselves only to reason, and if they receive religion from a religious philosopher, at once and of their own volition they recognize religion in general and from there more readily to the best species of religion included in that genus.[1]

Elsewhere he says:

What was Christ but, as it were, a living book of moral, nay of divine philosophy, and the very divine idea of virtue made manifest to human eyes.[2]

Ficino's influence survived his death and the dissolution of his Academy. His works were reprinted and studied throughout the sixteenth century. His concept of natural religion may well have had some bearing on the theology of the period of the Reformation. In England, Colet shows traces of Ficino's Platonism and the Cambridge Platonists carry on the philosophical tradition of the Florentines.[3] Florentine Platonism freed English thought of the narrowness and fetters of ecclesiastical tradition by confronting it with the question of the universal grounds of the *a priori* of religion. The Platonic concept of apriority became the instrument with which Whichcote and his followers attacked the whole intellectual world, and sought to undermine on the one hand the central position of English empiricism and on the other the views of the orthodox church system and various religious sects.[4]

About three hundred years after Erigena, the English Schoolmen who studied Aristotle in Latin, appear in history as opponents of Aquinas. Duns Scotus and William Ockham can hardly be claimed as Platonists. After Ockham, there was a gap and we may pass at once to the Renaissance proper, which reached England in the time of Colet and Erasmus. The flame which they kindled in England was lighted in Italy, where Linacre visited the Platonic Academy at Florence. At Cambridge the study of Greek was promoted by the teaching of Erasmus in 1512–13. Three or four years later Ascham found undergraduates reading Aristotle and Plato under John Clerke, the new Greek professor.[5]

---

[1] *Ibid.*, p. 28.

[2] Robb, *Ibid.* p. 86. (from Ficino, *De Christiana Religione*, ch. xxiii, p. 25).

[3] Kristeller, *Ibid.* p. 19. Cf. Preserved Smith, *History of Modern Culture*, (New York, 1930) p. 181.

[4] Ernst Cassirer, *The Platonic Renaissance in England*, tr. by J. P. Pettegrove (New York, 1953) p. 24. Cf. Festugière, *Ibid.* pp. 40–43.

[5] W. R. Inge, *The Platonic Tradition in English Religious Thought* (London, 1926), p. 36. Cf. Lewis Einstein, *The Italian Renaissance in England* (New York, 1902), pp. vii–viii, 179–228, 373–385.

The earliest signs of contacts with Italian culture to be detected at Cambridge appear about 1478, with the presence of an Italian Franciscan, Lorenzo Traversagni. His treatise in 1478 called *Rhetorica* was constructed on new lines and was obviously inspired by classical models: it shows a strong Ciceronian influence, together with a certain independence of the mediaeval schoolmen.[1] Another figure of note is John Doget, a Cambridge scholar who had studied in Italy. He may be considered important among early English humanists, chiefly because he was an average scholar, and as such was more representative of contemporary culture than humanists endowed with brilliant gifts and more under the influence of the Italians. It is apparent from the state of Cambridge scholarship at the close of Edward IV's reign that the University was beginning to break away from the mediaeval view of the humanities. Although this was due mainly to practical considerations, the superiority of modern Latinity over the earlier style was recognised. But Cambridge at this point accepted only the "surface" of humanism and for a deeper grasp of humanism we must look to the sixteenth century.[2] A sound knowledge of Greek enabled some of the most lively and inquisitive minds to study the Greek philosophies.

By the mid-sixteenth century no English edition of Plato or Plotinus had yet appeared, but all Plato's works had been issued in Venice in 1522, in Basle in 1534, in Paris in 1578 and by Ficino (with Porphyry's life) in Florence in 1492. Remembering that the circulation of books in the universities of Europe was as a rule rapid, we may assume that copies of these or some of them would be accessible at one or more of the Cambridge colleges; and thus the Platonic fire could be kindled, or if kindled already, could be kept burning.[3]

Erasmus was a figure of great significance and wide influence as a

---

[1] Roberto Weiss, *Humanism in England During The Fifteenth Century* (Oxford, 1941) pp. 162–163. Cf. H. A. Gelder, *The Two Reformations in the Sixteenth Century* (The Hague 1961), chs. IV, V. See also, Paul Meissner, *England Im Zeitalter von Humanismus, Renaissance Und Reformation* (Heidelberg, 1952), pp. 31–35, 176–178, *passim*.

[2] Weiss, *Ibid.*, pp. 163–167. Doget became Provost of King's College in 1499. Among other things, he studied Platonic writings diligently and produced a commentary on the *Phaedo*.

[3] F. J. Powicke, *The Cambridge Platonists*, (London, 1926), pp. 12–13. According to this author, Andrew Downes (1549?– 1628) was Greek Professor at Cambridge until 1625 after serving 17 years as professor. However, upon his enquiry at Emmanuel College, Queen's College and the University Library, Cambridge, he discovered no evidence that they possessed any copy of the editions of Plato or Plotinus at the period in question. He concludes that there must have been some private copies. However, Weiss, *Ibid.*, p. 163–165 reports that John Doget, Provost of King's College, Cambridge, from 1499, found several books on the subject in King's Library, among which were: Decembrio's translation of the *Republic* and Bruni's latinised *Phaedrus* together with other modern translations of Plato's works. It is interesting that this Provost of King's, Whichcote's predecessor in the same position, should have attempted, though uncritically, to enlist Plato as an apologist for Christianity.

representative of humanism. He is especially valuable for our purpose
since he visited England and taught at Cambridge University.[1] He is
a well-known representative of the "rational Christian spirit" before
the Reformation.[2] He was at once a great scholar and literary artist.
Erasmus was also a religious man with a deep concern for the religious
conditions in his day. He set forth clearly and in great detail the nature
of true piety and showed how it is to be attained: he insisted that no
man can live the Christian life by his own strength, he must exert
himself to the utmost, must have courage and confidence, must be ever
watchful and persistent in resisting the devil, but even so he cannot
overcome evil and live as he ought without divine help. He emphasized
the dignity of man, but only for the purpose of bringing out clearly the
unworthiness of vice and uncleanness. He based man's dignity not on
what he was himself, but on what he owed God who created him and
brought him with a great price, who created the world for his sake,
who made him as a son of God, an heir of immortality, a member of
Christ and of the Church, his body a temple of the Holy Spirit and
his mind the image and secret habitation of Deity.[3]

The "new learning," which was expressed by Erasmus, spread to
Germany and the Low Countries, to Italy and to England. In addition
to Erasmus, Wessel, Reuchlin, Staupitz and the Florentines showed
the influence of the New Learning on the Continent together with
Colet, Thomas More, Tyndale and others in England. The spirit of this
movement was to harmonise Christianity and natural truth – to interpret the Scripture like other books; to simplify Christian Doctrine
to the limits of the Apostolic Creed; to put the Bible before everything,
and to be content with simple truths evidently set forth in it as
necessary to salvation. It aimed at spiritual enlightenment rather than
dogmatic change.[4] Accordingly, in England, with the opening of the
sixteenth century, there was a genuine and decided awakening in
religious life, a new tone of religious thought, and a desire to renovate
the Church, and deliver theology and the study of the Scriptures from
the bondage of scholasticism. Colet and Tyndale are the most conspicuous representatives of this early movement. Colet actively co-

[1] McGiffert, *Ibid.*, pp. 381–383; Cf. Thomas Fuller, *History of the University of Cambridge*,
new ed. (London, 1840); See also D. F. S. Thomson and H. C. Porter, eds., *Erasmus and
Cambridge* (Toronto, 1963). This entire work contains a collection of Erasmus' personal letters
and papers during his stay at Cambridge University.

[2] John Tulloch, *Rational Theology and Christian Philosophy In England In the Seventeenth
Century* (London, 1872), I, 2.

[3] McGiffert, *Ibid.*, p. 389.

[4] Tulloch, *Ibid.*, I, 2–3.

operated with Erasmus in the promotion of the "new learning" while
Tyndale carried it on in his devoted labours in the English translation
of the Scriptures. The spirit of this movement was at once rational and
evangelical: Colet and Tyndale both loved truth, but had at the same
time a vital power and a divine faith to move them.[1]

Turning to Whichcote and his disciples, one remembers that they
dealt with questions which affect the very conception and structure of
the modern mind. They stand between the philosophical Italian and
English Renaissance and the general history of eighteenth century
thought. Their thought is an integrating factor and an important stage
in the growth of modern thought. The view of Plato we find in the
Cambridge Platonists, beginning with Whichcote, is that of the
Florentines. Ficino's views seemed authentic and exemplary to them.
They added no essentially new feature to this picture, nor did they have
the courage and capacity for historical criticism. Plato is for them the
living proof that true philosophy is never opposed to genuine Christianity. On the other hand there is something new and different in
English humanism which comes out in Whichcote and his school. Even
though humanism in England has its roots in Continental and especially
Italian humanism, it exhibits basic differences. Italian humanism at
first sought to make peace with religion; but this was mainly for the
purpose of increasing its influence over the Church. In the meantime,
there was a growing estrangement between the interest of humanism
and religion in Italy. Thus the great Italian humanists, like Lorenzo
Valla, looked upon the traditional objects of religious faith with a cool
and deliberate scepticism. They were free from the bondage of dogma
and were seeking freedom from the Christian ethic and way of life.
Fortunately in England, humanism takes the opposite course. It is as
critical of the scholastic system, but is never anti-religious. The
English humanists were anxious to further the interpretation of the
sources of Christianity.[2]

But as we shall see, Whichcote is also faced with the aftermath of the
Reformation. The voice of Erasmus would never have moved Europe
as Luther did. It needed the cry of an evangelist rather than the inquiry
of a biblical critic and rational theologian to spark the Reformation.
Lutheran theology hardened into dogmatism. Calvinism was dogmatic

---

[1] *Ibid.*, p. 38. For an account of the influence of Ficino and Erasmus upon Colet together
with his fresh approach to Scriptural exegesis, see Cassirer, *Ibid.*, pp. 12–14.

[2] Colet's place in the Platonic tradition is well established by Leland Miles in his, *John
Colet and The Platonic Tradition* (Lasalle, Ill., 1961). Cf. Cassirer, *Ibid.*, pp. 7–9.

from the beginning. Calvin adopted the same great lines of Augustinianism which Luther used without question. He was systematic in his treatment of theology. But this very dogmatism of Calvin prepared the way for a reaction by a series of rational theologians anticipating in many ways the position to be held by the Cambridge Platonists.[1] It is my view that the reactions of the Socianian and Arminian systems to the dogmatic position of the Reformers paved the way for the liberal and rational tendencies of the later theologians.

Socinianism entered England by way of Holland and influenced the Oxford rational theologians, i.e. Falkland, Hales and Chillingworth as well as the Cambridge Platonists. Whichcote, the leader of the latter group, takes his place among Christian humanists. How far he was influenced by Socinius is in question. But there is no doubt that the Cambridge Platonists belong to the liberalizing progressive theological forces of their day. In this sense they may be closely related to the side of the Socinian movement that stood for the principle of reason and tolerance in religion. However, the evidence is too slender to suppose that they were greatly influenced by Socinian theology. From the sources it is difficult to say just how much Whichcote derived from Socinius and from more contemporary writers, viz. Hooker, Hales, Chillingworth and Taylor.[2]

Arminianism seems to have begun in England after the visit of Grotius in 1613. By 1625 Arminianism had become extremely influential in England.[3] In the pre-Cartesian period Grotius together with Lord Herbert of Cherbury appears to have been among the first to introduce in England the notion of "innate ideas." Grotius' influence in England was extensive. Lord Herbert was especially influential among the liberals in the church. Grotius asserted that the law of nature originated *ex principiis homini internis*, and that the certainty of the principles within man were such that no further assurance, not even in the form of divine revelation, could strengthen them. Lord Herbert spoke of the human mind as a closed book in which much truth was already stored, even if the stimulus of sense – experience is needed to open the book and make the truth apparent, and he spoke

[1] Tulloch, *Ibid.*, I, 4–9; Cf. A. F. Mitchell, *Minutes of the Westminister Assembly of Divines* (London, 1874), pp. xvi-xviii. See also, Meissner, *Ibid.* pp. 467–514.

[2] H. J. McLachlan, *Socinianism in Seventeenth Century England* (London, 1951), pp. 4–6, 30–33, 97–100. Socinius' doctrines of the unipersonality of God and the humanity of Christ is foreign to Whichcote. See *Ibid.* p. 13.

[3] A. W. Harrison, *Arminianism*, (London, 1937) p. 122.
Cf. F. J. Powicke, *John Norris of Bermerton* (London, 1894), p. 129. See also R. L. Colie, *Light and Enlightenment* (Cambridge, Eng., 1957), pp. 23, 37, 144.

of certain "common notions" which have their existence in reason itself. Both, like Whichcote, were concerned with religious and ecclesiastical matters, and their "common notions" or "internal principles." These were devised to furnish a ground of certainty on which all contending parties in the church might unite.[1]

When Tuckney came to Cambridge as Vice-Chancellor in 1648, he was shocked at the reaction against Calvinism there. He found men who refused to receive the Gospel according to Geneva without question, but insisted upon submitting all to the bar of reason. The most influential of these men was Whichcote. Was he an Arminian? There seems to be no conclusive answer to this question. However, it appears safe to assume that indirectly the Arminian spirit helped to shape his ideas, but that he arrived at his conclusions independently.[2]

Under Elizabeth the leaders of the Church of England set out upon a *Via Media* determined to avoid equally the Romanists and the Genevans.[3] The theologian who gave force to this general position was Richard Hooker. Hooker gives to theological controversies of his time a rational and philosophic interpretation which in turn gives new meaning and illumination to the whole sphere of theology. He began his analysis of the primary and essential principles of all government. He said that divine laws are our only immutable guides in the ordering of the Church. Laws are not divine merely because they are found in the Scripture, but all law, as an expression of the original law, or reason, of the universe, is divine. Whether the law is revealed in Scripture, or in the rational constitution of human nature, makes no difference. Its sacredness is the same as springing out of the same fountain of all light and order. According to this idea the Church of England, in preserving the Catholic hierarchy of offices was defensible, not merely because it was there and there was nothing in Scripture against it, but because it was in itself a fair, seemly and rational order of government. It based itself on the divine reason, expressed in the rational consciousness, and sanctioned both by the national sentiment and the course of Catholic history. It was conformable to Scripture and the Christian reason, and had its origin directly in the growth and advance of reason. It was a spiritual order, capable of diverse forms,

---

[1] James Seth, *English Philosophers and Schools of Philosophy* (London, 1912), pp. 89–90.

[2] Harrison, *Ibid.*, pp. 166, 168–169; Cf. *Ibid.*, pp. 131, 141–142, 153, 147, 176. See also Tulloch, *Ibid.*, pp. 25–27. See Harrison, *Ibid.*, pp. 141–143. Here is an account of the English reaction to Arminian ideas. It is important to note that John Goodwin, a vigorous Arminian, dedicated his book *Redemption Redeemed* to Whichcote and others at Cambridge.

[3] J. R. H. Moorman, *A History of the Church of England*, (London, 1953), p. 202.

and tolerantly comprehensive of all Christian gifts and activities.[1]
According to Hooker, order is divine and discipline is needed
everywhere, but there is no necessity that it be everywhere the same.
He does not defend any particular order, but begins with a general
dissertation on the nature of law. The Church is left in possession of
rational freedom. It is guided by public reason. The Scriptures which
contain the supernatural light presuppose in the main the existence
of a natural light. Hooker, in a general sense, with many qualifications
may be considered as a Rationalist against the Scripturalist. He
vindicated the use of reason with certain limits. The supernatural light
presupposes the natural. Scripture comes to help in the further
enlightenment of reason. It is by reason we know the Scriptures to be
the word of God. This is the one thing we cannot know by the Scriptures
themselves, so that reason is the instrument of faith. When we speak
to men of God we suppose them in possession of a faculty to understand
and to judge something of what we shall tell them. Hooker defended
reason and the light of nature as able to teach us our duty, but not to
lead us to salvation.[2] It is a brief step from Hooker to Whichcote
concerning the role of reason and natural light.[3]

In the age following Hooker, or during the reigns of the first two
Stuarts, James I and Charles I, the Church of England lost much of
its original breadth and catholicity. Anglo-Catholic theology marks
the decay of the more genuine catholic spirit which united the Church
of the English Reformation to the other Reformed Churches. As a
definite system, however, it did not emerge till the seventeenth
century; and Anglo-Catholics, as a party, have no right to claim the
inheritance of the Church of England.[4] The original advocates of the
Church of England *via media* fought their battle with weapons of
reason and fair Scriptural enquiry. They had no exclusive theory of
divine right, and their sacerdotalism was not dogmatic. But now
Anglo-Catholicism allied itself with Arminianism and hardened into
a dogmatic position. They attacked Calvinism on the grounds of its
inconsistency with the ancient decrees of the Councils and writings

---

[1] Tulloch, *Ibid.*, pp. 51–52; II, pp. 82–83. Cf. John Hunt, *Religious Thought in England*,
(London, 1870) I, 57.

[2] Hunt, *Ibid.*, pp. 58–60. One of the limits Hooker puts on reason appears to be his
assertion that private reason should not depart from the decisions of public reason; for this
departure leads to confusion. We are not to consider our yes as good as the nay of all learned
men in the world. We should despise the judgment of grave and learned men. However, we
are not to be tied to authority when there is reason to the contrary.

[3] Cassirer, *Ibid.*, p. 35–36.

[4] Tulloch, *Ibid.*, pp. 54–55.

of the Fathers. While accepting the basis of faith in the Holy Scripture, they resolved to take the Bible as God gave it and allow full weight to the interpretation of ancient Catholic authority. They met the claim of the Divine Right for the Presbyterian polity by claiming a Divine Right for Episcopacy and by emphasising the individualism of Puritan theology and worship, the reality of Sacramental grace, of the power of Absolution, of the authoritative ritual of the Church. Of this school Andrews was the chief theologian and Laud was the great champion in action. Unfortunately, Anglo-Catholicism entered into alliance with the Stuarts and so with the policy of royal absolutism and the Divine Right of Kings. Thus the Anglo-Catholics believed that this alliance would act as a break-water against the waves of revolution and a means of enforcing their views on Church Order and Ritual. They threw themselves unreservedly in the cause of advancing despotism. But this proved a fatal mistake. With the sudden collapse of the Royal Absolutism their power also fell. The Calvinistic or Puritan Party, powerful especially in the middle classes and in the House of Commons, formed a bolder and happier alliance with the defenders of political liberty and triumphed over the High Church School, with a triumph which seemed permanent and complete.[1]

One of the most striking features of the Commonwealth period was the luxuriant growth of new sects. The various names given these sects do not represent sects in the modern sense of independent, organised, ecclesiastical systems. Seventeenth century writers often spoke of a sect where we should speak of a party or a school of thought. Pelagians, Arminians, Arians, Antinomians, Millenarians, and Latitudinarians were severally to be found in more than one of the various churches.[2] Richard Baxter describes four religious sects in a stricter sense, viz., the Vanists, Seekers, Quakers and Bohemists.[3] At any rate, it was against similar religious divisions with their enthusiasm and super-stition that Whichcote protested.

Whichcote reacted against Romanism on two main grounds: (1) Its claim to infallibility and general intolerance, and (2) Its Scholastic position. The very activity of the Roman Catholics at this time served

---

[1] Alfred Barry, *Masters of English Theology*, (London, 1877), pp. x–xii. For a fuller discussion on the struggle of Anglo-Catholics with the Puritans, and the subsequent triumph of Puritanism, see Tulloch, *Ibid.*, pp. 57–59. See also *Infra*, Chap. III.

[2] C. E. Whiting, *Studies in English Puritanism*, (London, 1931) pp. 233–234. This book contains a full description of the minor sects from 1660 to 1688 (pp. 233–322). Cf. H. G. Plum, *Restoration Puritanism* (Chapel Hill, N.C., 1943), p. 13.

[3] Richard Baxter, *Autobiography*, ed. by J. M. L. Thomas, (London, 1931) pp. 72–74.

to quicken in England a new type of thought. The Roman Church had never lost the hope of winning back the English crown and people to its old Catholic allegiance. Encouraged by the success of the Jesuits on the Continent, and well informed of the prevalent religious divisions in England, it posed itself as the remedy for the distractions of controversy by the claim to infallible authority.[1] Whichcote's reaction to the intolerant and dogmatic attitude of Popery may be easily understood; for it was a challenge to his moderate presuppositions of faith and practice. The other point of divergence between Whichcote and the Romanists had to do with the general Scholastic position. In this he shared the general spirit of the time. There was a demand for a new type of philosophic learning that would furnish Protestantism with the same intellectual support that Scholasticism had given Catholic doctrine. Whichcote rejected Aristotelian thought in his search for conceptions to develop his thought in accordance with the doctrine of two substances. The acceptance and application of Platonic and Neo-Platonic conceptions appear for him a logical step. It is to be remembered that though Whichcote adheres to the doctrine of two distinct substances, his real interest lies in the divine creative purpose, and the soul's capacity to share in the knowledge of that purpose, and thus participate in the divine life until it finally returns to God.[2]

The Reformation and the scientific movement were two aspects of the historical revolt which was the dominant intellectual movement of the later Renaissance. The appeal to the origins of Christianity, and Francis Bacon's appeal to efficient causes as against final causes, were two aspects of one movement. The seventeenth century inherited a ferment of ideas from the revolt of the sixteenth century and in it were developed systems of thought touching every aspect of human life. This "century of genius" provided intellectual activity adequate for the greatness of its occasion; it was crowded with new innovations of thought.[3] Bacon, Hobbes and Descartes are noteworthy representatives

[1] Tulloch, *Ibid.*, pp. 64, 74. Cf. Arthur Galton, *Our Outlook Towards English Roman Catholics and The Papal Court* (London, 1902), pp. 104–106, 118–124.

[2] J. J. De Boer, *The Theory of Knowledge of the Cambridge Platonists*, (Madras, 1931) pp. 9–10. Though De Boer is only concerned with Smith, Cudworth and Culverwel, I would maintain that his position is applicable to Whichcote also, though the reaction may have been stronger in these other writers.

[3] A. N. Whitehead, *Science and the Modern World*, (Cambridge, Eng., 1926), pp. 11, 55–57. Cf. F. J. C. Hearshaw, ed., *Social and Political Ideas of Some of the Thinkers of the Sixteenth and Seventeenth Centuries* (London, 1926), p. 32; R. S. Westfall, *Science and Religion in Seventeenth Century England* (New Haven, 1958), ch. V; Herbert Butterfield, *The Origins of Modern Science 1300–1800* (New York, 1959) pp. 77–95. See also Robert Hoops, *Right Reason in the English Renaissance* (Cambridge, Mass., 1962) p. 175; Lydia Gysi, *Platonism and Cartesianism in the Philosophy of Ralph Cudworth* (Bern, 1962).

of the genius of the seventeenth century. It is difficult to say how far Whichcote was influenced by Bacon and Descartes, but the negative influence of Hobbes appears more evident. Bacon's *Novum Organum* was published in 1620 but his philosophy did not reach the University or make any notable impression there for many years and Descartes' influence belongs primarily to the second half of the century.[1] The fecundity of Cartesianism manifested itself in England chiefly through the part played by it in the formation of the intellectual system of Locke.[2] It appears that Whichcote had his position well established before the impact of Cartesianism was fully felt in England. Yet it is possible that he had a casual knowledge of the thought of Descartes. The impact of Descartes appears more in the later Cambridge men, especially Henry More. There seems to be no doubt that Hobbes sparked a negative reaction among the Cambridge Platonists. It was inevitable that the radical speculation of Hobbes, alike in the spheres of metaphysics and of politics, should provoke a reaction, and that such a spiritually minded man as Whichcote should rally to the defence of higher and more spiritual aspects of human life.[3]

We turn now to a more positive influence upon Whichcote and his followers, viz., a band of scholars who had assembled at Lord Falkland's before the Civil War to consider the problems of theology and philosophy in a spirit of freedom. The most outstanding of this group were Falkland, Hales and Chillingworth. We shall present Chillingworth as a suitable representative of this group. *The Religion of Protestants* is his great work summing up his thought. He raises the question of the grounds of religious certitude, the basis of faith, or the arbiter of religious opinion. His opponent is a Romanist called Knott. Both Chillingworth and Knott accepted the fact of revelation and the necessity of the divine spirit. They differed concerning the medium and the interpreting spirit. To Chillingworth, Scripture and reason were the twofold source of truth, the one external, the other internal. The Gospel contains all truth possible and desirable among Christians. Beyond these facts – of which the Apostle's Creed is the summary, the

---

[1] G. P. H. Pawson, *The Cambridge Platonists* (London, 9130) p. 19.

[2] *Cambridge Modern History*, IV, 781–782, 791–792, 799. Cf. J. H. B. Masterman, *The Age of Milton* (London, 1897), pp. 221–222; Egg-Olofsson, *Ibid.*, pp. 43–44; J. H. Muirhead, *The Platonic Tradition in Anglo-Saxon Philosophy* (London, 1931), pp. 25–26.

[3] Seth, *Ibid.*, p. 79. Cf. Charles de Rémusat, *Histoire de la Philosophie en Angleterre depuis Bacon jusqu'à Locke* (Paris, 1875), II, 11; Gilbert Burnett, *History of His Own Time* (Oxford, 1838), I, 340–341; M. H. Carré, *Phases of Thought in England* (Oxford, 1949), p. 262; L. A. Selby-Bigge, ed. *The British Moralists* (Oxford, 1897), II, 286–288; C. M. H., IV, 291; J. B. Mullinger, *History of Cambridge University* (London, 1888), p. 110.

Christian has latitude. Christianity is belief in Christ – the great
facts of Christ's life and death for man's salvation – without a Sacra-
mentarian or a Calvinistic or an Arminian theory of the mode in which
this salvation is made effectual to man. Chillingworth recognises the
authority of God in religion, and no other. This authority is addressed
in Scripture to the individual reason and conscience. No other authority
has a binding effect over the Christian conscience.[1]

Jeremy Taylor and Edward Stillingfleet belong to the liberal
movement of the seventeenth century in so far as they contributed
by distinct and important works to its advancement. Yet neither their
reputation nor the prevailing character of their theology has identified
them with it. Taylor's *Liberty of Prophesying* is among the most remarkable works of the century. Stillingfleet's *Irenicum* is of less significance.
Yet it marks the height to which the liberal churchmanship of this
period had risen before the reaction set in at the Restoration. Taylor's
work appeared in 1647, ten years after Chillingworth's *Religion of
Protestants*, Stillingfleet's work in 1659, on the eve of the Restoration.
For our purpose, it will be sufficient to consider Taylor's *Liberty of
Prophesying*. According to Taylor, faith is a simple personal acceptance
of Jesus Christ and Him crucified. Profession of faith in the Apostle's
Creed is the sole essential of salvation and Christian communion.
Episcopacy is divinely sanctioned and appears to have been committed
to the apostles by Christ Himself. But it is not the essence, *esse* of the
Church; it only implies the well-being, *bene esse* of the Church. All
necessary articles of faith are clearly and plainly set down in Scripture.
When the meaning of Scripture is uncertain, we have no means of
determining its infallibility. No one is entitled to dictate to another
as to what he shall accept as the meaning of Scripture. Reason and
private judgment must be the last authority of every man in face of
Scripture. Divine revelation in Scripture is the ultimate source of
religious truth, but the question remains as to the interpretation of
revelation. Thus reason is the interpreter of revelation. In the process
of the interpretation of revelation a man follows his own reason, guided
not only by natural arguments, but by divine revelation and other
good means.[2] Taylor's work points in the direction of Whichcote's
position.

---

[1] Tulloch, *Ibid.*, pp. 343–345. Cf. pp. 281, 288–290, 305, 318, 330–332. Volume I of Tulloch's
work is a valuable analysis of the thought of Falkland, Hales Chillingworth and other
forerunners of the Cambridge Platonists. Cf. J. F. H. New, *Anglican and Puritan* (Stanford,
1964), p. 107.

[2] Tulloch, *Ibid.*, pp. 343–345, 379–408. Cf. John Hunt, *Ibid.* I, 340–341. For a comparative

In this chapter, it has been our purpose to trace the development of the Platonic tradition from its original source up to the time of Cambridge Platonism. Though to the present writer there appears to be sufficient evidence to assume Whichcote's indebtedness to this historical development of Platonic influence in religious thought, no conclusions are yet drawn as to the degree of the influence upon him from this source.[1] Further, it appears that a number of ideas and conditions since the Renaissance have culminated in his thought. The seventeenth century itself was rich in thought, scientific, philosophical, and religious, and much of the thought of Whichcote can be understood only in this context. The immediate religious cause which started this new school was the reaction to Puritan dogma. We have omitted a consideration of Puritan thought and activity in the present chapter to give full scope to our discussion both concerning Whichcote's Puritan background and reaction to this school of thought, in the following chapter.

study of the thought of Whichcote and Taylor, see De Pauley, *Ibid.*, pp. 41–43. Stillingfleet's contribution to liberal thought appears more important when considered in the context of Latitudinarian thought, which follows the Cambridge Platonists School in the 17th Century rational tradition. See C. R. Cragg, *From Puritanism to the Age of Reason* (Cambridge, Eng., 1950), pp. 61–63.

[1] See *Infra*, Ch. IX.

CHAPTER THREE

CONTROVERSY WITH A PURITAN

The history of English Puritanism is the history both of a theological movement and of a great national struggle. No one can understand the sources of the mixed civilisation of England without studying the great Puritanical movement of the seventeenth century. Britain was the national soil in which the seeds of the Reformation were destined to take the deepest and most enduring root. England could boast neither of a Luther nor a Calvin, but the spiritual impulses out of which the movement grew, and which constituted its real life and strength, found in Anglo-Saxon character their most congenial seat, their highest affinities, their most solid nutriment. Slowly and under many hindrances, they spread, unaided by the powerful influence of any great teacher, but sinking always more deeply and gaining a firmer hold on the thought and faith of Englishmen.[1]

During the time of Elizabeth, Puritanism did not want to overthrow the Church as the Romanists did but to transform it according to their own ideas of what the church should be. They could not be prevented from holding positions of power and responsibility in the Church. To them the Church that Elizabeth had established was tainted with Romanism and untrue to Scripture. The motive power behind the Puritans was Geneva and it was the Calvinistic system that they wanted to introduce in England. Thus when James VI of Scotland became James I of England, at the beginning of the seventeenth century, the Puritans expected sympathy from him in view of his coming from a Presbyterian country. They were soon disappointed with the new King, who immediately allied himself closely with the Anglo-

---

[1] John Tulloch, *English Puritanism*, (Edinburgh, 1861) (pp. 1–2) Cf. *Ibid.*, pp. 5–7, where the author asserts that the connection between Puritanism and Calvinism was at first more of an ecclesiastical than a doctrinal sympathy. Puritanism began with contention between rival bishops.

Catholics. He was followed by Charles I, who believed strongly in the Divine Right of Kings and sought to enforce it. But by taking this position he was out of sympathy with his most progressive subjects and by his alliance with Laud and the Anglo-Catholics he was opposed to the Puritans. The new century was an age of revolt against absolutism in England and elsewhere. Charles ignored this and refused his subjects a voice in the policy of the country.[1]

This condition led to the Puritan revolt in the 1640's. On June 12, 1643, Parliament issued an ordinance commanding that an assembly of divines should be convened at Westminster, July 1, 1644. The purpose was to alter the establishment. However, the resolution to abolish prelatical governments as soon as possible did not go far enough to extinguish episcopal rule, but left no doubt in the minds of the legislators that an end must be put to the ancient hierarchy. Ecclesiastical government was to be settled so as to be most agreeable to God's word, and adapted to procure and preserve the peace of the Church at home and to promote nearer agreement with other reformed communions abroad. The New League and Covenant of 1643 differed from former ones by the addition of an express resolve to extirpate prelacy as well as popery. The Covenant prepared in Scotland, having been adopted in England, the two countries entered into a treaty November 29, 1643. The Covenant took the form of a compromise and at the same time was meant to declare truth and to accomplish union. However, it received different explanation from different persons. It was used variously by Presbyterians, Independents and Cavaliers. Hence, in spite of Presbyterian activity and Parliamentary orders, great numbers refused and evaded the test.[2] In fact, while Tuckney was one of the Westminster divines, Whichcote was absent from the Assembly and refused to take the Covenant.

When Parliament exercised supreme power in the 1640's, only persons sympathetic with Puritan ideas received university appointments. To confirm this one need only observe the men appointed along with Whichcote in 1644. Hill, Master of Trinity, and Arrowsmith, Master of St. John's, were both old-fashioned Puritans and decidedly Presbyterian. Tuckney, another of the Presbyterians, was Master of

---

[1] Moorman, *A History of the Church of England*, (London, 1953) pp. 208, 221–226. Douglas Bush, *English Literature 1600–1660*, (Oxford, 1945) pp. 6–8; F. J. C. Hearnshaw, *Social and Political Ideas*, (London, 1926) pp. 34–35.

[2] John Stoughton, *History of Religion in England*, new and revised edition, (London, 1881), I, 267, 289–291, 219–220.

Emmanuel.[1] Emmanuel College was founded in 1584 as a Puritan College. This shows the determination of the Puritans not to desert the university but to propagate their views.[2] The Puritan approach to preaching is part of the *raison d'être* of Emmanuel College. Puritan preaching was called "spiritual" in contradistinction to the "whitty" preaching of the more conservative Churchmen. Thus Emmanuel College where Whichcote studied, taught and became fellow and where Tuckney was at various times student, tutor, fellow and master, was founded by Sir Walter Mildmay to encourage the Puritan type of preaching.[3]

Taking all facts into consideration, it seems safe to suppose that Whichcote developed in a distinctly Puritan environment. He most probably came from a Puritan home, his parents in turn sending him to Emmanuel College, "the nursery" or "the cradle" of Puritanism to be "established in the faith." Further, the fact that he was trained at Emmanuel College most probably explains his appointment as Provost of King's by a Puritan Parliament and his retention in this position in spite of his refusal to take the Covenant. It is significant that the greatest reaction against the dogmatism and intolerance of Puritanism came from within their own ranks and mainly from men trained at Emmanuel, the Puritan College. Thus, the law of reaction was at work, "for the stringency of Puritan and Calvinistic rule tended to create its own exception," and to drive men of "independent and antipathetic temper" into revolt. This "citadel of Puritanism and Calvinism became . . . the cradle of a movement animated by the spirit of Plato and devoted to the golden mean in every sphere of thought and life." [4] A casual acquaintance with Whichcote indicates why he rejected the Puritan position. He says:

> Every one do rest in his teacher a while . . . but yet let him not depend upon his teacher more than he needs must, nor than need require; for you ought not to think that you must be in the state of a learner all the days of your life. A child must believe what is told him at first, that this letter is so called, and that two letters put together spell so much; but after a while he comes to see reason

---

[1] *Ibid.*, II, 260–261, Cf. *Ibid.*, I, 485.

[2] J. B. Mullinger, *A History of the University of Cambridge*, (London, 1888) pp. 130–132.

[3] William Haller, *The Rise of Puritanism*, (New York, 1938) pp. 19–21. The difference between witty and spiritual preaching, between the "Wisdom of Words" and the "Word of Wisdom" marked the difference between Anglican and Puritan preaching. The Puritans professed to disapprove the citation of human authors and to depend solely upon Scripture. See *Ibid.*, p. 23. G. F. Nuttall, *The Holy Spirit in Puritan Faith and Experience*, (Oxford, 1946), pp. 22, 42–45.

[4] F. J. Powicke, *The Cambridge Platonists*, (London, 1926), p. 3.

thereof as well as his teacher . . . . He is a very unhappy man that hath lived twenty, thirty or forty years in the world, and hath never done that which is the peculiar and proper action of human nature, that is, to use reason, understanding and judgment; but lived all the days of his life . . . below his kind; having not put forth any of those acts which do most properly belong unto him, as a rational being.[1]

The central dogma of Puritanism as applied to the life of the men of the seventeenth century was that of an all-embracing determinism, theologically formulated as the doctrine of predestination. It postulates an absolute human depravity and a purely arbitrary human redemption.[2] Thus the Westminster Confession states that God ordained from eternity whatever comes to pass. Yet He is not the author of sin, nor is violence offered to the will by creatures, nor is the liberty of contingency of second causes taken away but rather established. God knows what may or can come to pass upon all supposed conditions; yet He has not decreed anything because He foresaw it as future, or that which would come to pass upon such conditions. Accordingly, by the decree of God some men and angels are predestined unto everlasting life, and others foreordained to everlasting death. The number of those predestined or foreordained is permanently fixed. Those of mankind that are predestined unto life, "God, before the foundation of the world was laid, according to his eternal and immutable purpose, and the secret counsel and good pleasure of his will, hath chosen in Christ unto everlasting glory." This has been done, "out of his mere free grace and love, without any foresight of faith or good works, or perseverance in either of them, or any other thing in the creature." There are no "conditions or causes in creatures moving God to his decree; all is to be attributed to His glorious grace."

Further, as God has appointed the elect to glory, so He has foreordained the necessary means, "wherefore those elected are redeemed by Christ; are "effectually called" to faith in Christ by His Spirit working in them." They are justified, adopted, sanctified, and kept by His power through faith unto salvation. Thus only the "elect" are saved. From the rest of mankind, "God was pleased to withhold his mercy; for the glory of His sovereign power over His creatures." He rejected them, dishonouring them with wrath for their sin "to the praise of His justice." According to the Puritans such a doctrine was "to afford matter of praise, reverence and admiration of God, and of

---

[1] Whichcote, *Works*, I, pp. 155–157. Cf. *Ibid.*, IV, p. 337.
[2] Haller, *Ibid.*, pp. 83–84.

humility, diligence, and abundant consolation to all that sincerely obey the Gospel.[1]

The Puritan doctrine was Calvinism with a difference. Calvinism was not so readily accepted in England as in Geneva, Scotland or Massachusetts. Thus Calvinism in England did not lead to a swift reconstruction of the Church but to the creation of a literature which expressed a way of life that eventually transcended all ecclesiastical and even religious bounds. Thus the Puritans set forth the doctrine of predestination in terms calculated to appeal to the English populace. English Puritanism may be called Calvinistic chiefly as a matter of historical reference. The Puritans though Calvinist in varying degrees, referred as often to Augustine as to Calvin and were reluctant to quote too frequently any merely human authorities whatsoever. However, Calvin's positive, clear, dogmatic intelligence was very suggestive.His most important effect upon them was to send them back to their Bibles. Thus there was more of Paul than Calvin in Puritan thought. They followed Paul in their teaching of the spiritual condition of the disinherited, aggrieved or oppressed. Thereby they attacked the special privileges, the vested interests, and class prejudice of the existing order. The spiritual equalitarianism of Paul was implicit in Puritan preaching. It seized the imagination of ordinary men. It created discontent among all those who had reason to be dissatisfied with the Stuart regime, and this became the central theme of revolutionary Puritanism. Thus the doctrine of predestination appears to have been the rationalised statement of this sentiment toward equality. It appeared as "a clear dogma answering with irrefutable logic to men's emotional need for something by which to be convinced." Accordingly, a favourite theme of Puritan preaching was equality for all men – "that God before whom all men are levelled is sure in his own time to uplift the low and humble the great." [2]

The Scripture was the basis of the Confession of the Westminster Assembly and recourse to it proved vital in their discussion. It was not the desire of the framers of the Confession to go beyond their predecessors in rigour and they took special pains: (1) to avoid mixing up the questions of the canonicity of particular books with the question of their authorship, where any doubt at all existed on the latter point; (2) to leave open all reasonable questions as to the mode and degree of

---

[1] A. F. Mitchell, *Minutes of the Sessions of the Westminster Assembly of Divines*, (London, 1847), pp. ii–iv. Cf. John Hunt, *Religious Thought in England*, (London, 1870), I, 200–201.
[2] Haller, *Ibid.*, pp. 84–86.

inspiration which could consistently be left open by those who accepted the Scriptures as the infallible rule of faith and duty; (3) to refrain from claiming for the text such absolute purity and for the Hebrew vowel points such antiquity as was claimed in the Swiss Formula Concordia, while asserting that the originals of Scripture, are, after the lapse of ages, still pure and perfect for all those purposes for which they were given; and (4) to declare that the sense of Scripture in any particular place is not manifold, but one, and so raise an earnest protest against the system of "spiritualising" the text which had been over-emphasized by some of the most eminent Fathers and mystics.[1]

The Westminster Assembly took the position, that "the light of nature" is just enough to leave men "inexcusable" for their sins, but not enough to give them the knowledge of God, and His will which is necessary to salvation. The light of nature may do men great harm, but it can do them no good. Thus what God wishes us to know is wholly committed to writing. The Holy Scriptures are given by inspiration and they come to us, not by the testimony of any man or church, but depend wholly upon God, and must be received as the word of God. Our assurance of its infallible truth and divine authority is from the inward work of the Holy Spirit. The work of the Spirit is now limited to giving a saving understanding of what is revealed in Scripture. The Scripture, in the original Hebrew and Greek, was immediately inspired by God, and by His care and providence kept pure in all ages. The Holy Spirit speaking in Scripture is the supreme judge; and the infallible rule of interpretation is to interpret Scripture by Scripture.[2]

In view of the fact that Tuckney represented the spirit of the Westminster Assembly, there is little wonder that he should disagree with Whichcote concerning the basis of religious authority. We have seen that Whichcote was probably a Puritan in Background, training, temper and intensity of conviction but not in sympathy with prevailing Puritan theology. He read Calvin and Beza, but his thought did not move in their direction. Instead of beginning with the inscrutable of God, he began with the fundamental nature of man. His interest was

---

[1] Mitchell, *Ibid.*, pp. xlix–li.

[2] Hunt, *Ibid.*, pp. 199–200. Cf. John Brown, *The English Puritans*, (Cambridge, England, 1910), pp. 154–155, M. R. Craff, *From Puritanism to The Age of Reason*, (Cambridge, England, 1950), pp. 36–38.

See also, J. S. McEwen, *The Faith of John Knox* (Richmond, Virginia, 1961), McEwen traces the main roots of later Scottish Calvinism back to the English Puritanism of the Westminster Assembly era (p. vii). He adds: "The interaction between Scottish Presbyterianism and English Congregational Puritanism culminated in the Westminster confession which partakes of a 'Calvinism more rigid than Calvin's.'" (p. 1).

psychological more than theological. He asserted that nothing is more intrinsically rational than religion.[1] Further, Whichcote could not accept the intolerance of Puritan theology. Puritan theology in the seventeenth century was both intolerant and highly theoretical. It could admit no rival; it was impatient of the least variation from the language of orthodoxy. It emphasized all the transcendent and divine aspects of Christian truth, rendering them into theories highly definite and consistent, but in their very consistency disregardful of moral facts and the complexities of practical life. Thus Whichcote and others with a reflective and tolerant mind looked on the one hand at this compactness of doctrinal divinity and on the other, at the state of the religious world and the Church around them. They sought a more excellent way and concluded that reason and morality are essentials of religion. They sought to soften down instead of sharpening doctrinal distinctions, to bring out points of agreement instead of differences in religious opinions. They tried to find a common center of thought and action in certain universal principles of religious sentiment rather than in the more abstruse conclusions of polemical theology. They became ecclesiastics against the theological dogmatism and narrowness of their time.[2] Stoughton makes the following observation concerning Whichcote and followers:

It is curious to find such men in the very heart of the Puritan age. They were founders of a new order of religious thought, new at least to the mental habits in general of the period. They did not assail puritanism, nor assume an attitude of opposition to other good men of any class, they preferred to build up rather than to tear down, to heal rather than to wound; but their sympathies did not run in Puritan lines. They appreciated the piety of many contemporaries at Cambridge and lived with them upon terms of friendship, but for their own part, they held broader views of theology than their brethren. Their interest in the study of Plato and Plotinus, and their elevation of what is moral over what is merely intellectual, gave to their method of inquiry, and to the conclusions which they reached, a certain cast, which plainly distinguished them from the kind of teaching found in the Westminster Confession, and in the standard works of Puritan divines.[3]

[1] Rufus Jones, *Spiritual Reformers in The Sixteenth and Seventeenth Centuries*, (London, 1914), pp. 290–291.

[2] John Tulloch, *Rational Theology and Christian Philosophy in England in The Seventeenth Century*, (London, 1872), II, 12–13.

[3] Stoughton, *Ibid.*, 266–267. Cf. Mitchell, *Ibid.*, pp. xliii–xliii. Here it is stated that Chillingworth was not at the Assembly. Neither were Whichcote or Cudworth; but they were held in "high esteem" by its members and were considered worthy of appointment in the University of Cambridge. Tuckney, Hill and Arrowsmith were members of the Assembly. Tuckney was on the First Committee; Hill and Arrowsmith on the Second Committee. Arrowsmith appeared on a Committee to join the Commissioners of the Church of Scotland to formulate a joint Confession of Faith. Tuckney's name was later added to the latter Committee. See *Ibid.*, lxxxii–lxxxiii. Much of the theology of the Confession was accepted just

We now turn to Whichcote's letters of controversy. They are valuable in that they state frankly the reaction that he took to the Puritan view. It is to Cradock, at that time a fellow of Emmanuel, that we owe the beginning of this valuable correspondence. In these letters we find the "germ" of Cambridge Platonism. Cradock became aware of the fact that certain seniors including Tuckney were giving unfavourable criticism of Whichcote's views. He ventured to suggest that his would-be critics were not dealing fairly with Whichcote by criticising him behind his back and that they should put their points of opposition clearly and frankly to Whichcote himself. But since Whichcote was at this time Provost of King's College and Vice-Chancellor of the University, there were few who felt willing and entitled to attack his views. Eventually Tuckney, Master of Emmanuel and formerly Which-cote's tutor, accepted the challenge of expressing his concern and opposition to the views of Whichcote, as a personal friend of long standing. Whichcote delivered on Sunday, September 7, 1651, a Commencement Sermon which set off the series of letters between himself and Tuckney.[1] Tuckney's initial letter and Whichcote's reply introduce the controversy. Thus Tuckney begins:

... Out of that ancient and still continued love and respect I bear you, to crave leave to tell you; that my heart hath bin much exercised about you: and that, especially since your being Vice-Chancellor, I have seldom hear'd you preach; but that something hath bin delivered by you, and that authoritatively, and with the big words, sometimes of "divinest reason," and sometimes of "more than mathematical demonstration"; that hath very much grieved me; and I believe, others with me: and yesterday, as much as any time I pass by many things in your sermon; and crave leave to note three or foure.[2]

Tuckney proceeds to present his criticisms under four main headings, as follows:[3]

(1) The notion that all differences between good men may not be determined by Scripture was considered by him as "unsafe and unsound."

(2) Whichcote had insisted that one should be confined to passages of Scripture in which all parties agree. Thus there would be more peace

as Tuckney produced it, but there is much "unworthy" of him. Though he accepted the basic thought of the Assembly, he rejected plans to enforce it upon others. This moderate view held by Tuckney may partly explain his continued friendship with Whichcote after their controversy. Cf. Edmund Calamy, *The Nonconformist's Memorial*, ed. by Samuel Palmer, 2nd ed. (London, 1802), I, 264–266.

[1] Whichcote and Tuckney, *Letters*, pp. 1–2. Hereafter in this chapter *Letters* only. Samuel Cradock was a former pupil of Whichcote, *Ibid.*, p. 1 (n).

[2] *Letters*, p. 2.

[3] *Ibid.*, pp. 2–4.

in Christendom, if fallible men would not press their disagreements. Tuckney considered this position "more dangerous" since Papists, Arians, Socinians and all sorts of heretics could be accepted as long as there is Scriptural agreement. According to Tuckney, this is not the kind of peace that "Christ purchased by his blood."

(3) The advice which Whichcote gives that men have the liberty to interpret Scripture. According to Tuckney, this would take away the peace that Whichcote has suggested. The principle of the *libertas prophetandi* would lead to even greater division and intolerance in Christendom.

And (4) Whichcote had suggested that reconciliation does not work on God but on us. Tuckney asserts this as "divinity his heart riseth up against." What does Whichcote mean? Does he mean that God overlooks sin so as to be reconciled to those that remain in sin? Or, does he mean that God's reconciliation is from something in us and not from His free Grace?

Thus Tuckney states his disagreement and expresses his concern for Whichcote's own position. He desires to keep youth from being tainted and Whichcote's reputation from being marred and in order that "his friends may not be grieved." [1]

In our treatment of the controversy we shall be concerned primarily with a clear statement of the issues involved, and a critical appraisal of them. Further we believe that the controversy first reveals Whichcote's thought, and marks the real beginning of the movement known as Cambridge Platonism.[2] It is not easy to fix upon a neat outline for our discussion since the criticisms set forth by Tuckney involve various related ideas of Whichcote. But it seems clear that certain concepts are of fundamental importance for both men. Thus we shall concern ourselves with the following: (1) the problem of religious authority; (2) Christian tolerance; and (3) the Doctrine of Reconciliation.

The problem of religious authority deserves first place in our discussion because it affects in a profound way all that is to follow.

---

[1] *Ibid.*, pp. 36–38. Whichcote's version of his Commencement Sermon is as follows: (1) All truly good men substantially agree in all things saving; (2) Some things wherein we differ, may be determined by Scripture, but not all; (3) The Proposal for peace; (4) The Proposal for progress and growth in knowledge; and (5) Reconciliation. We find here the justification for the assumption that he usually preached by outline. See *Ibid.*, pp. 11–13. Tuckney certainly based his criticisms upon Whichcote's outline, though there is the possibility that he did not grasp his full meaning.

[2] There are other detailed discussions of the controversy to be found in Tulloch, *Ibid.*, II, 49–51. Powicke, *Ibid.*, pp. 54–56; W. C. De Paulay, *The Candle of the Lord*, (London, 1937), pp. 28–30.

According to Tuckney, Scripture is the only rule of faith and for this reason its testimony is unquestionable. Divine truth is given explicitly in the Scriptures and it is "made Divine by the simple fact of being there." Of course, he did not exclude reason entirely. But its place was strictly subordinate. Faith takes the lead and accepts completely what Scripture lays down. She then calls upon reason to collect and compare its statements; to arrange them in due order; to deduce logical consequences; to clear up apparent contradictions; and to weave the whole into a system. Here the function of reason ends: to sit in judgment on the substance of what Scripture lays down is beyond her province. Thus, when faith acts, reason also acts; yet this is not to resolve faith into reason. But he is insistent upon the fact that men need an infallible authority and this is Scripture. Even if our reason cannot judge, Scripture is to be believed and obeyed.[1]

Whichcote's position seems to be just the reverse. Reason, he said, may and must come first, then faith. The reason of a man's mind must be satisfied for no one can think against it. Faith, when it is more than credulity, is an intelligent act. Faith follows reason – is simply Reason herself, yielding assent to the evidence which her own authority has made clear.[2] The reader should bear in mind from the outset that both men recognize reason as important but it appears that reason has become too important in Whichcote's thought for Tuckney's satisfaction.

At this point we should perhaps give some attention to Whichcote's assertion that his position was not new. The emphasis of Luther upon the right of private judgment shows the truth of this assertion. When Luther was at the supreme moment of his life, when retraction or death seemed the alternative, his plea was that what is contrary to reason is contrary to God. But Luther, and still more his successors, grew doubtful of this principle. Its seeming abuse led them to denounce its very use. Later he speaks of faith as strangling reason.[3] The reaction

---

[1] Cf. *Letters*, pp. 21–23.

[2] Whichcote, *Works*, III, 163 and *Infra*, Ch. IV. Cf. D. E. Trueblood, *Philosophy of Religion* (New York, 1957). According to Trueblood, the distinction between natural and revealed religion is not nearly so sharp as it formerly seemed to be. The contrast between reason and revelation is now seen to be more of a matter of object than method. Reason and revelation need to go together at all times; for revelation needs to be tested by reason for the simple reason that there are false claims to revelation. (pp. 28–30).

[3] Charles Beard, *The Reformation of the Sixteenth Century in its Relation to Modern Thought and Knowledge*, Hibbert Lectures, 1883 (London, 1885), p. 153. Cf. B. A. Gerrish, *Grace and Reason: A Study in The Theology of Luther* (Oxford, 1962), pp. 25–27. See also, Heinrich Bornkamm, "Faith and Reason in The Thought of Erasmus and Luther"; *Religion and Culture*; *Essays in Honor of Paul Tillich*; ed. by Walter Leibrecht (New York, 1959).

against reason grew. *Credo quia impossible* became a favourite motto and the result was to present the whole matter of Faith as a tissue of Mysteries. In particular, Calvinism was the result – not the Calvinism of Calvin so much as that of his rigorous disciples who shaped it into the dominant creed. But let reason come to its own again and this creed with a great deal besides would topple to the ground; and Tuckney knew this well. It is true that the Reformation on its intellectual side was but an aspect of the Renaissance, and we have seen how Whichcote was directly influenced by the Renaissance. It would appear that the attitude of both men in this controversy goes back to the Renaissance-Reformation period, Whichcote being more directly under the influence of the Renaissance on its intellectual side [1] and Tuckney more under the impact of the line of development resulting from a reaction to reason through the Reformers. So important is their difference as to the nature and importance of reason that it will be necessary to return to this theme often for it is the key to an understanding of the entire controversy.

Scripture is an authority for both men, but here also their differences are outstanding. The important role Whichcote assigns to reason naturally makes him more critical than Tuckney even in his use of Scripture. Thus it was consistent with his general attitude towards Scripture for Whichcote to suggest that all differences between Christians may not be determined by Scripture and for this reason they should hold to passages of agreement, since there is substantial agreement "in all saving things." [2] On the other hand, Tuckney who considers Scripture as his only religious authority finds Whichcote's position extremely disturbing. He argues that interpretations of Scripture by councils and synods and the commentaries and creeds resulting therefrom, are not additions or alterations of Scripture and these are necessary because

---

[1] Etienne Gilson, *Reason and Revelation in the Middle Ages*, (London, 1955), pp. 69–71. De Pauley has observed that the thought of Calvin and Whichcote stem from a single source – from the Alexandrian tradition and Augustinian theology, but their reactions have been different. See, De Pauley, *Ibid.*, pp. 231–233. Similarly, Tuckney and Whichcote have a common background and for this reason there is at once continuity and discontinuity to be observed in a comparative study of their thought. The general attitude of the debasement of reason to make way for faith has often occurred in the history of thought, and Tuckney is not alone in his general position. Cf. Tertullian, "The Prescription Against Heretics," *The Ante-Nicene Fathers*, ed. by Alexander Roberts and James Donaldson, revised by A. C. Coxe (New York, 1896), III, 243–265. S. Kierkegaard, *Concluding Unscientific Postscript*, trans. by D. F. Swenson, ed. by Walter Lowrie (Princeton, 1941), pp. 188–189, Jaroslav Pelikan, *From Luther to Kierkegaard* (St. Louis, Mo., 1950), pp. 1–14, 113–118.

[2] Here reference is to everything essential for salvation. Cf. *Letters*, pp. 11–12, 21–23. See also, John Milton, *De Doctrina Christiana*, tr. by Charles Summer (Cambridge, England, 1825), pp. 469–470.

of the imperfections of our understanding. Tuckney accepts orthodox explications of Scripture (to Scripture). This position is natural in view of his role in the Westminster Assembly. This also explains his fear that Whichcote had read too much Arminian literature, for he had understood him to imply that he would accept the minimum in Scripture of "those things saving" and discount the use of confessions of faith and catechisms which explain them. At first it would appear that Tuckney wishes to have things both ways, but to him Scripture is to be interpreted by Scripture. It is difficult to see how even this could be done without the use of reason, but it would be counter to Tuckney's purpose to admit it.

Whichcote agrees that matters of faith are matters of divine revelation. But to him, the first task is to prove the divine authority of Scripture since Scripture is not to be produced as a witness for its own truth. He would accept the same aids to an understanding of Scripture as Tuckney, but even these must be examined by reason in view of disagreements. Finally, whether one relies upon Scripture itself or upon councils, confessions, and the like, the individual must reserve the right to judge for himself. To Whichcote Tuckney had actually weakened his position by bringing into the discussion these extra-biblical "explications," for the Scriptures themselves are more authoritative than these.[1] It is Whichcote's belief that if a man has good intentions as he studies the Scriptures, he will not miss "anything saving."Fundamentals are so clear that there is little danger of good men differing about them. If a man is satisfied on fundamentals, he should appreciate discussion with those who differ. This is healthy, for it leads to a re-examination of one's own thought.[2] The obvious advantage of Whichcote's more liberal view is that it gives greater freedom for discussion and the development of a fuller rational understanding of one's faith. Here Whichcote recaptures the spirit of Christian-Platonism and one recalls the "faith seeking to know" of Augustine and the *Credo ut intelligam* of Anselm.[3] This leads us logically into our next consideration, what is described as the *Libertas Prophetandi*, which we have subsumed under the general heading of Christian tolerance.[4]

Powicke has singled out Whichcote from among the Cambridge

---

[1] *Ibid.*, pp. 42–44, 49–51.
[2] *Ibid.*, pp. 52, 55.
[3] Gilson, *Ibid.*, Ch. I. Cf. J. A. Hutchinson, *Faith, Reason and Existence* (New York, 1956), pp. 97–99.
[4] See *Infra*, Ch. VIII.

Platonists as being conspicuous for his Christian tolerance.[1] Whichcote has asserted in his Commencement Sermon that men have the liberty to use reason as a criterion of faith.[2] He has also asserted that a Christian, "after application to God, and a diligent use of means to find out truth might decide upon what, as a result of his search, he finds cause to believe and to venture his soul." [3] Now, according to Tuckney, Whichcote places too much stress on *Theologia Naturalis*, and exalts the natural reason above "the purely supernatural and evangelical." He quoted too often Proverbs 20:27, and misunderstood Romans, Chapters one and two.[4] Further, there is the danger that such liberty suggested by Whichcote might lead to various unwholesome divisions among Christians. Tuckney points to Socinians, Arminians and the many Sects as ample justification for his concern.[5]

At this point Whichcote finds it necessary to state more clearly his general position. Religion itself is the truest and highest reason. In the nature of things, there is necessity and contingency, the latter is determined by God out of His power, but the former is eternally fixed. Then, there is that which is declared by God. The first is in *ratione rei;* the second in *materia libertatis et beneplaciti Dei;* and the third is *materia fidei.* Scripture is knowable and does not stand only upon the foundation of revelation. Natural light and conscience also condemn iniquity, and give testimony to righteousness. Calvin himself acknowledged that faith agrees with reason, that the principle of reason does not destroy the knowledge of God. *Materia theologia naturalis* is demonstrable by reason; and *materia fidei sacris litteris contenta est summe credibilis* is satisfactory to reason. Thus "unbiased reason, not in compromise with sense, not engaged in worldly design" is valid. Meanwhile, one should receive "what God speaks of Himself, of His own affairs as acts of His infinite wisdom and power"; for what God speaks transcends

---

[1] Powicke, *Ibid.*, p. 50.

[2] *Letters*, pp. 3–4.

[3] *Ibid.*, p. 13.

[4] *Ibid.*, p. 20. This controversy reminds us of a recent controversy between Brunner and Barth where Brunner conceives a relation between nature and grace as the basis of a *theologia naturalis*, but Barth's reply to his proposition is an unqualified "No!" Brunner's view concerning a "general revelation" in Nature and a "special" revelation in Christ is similar to Whichcote's scheme of "truths of first-inscription" and "truths of after-revelation." On the other hand, there is much in common between the approach of Barth and that of Tuckney on the same subject. In both cases the two modern thinkers are far in advance of these 17th century thinkers. Our only purpose here is to indicate tendencies. Cf. K. Barth and E. Brunner *Natural Theology*, ed. by John Baillie, tr. by Peter Frankel, (London, 1947).

[5] *Ibid.*, pp. 29–31.

our rational understanding. But such "transcendency" is supra-rational and not irrational.[1]

... Reason is so far from doing disservice to Christian faith, that it fits men to receive it .... Therefore the use of reason in matters of religion is so far from doing any harm to religion, from being prejudicial to any articles of faith, that it is the proper "preparatory" for men to look to God; and taking up the Bible, and finding that God is in Christ reconciling the world to himself; reason saith, I did expect it, I did believe such a thing from the first and chiefest good; and now I am assured of it by the gospel.[2]

The common end which both Whichcote and Tuckney have in view is peace in Christendom, but the manner of attaining this peace is conceived differently by each man. It was Whichcote's belief that Tuckney had confused the use of reason with the principle of reason. And while he was willing to concede the possibility of the misuse of reason, he would not denounce the principle. Reason, says Whichcote, in the hand of God is His "candle." [3] Further, Whichcote is prepared to recognize all truth, both natural and revealed. The University is the place where truth should be sought wherever it may lead. The foundations of truths necessary to salvation are so "immoveably" laid by God and the light of them is so "full and clear" that no "ingenuous and teachable mind" can be mistaken about them. Truth is of God, "He is the Superintendent over truth in the world." [4] It is consistent with his broad outlook to study philosophy. This does not in any way affect his love of Scripture and though he must admit that the philosophers are good as far as they go, yet in Christ we have a "fuller light." This, however, does not make them enemies of the Gospel; on the contrary, at times their insights challenge the Christian to live up to his profession of faith in Christ.[5]

Natural light and conscience condemn iniquity and give testimony to the ways of righteousness. Christianity is beyond all control of human Reason, for truth delivered by God concerning Salvation by Christ is amiable, grateful, acceptable by mind and understanding and such as speaks itself from God and to this purpose human reason was made use of, as a Receiver, discoverer, a principle to be mistrusted and taught not as an author or inventor or controller of what God speaks, divine truth always carries its own evidence so that the mind receiving it is illuminated, edified and satisfied. I receive the Christian Reve-

---

[1] Ibid., pp. 44–46. Cf. Calvin, Institutes ed. by Thomas Morton (London, 1611), II, ii, 12, 26; I, xv, 6; III, xxv, 2 passim.
[2] Whichcote, Works, III, 184.
[3] Letters, pp. 49, 113.
[4] Ibid., pp. 56–58. Cf. Whichcote, Works, IV. 340.
[5] Ibid., pp. 60–62. He says: "In some Philosophers especially Plato and his scollars ... I find many excellent and divine expressions." See "Philosophical and Theological Reflections," "Sloane" (MS) in (BM), 2716.

lation in a way of ... Choyce, I myself am taken with it as a welcome guest, it is not forced upon me but I let it in. Yet so as taught of God I see Reason to embrace it; I have no Reason against it, but rather the highest and purest Reason for it.[1]

Whichcote appears to anticipate the conclusions of Brunner who asserts that:

Revelation is only a stumbling-block to that reason which proclaims itself as a final court of appeal even before God. Hence the stumbling-block is not so much to reason itself, as to the arrogance of reason, our self-sufficiency in virtue of reason.[2]

One would think that Whichcote's apparent subordination of reason to revelation would have satisfied Tuckney, but obviously it did not. Tuckney agrees that faith is the act of an intelligent and rational creature and thus understanding and reason are necessary. But this has little to do with bringing peace into Christendom; for the most divisive doctrines are, in fact, those which are beyond the grasp of reason. For instance a "trinity-in-unity" is revealed in Scripture as a divine truth as also are the "divine decrees" and these must be "humbly believed" since "reason's judging" of them is inadequate.[3] It seems that both men agree that *materia fidei* is not contrary to reason, but their attitudes toward supra-rational matters are different. Tuckney insists that these matters of the Christian faith which are beyond the comprehension of reason must be believed as firmly as those within its grasp.[4] On the other hand, Whichcote offers reason even as the receiver of revelation and this he believes is in the interest of *de certitudine et dignitate Christianae religionis*. But to Tuckney this *dignitas et certitudo* is more demonstrable by Scripture than by reason. Scripture should be distinguished from what is properly called Christian religion, as that which contains it and may be therefore considered as the full proof of Christianity. There is much good matter in heathen writings, Tuckney agrees, but these cannot be compared with Scripture which is confirmed by miracles and other divine testimonies. Thus the truth of the Christian religion is not by reason, but by the divine authority of Scripture and this testimony is to be received by faith.[5]

---

[1] "Philosophical and Theological Reflections," *Ibid.*

[2] Brunner, *The Philosophy of Religion*, tr. Farrer and Wolf, (London, 1937).

[3] *Letters*, pp. 66–68. Cf. J. K. S. Reid, *The Authority of Scripture*, (London, 1957), pp. 29–55 where Reid explains the views of Calvin concerning scriptural authority and (pp. 194–233) where the positions on the same subject held by Barth and Brunner are discussed.

[4] *Ibid.*, pp. 68–69.

[5] *Ibid.*, pp. 70–72. Cf. Pascal, *Pensées*, tr. and ed. by Stewart (New York, 1947), *Pen.* 236.

To Tuckney, Whichcote's insistence upon reason as a religious authority explained much of the confusion in the University.[1] It is his desire rather to be called a Calvinist than a Socinian or Arminian. Because of Whichcote's emphasis on reason the unwholesome views of Chillingworth and Hooker are reflected in his thought.[2] In his zeal for liberty of comprehension of truth, Tuckney believes Whichcote, though an honest seeker of the truth, to actually cast his lot with the Socinians and Arminians who hold the same principle. Further, there is the danger that Whichcote's position is most likely to harm the "yonge auditors." [3] Divinity students should be so fully occupied "seeking to understand revealed truth still hidden, that they should desire no such liberty." That is, they should have no longing,

... for the liberty of opposing, or doubtfully disputing ... much more without a Cartesian ἐποχή supposing them for errours, or not established truths; till I come *de novo* without anie prepossession of them, shall study and reason my selfe into a beliefe of them.... [4]

Whichcote assures Tuckney that it is with the many divisions among Christians in mind that he offers reason as a religious authority and as the principle of the "liberty of interpretation." He believes that truths of "high importance" are of clearest "evidence and assurance" – knowable.[5] There is no opposition between the rational and the spiritual; for the spiritual is most rational. However, there is a distinction between the rational and the "conceited, impotent, affected canting" that makes no impression upon the understanding nor the inner life. So that the real threat to faith, as Whichcote sees it, is not reason but passion and excess enthusiasm in religion, since where the Spirit is truly present, there is the highest and purest reason to "satisfie, convince, command the minde." The spirit is present when things are most clearly under-

---

[1] *Ibid.*, pp. 70–72.

[2] *Ibid.*, pp. 79–80. Cf. *Supra*. Ch. II.

[3] *Ibid.*, p. 85. Cf. *Ibid.*, p. 94.

[4] *Ibid.*, pp. 86–87. If Whichcote were under the full impact of the thought of Descartes, especially his concept of "initial doubt" perhaps Tuckney's fears would be justified. However, there is insufficient evidence to take Tuckney seriously here. Even Henry More who corresponded with Descartes and who was at first an enthusiastic disciple of the Frenchman, soon discovered the disharmony between the fundamental presuppositions of Descartes and those of the movement to which he and Whichcote belonged. Thus it appears that here as at many other points, Tuckney uses the method of over-statement to attempt to bring his former pupil back to the Puritan fold. This is my view notwithstanding De Pauley's attempt to quote isolated passages from Whichcote's writings to establish a direct and significant connection between Whichcote and Descartes. See De Pauley, *Ibid.*, pp. 4–6, Cf.Descartes, *Discourse on Method*, 4th ed. (Edinburg, 1870), pt. iii, pp. 65–67. See also *Supra*, Ch. II. See also R. L. Colie, *Light and Enlightenment*, (Cambridge, England, 1957), p. 52, *passim*.

[5] *Ibid.*, pp. 103–107.

stood. In the Bible, the prophets and apostles as well as our Lord, present their message rationally, so that matters of "pure revelation" are also rational. Only reason reaches the mind and that does not affect and command the heart, "which does not satisfy and convince the mind." To admit reason its proper role under the guidance of God's Spirit is not to deny God. On the contrary, to nullify man would be to dishonour God.[1] Whichcote asserts that true faith may be known by our best use of reason. Arthur E. Murphy has put this view in a modern context:

> What we need now . . . is the wisdom to find a faith that can maintain itself in practice and in the open, as the spokesman for a good that is in fact what it purports to be and can perform what it promises, and what its disciples profess. For the attainment of such a faith we shall need the best use of all our powers, those of rational discrimination and comprehensive understanding not least among them. While, therefore, we shall welcome any aid that faith can bring to reason, we shall have to ask that faith to identify itself and present its credentials.[2]

Whichcote makes it clear that he is as much concerned about peace among Christians as Tuckney could possibly be and he believes this principle of liberty of interpretation is the only means to arrest the growth of religious sects so prevalent. Recently, Paul Tillich has agreed with Whichcote in substance as he insists that no foundation will last unless the existential reason has sincerely seen and surrendered to all available knowledge.

> If rational truth, with its contributions to the different realms of knowledge, is excluded, Christian faith necessarily becomes sectarian and exclusive.[3]

On the other hand, Whichcote believes that the use of Scripture alone as a religious authority encourages religious intolerance. Matters of faith are clearly stated in Scripture, but the problem arises because some try to "determine beyond Scripture" and then impose their conclusions on others. These have "enlarged Divinitie" but have "lessened Charitie, and multiplied Divisions." Thus it is for God to maintain truth, and for us to preserve charity.[4]

---

[1] *Ibid.*, pp. 108–113.

[2] A. E. Murphy, *The Use of Reason*, p. 12 (quoted by N. F. S. Ferré, *Faith and Reason* (London, 1946), p. 23.

[3] Paul Tillich, *The Christian Answer*, p. 33 (quoted by Ferré), *Ibid.*, p. 206.

[4] *Letters*, p. 118. Whichcote has taken the offensive at this point and he is alarmingly close to the real facts concerning Tuckney's part in the Westminister Assembly, the formulation of its Confession and its attempt to impose conformity upon others. Elsewhere in the controversy Tuckney had apparently anticipated this attack by stating that he voted against "tendering" the Covenant. Cf. *Ibid.*, p. 76.

... Persons valuable for their love and desire of truth, differing from us, generallie meane better than our prejudice, occasioned upon this difference, admits us to conceeve them; for I make account, that Scripture is so cleare and satisfactorie, in matters of weight ... that none but they, who unworthie practise and design upon truth; can be mistaken: and these in religion are not considerable; as being under the power of it, but serving ends: but, sure enough where the love of truth rules in the hearte, the light of truth will guide the minde. I believe it is not to be found in Scripture, or otherwise, that honestie, uprightness, integritie, are in conjunction with haeresie: and the Scripture way is, to rectifie simple misapprehensions with tenderness. Indeed that principle, of Scripture's perfection sufficiencie and perspicuitie, inclines me to think, that they, who fullie come up to Scripture: and set themselves with ingenuitie to find out the sense; seeking to God, to guide them; being not under the power of any lust, or corruption, or worldlie interest; will not substantiallie differ, in their resolved judgments about verie materiall things; as you seem to suppose.[1]

It is obvious that Whichcote is reacting, at once against the dogmatism of Puritan scripturalism and the intolerance which followed in its wake, and against the sectarianism resulting from excessive enthusiasm in religion. By asserting reason as a religious authority and by exalting the principle of "liberty of interpretation" he believed both of these unwholesome tendencies could be checked. While Tuckney appears more moderate than many of the Westminster divines, both in the spirit of his discussion with Whichcote and his reluctance to force his views on others, he nevertheless was much closer to the principle of the Reformers, *sola scriptura – sola gratia* and was convinced that his friend and former pupil was heading for great danger. It is not for us to pronounce either man as being right or wrong, but to use history as a standard of judgment is instructive. Within the historical setting of seventeenth century England, the progress of the immediate future belonged to Whichcote's view. Whichcote's thought and that of his disciples accelerated the growth of toleration in Church and State. On the other hand, when we go into the eighteenth century, the Age of Reason, it is obvious that this tendency toward a moral, rational and liberal approach to religious comprehension gets out of control. This rationalism which Whichcote attempts to root securely in Scripture and to use as the receiver of revelation, loses its balance and separates itself from the source that gives it life. But consequences and ideas always have a tendency to change as they move through time and for this reason the rationalism of the eighteenth and nineteenth centuries does not invalidate the original intention of Whichcote. He had clearly left the door open for further developments of thought, and to any illumi-

[1] *Ibid.*, p. 119, Cf. Whichcote, *Works*, IV, 240.

nation of reason by means of revelation. For him reason may point beyond itself, that is to say, truth may go beyond right reason even while using it as fully as possible both critically and creatively.[1]

The final issue in the controversy which we propose to treat concerns reconciliation. According to Tuckney, Whichcote had proposed the notion of "inherent" righteousness instead of the Puritan notion of "imputed" righteousness. Whichcote had asserted "that Christ does not save us, by only doing for us, without us." There must be repentance before forgiveness of sins. Christ is to be acknowledged as a principle of grace in us as well as an Advocate for us. According to Whichcote, Scripture presents Christ to us under a two-fold notion: (1) He is to be felt in us, as the new man in contradiction to the old man; as a divine nature to replace the degenerate and apostate nature; and as a principle of heavenly life contrary to the life of sin: (2) He is to be believed by us, as a sacrifice for the expiation and atonement of sin; as an Advocate and means of reconciliation between God and men. Christ performs both of these offices at once, for reconciliation between God and man involves both. There can be no reconciliation without our becoming god-like. God is supreme good and before we become reconciled to Him, we must surrender to the rules of goodness. God is pleased only in so far as goodness takes place in us. Whichcote makes it clear that he does not oppose "free grace" but wishes to take precautions against those who would turn the grace of God into wantonness. The true notion of salvation is a Saviour to give repentance and forgiveness. Some look upon salvation "as a thing at a distance from them... exemption from punishment; freedom from enemies abroad; but it is the mending of our natures, the safety of our persons, our health and strength within." There is in this view no attempt to leave out the Author of our salvation. "Our good state and condition with God; the work of grace and favour towards us; our being restored to righteousness, goodness and truth, all indicate our reconciliation to God by Christ and that the Kingdom of God is within us." [2]

Whichcote's view of reconciliation appears unsatisfactory to Tuckney. The former has denied Christ's working upon God in our reconciliation.

---

[1] Ferré, *Ibid.*, pp. 22–24. Cf. A recent statement by the same author, *Reason in Religion*, (Edinburgh, 1963), pp. 116–117. "Reason," says Ferré, "is an indispensable part in the religious life and thinking, but reason in ... religion, is not master and judge, but servant and judged. The function of reason is to provide clarity and consistency within man's totality of experience in relation to reality."

[2] *Letters*, pp. 13–16, Cf. "Reflections," *Ibid.*

Whichcote had asserted "that Christ is held out to us in the Gospel as first felt in us, as the new man; before he is believed in by us, as sacrifice and advocate." Tuckney asks, does this mean that when God works we are aware of what He brings to pass in us, before we are brought to the assurance of our peace and pardon by the work of the Spirit? Does Whichcote mean by belief, faith's reliance and dependence upon Christ's mercy? If he implies the latter meaning, Tuckney would agree that many sinners have believed in Christ as a sacrifice and advocate before they have felt the new man in themselves. Certainly repentance is before forgiveness. But it is necessary to add "that God, not only in His eternal election has before purposed, and by the death of His Son after, purchased our reconciliation; but even in the execution of that purpose, and the application of that purpose, He is before us; and is setting out first that happier meeting of our fuller reconciliation." It is not contrary to God's goodness, "freely to justify the ungodly." [1]

Tuckney wishes to know the source of Whichcote's notion "that God's work within us precedes his work about us." [2] Was it from a pagan source? Tuckney would admit that there are some "excellent and divine expressions" in "Plato and his scholars," but cautions against too much admiration for Plato.[3] Whichcote had gone too far in advancing the "power of nature in morals" and had given reason too much authority in the "mysteries" of faith. Whichcote seldom mentioned heart and will. The "decrees of God" were questioned because they could not be comprehended by reason. Thus Whichcote had even considered some philosophers and heathen "fairer candidates of heaven than the scriptures seeme to allowe" and because of their virtues had preferred them before Christians, who were overtaken with weaknesses. According to Tuckney, this is a kind of "moral divinity" with only a little of Christ added. It is "a Platonic faith which unites to God – an inherent righteousness which takes no account of imputed righteousness." As a result God and Christ become only a "notion and speculation." [4]

Whichcote replies that truth declared by God, concerning our relief by Christ is "amiable, grateful and acceptable to mind and under-

---

[1] *Ibid.*, pp. 32–34.

[2] *Ibid.*, pp. 34–35.

[3] *Ibid.*, p. 38.

[4] *Ibid.*, pp. 38–40. Tuckney accuses Whichcote of uttering Latin sentences and axioms in logic, philosophy, law and divinity of his own making. Cf. *Ibid.*, pp. 35, 96.

standing." [1] The truth of salvation is satisfactory to the mind; the Holy Spirit contributes to the mind's assurance and satisfaction; the Christian religion is received in a way of illumination, affection and choice.[2] Thus his emphasis upon reason merely strengthens his belief in the saving work of God in Christ. The beginnings of grace are wrought in us before God actually justifies sinners. He never leaves God out of his scheme and always gives him his principal place. God is his all and there is nothing more real in his experience than his dependence upon God. Christ enables us to repent, but repentance is truly an act. God does not repent in us, but works repentance in us.[3]

Tuckney is still unsatisfied concerning Whichcote's exaltation of the philosophers. Philosophers are seldom mentioned in the Scripture as the "wise men of the heathen" or "with approbation and honour," but generally with "dislike and contempt." Therefore we should follow the scriptural pattern and speak more of their "darkness, ignorance and their refusal to come to Christ" than in "admiration of their advancement, knowledge and virtue, which at best were but dim and dead, while not enlightened and enlivened" by Christ. Whichcote had insisted that they were good as far as they had gone, but Tuckney considered the few he had read as "scattering a great deale of what is bad, with what is good in them." Further, Whichcote felt that they were "never enemies of the truth of the gospel." Tuckney replies that the early Christians found them "amongst the chief and most subtle enemies they had to resist."[4] Our Saviour did not come to destroy the moral law; and therefore he could not be against moral duties. His stress upon inward grace and outward obedience was great, but it all comes by free justification and by the imputation of Christ's righteousness rather than by any inherent righteousness and holiness. He that has faith working by love cannot but join love with faith; but love cannot be above faith in this life, this can happen only in the next world. Faith is above reason and is the condition of the covenant of grace. Tuckney would lay stress upon the impotency of nature rather than its strength.[5]

Whichcote answers that God consults not with us, but with His own wisdom and goodness for the remedy of our sins: "yet God proposeth, with respect to our understandings, viz. what they can receive and are able to bear. What he proposes, viz. expiation of sin, in the blood of

---

[1] *Ibid.*, pp. 47–48.
[2] *Ibid.*, p. 49.
[3] *Ibid.*, pp. 57–59.
[4] *Ibid.*, pp. 92–93.
[5] *Ibid.*, pp. 95–96.

Christ and our reformation by Him into his divine spirit are things grateful to the mind and expected by the mind." [1] He is convinced and clear concerning our acceptance by God, in and through Christ. He is surprised that Tuckney should balance knowledge against goodness; that he should insist upon Christ less as a principle of divine nature in us than as a sacrifice for us. It is easy to say that Christ died for one. "Self-flattery" may say this as well as faith. The greatest sinner can say this even if his whole self rises up against self-surrender to the will of God and the "transformation of himself into the spirit, image and nature of Christ." And further, "there is no real affirmation unless confirmed by the transformation of life." [2] If Christ be "more known and freely professed, let him also be inwardly felt, and secretly understood as a principle of divine life within us, as well as a Saviour without us." [3] Whichcote sums up his position as follows:

I am verie free to acknowledge Christ, the onlie foundation; since the apostasie and sinne of man: Hee alone gave the stoppe to God's just displeasure; His interposing prevayled with God, not to take the forfeiture; or, if taken, Hee procured the restauration and recoverie. Upon this account I acknowledge Christ, in parts of nature, reason and understanding; as well as in gifts of grace; so that Christ is not by mee anie where left out, nor faith neglected; no, nor not advanced to Superioritie and super-eminencie everie where; for I beleeve that I hold and enjoy my reason and understanding, by and under Christ. And what I have meant expressed and endeavoured all along, hath bin; to call men to the due and carefull use, employment and improvement of what they hold by and under Christ ... I attribute to the creature, upon itt's own accounte, nothing but unworthiness, inabilitie and insufficiencie; and look at Christ, as the onlie ground of acceptance; and his spirit, as the onlie principle of enoblement, power and sufficiencie. [4]

Because of the fundamental importance of the difference between Whichcote and Tuckney, we feel that we have been justified in this prolonged discussion of this aspect of the controversy. We have seen how the previous points of difference have entered into the way they view reconciliation. Whichcote, who from the outset, has given signal importance to human reason in the comprehension of truth, has here stressed the responsibility of man both in the beginning of the saving process and its continuation – by repentance and holy living. On the other hand, Tuckney, who from the outset set forth the basic principle

---

[1] *Ibid.*, pp. 104–105.
[2] *Ibid.*, pp. 123–124.
[3] *Ibid.*, p. 125. Cf. *Works*, I, 69–70; *Ibid.*, III, 282, where Whichcote seeks to justify his views on Reconciliation and his preaching a "moral gospel."
[4] *Ibid.*, pp. 126–217.

of *sola scriptura*, has in his concept of reconciliation added the logical corollary to the former principle, viz., *sola gratia*. The differences between these two men as we indicated at the outset of the discussion stem directly from the Renaissance-Reformation period. Whichcote, being greatly influenced by the Renaissance doctrine of the dignity of man and its corollary the exaltation of human reason, has made this influence felt throughout all his thought. Tuckney, on the other hand, derives his direct inspiration from the thought of the Reformers and more specifically, as interpreted by the Puritan Party of his day. This does not by any means deny the possibility of Whichcote being influenced by the Reformation or Tuckney by the Renaissance, but these observations seem to indicate the dominant influence in each case. We believe this explains both the agreements and differences between these two men as the controversy proceeds. Both men acknowledge reason and scripture as having importance, and in their controversy over reconciliation, both recognise the need for "free grace" and holy living, and both desire peace in Christendom. The difference in each instance is either in emphasis or approach. Between Tuckney and Whichcote we have what Collingwood conveniently describes as "a distinction without a difference," or a difference of "degree" rather than "kind." [1] And though their points of view were too far apart, on what they considered as fundamentals, to compromise – yet these conclusions help us to understand the spirit underlying their disagreements. [2]

The fourth letter of each man is a valuable index to the character of the two men. Tuckney writes:

> In the bodie of your after-discourse, in some things I find you immoveable; you being, as you write, under the power of them; and therefore, itt would bee in vayne, as to them, for me to move anie farther; itt is enough, that I have faithfullie expressed myself about them. [3]

And Whichcote replies:

---

[1] R. G. Collingwood, *An Essay on Philosophical Method*, (Oxford, 1950), p. 50. Milton is a good example of a Puritan who believed firmly in the Puritan doctrine of Scripture, but whose concept of reason was almost identical with that of Whichcote. It is obvious that he had, more than is true in the case of Tuckney, taken seriously the Renaissance doctrine of man and its corollary the centrality of reason in the comprehension of truth. This tendency in Milton is evident alike in his poetic and prose works, i.e. *Paradise Lost* and *De Doctrina Christiana*. Cf. Haller, *Ibid.*, pp. 309, 334.

[2] The friendship between Whichcote and Tuckney continues after this controversy, as we eoberve from their work together at Cambridge. Cf. *Supra*, Ch. I.

[3] *Letters*, pp. 131–132.

... I cannot practise upon my judgment; nor use anie force to command my understanding into other apprehensions, in the matter debated betwixt us; than I have expressed to you.... Wherefore if in this poynte of discerning, we differ; there is no helpe for it; we must forbear one another: and nothing is to be done, unless so farre mutualie to value each other's judgments; as to think that from such difference there is occasion given to each of us to examine our own spirits. ...[1]

The basic principles of Puritanism, namely, the supreme authority of Scripture and the doctrine of Predestination, are under attack by Whichcote. Tuckney represents a group of Puritans who consider the position of Whichcote a threat to the very foundations of their viewpoint. Indeed, the "germ" of a new movement is contained in Whichcote's position. And though Tuckney appears to "agree to differ" and to close the correspondence with unusual understanding, the next year, July 4, 1952, his Commencement Sermon is obviously in remembrance of his controversy with Whichcote. Tuckney says:

... Salvation is only by Christ, therefore in all matters of salvation, with a single eye let us look to Christ and to God in him, as Elected in him, Redeemed by him, Justified by his grace, and the imputation of his righteousness, in which is the ground of comfort, and sanctified by his spirit, not by a philosophical faith; or the use of right Reason, or a virtuous morality, too much now-a-days admired and cried up. As of old, the Temple of the Lord, the Temple of the Lord. So now, the Candle of the Lord, the Candle of the Lord. I would not have that Candle put out, I would have it snuffed and improved as a handmaid to faith, but not so (as when the Candle is set up) to shut the window, wither wholly to keep out, or in the least to darken the Sunshine, as it is with men's eyes, who can read better by a candle in the night, than by day-light.... Whatever Nature and Morality may be to others, yet to us let Christ be all in all. Nor let us be Deists, but Christians; let us not take up in such a Religion, as a Jew, or Turk, or Pagan, in a way of Nature and Reason only may rise up unto, but let us indeed be what we are called Christians, Christians.... Not a philosophical dull Morality, but the law of the Spirit of life, which is in Christ Jesus... not that Candle light, but the Sun of righteousness, that will guide our feet into the way of peace.[2]

The remainder of this study may be considered as Whichcote's answer and his justification for his departure from the rigid doctrinalism of Puritanism.

---

[1] *Ibid.*, pp. 132–133.

[2] Tuckney, *None But Christ*, (Cambridge, England, 1654), pp. 50–51. According to Haller, Calvinism ran counter to humanism and mysticism. It ran counter to the Renaissance Neo-Platonic idealism and to the rationalism promoted by the knowledge of ancient philosophy, literature and history. See Haller *Ibid.*, p. 194. It is wise, however, to bear in mind the difference between Calvin and Calvinism (esp. Puritanism). Brunner observes that there is a "platonic" element in Calvin's thought and even in Barth's *Epistle to the Romans*, see Brunner. *Ibid.*, pp. 34–35. Thus Platonism has a tendency to be reflected in the most unexpected places.

RELIGION OF FIRST-INSCRIPTION (I)

"The Reason of man is the Candle of the Lord"

As we begin our discussion of Whichcote's view of natural religion, we must remember that for him natural religion is subsumed under the more comprehensive notion of revealed religion. The "light of the creation" is preparatory to a "fuller" light and the latter is in a real sense the fulfilment and consummation of the former. Thus our separation of the two concepts is primarily for convenience of discussion. This fact will become increasingly evident as we proceed with our study.

It is not easy to fix upon a precise meaning for the term "reason" as Whichcote employs it. It would appear that he makes it include both the mental processes by means of which we arrive at a conclusion, and also the insight we possess into self-evident principles which condition these processes. It seems to stand, too, for our capacity to acknowledge God, the source and sustainer of all that is good, beautiful and true. Furthermore, reason appropriates these values and incorporates them within the soul in such wise that they form its disposition and become its temper; and so it is the governing principle which directs our appetites and controls our passions.[1] There is no question, but that for Whichcote reason is the highest and noblest of our faculties [2] – the faculty which marks us off from all other created beings as personal, and fits us to enter into fellowship with God.

Reason is the instrument we have to work with; it is uniform and the reason in one man speaks to the reason in another.[3] It is a law

---

[1] De Pauley, *The Candle of the Lord*, (London, 1937) pp. 10–11. Cf. A. N. Whitehead, *The Function of Reason*, (Princeton, 1929) p. 2; *Infra*, Ch. VI.

[2] Whichcote, *Works*, IV, 286. Whichcote's *Works* will be referred to hereafter by volume and page only unless greater detail is indicated. *Aph.* will be used to indicate Whichcote's *Aphorisms*. Cf. B. Pascal, *Pensées*, ed. and tr. by Stewart (New York, 1947), *Pens.*, 157, 158. See also, Richard Baxter, *The Reasons of the Christian Religion* (London, 1667), p. 4. The entire first part of Baxter's work may be favorably compared with Whichcote's views on natural theology.

[3] *Aphs.* 459, 1191.

which none may transgress; for it is used by God in His communications with men. It discovers the natural and receives the supernatural.[1] Reason is the perfection of our souls as well as the law and rule of men's minds. To go against reason is to go against God, while to follow reason is the same as to obey God. God is the highest Intelligence and reason is His voice, and the principle by which He governs the world.[2] Reason is the only rule in natural knowledge and it is the foundation of nature.[3] Whichcote concludes that nothing without reason is to be proposed and nothing against it is to be believed.[4] The concept of reason is central to all Whichcote has to say.

There is one aspect of reason, however, to which Whichcote repeatedly draws our attention, namely, that reason is not a self-sufficient endowment equipped either by God or by nature to fulfil its own functions. It has been adapted to work with God and in harmony with Him to reflect His mind. Reason, in so far as it speaks true, is the voice of God speaking within the human soul; and contrariwise, it is man's witness that what God says is good and true.[5] Thus "reason" is the "candle of the Lord, lighted by God and lighting unto God." [6]

Divine truth allwaies carried it's own light and evidence; so as that the mind receiving itt is illuminated, edified, satisfied.... It speaks for itt selfe, it recommendes itt selfe to its owne enterteinment, by it's owne excellencie. I adde allsoe, that the persuasion of the holie spirit contributes to the minde's assurance and satisfaction.[7]

The proper employment of intellectual faculties is to seek God.[8] The mind is the faculty by which man is capable of God, and unless a man brings his reason with him, he cannot receive the principles of religion.[9] A man is by no means confirmed in religion until his religion and reason are one. If this union is proper, when he thinks he speaks reason, he speaks religion; or when he thinks he speaks religiously, he speaks reasonably.[10]

In the state of religion, spirituals and naturals join and mingle in their subjects; so that if a man be once in a true state of religion, he cannot distinguish

---

[1] *Ibid.*, 99.
[2] IV, 401.
[3] *Aphs.* 778, 1021.
[4] *Ibid.*, 880.
[5] III, 163.
[6] Prov. 20:27. See W. O. E. Oesterley, *The Book of Proverbs* (London, 1929), p. 174.
[7] *Letters*, p. 48. Cf. Aug., *Trin.* xiv, 14.
[8] I, 149.
[9] IV, 139–140.
[10] *Ibid.*, p. 144.

between religion and the reason of his mind; so that his religion is the reason of his mind and the reason of his mind is his religion. ... The products of reason and religion are the same, in a person that is truly religious; his reason is sanctified by his religion, and his religion helps and makes use of his reason: so that in the subject it is but one thing; you may call it, if you will, religious reason, and the reason made religious; they are not divided or separated; but the union is more intimate and near, as the principles are more immaterial and spiritual; whereas gross and material things keep at a distance, because of the impossibility of penetration.[1]

Closely associated with the relation of reason and religion is Which-cote's treatment of natural truth, or truth of "first-inscription." Such truth is "connatural" to man, for the knowledge of truth is drawn out of us, not brought in to us. There are "common notions" [2] or "notions of truth," which light up and adorn the mind. These truths are knowable,[3] necessary and immutable in their nature and quality,[4] they are the first "emanation" [5] of divine truth in the moment of creation as the candle which God lights in man.[6] Truth comes to us by way of descent,[7] as a "ray" or "beam" from God.[8] Truth is akin to man's soul and speaks the same language and it is so near to the soul that it is the soul's image or form. Just as the soul is derived from God, even so truth comes from Him by communication. This explains the proper relationship between the soul and truth.[9]

At first glance it may appear that truth for Whichcote is somewhat subjective, that truth is subjectivity – to use the phrase made famous by Kierkegaard.[10] This tendency toward solipsism is foreign to Which-cote, who believes truths to have objective reality answerable to the idea of them in the divine mind. When these truths are grasped by the mind, the mind is acting according to its true nature; for God created the mind to comprehend reality. Truth belongs to those things which have eternal and immutable existence prior to the mind's

---

[1] *Ibid.*, p. 147. It was upon the principle of the "Impenetrability" of matter and other related concepts that Henry More offered to challenge Descartes in his correspondences with the Frenchman. Cf. Henry More, "The Immortality of the Soul," *Philosophical Writings*, ed. by F. I. Mackinnon (New York, 1925), I, iii, V.

[2] II, 13.

[3] III, 215. Here we are reminded, at once, of Platonic "recollection" and the "common notions" of Lord Herbert of Cherbury.

[4] *Ibid.*, p. 20.

[5] It is characteristic of Whichcote to use Neo-Platonic words and phrases.

[6] III, 29.

[7] *Ibid.*, p. 20.

[8] *Ibid.*, pp. 54–55.

[9] *Ibid.*, p. 15. When Whichcote speaks here of truth as an old friend and "ancient" acquaintance of the soul, we are again reminded of Platonic "recollection."

[10] The present writer is not here proposing to define the phrase as Kierkegaard uses it. See my art. "Kierkegaard on the Subjectivity of Truth," J RT, vol. XVIII, no. 1 (Winter-Spring, 1961) pp. 41–56.

apprehension of them and the mind's apprehension of them properly agrees with their objective reality.[1]

Cudworth's commentary at this point is so important that we consider it justifiable to present the substance of it here. He asserts that either understanding may be looked upon as a *tabula rasa* or it may have certain intelligible forms by which things are understood and known. The former theory is impossible, for how can the understanding being given a single individual image, connect this with others as cause or effect, or regard it as possible or impossible, when these ideas cannot be given by sense? [2] The latter theory is true, viz., that such (νοήματα) are implanted upon the mind as "anticipations" or (προχήψεις); not, indeed, actually present, but always potential, ready to fit any sense – presentation with its notional unity, and thereby give this composite object its true place in our objective experience.[3] If knowledge is possible, there must be something permanent and immutable, else the mind could have naught to fix itself upon and all communication between men would be impossible. The immutable must lie in the fitting of the (νοήματα) to the contributions of sense. Therefore, the (νοήματα) themselves are immutable. Though the (νοήματα) and essences of things exist in the mind, they are at the same time independent of any created mind and have a constant and never-failing entity of their own, i.e. in the mind of God. Since these (νοήματα) are modifications of mind, and at the same time eternal and independent of our minds, there must be some eternal mind existing, as it were, to contain the ideas. These essences of things must be either substances or modifications of substances. They are not substances, because they are "true of something," which something thus acts as their substance,[4] and for this reason they are modes. But all modes are of matter or of mind. They cannot be modes of matter, because matter is mutable, while ideas are immutable. Therefore they are modes of mind; but they are eternal, therefore they must be the modes of Eternal Mind, viz., God.[5] This discussion is important not only because it indicates Cudworth's attempt to clarify the nature of truth and its compre-

---

[1] III, 370–372.

[2] Ralph Cudworth, *A Treatise Concerning Eternal and Immutable Morality*, ed. by Edward Duresme (London, 1731), bk. IV, ch. I, sec. 8.

[3] *Ibid.*, bk. IV, ch. II, sec. 1.

[4] *Ibid.*, ch. IV, sec. 9.

[5] *Ibid.*, ch. II, secs. 12, 13. Cf. Henry More, *Theological Works*, ed. by Joseph Downing (London, 1708), pp. 765–767; John Smith, *Select Discourses*, ed. by H. G. Williams, 4th ed. (Cambridge, Eng., 1859), pp. 1–2.

hension as grasped by Whichcote, but it is also considered by Cudworth as the "first proof" of the existence of God.

It is interesting that Cudworth's argument arrives at approximately the same conclusion as Whichcote.[1] This fact may be explained, it seems to me, by the fact that the two men have the same fundamental presuppositions, but different purposes. Cudworth is here concerned with epistemology, ethics is secondary for him at this point, and this treatise was for him merely a *prolegomena* for a projected work in ethics which never appeared. On the other hand, Whichcote with the same presuppositions and basic conclusions, loses sight of epistemological subtleties in pursuit of his ethical purpose and at the summit of his vision of virtue, truth and beauty unite. Whichcote says:

> The understanding, as it comes into the world . . . is as *rasa tabula*, or a "white sheet of paper," whereon nothing is writ; but when it doth receive notions of truth, it is then beautified. . . . Such is the understanding when it is illuminated: truth, it is glory, light and beauty to the soul to shine and to appear fair and beautiful. . . . But on the contrary, as one shut up in a dungeon of darkness. . . so is one who is in a state of ignorance, or hath his mind depraved by vice.[2]

Truth is universal, and there is a remarkable agreement between divine truth and the ideals set up by non-Christian religions and their ethical systems. Whichcote adds that in their ethical ideals not only are we unable to speak beyond them but many adherents to these ideals act so well as to shame those who only profess to live by the fuller revelation in Christ.[3] If the objection be offered that many non-Christians fail to live up to such a high standard, Whichcote would answer by limiting what he means by universal acknowledgement. Universal acknowledgement as he employs it, does not depend upon universal acceptance, but upon the affinity it holds with the universal reason of mankind. The claim he would make for universal reason is that men, "improved in their intellectuals, and refined in their morals hold certain common notions on the ground of reason." It follows that truths of first-inscription are fully agreed upon by all persons that have lived up to their true nature, and this for Whichcote amounts to universal acknowledgement.[4]

---

[1] Whichcote, II, 4.

[2] III, 215.

[3] *Ibid.*, p. 30. After a personal dialogue with "cosmic" personalities, men who were as much saint as sage (i.e. Prof. Abe, a Zen Buddhist at Kyoto, Japan and Prof. Yamunacharya, a Vedantian of Mysore, India, to name only two), I am convinced that God's revelation to men through non-Christian religions is more than a general revelation in nature – it is personal and has received a personal response in such saintly lives. Whichcote appears to point in this direction and is remarkably advanced in this regard for his age.

[4] *Ibid.*, pp. 31–35.

Whichcote justifies this claim for natural light upon passages from the first stages of St. Paul's argument in Romans. Here is to be found the *locus classicus* of natural religion. It declares that God speaks to man's conscience, and makes him to perceive His invisible things through the things that are made; and that all who live contrary to reason are without excuse. Of certain verses in chapters i and ii, Whichcote says that they "have forced upon me all those notions I do entertain, or have publically delivered; concerning natural light, or the use of reason." [1]

The question concerning the validity of non-Christian religions arose in response to Whichcote's view of natural truth. [2] For instance, what about the validity of the Islamic faith? According to Whichcote, Mohammed bases his faith on "gentilism" and Judaism, but his additions are contemptible to sober reason as well as contrary to his extractions from the Old Testament. He may easily be detected as an imposter, for apart from what he borrowed from the Bible, the remainder opposes reason. When God bears witness to a religion, it is reasonable. Further, God only reveals truth in a way of purity and holiness, and never in agreement with immorality and irrationality. By these standards, history has condemned Mohammed, who, even in his own lifetime, became immoral. The only valid representation of divine truth is that which satisfies reason and acquaints us with the nature of God. [3]

There is for Whichcote an unbroken transition from natural truth to revealed truth, the latter being actually an "addition" to the former. Revelation is "grafted on" this natural foundation, and the former is in a real sense, preparatory, and a necessary prerequisite for the latter and fuller revelation of God in Scripture, and more specifically in Christ. [4] This intensifies the importance of Whichcote's assertion that the several truths hang together by mutual dependence and lead one to the other.

---

[1] *Letters*, p. 9. Cf. Rom. 1:18–21, 28, 31; 2:14.

[2] Cf. Tuckney, *None But Christ*, (Cambridge, Eng., 1654), pp. 50–52.

[3] Whichcote, III, 36, 40. It is interesting that Whichcote and his followers use the same ideas to attack Romanism and the fanatic Sectaries within Christendom as he uses here against Islam. Cf. Baxter, *Ibid.*, pp. 198–200. If Whichcote had acquired a deeper understanding of Islam he would have known that Greek philosophy was used in the formulation of Islamic thought also.

See, A. E. Affifi, "The Rational and Mystical Interpretations of Islam," K. W. Morgan ed. *Islam–The Straight Path* (New York, 1958), pp. 144–179. Cf. R. Klibansky, *The Continuity of the Platonic Tradition During the Middle Ages* (London, 1939), pp. 13–37.

[4] *Infra*, ch. VI. Here we devote a section to a treatment of the relation of natural to revealed truth.

By truth already received, we have a double advantage for receiving more. . . .
The way to understanding which was obstructed is open. . . . The mind is
brought into disposition and preparation to receive all divine truth.[1]

Whichcote was very sensitive to the atheistic tendencies of his
time.[2] For him, atheism is the most unaccountable of all things
since the existence of God is so self-evident, while atheism is so
irrational.[3] This is where Cudworth's approach to the same subject
varies from Whichcote's, for to Cudworth atheism requires polemical
disputation. Thus Cudworth devotes the first book of his most celebrated work, *The True Intellectual System of the Universe,* to an
argument against atheism. The seriousness with which Cudworth
viewed this problem of atheism is indicated by the fact that he argued
against atheism more than in favour of theism, and he devotes the
first three of five chapters of book one to a statement and refutation
of several atheistic systems as conceived by him. Though he begins
a more positive approach in the fourth chapter of book one, it is only
in the fifth and last chapter that he approximates a statement of
argumentative evidence for the being of God. This essentially negative
approach of Cudworth may be compared with Whichcote's more
positive and self-confident assertion that it is the most self-evident of
all truths, that God is, and that conversely atheism is the most
unreasonable of all things.[4]

Whichcote's attitude towards atheism does not indicate any indifference concerning the fact of atheism or any lack of insight into its

[1] II, 12.

[2] I, 65.

[3] II, 57.

[4] At this point it would not be amiss to say that Whichcote is more biblical while Cudworth
is more philosophical in the approach to the problem. The message of the Bible throughout is
that God exists without any necessity for rational proof, while the philosophical approach is
to offer proofs for the existence of deity. The difference here between Whichcote and
Cudworth seems to be merely one of emphasis. Cf. E. S. Brightman, *The Problem of God*
(New York, 1930) pp. 139–165 with A. C. Knudson, *The Doctrine of God* (New York, 1930),
pp. 203–241. Both Brightman and Knudson are personalist thinkers and yet the differences
in their approach to the problem of the existence of God remind us of the divergence between
the approach of Cudworth and Whichcote to the same problem. See also, E. L. Mascall, *He
Who Is* (London, 1943), pp. 30–39 and his, *Existence and Analogy* (London, 1949), pp. 18–121;
where he contrasts the essentialist and existentialist approaches to theism and presents St.
Thomas' doctrine of analogy. We need only mention here Bishop John A. T. Robinson's
Honest to God (London, 1963) which was a challenge both to theism and ethics. It is based on
ideas drawn from Buber, Tillich, Bonhoeffer and others. Robinson attempts to make these
views relate to each other without placing them in context or being aware of the disagreement
between those from whom he receives his ideas. The bishop by his attack upon the fortress of
Christian faith and ethics and mostly by the sheer weight of his office has helped to create a
real crisis in the West from which Eastern religions may profit (i.e. Zen and Vedanta). Cf.
D. L. Edwards, ed., *The Honest to God Debate* (London, 1963) and Bishop Robinson's own
apology for his "new morality" in his *Christian Morals Today* (Philadelphia, 1964).

unwholesome implications. He asserts that a man may be an atheist by neglect, the failure to use reason to know God, or by contempt, the desire for the non-existence of God.[1] To deny God's existence is to deny absolute moral distinctions, and to consider all moral decisions as relative. In this sense, atheism is a perversion of human nature since man is made to know, love and obey God.[2] Further, atheism results in giving first place to temporal things instead of subordinating them to spiritual realities.[3] In fact, the denial of God is the denial of one's own soul and its immortality, for self-denial and atheism are a single attitude.[4] For Whichcote, the essential being of man as man is identical with his relation to God.[5] Whichcote captures the spirit of Berdyaev who says, "where there is no God there is no man." [6] It is consistent with the trend of Whichcote's thought to conclude that when man ceases to be rooted in God, he relapses inevitably into the sub-human.[7] Thus Whichcote conceives the plight of the atheist as a very serious one.

He that affects to be an atheist is no longer at rest than God will give him leave; God will be there to awe and command at his pleasure, where he is refused as to love and affection.... No men ever stood more in fear of God, than those that most deny and least love him; and so it will be if men do affect to be atheist that so they may live exorbitantly and loosely; there is more slavish fear of God in these men ... than there is in them that fear, obey and love God.[8]

Since Whichcote assumes a Christian world-view, *Weltanschauung*, for him the existence of God is self-evident. Therefore, his proof for the existence of God is in the interest of those who need proof. But a man does not need to look beyond himself for such proof since a man is himself the best possible evidence of the existence of God. The best proof of God's existence is a man's awareness of his self-activity. Descartes' *cogito ergo sum* becomes for Whichcote, "I act, therefore I am; I do, therefore I have being." Though the concept may have been suggested by Descartes, it is obvious that Descartes begins his ontology

[1] III, 238–240.
[2] *Ibid.*, pp. 240–242.
[3] *Ibid.*, pp. 276–278.
[4] IV, 320.
[5] Emil Brunner, *God and Man*, tr. by David Cairns (London, 1936), pp. 155–159.
[6] N. A. Berdyaev, *The End of Our Time*, tr. by D. Atwater (London, 1933), p. 80.
[7] Cf. John Baillie, *Our Knowledge of God*, (London, 1939) p. 42.
[8] Whichcote, III, 61. Cf. H. More, *Antidote Against Atheism* (London, 1662) and *Immortality of the Soul* (London, 1662). In both works the author has a similar aim, viz., to present the proper notion of spirit, to prove its existence and its special nature and qualities. Though More goes to extremes in his witness to witchcraft and apparitions, his intention is sound, for he attempts to establish the fact of the existence of God by defending the reality of spirit. See also his *Explication of the Nature of Spirits*, etc... (London, 1700).

by self-reflection while Whichcote sets out from self-activity.[1] Whichcote presents his argument as follows: If I am, either I made myself, or
I was made by another. I did not make myself; for if I made myself
at my own will, I could continue myself in being during my own
pleasure and this I know I cannot do. It takes less power to continue a
thing which has being than to call a thing out of nothing, *ex nihilo*, into
being; therefore I was not made by myself, but by Another. And that
Other must be neither my equal nor my inferior; for I can do more
than my inferior and as much as my equal. It follows that I was made
by a Greater than myself both in wisdom and power and this First
Independent Being is God.[2]

Though Whichcote is partially influenced by the negative approach
to the existence of God as set forth by many Christian Platonists before
his time,[3] his emphasis is more positive. God's existence is attested by
universal reason and even if He cannot be comprehended in essence,
yet He is universally known by His moral perfections and providence.
Thus what our author implies by knowledge of God involves likewise
support for his assertion that God exists.

The roots of God are in the soul and by sheer force of mind one
knows that God made the world and governs it. The first knowledge
is that God exists. If God did not make us to know that He is, then He
cannot judge us nor make demands upon us. We are not merely taught
to know God, but we are made to know Him, or we could never know
Him. There is no basis for divine faith save divine authority. It is
for this reason that we are not capable of faith unless we know that
God is. His existence must precede faith, and without natural know-

---

[1] R. Descartes, *Meditations*, tr. by John Veitch (Edinburgh, 1881), Med. III, pp. 115–132.
Cf. D. E. Trueblood *Philosophy of Religion* (New York, 1957) where Trueblood points up the
importance of Descartes' method and concludes: "I care, therefore, I doubt" is at least the
beginning of a valid method in the philosophy of religion (p. 45). Both Descartes and Whichcote base their ontology on personal experience even if it is viewed differently. However,
Descartes' fundamental proof for the existence of God is rooted in his more comprehensive
conception of initial doubt and upon his notion of clear and distinct ideas. God as a Perfect
Being is for Descartes a clear and distinct conception. Cf. Anselm, *Proslogion*. What Whichcote, Descartes and Anselm have in common is an anxiety to satisfy reason and to assert that
thought leads by logical necessity from their respective presuppositions to the existence of God.
For criticisms of this general approach to proving the existence of God, see Aquinas,
Contra Gentiles, i, 11; Kant, *Critique of Pure Reason*, tr. by N. K. Smith (London, 1918), p.
505, and Casserley, *The Christian in Philosophy* (London, 1949), pp. 60–62. Hartshorne sheds
new light on Anselm's ontological proof for the existence of God in his introduction to *Saint
Anselm: Basic Writings*, tr. S. W. Deane, 2nd ed. (La Salle, Ill., 1962), pp. 28–117.
[2] *Ibid.*, pp. 241–242. Cf. Arist. *Meta*, xii; Baxter, *Ibid.*, p. 32.
[3] E.i. Aug. *Trin.* viii, 3, 2. Casserley asserts that the Christian is committed to two ways of
conceiving God: (a) a biblical way of affirmation, and (b) a philosophical way of negation
which keeps us aware that the glory of God exceeds even His self-disclosure in Christ. *Ibid.*,
pp. 36–38.

ledge of God, faith is impossible.[1] Thus with the author of the Book
of Hebrews Whichcote agrees, "he that comes to God must believe
that He is." [2]

When Whichcote reasons from the "effects" in the natural world
and in the moral experience of man to the God behind them, we are
reminded of the Prime Mover of Aristotle [3] and the cosmological proofs
for the existence of God set forth by Aquinas.[4] In each case, the
argument is from phenomena in the world to a Cause behind things
outside of the world. However, Whichcote argues from the incompre-
hensibility of these effects by our finite minds to the existence of an
Infinite and Eternal Mind which fully comprehends them. He asserts
that if a man acknowledges a being more able and wise than himself,
he acknowledges deity, for things which excel human knowledge may
be known only by an eternal Mind which is the original of our mind.
He reasons thus: if the mind of man is transcended, there is no creature
below him capable of explaining this fact. This being so, and the fact
that man is "overborn" by these transcendent realities the cause of
these realities as well as the comprehension of them must be in a
primary, original and independent Intelligence.[5] Once again Whichcote
attempts to establish the fact of God's existence in a rational manner.
But the weakness of any such attempt is in the fact that all men do not
have the same presuppositions. For instance, in this argument, in
order to agree with Whichcote's conclusions, one would have to accept
most of his intellectualism and especially the dignity he attributes to
man.

But though God's existence is knowable by reason, according to
Whichcote, yet our knowledge of God also transcends reason. Beyond
a certain point our reason will not carry us and we must believe, where
we cannot prove. However, this limitation should be admitted only
when we shall have reasoned to the top of our minds, for after all, God
is more knowable than all else besides. First, God is more knowable
because of the "fulness" of His being, while things unknowable are
so because of their "littleness" of being. Since God is the fullest Being,

---

[1] Whichcote, III, 142–144, 160. Cf. E.R.E., XII, 324.
[2] Heb. 11:6.
[3] Arist. Ibid., Cf. Plato, Laws, x.
[4] Aquinas, Contra Gentiles (Eng.tr.), i, 13. Cf. Summa Theologica (Eng.tr.), Pt. I, Q. 2, Art.
3. In Aquinas the cosmological proofs take the place of the ontological proof of Anselm.
Whichcote makes use of the cosmological approach as well as the ontological. Cf. Aristotle,
Ibid. See also Mascall's He Who Is and Existence and Analogy introduced earlier in this
chapter and Daniel Jenkins, The Christian Belief in God (Philadelphia, 1963), pp. 46–41.
[5] Whichcote, III, 164–170. Cf. Cicero, De Natura Deorum, ii, 6; Aug. Trin. xv, 1.

He is the most intelligible.[1] Second, the ways of knowing God are the most dependable, that is by perfection or negation. By ascribing to Him perfection, we cannot attribute too much perfection to Him since God is the Best, and infinitely Perfect. Conversely, by means of negation, we cannot remove too much imperfection from God. Our very words must be purified of all limitations before we can say clearly what God is not.[2] Third, God is not knowable by virtue of our relation to Him since we are closer to God than to anything else. God is more inward than our souls, more than what is most ourselves. And, fourth, God is most knowable because of our dependence upon Him. There is such a "naturalness" between our souls and God, that it is impossible not to know Him.[3]

Though the mind does not have the power to get final knowledge, yet further knowledge comes through illuminations from God.[4] God who made "finite and fallible" spirits, guides and directs them. When Whichcote asserts that "the spirit of man is the candle of the Lord," he asks us to add that a candle is first "lighted and then lighting," that is, the mind is first illumined by "divine influences." It is only when a man's mind has been exposed to such divine illumination that he is enabled to know truly God in creation and providence. God is the Father of our spirits and to us He is "all in all, original, final, and the center of our souls. Our faculties are sagacious and the nearness of the light of knowledge is ours. If we are without a sense of deity, it is our fault." [5]

We have already implied that for Whichcote many of the divine perfections remained incomprehensible, i.e. omnipotence, eternity, ubiquity and the like. But while making this admission, he insists that

---

[1] Though Whichcote is consistent with his Neo-Platonic background, Paul Tillich is quite critical of this view. Whichcote speaks of God in terms of superlatives, and here God is conceived as the "fullest" Being and therefore, the most knowable. But for Tillich, God is being – itself, and has the infinite power of being, and therefore the being of God cannot be understood as the existence of "a" being alongside others. If God is "a" being, He is subject to the categories of finitude, especially to space and substance. When applied to God, superlatives become diminutives. They place Him on the level of other beings while elevating him above them. But whenever infinite or unconditional power or meaning are attributed to the highest being, it has ceased to be "a" being, and has become being – itself, or the ground of being. *Systematic Theology*, (London, 1953), I, 261–263. This general criticism will apply to most of Whichcote's thoughts of God, metaphysical and ethical as well as theological.

[2] By his two-fold method of seeking knowledge of God, Whichcote is at one with the early merger of Christian and Neo-Platonic strands of thought, i.e. in Pseudo-Dionysius and Augustine.

[3] Whichcote, III, 176–180.

[4] Cf. P. O. Kristeller, *The Philosophy of Marsilio Ficino*, tr. by Virginia Conant (New York, 1943) p. 253. See also, Aug. *Trin.*, xiv. 14.

[5] Whichcote, *Ibid.*, pp. 187–189.

other divine perfections are knowable, especially moral perfections and the knowledge of these latter is fundamental to religion and morality. Thus his treatment of the attributes of God is limited almost exclusively to what he calls moral perfections, such as goodness, wisdom, liberty, justice and power.[1] These moral perfections of God are at the heart of His entire scheme of thought, for the "copy" of these principles is for him the evidence in man of his "divine likeness."

When Whichcote speaks of God as the greatest good, *summum bonum* his meaning is closer to Plato than to Plotinus.[2] The latter places the One above good and evil, while Plato conceives the absolute and final reality and ultimate unity as the Good or the "Form of the Good." [3] Whichcote asserts that goodness is God's prime perfection and our truest conception of God is as Almighty Goodness.[4] The divine nature is goodness, infinite goodness. God is as good as good can be, and will not fail in any act of goodness. The true effect of goodness is known by communication, and thus we know God to be the highest Good by His communication of goodness to us.[5] It follows that God is "necessarily the Best as he is the Greatest." [6] To accent his ethical concept of the divine nature, Whichcote includes holiness and truth in divine goodness. When speaking of the divine nature, holiness and righteousness are synonymous, and so are truth and faithfulness.[7] All the ways of God are ways of goodness, righteousness, and truth.[8] Now, these divine attributes are the very foundation of religion and, unless they are a part of the nature of God religion is groundless since religion is the imitation of God in these.

Divine knowledge is true wisdom since it is from God, and is perfected only in Him.[9] In this connection Whichcote fails to do justice to the concept of wisdom in God. However, we will meet the notion later in his views concerning Scripture.[10] Whichcote's main concern here is to establish God's dealings with us, as also our response to Him,

---

[1] *Ibid.*, I, 381; Aph. 85.

[2] Plotinus, *Enneads*, vi, 9, 3, 4.

[3] Plato, *Republic*, vi. There is no question but that for Plato the idea of the Good is the highest Idea, but as to whether he identifies the Idea of the Good with God is less certain, though the trend of his thought is often in this direction. As for Whichcote, God is certainly the *Summum Bonum*.

[4] Whichcote, I, 22.

[5] II, 343.

[6] *Aph.* 320.

[7] I, 381.

[8] *Aph.* 995.

[9] IV, 280–281.

[10] *Infra*, ch. VI.

as rational. Man's reason is a derived light, lighted by a Greater Light the infinite wisdom of God. God knows infinitely and teaches man by His wisdom.[1]

Concerning the liberty of God, Whichcote ascribes to God mastery of His own right, that is, God does as he pleases and His will is a law to Him.[2] But a necessary distinction is to be made between His secret will and revealed will only in the superficial sense that the former is unknown while the latter is known, actually they are the same.[3] Having made this statement, he goes forward with his assertion that God's freedom is limited by His goodness.[4] There is that in God, which is more beautiful than will,[5] viz., goodness. Thus, God is certain because in Him there is, at once, the fulness of liberty and all other moral perfections.[6] God only can say He will, because He will in view of the complete agreement between His will and the right.[7]

God's justice is the basis of His integrity and uprightness, and these agree with reason and right.[8] When Whichcote uses the example of God's punishment of sin to describe justice, other moral perfections merge with justice and we see their interdependence. If God punishes sin, it is just, for sin deserves punishment. But we cannot say that it is necessary for God to punish sin, for this would be to impinge upon His liberty. Punishment for sin is just, if it is carried out and just if it is not. This must be true since otherwise we make a law for God and He is not bound by it. Since God has the right of an owner over man, He can forgive sin if He pleases. However, God does this only if the sinner repents, since to do so for an impenitent would bring God's will in conflict with His goodness. On this point Whichcote captures the

---

[1] "Reflections," *Ibid.*, IV, 264.

[2] I, 28; *Aph.* 158.

[3] *Ibid.*, p. 223.

[4] *Ibid.*, p. 251.

[5] II, 397.

[6] *Aph.* 158.

[7] *Ibid.*, 413. Whether it was his intention or not, Whichcote has, to a certain extent, offered a finite God. In the case of Edgar Brightman, the evil in the world prompted him to seek an explanation.

Brightman concludes by asserting the necessity of a God limited in goodness or power to explain the vast amount of evil in the world, and the result is his doctrine of a finite God. Whichcote, on the other hand, conceives a self-limitation of God as necessary for self-consistency in the divine nature conceived as morally perfect. Cudworth unhesitatingly declares God's wisdom and goodness to be above His will, and therefore morality does not depend upon divine commands. *Eternal and Immutable Morality*, i. 3. 1, 8. It is only a brief step from Cudworth's position to Kant's "categorical imperative" which requires the service of God only to guarantee that the commands of the moral order will be obeyed, and a thing is not good because it is the will of God, but God wills it because it is good.

[8] I, 28.

essential spirit of Origen, namely, "God by goodness punishes impenitency and by justice relieves penitency." [1] Thus justice is to be conceived in the divine nature not only as being in agreement with reason and right, but also in conjunction with the liberty and goodness of God.

God is self-sufficient and His sovereignty puts Him out of fear; He is always clothed with omnipotency.[2] Power is "a" perfection of God, but of the three eminent perfections of God, power comes after both goodness and wisdom. Power, therefore, does not exclude other divine perfections.[3] God's power is always in relation to His righteousness and holiness, but it is sufficient to do what is "needful and fulfil His promises." [4] God does not by virtue of His omnipotency, deal arbitrarily with us, but according to right and reason.[5] It follows from this that, in spite of the fulness of God's liberty and power, we can be more certain of His righteousness and equity than of all other beings.[6] God's creation in infinite wisdom and power speaks goodness in principle. The variety, order and fitness of things, declare the wisdom of God and to bring things remotely distant together, *non ens* to *ens*, declares His power.[7]

From what has been said, it is evident that God is conceived by Whichcote as personal. Galloway has pointed out that between the notion of personal and that of ethical, an intimate relation subsists, and the one implies the other.[8] Further, reverence is possible between persons but not between persons and things. Thus on the level of spiritual religion the idea of God as personal and ethical is dominant, and this is clearly expressed in the character of worship. The vitality of religious consciousness is bound up with the conviction that the object of reverence

---

[1] IV, 15–16; Cf. Orig., *De Princ.* ii. 10.

[2] II, 344–345.

[3] III, 66. For Brightman power is never an intrinsic good, but only an instrumental good at best. The use of power, therefore, determines its moral quality. It appears that Whichcote desires to make some such assertion to counteract Hobbes' Absolutism as more recent philosophers have attacked the concept of the Will to Power as set forth by Nietzsche. Whichcote certainly provides a safeguard to his concept of power by subordinating it to goodness, wisdom and the like, as he applies it to his notion of the divine nature.

Thus without any undue limitation of power in God, he assures us that even power in God is virtuous, because it is always consistent with the other ethical attributes of the divine nature, and because it enables God to work for good in nature and history. Cf. Knudson,*Ibid.*, pp. 242–284.

[4] *Ibid.*, pp. 349–350.

[5] *Aph.* 417.

[6] *Ibid.*, 685.

[7] I, 30.

[8] Galloway, *The Philosophy of Religion* (Edinburgh, 1914) p. 492.

is a personal Being.[1] If C. J. Webb is right when he asserts that personal nature is identical with rational nature, we have further support for adding the personal element to Whichcote's conception of God.[2] Professor H. H. Farmer often speaks of the "radical personalism" of the Christian religion and the awareness of God as personal as the essence of all living religion. He says: "The essence of religion in all its forms is response to the ultimate as personal." [3] One meets a similar view in the writings of Brunner, John Baillie and Ferré, but what we meet in these men is not the personalism of Brightman. Ferré has in no uncertain terms attacked the school of personalists and asserted that impersonalism and personalism alike detract from the fulness of the Christian faith.[4] By considering, then, only the natural theology of Whichcote we have good reason to believe that for him, God is personal. This fact will become more obvious as we pass on to a consideration of providence.

Whichcote conceives God as active in nature and history.[5] We have the assurance that we are in the hands of a good God, whatever the appearance of things may be. The God who governs the world is a mild, gentle and loving spirit. God is at work in the world [3] and all things are in some way under His management. All things are either willed by God or permitted by Him. That is to say, God permits some things out of wisdom, which He does not prevent by power, and even the things merely permitted by God are for our instruction in goodness. All God's acts in nature and history are purposeful and especially designed to lead men to growth in goodness.[6] Here we are reminded of Ferré's convenient observations upon what he calls the general and special providences of God. The former allowing for a belief in an "open" universe, (an idea made famous by Bergson and William James), and in human freedom. General providence is conceived as permissive rather than intentional, but it is nevertheless purposive. Thus God allows accidents to happen not against His will but according to His

---

[1] *Ibid.*, p. 491. Galloway has made a convenient distinction between what he calls the metaphysical attributes of God, i.e. omnipotence, omnipresence and omniscience, and the personal and ethical attributes of God. Whichcote comes close to this distinction except in his reference to the personal-ethical attributes as ethical only. However, it appears obvious that these ethical attributes are personal also.

[2] C. C. J. Webb, *God and Personality* (London, 1918), pp. 109–111. Here it is stated that it is because personality is ethical as well as rational that Bosanquet attempts to place God above personality in order to make Him transcend all moral distinctions, since personality and morality go together. *Ibid.*, pp. 124–126.

[3] H. H. Farmer, *The World and God* (London, 1955), pp. 27–28.

[4] Nels Ferré, *The Christian Understanding of God* (London, 1952), pp. 11, 26, 31–33.

[5] Whichcote, I, 62.

[6] *Ibid.*, pp. 124–127.

general will. On the other hand, the special providence of God is in keeping with God's personal purpose and by this means God releases in nature and history His redemptive being and force. It follows that the closer one draws to God spiritually the more one comes under the direction of His special providence, and it is to be remembered that God's general providence is likewise under His control, and He may change its course at will.[1] It appears that Ferré has in many ways enlarged upon and provided a necessary supplement to Whichcote's view of providence.

Whichcote conceived God as the Creator and Governor of the world in nature and history. If a man will only use his reason, the work of God may be easily discerned all around him. The prerequisites of the proper interpretation of providence are: reason, scripture and a good life.[2] Whichcote believed one common misunderstanding of God to stem from unworthy notions of God.[3] A good example of an unworthy notion of God is considered by him to be the doctrine of predestination. He asserts that God has not pre-determined our sin or our misery. Such a belief makes one unwilling to be reconciled to God, and the idea is false since God does not will the death, but the salvation of a sinner.[4]

To believe there is a God is to believe the existence of all possible Good and Perfection in the universe, and that things finally shall be as they should be.[5] Here Whichcote is in essential agreement with William James who gives us the assurance that the world is safe in God's care and that no matter how much it might zigzag in its course, He can bring it home at last.[6] Just as created beings provide for their offsprings, even so the Creator will not fail to provide for His creatures.[7] But to Whichcote, God is more concerned in the moral order than He is in the natural, and this is because the moral order has greater possibilities for good or for ill. The proper use of rational and voluntary nature is of the greatest importance, but its perversion is more destructive. It follows that God's "superintendency" should be more evident in the moral than in the natural order.[8] Thus Whichcote's confidence in providence is

---

[1] Ferré, *Ibid.*, pp. 139–153.
[2] Whichcote, I, 128–133.
[3] *Ibid.*, pp. 338–341.
[4] II, 359.
[5] *Aph.* 70. Whichcote is here in essential agreement with Leibniz's *Theodicy*, viz., that this is the best possible world. Voltaires sceptical but challenging reply to Leibniz in his *Candide* might be considered here also.
[6] William James, *Will to Believe* (New York, 1898), p. 182.
[7] Whichcote, *Aph.* 533. Cf. Lu. 12:22–31.
[8] III, 173–174.

unquestioned. God is the "Original of our being, the Father of our spirits, the Centre of our souls, and our utmost End." [1] He is the Universal Father and the whole world is His family. He maintains, settles and establishes the order and government of things, and His concern is to control evil and maintain right.[2]

> There is no Fate; but on our part Reason and Prudence; on God's part Providence; and this Providence, and all necessary Help, are as sure and certain as the Existence and Perfections of God.[3]

But when we face up to reality – to the hard facts of this life, is the proper understanding of providence reasonable at all times, or isn't it really a matter of faith? In spite of Whichcote's words, there are times when it is hard to believe in a providential God apart from the faith and patience of Job.[4] One wonders if this is not one point where the rigid intellectualism of Whichcote breaks down. Indeed, it would seem that his rational approach is a faith in God which transcends his rational explanation. Further, as Farmer reminds us, there is a great danger in searching out in the lives of others, the course of history or the order of nature evidences of God's providence, for such evidence is bound to be insecure. The rationalist theologians who conceived it possible to demonstrate a beneficent and contriving agency in nature providing for the well-being of all creatures including man, had their argument wrecked by the natural abnormality of the Lisbon earthquake.[5] If we appeal solely to scripture as the basis of our interpretation of providence, then there is always the danger of biblical literalism which may prove disastrous.[6] There is also the question of approach. In Bultmann's opinion, any consideration of God's work in nature or history should begin with the revelation of God in Christ, for to begin from man and his experience can never lead to the truth. Thus with the wrong starting-point one can only expect to arrive at the wrong conclusion.[7] However, I would maintain that when one takes into account the whole sweep of Whichcote's thought, his view of providence is sound and praiseworthy. His view of Gods relation to the world is obviously what is sometimes called "panentheism," now held

---

[1] II, 187.
[2] IV, 100.
[3] *Aph.* 974.
[4] Job 13:15; Cf. Ferré, *Ibid.*, pp. 143–144.
[5] Farmer, *Ibid.*, pp. 231–232.
[6] E.i. Those who believe in the inevitability of war simply as a result of their literalistic interpretation of scripture, viz. Matt. 24:6; Mk. 13:7.
[7] Rudolf Bultmann, *Essays Philosophical and Theological*, tr. by J. C. G. Greig (London, 1955), pp. 90–118.

with varieties of emphasis by writers like Tillich, Hartshorne and S. L. Frank. God is at once immanent in the world, and transcendent to it; the world as Farmer describes it has "relative independence," but since God is the all-including reality, He grants it being and continues it in being.[1] It is in this spirit that Whichcote describes the providence of God.

What is man? The answer to this question is of great importance to the entire scheme of Whichcote's thought. The "image of God" is in man and man is in some sense a "middle being" to Whichcote, a view characteristic of the Renaissance especially when the Neo-Platonic or Christian-Platonic strands have been most evident.[2] In respect of his higher faculties, man is rational and free, and by virtue of his possibilities transcends the whole creation below him. The real exaltation of man is by virtue of his reason and as Pascal has so well said, "man is only a reed, but he is a thinking reed."[3] To Whichcote man is the masterpiece of creation, and is more valuable than all the rest of creation.[4] Man is made in the image of God and though he is of the "earth earthy"; yet because he partakes of the image of God, imago Dei, he is no less "heavenly."[5] The "generation" of man is by "superinducing" the rational soul upon the "sensitive," and thus man is more than animal.[6] Whichcote's concept of the image of God is inseparably bound up with his assertion that the "reason of men is the candle of the Lord; lighted by God and lighting unto God. Res illuminata illuminans."[7] So important is this concept of the "image" of God in man to all Whichcote has to say that it deserves special attention.[8]

In Whichcote's conception of the image of God it is obvious we have an eclecticism of many strands of thought. As we have seen, he combines in his conception (Gen. 1:26–7), man's being made in the "image and likeness of God" with (Prov. 20:27) the spirit of man as "the candle of

---

[1] Duthie, God in His World (London, 1954), pp. 53–54.
Cf. D. J. Elwood, The Philosophical Theology of Jonathan Edwards (New York, 1960), pp. 19–22.

[2] Robb, Ibid., p. 87. Cf. Whichcote, I, 195; Aph. 8.

[3] Pascal, Ibid., Pen., 161.

[4] Whichcote, I, 298–300.

[5] II, 43. Cf. Gen. 1:26–27. See also, Gene Rice, "Let us Make Man," J R T, vol. XXI, no. 2 (Winter, 1964–65), pp. 109–114.

[6] Aph. 855. Cf. Bergson's criticism of the traditional classifications of life, viz. vegetative, instinctive and rational life, see Creative Evolution tr. A. Mitchell (New York, 1911), p. 135.

[7] Ibid., 916. There is no question but that the dignity of man as he conceives it is based on "reason."

[8] The best source to my knowledge on the subject is David Cairns, The Image of God (London, 1953); Cf. Leif Egg-Olofsson, The Conception of The Inner Light in Robert Barclay's Theology (Lund, 1954) and T. F. Torrance, Calvin's Doctrine of Man (London, 1945).

the Lord." And as it is his custom to "run through" the Bible, he adds at least one supporting passage from the New Testament (Mark 12:16), where Jesus upon asking for a penny inquired as to whose "image or superscription" was upon it, and commanded "Render unto Caesar the things that are Caesar's and to God the things that are God's." Whichcote concludes that God's "superscription" is upon man, and for this reason man's nature and destiny are inextricably bound up with God.[1] It is obvious that if we applied critical biblical exegesis or the rigours of the modern historical method to Whichcote's use of the Bible, we could easily condemn him for misuse of the Bible, for he has approached the Bible with his own preconceived ideas. Further, he has made use of his knowledge of the history of thought, philosophical and theological, to arrive at this synthesis. The Platonic-Stoic, Jewish-Hellenic, and Christian-Platonic strands of thought converge in Whichcote's concept of the "image of God" in man. It will be necessary for us to return to this subject again when we consider his doctrine of revelation and especially his doctrine of sin.[2] Our purpose here has been to underline the centrality of the idea, and to suggest the several channels through which the idea perhaps reached our author. Finally, it has been our present purpose to indicate the centrality of the concept to all that is to follow in this study.

Man by virtue of his rational and free nature is a moral agent. Whichcote adds to this assertion a belief in man's "dei-form" nature or a natural sympathy in man for true morality and religion.[3] But for Whichcote, man's real moral responsibility is based upon man's endowment with "self-reflecting" faculties capable of making moral distinctions.[4] It is natural for man to choose good and avoid evil for it is the same thing for moral agents to observe and comply with reason, as for inferior creatures to act according to sense.[5] It is only necessary at this point to state Whichcote's view of man as a free moral agent since the further implications of this notion are treated elsewhere.[6]

However, the question as to the nature of human freedom deserves some attention here, even though it will emerge again in relation to Whichcote's moral theory. Whichcote is here in essential agreement with Kant in asserting that "I ought" implies "I can." But man's

---

[1] Mk. 12:16. Cf. Cairns, *Ibid.*, p. 30.
[2] *Infra*, ch. VI.
[3] Whichcote, *Aph.* 1133.
[4] I, 131.
[5] *Ibid.*, p. 212.
[6] *Infra*, ch. V.

freedom is a limited freedom since man is not free to disregard reason or the moral order. However, the very fact that God created man as a rational being implies that man has freedom to direct his own faculties, or God would necessarily control His own "workmanship." This is not in keeping with God's true relation to man, for on this basis man could not be a real person nor a moral agent. On the other hand, will in man, as in God, is properly used only in relation to reason and right, and for this reason a man is not free to will because he will.[1] It is easy for us to tend toward arbitrariness, but this is not liberty in a true sense, but servitude to unwholesome desires.[2] Free-will is not an absolute perfection in this unlimited sense, for even though it does include the power to choose evil, such choice is not a perfection.[3] To clarify his position further, he speaks of the two possible acts of man, viz., the internal and external acts. The external act is less an act of man because it may be coerced, while the internal act cannot.[4] He concludes that the one thing which we can really call our own is the consent of our minds,[5] but it is to be remembered that if we are free, others must be as free as ourselves.[6] We will return to this concept both in Whichcote's theory of morality [7] and his doctrine of sin.[8] It appears that Whichcote means by human freedom neither complete determinism or indeterminism, but a self-determination: that is, within certain limits man has the freedom to determine his own destiny.[9]

---

[1] I, 253.
[2] *Ibid.*, p. 185.
[3] *Ibid.*, p. 251.
[4] *Ibid.*, pp. 345–346.
[5] III, 209–210.
[6] *Aph.* 55.
[7] *Infra*, ch. V.
[8] *Infra*, ch. VI.
[9] Galloway, *Ibid.*, pp. 531–533. Ralph Cudworth has worked this problem out more carefully than Whichcote, see, *Treatise on Free-Will*, tr. Allen (London, 1838). Cf. Austin Farrer, *The Freedom of the Will* (London, 1958) pp. 253–277. See also Jonathan Edwards, *Freedom of The Will*, ed. by Paul Ramsey (New Haven, 1957), pp. 239–269. There is a remarkable difference between the Cambridge Platonists and Edwards on this important subject. Those who see an unqualified similarity between Edwards and the Cambridge Platonists should take notice. Edwards is much closer to Calvin, see J. K. S. Reid's introduction to John Calvin's *Concerning The Eternal Predestination of God* (London, 1961), pp. 9–44.

W. Montgomery Watt provides a helpful comparison between free-will in Christianity and Islam. According to Watt, the conception of free-will, in the strict sense, does not occur at all in Muslim thought. It is replaced by the slightly different conception of man's power to act and to determine the course of events. The conception of predestination does occur, but not so often as might be expected. The Muslim is much more interested in what God is doing in the present. Salvation is linked to the community and punishment also.

Thus there is no adequate explanation for the fate of individual men. A partial explanation for these differences is that generally the East has tended to over-emphasize the sovereignty

According to Whichcote the body is inferior to the soul, even at its best. When the mind raises itself to a contemplation of immaterial things, the imagination suggests the corporeal, which are the things of inferior nature. The matters of greatest ethical and spiritual importance are imperceptible to the body.[1] It follows that we should give more attention to the refinements of our minds than to the concerns of our bodies, and this should be done to the extent in which our minds transcend them. This would not be to deny their relation; we have this treasure of the mind in an "earthen vessel," the body. The vessel deserves the best of care, in view of the treasure it contains.[2] The relation of mind and body is one of interdependence and for this reason any unnatural use of either has an unwholesome effect upon the other. Nevertheless, the body is to be subordinated to the mind and all its lower passions, and appetites are to be under the constant control and direction of the mind.[3]

Even though man is of the "earth earthy," yet by virtue of the "image of God" in him, he is "heavenly." God lays his foundation in the body in all its lowliness in order to indicate the excellency of the body when it shall be glorified. Man is made of dust, the most contemptible of all things, but it is the image of God in man that enhances his value. We are body and soul and these are so inextricably bound together that we must glorify God with both at once.[4] Thus Whichcote conceives the body as the soul's dwelling place and instrument. The house is rendered suitable for the inhabitants and not the reverse, while the value of an instrument lies in its fitness to fulfil its function. The body, then, deserves the proper care that it may be appropriate as a dwelling place and instrument of the soul.[5]

Certain points are obvious as we study Whichcote's conception of the nature and relation of body and soul. He makes no real distinction between the mind and soul and uses these terms interchangeably. Further, he makes use of the Platonic, Old Testament and the New Testament views on the subject. At times he oscillates from the Platonic to the biblical views. For instance, his concept of the body as at best a hindrance to the proper freedom and development of the

---

of God, whereas the West too often lays too much stress on the will of man. See his *Free Will and Predestination in Early Islam* (London, 1948) pp. 1–2, 33–34, 45, 137 *passim*.

[1] Whichcote, III, 103–104. Cf. Baxter, *Ibid.*, p. 4.
[2] *Ibid.*, pp. 146f., 360.
[3] IV, 12f.
[4] II, 42f.
[5] *Ibid.*, p. 214.

mind is radically Platonic; his notion that man is made from dust and that his value is in the "image of God" within is most probably taken from the Old Testament; and his view that the body and soul are interdependent, that the body is in some sense the dwelling-place and instrument of the soul, together with his belief in the glorification of the body, is almost assuredly Pauline.[1] There will be ample opportunity to draw our further implications of this subject as we proceed with our treatment of Whichcote's thought.

The real emphasis of Whichcote's discussion concerning man is not concentrated upon what man is himself, but upon man in relation to God. Man is dependent upon God and the recognition of this should lead to the submission of man to God.[2] Man as a finite spirit was created with the provision of being related to and communicating with the divine Spirit,[3] and for this reason our highest faculties are capable of divine communion, "spirit with spirit can meet." [4] Since we are only "second causes," we are sufficient only in God the First Cause.[5] A self-sufficient creature is a contradiction *in subjecto*, for all things are derived from and refer to their original. It follows that there is absolute insufficiency in every second cause, and it is impotent and ineffective when the First Cause is absent or inactive. Man's dependence upon God, then, implies the necessity for a proper God-relationship, to put it in Kierkegaardian terms. Whichcote says:

To this man is made; this was the very end and design of his creation, to have a sense of God as the first cause; and to have rest in him as the centre: and to have intention of God as the last end.[6]

God deals with us as persons, as free and responsible moral agents.

God deals with every creature according to its nature. Therefore, he deals with man by means of illumination, persuasion, mental conviction and satisfaction since intellectual nature cannot be divested of intelligence and freedom without which man ceases to be man.[7]

It is reasonable as befits our God-relationship that we should obey God. This is based upon our relation to God and our capacity to

---

[1] Cf. J. A. T. Robinson, "The Body", *Studies in Biblical Theology*, Ch. I. See also Henri Bergson, *Matter and Memory* (tr. Paul and Palmer, 1911), pp. 295f., 234f.

[2] Whichcote, I, 74.

[3] *Ibid..* p. 150.

[4] *Ibid.*, p. 197f.

[5] *Ibid.*, p. 217.

[6] *Ibid.*, pp. 298f., 220.

[7] *Ibid.*, pp. 336f.

acknowledge God and serve Him.[1] The fact that God has made us capable of Himself, means that he will "fill" our capacities for receiving Him and fulfil His relation to us. We are made in His image, not only morally, but naturally and intellectually. God will not forsake this image-foundation in man but will, if we permit Him, build a super-structure upon it.[2] Since God has made man in a special relation to Himself, He will comply with it [3] and, conversely, the "activity" of man should answer the "influence" of God.[4]

> Look we upon ourselves, as subordinate and subservient: take no more, than place and proportion of second causes. God will do the work of the first Cause; but expects we should do the work of the second Cause. There is a Conjunction of the first and second Cause to the same effect, in their several Orders.[5]

Whichcote conceives our God-relationship almost in the mystical sense of our souls in communion with God. Our souls upon communing with God, discover their virtues and display their powers. God is their proper object and we know not our powers or faculties, but by their acts; and we cannot act save in the presence of the object. Thus when we give ourselves to meditation, we ennoble and enlarge our faculties.[6] Our souls are used to their maximum only in the enjoyment of God and all else is beneath the possibility and capacity of the soul. To fix our souls upon any thing less than God can only lead to great loss.[7]

> God is our proper object, our chief concern. Were it not for man's capacity for God; if our rational faculties had no employment about God, but were intended only for drudgeries of the world; it would have been better for man to have been made in a lower order. Had man had his fulfilment in things of earth; had he been made to converse with creatures – he would have been happier if he were equal to them. There is no free converse, where there is inequality. A man cannot communicate with creatures below him. They cannot understand him as their equal; but as their governor. Man would have been made less; if he were made to be concerned with beasts. But in relation to God is our nature. Our motion should be Godward, upwards. Our converse is with spirits. The mind of man is made for communication in the rational and spiritual world.... The reasonable part in men is God's mansion: it has the impression of God upon it: it has a peculiar reservation for God – to be used in his service – in acts of faith and trust, homage, and employed about God.[8]

---

1 *Ibid.*, p. 385.
2 Emil Brunner, *Natural Theology* (Londen, 1946), pp. 24, 32.
3 Whichcote, II, 93f.
4 *Aph.* 176, 224.
5 *Ibid.*, 1128; Cf. Arist. *Meta*, xii; Plato, *Phaedrus*, xxiv (D).
6 IV, 195f.
7 *Ibid.*, pp. 301f.
8 *Ibid.*, pp. 73f.

Any proper estimate of man must take into account his future life.[1] Less of man is here and more of him is in another world and that which is most our own may be least in worldly appearance. A man is infinitely more valuable than appearances seem to indicate. This is true for instance in regard to his duration or longevity of life, his possibility- and his opportunity. In many ways man is at present immature and the present life does not afford him sufficient time to realise self-fulfilment. Further, such development as is possible for man, in the present, is curtailed by hindrances of the body, by the "non-use" and "misuse" of himself, and as a result man is not as he ought to be or as he desires to be because of the tendencies and limitations of his mortality. But man is really made for immortality, his soul is divine and continues after the death of the body.[2] Accordingly, man's destiny and God-relationship are of a piece.

By understanding and knowing God, we come to a true self-enjoyment. There is no happiness apart from composure of mind, and this state can only be realised by communion with God. And it is worth remembering that man's proper relation to God is one of communion rather than union.[3] Vital happiness within us consists in a personal act whereby we enjoy God. Objective happiness presupposes God as the Object we seek and fruition and enjoyment belong only to the attainment of the end. God is the ultimate End – the Object of happiness, all else is means. Here Whichcote speaks of God paradoxically in the sense of a "Beyond within." God is in one sense already within the soul of the believer, and by his own mental activity, a man is capable of an awareness and enjoyment of God, in this sense God is "closer to us than breathing." But, on the other hand, God is in a real sense the "Reach which exceeds our grasp." [4] In conceiving man's happiness in God alone, Whichcote exclaims in a passage reminiscent of Augustine:

O God! Thou hast made us for thyself, our souls are unsatisfied and unquiet in us; there is emptiness, till thou dost communicate thyself, till we return unto thee.[5]

Souls that are properly related to God have a great deal of internal peace, quiet and satisfaction and they feel often such "influences and

---

[1] I, 273.
[2] *Ibid.*, pp. 274-298; Cf. *Infra*, Ch. VII.
[3] Cf. Emil Brunner, *Revelation and Reason* (London, 1947), p. 79.
[4] Whichcote, IV, 301.
[5] *Ibid.*, pp. 314f.; Cf. Aug., *Conf.* i, 1.

communications" from God as give delight and satisfaction which transcend the pleasure of sense.[1] Thus human happiness is to be found only in communion with God.

In this chapter we have attempted to examine Whichcote's view on natural revelation in relation to his doctrines of God and man. Whichcote gives a convenient summary of his observations on the proper relation of God and man as follows:

We are to acknowledge God, as the Original of our Being and the Father of our Spirits; to be thankful to Him, as preserving and maintaining us; to be governed by Him, He being Supreme and Sovereign; to serve Him, as our Lord and Owner; to reverence admire and adore Him, as the most Perfect Being; to believe in Him, as most Certain and Infallible; to trust in Him, and commit our Selves and our Concerns to Him as being most Faithful; to love and delight in Him, as the first and chiefest Goodness; to rest in Him, as the Centre of immortal Spirits; in all things to refer our-selves to him as being Ultimate and Final.[2]

---

[1] *Ibid.*, p. 302.
[2] *Aph.* 1173.

CHAPTER FIVE

RELIGION OF FIRST-INSCRIPTION (II)

Natural Ethics

Whichcote believed in the permanence of moral distinctions. He arrived at a similar conclusion to those in our time who believe in moral absolutism as opposed to moral relativity. To him the great rights of the world which govern all human life and experience are determined by the relation of things and therefore may not be altered at will. These rights are a law with God because they are according to His nature.[1] The germ of this idea which is to be developed by his disciples, especially in Cudworth's *Eternal and Immutable Morality* and More's *Enchiridion Ethicum*, is found in Whichcote.[2] This stable moral order places upon man a responsibility to recognise and obey its commands. To this end man has his reason to enable him to observe the moral law in its particulars and failure to do so leads to self-condemnation.[3] Truth and goodness are in things themselves and our duty consists in the obedience with which we comply with their demands.[4] Thus, for Whichcote, morals consist of things good in themselves, in their nature and quality.[5] According to him, "things themselves speak to us, and offer notions to our minds; and 'this' is the voice of God." [6] The moral

---

[1] Whichcote, *Aph.* 250.

[2] Cudworth has developed the epistemological discussion of the concept beyond our author, but he is rather brief in his application of the theory mainly because his projected work for this purpose never appeared. More, on the other hand, has done a better job in developing a more comprehensive ethical work than either Whichcote or Cudworth.

[3] The present writer is aware that citations from modern ethicists supply no satisfactory criterion by which to judge Whichcote's moral theory. Social conditions, ideals and problems today bear little resemblance to those of his period. Further, many such problems received little serious thought or study in the seventeenth century. But these facts only render the favorable comparison between Whichcote's moral theory and the thought of some of the most outstanding moralists of today more remarkable.

[3] Whichcote, I, 40.

[4] *Ibid.*, pp. 68–70.

[5] *Ibid.*, p. 122.

[6] *Aph.* 482.

order is composed of absolute perfections, always the same everywhere and for all time.[1]

There is a distinction between natural principles and moral duties, but they are interrelated. By the former is meant impressions originally stamped upon the nature of things necessary for the fulfilment of their created purpose. The most universal principle is self-preservation expressed in man by his desire for happiness. On the other hand, the means to this end may be conceived as a moral duty. Duty in a moral sense derives its necessity from the effectiveness with which it promotes the end. Happiness, then, the supreme and ultimate end to which all else must be subservient by natural necessity, is the foundation of moral duty. All men naturally seek happiness but some, for lack of understanding, substitute something else in its stead. But if all men were firmly convinced that God was their real happiness, they would necessarily love Him.[2] It is wise to remember that for our author there can be no true happiness for an individual apart from the proper relation to one's fellows and to God.[3]

We have a moral obligation to be intelligent and there is an obligation for an intelligent person to be informed as to the effect of his conduct. In order to do our duty, we must know what our duty is. Thus, an intelligent man needs to scrutinize not only the motives which prompt him to act, but also the situation in which his action will take place. It is the duty of each person to seek truth and make full use of his powers of judgment. We are to recognize the permanence of the difference between good and evil and use our faculties to the maximum in moral decisions.[4] Whichcote makes it clear that he is aware of the

---

[1] III, 92. Harold Titus has conveniently divided ethical theory into four main types, viz., Formalism (Kant); Utilitarianism (Mill); Naturalistic Ethics (Spencer); and Self-Realization (Aristotle, Dewey).

It is difficult to fit our author neatly into a category because of the eclectic nature of his ethical theory. He agrees with the Formalists that rightness is an inherent quality of the act itself, that right and wrong differ absolutely, but he does not stand diametrically opposed to the good in other types mentioned by Titus, i.e. Self-Realization. See *Ethics For Today* (New York, 1936), pp. 41–43.

[2] *Ibid.*, pp. 328–330.

[3] With Hobhouse, Whichcote does not separate social theory and individual conduct, but suggests that there is an objective standard of morality in place of individual arbitrary choice, which places demands upon the individual and society alike. See *Elements of Social Justice* (London, 1922), pp. 15–16.

Cf. John MacMurray, *The Self as Agent* (London, 1956), pp. 84–103 and his *Persons in Relation* (London, 1960), pp. 127–146.

[4] Hobhouse, *Ibid.*, p. 15. Cf. Whichcote, I, 152–153; Titus, *Ibid.*, ch. XV, pp. 232–234. According to Titus, the effort to meet moral obligation with diligence is the principle of "due care." See *Ibid.*, pp. 235–236. Cf. Whichcote, I, 157–158.

fact that some moral decisions are hard to make, because the line between good and evil, right and wrong, is at times obscure.

In many cases it is hard to fix the utmost bounds of good and evil, because these part as day and night which are separated by twilight, so that there is a dim day – light between both. Thus it is a very nice point for a man to know how far he may go and farther he may not.[1]

The sheer difficulty of making moral decisions makes the proper development of our moral faculties the more important. This fact is intensified by the fact that man is born only with faculties possessing potential power for moral decision and action. And these faculties (by which Whichcote means mind and conscience) develop through education and the acquisition of habits. Man, then, is endowed merely with moral possibilities, but these faculties, capable of moral judgments if developed, are not to be trusted unless they are "qualified and seconded." [2] One cannot help but wonder if our author is not heading for a contradiction in his assertion that human nature is naturally good. If we divide the three general attitudes towards human nature into categories, those who hold that it is essentially evil (Augustine), those who hold that it is good (Rousseau); and those who hold that it is neutral (Titus), then Whichcote's position cannot be strictly classified since he has elements of the last two views in his total view of human nature. This point seems to be of the utmost importance, affecting his theory of social morality as well as his concept of true religion, i.e. the doctrine of the Fall.

Titus' evaluation of the three usual approaches to the subject as listed above is instructive and explains, I believe, why Whichcote has asserted that man is born morally neutral with possibilities for good or evil. According to Titus, the notion that human nature is radically evil appears untenable. This position is refuted by historical and scientific evidence and has no foundation. The doctrine also attributes to God practices which would be disapproved or considered immoral if done by human beings; for men do not consider it moral to punish one person for the sins of another. There can be no immoral act apart from persons who are guilty of committing acts of misconduct. To submit to such a view would be to admit that many social evils are inevitable. There is in this same camp, those who base their conclusions on men's biological or psychological inheritance. They assume, for example, that due to some force called "instinct" inherent in human beings, a certain widespread pattern of conduct may be explained. Since men fight,

---

[1] Whichcote, I, 189; Cf. *Aph.* 507.
[2] *Ibid.*, pp. 158–159.

there must be an instinct of pugnacity and thus it is futile to speak of non-violence or the abolition of war. The view that man is naturally good, in some sense held by our author though he has his own version of the Fall, is at once true and false. That is to say, many human traits, such as generosity, sympathy, sociability, and the like, are desirable, while others such as selfishness, combativeness, and jealousy are un-desirable. Apparently, all these qualities are found in man, now one, now the other. Human nature is many-sided and plastic and any idea that it is rigid and of only one quality is a false conception.[1] This general conclusion appears to be entirely consistent with Whichcote's general view on the subject. Within this framework he urges us to develop our moral faculties and use them to discover the good and live by it.

Another important consideration in Whichcote's moral theory, is his emphasis upon the end or intention of a moral action as all important. He asserts that the intention is of first importance and the means is significant only as it contributes to the fulfilment of the end. The end exists in the mind prior to choice or action, that is, the last in action is first in intention. A decision to seek a good end rightly precedes the selection and employment of means. This is why so much care should be used in the choice, alike, of immediate and ultimate ends; for immediate ends should be warrantable and ultimate ends should be universally good. The good life is one over-ruled by a good intention and carried forward by a certain purpose.[2] There is no excuse for failure in intention; for every man knows the reason for his action. Man as a moral agent is responsible for intentional behaviour and nothing is virtuous which does not stem from a mind actually con-senting to the good.[3] It follows that the intention and quality of a moral act are inextricably united and a morally good action must spring from a good intention.

Knowledge is absolutely essential to goodness; for the heart cannot

---

[1] Titus, *Ibid.*, XII, pp. 185–187. From this discussion it appears that Whichcote is quite modern in his view and is in line with most sociologists, psychologists, educators, moralists and many biologists of today.

See also Knight Dunlap, "The Principles of Human Nature," *Religious Education*, Vol. XVIII, (1923), pp. 18–19; Julian Huxley, "The Biology of Human Nature," Y.R., Vol. XXII (Dec., 1932), p. 337. See also D. E. Roberts, *Psychotherapy and a Christian View of Man* (New York, 1950) pp. 110, 104–5.

[2] Whichcote, II, 163–165.

[3] *Aph.* 590. It appears that Whichcote does not give enough attention to the "means," its proper nature and relation to the "end." It is too often true that a good end is spoiled by an improper means. John MacMurray's discussion on human action as "intentional" is a valuable supplement to our author's partial treatment of the subject. See *Clue to History*, (London, 1938) pp. 8–18 *passim*.

attain the good without it. However, knowledge alone is not the totality of the good life though knowledge precedes virtue. Here Whichcote is asserting that moral activity is rational and all truly moral decisions are to be made under the direction of reason.[1] Our author implies that there are at least a few acts of "non-attendancy" which do not come under this general rule. These actions are merely natural and are morally indifferent or neutral. For example, when men walk together, morally speaking, it does not matter whether they walk backwards or forward, but what they do and say to each other has moral implications and is therefore subject to the direction of reason.[2] Our author's real point here is that knowledge in the mind should activate will and affections and produce obedience. We are to begin by knowledge and end in practice. Truth and that which follows upon it are materially the same and they are called by different names to indicate their varied functions. The understanding is not finally enlightened for itself but for service. It receives and discusses moral issues, but then they are to influence life and practice. First the understanding satisfies reason, then the will consents and finally the notion becomes a way of life.[3]

According to Whichcote, conscience is God's "vice-gerent," or the God within us.[4] It will render a man miserable if he is not governed by the right judgment of moral distinctions.[5] We cannot go against conscience without serious consequences to ourselves. The morally wrong is the morally "impossible" or "we should not" is morally "we cannot." [6] One cannot escape the condemnation of conscience even in secrecy. Our author warns us that "we never do anything so 'secretly' but that it is in the presence of two witnesses; God and our Conscience."[7] One wonders if this significance given to conscience in moral decision in any way conflicts with the unique and all-important role of reason for the same purpose. Further, is conscience to be trusted as an infallible moral guide, in view of the fact that our author has just asserted that we are born only with potential capacities for moral decision? Putting our author's views together, which he has not satisfactorily done himself, it appears that reason and conscience are

[1] Whichcote, I, 152–154.
[2] *Ibid.*, pp. 318. What Whichcote means by acts of "non-attendancy" is acts outside the realm of moral judgment, unmoral or amoral acts. See Titus, *Ibid.*, pp. 3–5.
[3] III, 214–216.
[4] *Aph.* 1055.
[5] *Ibid.*, 386. Cf. Paul Tillich, *Morality and Beyond* (N.Y., 1963) p. 65–81.
[6] *Ibid.*, 397.
[7] *Ibid.*, 660.

co-partners for moral decision and action, both of which are to be properly developed by education and wholesome experience. Without this safeguard, it would appear quite dangerous to rely upon an undeveloped conscience or one developed in the wrong way.[1]

When Whichcote speaks of the problem of evil he is primarily concerned with moral evil. He makes casual reference to natural evil but makes little effort to explain it. Moral evil is for him the greatest of all evils because of its malignity and consequences.[2] As we follow his discussion concerning moral evil, it will be helpful to recall some of the presuppositions of his moral theory. He has presented the notion that man is a free moral agent; that man is born only with moral possibilities; that the intention of the mind determines the goodness or badness of a moral action and as a corollary to this last notion, that the same thing in man is potential virtue or vice.[3] From all this we can see both the freedom and responsibility of man as a moral agent.

Whichcote's fundamental assertion as he approaches the problem is that God is not the author of evil. Antecedent to the existence of evil, God does what infinite wisdom directs or goodness moves to prevent it, by declaring against it, by warning and admonishing, by frustrations, and cross-providence. Subsequent to evil, He brings good out of evil according to His goodness and pleasure. Evil is to be explained primarily by the fact that man is in a probation-state and is necessarily free and for this reason evil is unavoidable. But God is the judge of evil rather than a partner to it. Some evils are natural, that is, they follow upon the condition of matter. Then, men bring some evils upon themselves by the abuse and misuse of themselves. Some evils result from the activity of malicious causes opposed to God.[4]

But Whichcote would insist that the main explanation for evil is the fact that God created "second causes" or "rational and voluntary" beings who are also "finite and fallible" and permits many things to go according to these second causes. These free moral agents are free to choose evil as well as good. Since God is not the author of evil, the greatest evil that we encounter may be our own fault or attributed to other second causes, that is, other men or fallen angels.[5] Evil results

---

[1] Cf. See my "Christian Conscience and Legal Discrimination," J. R. T. vol. XIX, no. 2 (1962–1963). Titus, *Ibid.*, pp. 18–20. Cf. A. K. Rogers, "Art and Conscience," (Jan., 1931), p. 146; J. S. MacKenzie, *Manual of Ethics*, 4th ed. (London, 1900), pp. 117–118.

[2] Whichcote, *Aph.* 514. Hastings Rashdall, *Is Conscience an Emotion?* (New York, 1914), pp. 1–51 and K. E. Kirk, *Conscience and Its Problems* (London, 1927) pp. 57, 59–70, 215–254.

[3] *Ibid.*, 1052.

[4] III, 290–292.

[5] *Ibid.*, 292–305. Cf. Nels F. S. Ferré, *Evil and The Christian Faith* (London, 1947),

from man's choice and the man who embraces evil is self-condemned by reason and conscience before he is judged by God. He has deliberately rebelled against the light of God's creation which is ample to lead him to lay hold of the good according to his nature.

It follows, also, that evil cannot be kept out of the world except by force, which God will not use against his creative design. His design in creation was to make free moral agents. However, since these beings are finite, there is also the possibility of their transgression of His commands and their abuse of their nature in view of their freedom to do so. This "peccability" of man arises from the imperfection of free-willed causes being left to themselves. Our present state is one of trial in which we must not be with-held *ab extra* from doing worse as well as better; for if we were, there would be no possibility for merit or demerit in the moral life. Whichcote has a slight tendency to try and explain some of the moral evil and perhaps some of the natural evil, which is not explainable to his satisfaction by man's apostasy, by fallen angels. However, this tendency in his writing is very faint and is not to be compared with the same tendency in a Puritan like Milton, i.e. *Paradise Lost*. Whichcote appears to be more anxious to relieve God of all responsibility for moral evil by placing all responsibility upon man and to a lesser degree upon "other second causes," i.e., fallen angels, who have abused their freedom, than to find any solution for the problem of evil.[1]

When Whichcote attempts a definition of virtue, he is not as clear

pp. 139–165 where Ferré discusses the Christian conception of God as Agape in relation to the problem of evil and J. L. Mackie, "Evil and Omnipotence," *Good and Evil*, ed. by N. Pike (Englewood Cliffs, N.J., 1964), pp. 46–60, H. J. McGlaskey, "God and Evil," *Ibid.* pp. 61–84.

[1] IV, 356. The total picture of Whichcote's view of evil cannot be clearly seen until we treat his doctrine of sin. See *Infra*, ch. VI. However, this brief discussion on the problem places Whichcote in a great succession of thinkers, philosophical and theological, who have struggled with his problem. In modern times such notables have treated the subject as Kant in his pamphlet, *Ueber das Misslingen aller philosophischen Versuche in der Theodicée* (1791), (cited by E. S. Brightman, *A Philosophy of Religion* (London, 1947), p. 147 (n. 15); Leibniz's *Essais de Theodicée* (1712), and Voltaire's *Candide* (1759) as well as more recent writers like A.M. Fairbairn, *The Philosophy of the Christian Religion* (London, 1902), Bk. I; Elton Trueblood, *Philosophy of Religion* (New York, 1957), pp. 23–255.

While the present writer is not satisfied with Brightman's "finite-infinite God" (*Ibid.*, IX, 155–170) or with his "Given" (*Ibid.*, pp. 167, 199, 202, 210, 223), it appears that he has put his finger on a fundamental criticism of those who seek to explain all moral evil by human freedom or the freedom of rational beings; i.e. men and angels. This view leaves much evil, even moral evil, unexplained. Freedom, as Brightman asserts, explains moral evil but it does not explain either the force of temptation or the debasing consequences of moral evil. See *Ibid.*, p. 147. Cf. F. H. Ross, "Personalism and the Problem of Evil," *Yale Studies in Religion*, No. 11, 1940. This is a critical appraisal of the views concerning the problem of evil of Brown, Knudson and Brightman. See also, Harting Rashdall, *Theory of God and Evil* (London, 1924), I, 287–288 and C. S. Lewis, *The Problems of Pain* (New York, 1948), p. 14–16, 21.

or as definite as we would like, but he presents a working concept of the term. He asserts that in a strict sense, it signifies any moral perfection, while philosophically and theologically speaking, it refers to the good. He speaks of the intellectual and moral virtues natural to man, and these are held by the best men outside the "pale" of the Church.[1] The several virtues are "connatural" to man, that is, they agree with the reason of his mind. But, even though virtue is good-in-itself, it is good for me only if I do it out of a good motive. We repeat our author's assertion that two things may be materially the same and yet they may differ because of the motive. A thing is virtuous only if it is done because it is good or avoided because it is evil.[2] Thus virtue originates in the mind and then issues forth into action.[3] For instance, an unselfish deed may be done out of a selfish motive, thereby diminishing its virtue. But the concept which is central to Whichcote's total moral theory is his assertion that virtue is natural to human nature, while vice is unnatural. This is intensified by the fact that virtue is rational, while vice is illogical and has no affinity with man as a rational being.[4] It follows that virtue is the basis of our peace and happiness, while vice is the foundation of misery. Vice, like all evil, has within itself the seeds of its own destruction, and misery follows upon its path as surely as the night follows the day.[5] These assumptions are at the heart of our author's moral theory and for this reason they will be met frequently in our discussion.

In his inadequate discussion of virtue, Whichcote appears to involve himself in a partial contradiction: if he believes in objective and absolute moral values, how can he make them contingent upon human motives? But when we consider that, for him, virtue is virtue according to the intention of free moral agents, then it appears consistent. By virtue he does not refer to moral perfections, which are good in themselves but the reaction of free moral agents to them, in their attainment and use. And he would want to get behind a particular moral decision or action to the proper attitude of life; for to him the moral life consists of "a good mind and a good life." One wonders if his belief in the natural goodness of man cannot be partially explained by his own sweet disposition. If he had been the victim of violent temptations like

---

[1] IV, 120–122. When Whichcote speaks of moral and intellectual virtues, he appears to be quoting directly from Aristotle. See Aristotle, *Eth.* i, 13, 20; ii, 8; vi, 12, 4.

[2] I, 246–248.

[3] *Ibid.*, p. 51.

[4] III, 148–150.

[5] IV, 195–197.

Augustine or even Pascal,[1] one wonders if his whole system of thought would not have been different. Often the psychological factor does explain the trend of a man's thought. It seems that our author clearly belongs to the "once-born" in contradistinction to the "twice-born" of William James' *Varieties of Religious Experience*. As a spiritual personality Whichcote is more like Pelagius than Augustine – closer to Erasmus than Luther.

Our author in his discussion of natural ethics is concerned almost exclusively with an explanation and application of these three terms: sobriety, justice and piety.[2] It is instructive that he goes to the Bible to find a basis for his moral theory as he has done for the ground of his theory of knowledge. Though the text fundamental to his ethics is found in the New Testament, it is obvious from his writings that he is strongly influenced by ethical monotheism expressed by the Old Testament prophets of social justice, i.e. (Micah 6:8). As he employs these three terms, sobriety is primarily personal; justice, social; and piety, religious. Nevertheless, it is wise to remember that though this classification is convenient for our discussion, it is obvious that we have here what Collingwood describes as an "over-lap" of classes,[3] that is, they are interrelated and interdependent concepts as used by our author.

Sobriety implies a moderate use of our natural appetite and the avoidance of the abuse of ourselves through excessive use of material things.[4] Sobriety refers partly to the mind and partly to the body. Mental sobriety is known as modesty or humility, while the soberness of the body is called temperance. The sober-minded man is uniform and does not involve himself in contradiction; for he has the assurance that truth will finally prevail. He is reasonable even in eating and drinking and avoids all excess. The body should be thought of as the dwelling place of the soul and for this reason all should be done in the interest of its health. Further, we should do nothing contrary to reason. Thus mental pride and bodily intemperance are to be avoided not only because they are harmful to body and mind, but also because they are unreasonable and therefore against our true nature.[5]

Our faculties are our own and yet we have no right to use them so

[1] Aug. *Conf.*, viii. 12; Pascal, *Pensées* ed. by (Stewart), "Adversaries," *Pen.* 1. Cf. *Erasmus and Luther, Discourse On Free Will*, ed. by E. F. Winter (New York, 1961), pp. ix–xi, 22–24, 134–136.

[2] Whichcote, I, 40–41; Cf. Titus 2:12.

[3] Collingwood, *Philosophical Method* (Oxford, 1933), pp. 26–28, 49–51.

[4] Whichcote, I, 41–43.

[5] II, 211–215.

as to indispose them for the ends and purposes for which they were created. In a real sense we destroy our faculties when we abuse them. Sobriety is fundamental to our nature and actually conserves our faculties. To Whichcote a person given to excess is a moral "monster" and such a person is not a valid example of a man true to his real nature. He insists that drunkenness is not a "beastly" sin, it is even worse. Beasts live according to their true nature and for this reason do nothing which is unnatural to them. Thus to speak of a man involved in sub-human acts as beastly is to "bely" or underestimate the true behaviour of beasts.[1] Excessive drinking impairs man's moral faculties and leaves him defenceless against all other evils.[2] A recent moralist has well said:

> Morality demands that we live at our best and bring our lower natures under the control of reason or our higher natures. Inasmuch as alcohol acts as a narcotic it tends to deaden the higher centres first. The higher faculties are stupefied, and the impulses and emotions are less restrained.... Duty demands that we preserve our health and strength of body and exercise diligence in respecting the rights of others.... The evidence as to the harmful effects of the excessive use of alcohol appears conclusive.[3]

Throughout our author's discussion on sobriety one recalls the "golden mean" of Aristotle,[4] but one wonders if this concept, whether presented by Aristotle or by Whichcote is adequate as a comprehensive standard of moral judgment. Especially since Whichcote is so insistent upon things good-in-themselves, intrinsic goods; how can he base his view of personal conduct so completely upon the principle of the "happy medium"? For if we follow his moral theory consistently from his presuppositions to his conclusions surely there must be, morally speaking, decisions based not merely upon finding the "mean" between "excess" and "defect," but a choice between intrinsic good and intrinsic evil, where the difference is not merely one of "degree" but of "kind." [5] And while his theory may be tenable in selecting values, relative or instrumental, it appears woefully inadequate as a standard of judgment when one is making decisions in the area of what he considers to be eternal and immutable. Further, our author has failed to give us guidance when faced with a choice between two evils.

The step from sobriety to social justice is direct, for, according to

---

[1] IV, 422–423.
[2] II, 218.
[3] Titus, *Ibid.*, p. 228.
[4] Aristotle, *Eth.* ii, 2, 6–7.
[5] Collingwood, *Ibid.*, pp. 54–56.

Whichcote, unless a man governs himself by sobriety, he is incapable of social justice or true piety.[1] Thus the relation in which we stand to one another is properly one of just and equal dealings.[2] Let us note that Whichcote wishes to distinguish between justice and equality. What is allowed by law or reason is just, while equity appears only when all circumstances are duly examined. It is in this way that equity moderates the rigour of the law. Thus, we can find justice without equity though sometimes we find both together. However, when there is a conflict between the two, equity should prevail. Equity should have first place not only because it is reasonable, but also because it suspends judgment until all the facts are in and then acts accordingly.[3]

> There is that which may be called just...; of which if a man will abate nothing; the law will allow it, nor none call him an unrighteous person if he will have it. And there is that which is equal and fit and good to be done, and which becomes a good man to do.... The righteous man is a man of strict right, he will do no wrong, but he hath hardly that largeness of spirit to do good, he will do nothing but what the law will admit, that which another man can neither hinder nor call him in question for doing it: but the other, the "good" man, he will do that which is equal and fit; he will abate of strict right, he is willing to do courtesies, to perform all mutual offices....[4]

This distinction made by Whichcote is, I believe, quite significant. The attempt to place equity above strict justice as he uses the two terms, is consistent with his view that man is fallible, that morality is rational and that punishment should be remedial. The assertion that all relevant facts should be weighed as the basis of judging the behaviour of others is becoming increasingly widespread in modern times. This principle is being employed by lawyers, psychologists, social workers and churches engaged in constructive social action; it is being used in passing judgment upon the misdeeds of juvenile offenders and mentally incompetent persons as well as in deciding the form of correction to be used in such cases. The term "equity," as used by our author, most adequately describes the principle.

Right is determined by the relation of things, by voluntary determination or constitution as viewed by a proprietor or law-giver. That is to say, a man may dispose of his property as he wills and one with power to make laws may determine their operation. But lest we should accuse him of absolute wilfulness, Whichcote hastens to add that even here

---

[1] Whichcote, *Aph.* 764.
[2] I, 384; Cf. Mich. 6:8.
[3] II, 64–67.
[4] IV, 5–6; Cf. More, *Enchiridion Ethicum* tr. by E. Southwell (New York, 1930), p. 128–29.

reason must prevail. By "the reason of things" he means these rights which are eternally fixed, which are a law with God, consistent with His nature and as unalterable as He is.[1] When right is determined by positive constitution, the right of property or authority is implied and by such a right a man may do with his own as he wills. But a right which begins thus may have great moral implications as it affects others. Thus by the right of authority one has the power to make laws and enforce them. However, the man who disobeys these laws is in the wrong only if they are in keeping with universal reason, rather than the fiat of a particular will.[2] To obey law irrationally is not only to go against one's own rational nature and this is why it is so difficult, and indeed unjust, for man to obey laws contrary to or even without reason. Thus a non-moral right, such as right of property or authority, when applied to others becomes moral and must at once come under the judgment of reason. Here we see clearly Whichcote's reaction to the concept of Absolute Will, alike in Calvinistic and Hobbesian thought, and how his concept of reason emerges as supreme.[3]

This leads us to re-examine Whichcote's view of personal freedom and its relation to social responsibility. He asserts that where a situation involves a man's own right, a man is free to act without regard for his fellows or God. Behind this assertion is the conviction that a man's true rights are in accord with reason and with God. The freedom we have is to do good, promote friendship, love and good-will, but there is no freedom of self-will which forfeits others of their rights.[4] Thus will alone must never be insisted upon for the justification of right and especially when it is unsupported by reason.[5] Is Whichcote really consistent here with his assertion that men are free to do good or evil? This problem is obvious unless we think of him as using the concept in a different context and therefore with a different meaning. Freedom here seems to mean "moral freedom" in a strict sense as distinguished from "immoral freedom" on the one hand, and from "non-moral" freedom

---

[1] *Ibid.*, pp. 6–11.
[2] *Ibid.*, pp. 13–14.
[3] By this I mean that Whichcote is opposing by his concept of reason in his moral theory, on the one hand, the notion of Hobbes concerning the state as absolute, as being controlled by the absolute will of the ruler whose power is by "social contract," and on the other the Puritan version of the absolute will of God as they understood it from the writings of Calvin. Cf. I, 258–259; IV, 214–215, 257. See also, S. I. Mintz, *The Hunting of Leviathan* (Cambridge, Eng., 1962), pp. 80–109; J. D. Eusden, *Puritans, Lawyers, and Politics in Early Seventeenth Century England* (New Haven: Yale U. Press, 1958), pp. 25–32.
[4] II, 162.
[5] *Ibid.*, p. 402.

on the other.[1] We do have freedom to go against reason, but this can only lead to self-condemnation and self-destruction, for this is to go against our own nature. Then we have freedom to act arbitrarily concerning non-moral acts. But to speak of moral freedom implies that we are restricted within the bounds of reason. This is one point where, I believe, Cudworth learned from Whichcote, but as we shall see later in this study, Cudworth contributes much to a clearer understanding of the concept.[2]

The love for justice and equality frees a man from severity of punishment; for he remembers that it is remedial rather than punitive. To be governed by these principles removes all arbitrariness or self-will in the act of punishment.[3] We are under a moral obligation to forgive those who repent of wrong actions. Further, there should be plain and open dealing with the offender,[4] but all have the right to just and equal treatment and this for our author means the practice of the Golden Rule.[5] We should use moderation in censure or punishment; for when a man is punished he condemns himself to a certain extent because having done wrong he has dissatisfied his internal judge, his conscience. If he is punished *ultra meritum*, beyond desert, he is vexed; for he concludes that he is not suffering as a malefactor, but rather as a martyr being overcome by power. Outstanding here is Whichcote's firm belief in the moral competence of the conscience and in the natural sympathy of man toward goodness.

Much extreme punishment may be explained by the fact that persons are too easily provoked in their dealings with others. It is for this reason that a man should be slow to take offence and should always apply the best possible meaning to the speech or action of another. As a matter of fact, one whould hesitate to be exposed to provocation for upon becoming provoked, one is no longer free and rational. If however, in spite of all, one does become provoked, one should even in this emotional state seek to be moderate and as reasonable as possible. To assure the triumph of justice and equality in such cases, one should invite a third person, morally trustworthy, who is also a disinterested party, to serve as judge. Another suggestion is that one should actually, as far as is possible, put oneself in the other's place. However, a proper third person is the best judge and even more praiseworthy still is the

1 Titus, *Ibid.*, pp. 3–5.
2 *Infra*, ch. IX.
3 Whichcote, II; 69–70.
4 *Ibid.*, p. 72.
5 *Ibid.*, p. 229.

possibility of ignoring rather than resenting an evil intention and thereby nullifying it. This latter method is most effective for it makes enemies friends and the person with evil intentions condemns himself.[1] Though the general spirit of the ideal here set forth by our author is consistent with his natural morality, the possibility of its realisation seems to be beyond our natural powers. This fact illustrates the essential unity of Whichcote's thought; for it is the same man who speaks as a moralist and as a Christian preacher.

According to our author there should be no oppression anywhere. Where anyone happens to have advantage or power, these should not be used for cruelty or oppression. All men are created in the image of God and therefore have an inherent right to dignified treatment.[2] Further, power in itself is not good, and must always be used in relation to goodness. Having stated his principle for social justice he proceeds to apply it, first to domestic relations and then to political relations. By the former he means parent-child, husband-wife and servant-master relations and by the later he refers to the magistrate and the type of government he fosters.

Just as God is original to man, even so the parent is original to the child and yet this does not entitle parents to mistreat their children. Children are to be dealt with with reasonableness and tenderness. On the other hand, the child must obey and honor his parents.[3] The relation of husband to wife is similarly treated. Though the husband is the head of the family, he must not be unfair or unreasonable in his treatment of his wife and must always consider her as his equal with a different but equally important function in the life of the family as his own. On the other hand, the wife is to be kind and gentle with her husband and by her devotion to her husband and children fulfil her responsibility in this relationship.[4] It needs to be said that though Whichcote has introduced a valuable subject in the proper spirit, he has not done justice to his treatment of it. It seems to me that Brunner has made a summary of the family relation which might add clarity to what has been said.

All members [of the family] belong to each other – the father to the child, the child to the father, the mother to the child, the child to the mother, just as the husband belongs to the wife and the wife to the husband. But the manner of belonging is not the same. The child belongs to the father otherwise than to the

[1] *Ibid.*, pp. 224–28.
[2] III, 382.
[3] I, 283–284.
[4] *Ibid.*, pp. 254–255.

mother. This "otherness" is determined by the divinely created order of nature. It establishes an unequivocal hierarchy of the family which, without prejudices to the equal human dignity of each member, is determined by the functions of the individual members.[1]

Whichcote gives us no guidance for the problem child or divorce. Perhaps it was because his wife was ideal according to his conception and he had no children, that these problems were of no great concern to him. It is to be remembered also that he spent the most active part of his life in the University environment which at times may be an artificial climate apart from the real struggle of human life.

Next Whichcote considers the master-servant relation. Without labouring the point, our author simply applies the same principles of dignified treatment, reasonableness and fair dealing to this relationship as to the family relation. He points up the mutual dependence of master upon servant and servant upon master and that each should render to the other his due. The master should treat with respect his servant and the servant should reverence and obey his master.[2] Sometimes he uses the more general reference of the relation of "superiors" to "inferiors," [3] but his conclusions are the same. He extends his concern to all creatures, even those below man.[4] Thus, he appears to anticipate Schweitzer's principle of "reverence for all life." [5] From the general position of our author we may rightly conclude that he accepts the existing stratification of society. In other words he would in his day accept the master-servant relation as Paul in his accepted the master-slave relation. However, in both cases the social-form is retained, but the social-content is challenged. Philemon may reclaim his slave as a slave according to Paul, but he must treat him as a "brother in Christ." [6] In like manner Whichcote, who himself was rich all his life, considers it in keeping with the "reason of things" to keep his servants, expect obedience from them, expect them to do all the menial work for him, but at the same time, recognise their human dignity and their right to humane treatment. This seems to me to state Whichcote's real position.

---

[1] Brunner, *Justice and the Social Order* tr. by Hottinger (London, 1945), p. 131.
[2] Whichcote, *Ibid.*
[3] II, 220–222.
[4] I, 255–256.
[5] A. Schweitzer, *The Decay and Restoration of Civilization*, (London, 1923), pp. xiii–ix. Cf. Kenneth Saunders, *The Ideals of East and West* (Cambridge, Eng., 1934), p. 129. Cf. Howard Thurman, as a Negro, has rejected the Pauline ethic in favor of the ethical teachings of Jesus who from birth to death identified himself with men "with their backs against the wall," see, *Jesus and the Disinherited* (New York, 1949).
[6] Philemon.

Is this position really consistent with his moral theory? Is it really Christian? Brunner going back to Aristotle's distinction between contractual and proportional justice,[1] makes a good case on purely natural grounds for what Brunner calls equitable treatment or equal-unequal treatment. When we take into account that all men are equal merely because they are human, but according to endowment and circumstances they are in fact unequal, then we can see the reasonableness of this position.[2] When Whichcote observes in Aristotle that equity is the truest justice and that there is no justice without equity,[3] we realise how close he is to Brunner and to Hobhouse [4] on this principle. The two questions we have raised above apply in a combined sense to Whichcote for being a Christian preacher he has read his Christian concepts even into his natural ethics. It is presupposed behind all that our author has said that he is convinced that the real basis of human equality is not philosophical but in the creation-act of God who created all men in the same image, in His image and Who reveals Himself in Christ as the Redeemer of all men and all peoples.[5] When this biblical concept of justice is taken seriously, it does not merely accommodate itself to an existing order of society, or merely seek to purge its contents, but cuts away at the very roots of inequality and injustice in the structure of society itself. Inequality based upon class, race, religion and the like are inconsistent with any system of ethics which takes seriously the message of the Bible, and this Whichcote claims to do. Aristotle [6] and Plato [7] may sincerely have accepted inequality and the Stoics [8] by virtue of their concept of an impersonal spiritual principle, a *nous* or *logos* pervading all things may take equality for granted, but the Christian may not take either for granted. While it is easy for a man of Whichcote's stamp to accept his exalted status as the will of God, it is not easy nor desirable for the disinherited masses to do so. It may be true that differences between men is the condition of community of natural created beings, but whenever sinful man makes himself the judge of these differences, there is always inhumanity and injustice. This seems to be because the principle employed is not usually mutual helpfulness but a superiority-inferiority relation with

---

[1] Aristotle, *Eth.* V. 7.
[2] Brunner, *Ibid.*, p. 30.
[3] Whichcote, IV, 18.
[4] Hobhouse, *Ibid.*, pp. 94–96.
[5] Brunner, *Ibid.*, p. 37.
[6] Aristotle, *Politics*, i, 4.
[7] Plato, *Rep.* V, 469; *Laws*, vi, 776–777.
[8] Brunner, *Ibid.*, p. 41. Cf. Paul Tillich, *Love, Power, and Justice* (London, 1954), pp. 78–86.

those who judge at the top of the scale of privilege and power. And though Whichcote has denounced oppression he has accommodated himself to the very type of social structure which perpetuates it. Brunner has well said:

Man does not derive his "dignity" from his service to the whole. His dignity as a person is anterior to fellowship because every individual is called by God Himself and is personally responsible to Him. The corporate community does not stand above the individual, making him a dependent, subordinate part of a higher whole, but fellowship is only truly personal when it is a community of independent, responsible persons.[1]

To Whichcote, the governor is a minister of God for the public good, and the governed are to obey his commands.[2] The purpose of government is to maintain peace, preserve the rights of its citizens and to promote good-will among men. It is the function of the governor to see that the political order fulfils its purpose.[3] Government has a good foundation, for it belongs to the orders of creation. He agrees with Paul that the "powers that be are ordained of God." [4] There must be mutual responsibility and respect between the magistrate and his citizenry in order to maintain order. It is dishonourable for any magistrate to allow disorder to prevail in his realm, and in each province government should be consistent with God's government of the entire world. The whole world is God's family and He is the Governor of the world. God's providence is thus to be the pattern of political order and the magistrate rules not by his personal will but by authority invested in him by God. The ruler, as well as the ruled, is accountable to God. The governor is responsible, therefore, to maintain justice in his realm between the citizens. Within his realm there should be no disorderly conduct allowed, no oppression of one class by another, no strife between rich and poor. All should in fact accept their condition as it is and deal peaceably and fairly with each other. Man is naturally kind and this is the principle by which government should be directed.[5] It is because all, including the governor, are made in the same image, the image of God, that cruelty and oppression are not to be permitted. This assertion is strengthened by the fact that the governor receives his authority from God and rules under providential guidance. It is obvious that Which-

---

[1] *Ibid.*, p. 45.
[2] Whichcote, II, 219–220.
[3] IV, 207–208.
[4] Rom. 13:1.
[5] IV, 371–373.

cote has struck a powerful blow at the Hobbesian political theory.[1]
The weakness of our author's theory seems to be in his optimistic view
of human nature together with his static view of society. In our time
with social mobility greater than ever before and with peoples who have
been content with their inferior lot awakening from centuries of indifference to demand the rights belonging to them as human beings,
the more conservative view of our author appears out-dated. Then there
is the more serious question, as to whether the class system itself is not
immoral and unchristian. Do the poor not have a right to better living
conditions and equality of opportunity? Should not be a general
levelling of society? Is it the will of God that a political order based
upon unfair inequalities should remain undisturbed? How is the
governor to keep order in his realm when men become aware of the
image of God within and the rights appertaining thereto and demand
their portion of these rights? Notwithstanding the good implicit in
Whichcote's political theory, in my view, it will not stand the practical
test in our time, nor the Christian test at any time.

Whichcote believes that man is naturally benevolent. He attests to
this by his life as well as by his thought. We described him in our first
chapter as a man of good nature and his contemporaries acknowledged
him as a man with an unusually pleasant disposition. This should give
added authority to the admonition to mutual helpfulness among men
so often repeated in his writings.[2] He never tires of reminding us that
man is by nature "a mild, gentle, calm and loving creature." [3] As a
result of his benevolent attitude, he exalts the benefactor as a representative of God.[4]

Nothing is deeper in human nature than righteousness, fairness, benevolence,
and this ingenuity of carriage... Universal benevolence, which God... did sow
in the nature of man when he made man.... That universal benevolence which
spirits the intellectual world, doth require each man towards another, faith
and truth.[5]

He asserts that this spirit of benevolence is the true genius of humanity. In spite of what some have said (most probably alluding to Hobbes)
there is a bias in man toward mutual helpfulness, there is a "secret
sympathy" in man for virtue and honesty. The mere fact that we are

[1] Hobbes, *Leviathan* (London, 1914), pt. II, ch. XVIII, pp. 90–92.
[2] Whichcote, II, 178–179.
[3] IV, 375–376.
[4] II, 220–221.
[5] IV, 43–44.

naturally members of one big family proceeding from the same source means that a foundation is laid in our natures for mutual good-will.[1] Now Whichcote's optimism concerning human nature indicates at least a partial truth. But living the good life and helping his fellows appears so easy for him that he cannot see the problems of the mass of people who find both quite difficult. For instance, as we ponder his stress upon intention as determining the moral quality of an act. The question arises as to whether many benefactors do not act unselfishly out of selfish intentions and thereby make the act morally void. Even if we take the universal fact of man's mutual helpfulness in times of sudden and great disaster, i.e., war, famine and the like, there is doubt even then if all intentions are morally pure. To be truthful, we would need to assume the possibility of unconscious selfishness; for it is impossible to judge adequately a single act apart from a man's total attitude toward life. And even more serious is the fact that "for all the centuries of experience, men have not yet learned how to live together without compounding their vices and covering each other with mud and blood."[2] Somehow we must not only take into account man's humanity to man, as Whichcote does, but also man's inhumanity to man.

Man is a social being and his needs demand a social order. For years after birth man is dependent upon the love and care of others. Man's necessities are greater than those of other creatures and these cannot be supplied without the assistance of others. Thus proper social relations are essential to personal well-being. Man can master the lower animals, but without the contribution of others in the same image, his fellows, he is of all beings the most miserable. Society, then, is a necessary supplement and security for man, for men are mutually dependent throughout life. It follows, that by good human relations, the status of all men is improved. This means that a personal contribution to social betterment is a moral and religious duty.[3]

Conversation is a peculiar excellency and privilege of rational nature. The only way to make a man's notions his own is to communicate them. Such exchange of ideas among men leads to self-improvement.[4] The real purpose of speech is the communication of truth. A man does not need speech for himself or to speak to God. God may be worshipped

[1] Ibid., pp. 212–218; Cf. Hobbes, Ibid., pt. I, ch. XIII, pp. 63–65. Cf. Henry Hazlitt, The Foundations of Morality (Princeton, 1964), pp. 90–91.
[2] Reinhold Niebuhr, Moral and Immoral Society (London, 1933), p. 1.
[3] Whichcote, IV, 75.
[4] Ibid., pp. 390–392.

by mental devotion unless worship is observed publicly. Thus speech is essentially a social instrument.[1]

> Man is a conversable creature; forasmuch as he is invested with intellectual nature, and is qualified with principles of reason, and with a power of speech; for all these he is enabled and disposed for converse: the principles of reason work inwardly, conceive the notions of things, and prepare matter. By the power of speech man is able to deliver his thoughts, direct, communicate, resolve, satisfy, instruct and make others partakers of his knowledge.[2]

There is no question in Whichcote's mind but that we should always communicate the truth. Without truthfulness among men there can be no trust nor integrity. One's word is a sacred trust and one has no greater assurance to give than one's word. One's word is the basis of all security between oneself and one's neighbour and upon this mutual trust society depends.[3] However, Whichcote seems to contradict what he has put so well, at least to a certain extent, by his rigid "class consciousness." He makes a distinction between conversation with equals and inferiors.[4] Though he insists that the latter should be heard in a spirit of kindness and answered accordingly, one gets the feeling that here as elsewhere, Whichcote has accommodated himself to the view that inequalities among men are almost a part of providential design. Thus, in spite of what seems to me to be his advanced view of society, I fail to comprehend what He can possibly mean by "social betterment" for the disinherited.

When Whichcote comes to emphasize the relation of morality to religion, he takes some of the wind out of the sails of our criticisms. He asserts that even our social relations are a part of our imitation of God.[5] Everyone is born with the right to be fairly treated, has the right to expect it, and even demand it. The right to fair treatment is absolute and is far above the duty felt by the rich to provide charity for the necessitous. This is within man's power to give and he who bears goodwill imitates God Who is love and Who bears good-will to all. A man does not love God who does not love his brothers. This is an argument of the denial of the less to the denial of the greater. Every virtuous action depends upon one attitude of life, for all moral virtues are united and the exercise of one virtue requires the "temper" which is productive

---

[1] *Ibid.*, pp. 358–360.
[2] *Ibid.*, pp. 376–377.
[3] II, 211–213; *Aph. 296.*
[4] *Ibid.*, p. 220.
[5] I, 32–33.

of all the rest. Accordingly the man who fails in easy duties, i.e. general good-will, will certainly not perform the more costly duties, i.e. payment of debts.[1] But is it not true that many people find it far easier to pay their debts than to love their neighbours? The testimony of history is in fact that it frequently is and this is not to consider the even more difficult problem of loving one's enemies. However, Whichcote's principles themselves appear remarkably sound. This is especially apparent when he insists that we should "universalise" ourselves, should use wisely our time and opportunity to glorify God in the world by helping others and that concern for the needs of others should be considered above our personal well-being.[2] He puts our human relations firmly within a religious context when he writes:

> He that wrongs any creature, sins against God, the Creator: because God is the Owner of the Creature, the Maintainer of Right, the Avenger of Iniquity, the Ruler of Obedience, in His Nature, or by His Will.[3]

True religion is consistent with the reason of mankind [4] and it includes moral principles also, for God illuminates our understandings for moral decision and action.[5] Those who are handicapped by material things need "divine affection" to quicken them and then they would be ready to imitate God. This is actually what the divine light does, it clears the mind and changes the affections. Knowledge is the first step to virtue, but then goodness follows by "delight and choice." [6] Whichcote is, therefore, quite anxious to give reason and moral principles their rightful place in natural religion.

We are tempted to be proud of our wisdom beyond bodily strength because it is within and because of its permanence. According to Whichcote, there are three types of wisdom: first, skills and professional knowledge; "carnal policy," by which he means a selfish cleverness; and third, divine knowledge, which is true wisdom because it brings us to God. The first type of wisdom is good as far as it goes, the second completely degenerate, and the third completely good.[7]

So important is Whichcote's concept of "vocation" as a part of the

---

[1] IV, 386–390.
[2] IV, 325–326. Here the notion of "universalizing" one's moral perspective reminds us of a similar concept to be developed by Kant. Cf. *The Metaphysics of Ethics*, tr. by T. K. Abbott (London, 1916), pp. 97–99.
[3] *Aph.* 1053.
[4] I, 174–176.
[5] II, 20.
[6] III, 103.
[7] IV, 274–282.

divine purpose of one's life that it deserves separate treatment. He asserts that the more one prepares oneself for a particular skill or profession the more one fulfils God's purpose for one's life and the more useful one becomes toward helping others. It is the duty of parents to educate their children and he considers this high purpose of education the justification for institutions of learning. It is his firm conviction that stemming from the providential design of the world and from the very nature of community among men, is the necessity for everyone to be prepared to make a constructive contribution to the whole. But he warns us that our vocation must not be the occasion of pride, for it is not a means to ultimate happiness. A man must not stake his eternal well-being upon "earthly wisdom" however useful it may be in this life. This is obvious for these reasons: it is inadequate for the unlimited possibilities of man: it is temporal only and man is born for eternity though he passes through time first.[1]

Now we look at the use of our skilled or professional knowledge. It is virtuous for a man to employ his faculties to help others. The more one is skilled or talented, the more one should help his fellows.[2] A man should do his work whole-heartedly; for one man's skill should be another man's security. The man without has a right to expect education from the educated man. That Whichcote believed this is evident from his own life, in that he paid for the education of several children at Milton and in his support of Smith.[3] Further he seems to anticipate the need for specialisation, when he asserts that it is not competent for one man to know all. Division of labour, by which he means various trades and professions apparently carried on by experts, is for the good of mankind. Modern interdependence seems to be visualised by him as he asserts that we must depend upon the skill and fidelity of others.[4]

These several distinct excellencies, and perfections, are the ornaments and endowments of human nature.... They are so many rays and beams of the infiniteness of the divine knowledge and wisdom; the flourishes of God's liberal and bountiful creation. These also recommend us to one another as needing each other in several ways, and to different purposes.... By a joint contribution of our several divided perfections, we make one body complete. Whereas an absoluteness and self-sufficiency is not found in any particular.[5]

[1] *Ibid.*, pp. 283–287.
[2] *Ibid.*, pp. 122–124.
[3] *Supra*, Ch. I. Cf. Whichcote, III, 318–319; *Aph.* 1194.
[4] IV, 386–387.
[5] *Ibid.*, 127. Though the doctrine of "vocation" was restored by Calvin and Luther, it appears that our author does not only look back to the Reformers, but forward to the future

When Whichcote turns to a direct consideration of divine knowledge he reminds us that such knowledge is only perceivable by those who have a "deiform" soul, a soul reconciled to God and at the same time holy and pure. To convey his thoughts on this subject he turns to Platonic metaphysics. He asserts that the mind must be prepared for the knowledge of God by abstraction from matter and separation from impurity. By the former requirement, he means that we must be aware of the mind's superiority over the body and their essential distinction. And by the latter requirement he agrees with the Platonists that it is impossible for the pure and impure to unite, that the disposition of the receiver determines the nature of the thing to be received. It follows that only the man with a good life and pure mind can discern divine truth.[1] John Smith clearly states the same views as he says:

> Divine things are to be understood rather by a spiritual sensation than a verbal description, or mere speculation. Sin and wickedness are prejudicial to true knowledge. Purity of heart and life, and an ingenuous freedom of judgment are the best grounds and preparations for the entertainment of truth.[2]

He adds:

> The reason why ... truth prevails no more in the world is we so often disjoin truth and true goodness, which in themselves, can never be disunited; they grow both from the same root, and live in one another.[3]

Whichcote firmly insists that since God is the Highest Good, to do a thing because it is good is to do it out of love for God, while to avoid it because it is evil is the same as not doing it because evil offends God.[4] Thus religion is divine participation, or the imitation of Him Whom we worship.[5]

> Religion doth possess and affect the "whole" man: in the Understanding, it is Knowledge; in the Life, it is Obedience; in the Affections, it is Delight in God; in our Carriage and Behaviour, it is Modesty, Calmness, Gentleness, Candour, Ingenuity; in our Dealings, it is Uprightness, Integrity, Correspondence with the Rule of Righteousness: Religion makes men "Virtuous," in all Instances.[6]

At certain points in Whichcote's natural theology he reaches the heights of the mystic. He asserts that when the mind is employed in

to the "ministry of the laity." Cf. W. R. Forrester, *Christian Vocation* (London, 1951), pp. 146–148. See also Calvin, *Institutes*, T. Norton, ed. (London, 1611), bk. III, ch. X, sec. 6.
[1] *Ibid.*, pp. 314–323; Cf. Matt. 5:8.
[2] John Smith, *Select Discourses* ed. H. G. Williams, 4th ed. (Cambridge, Eng., 1859), p. 1.
[3] *Ibid.*, p. 4.
[4] Whichcote, I, 248.
[5] *Ibid.*, p. 311.
[6] *Aph.* 956.

meditation and extracting spiritual notions from material things, it is properly employed. There is more satisfaction in meditation, devotional reading and prayer, than in all possible bodily pleasures. There is sufficient divine light in the world to be seen by the mind prepared for its reception. Nothing in human experience is more knowable than God and it is our own fault if we are estranged from Him.[1] A truly religious man is "an instrument in tune."[2] When our minds are transformed by religion, we feel, at times, strong and vigorous inclinations toward God. It is in this way that our minds are best satisfied since this is most suitable to our nature and the highest use our faculties are capable of; for it is in contemplation of God that we find our highest fulfilment and happiness.[3]

Our author sums up what he means by natural religion in reference to personal and social morality as follows:

... The *majora jura, pietatis, justitiae, sobrietatis*, the greater rights of piety to God, reverence, regard, duty, observance of him; fairness, justice, equal dealing with men; sobriety, chastity, temperance, the government of the body, so to be subservient to the temper of the mind; and the mind living in love, dwelling in peace, well-composed, fitted for mental and spiritual acts; these are such bright lights as the eye of reason cannot but see them. No man can make an excuse for being immoral, in any kind whatsoever. For these are of universal acknowledgement, in all times, in all places; there is nothing in religion and conscience where these things do not take place. The principles of reason, and the further light of revelation agree in these things.[4]

He properly concludes:

... The sum of all religion ... lies in this, to imitate him whom we worship, and endeavour after those excellencies and perfections, which we attribute to God. The state of religion consists in a God-like frame and temper of mind and expresses itself in life and actions conformed to the divine will.[5]

In our examination of Whichcote's view of morality, his personal and social application of this and of rational principles, we have penetrated to the heart of his entire scheme of thought. At many points we have found what appeared to us to be weaknesses, but what has impressed us most has been the remarkable spirit and insight of the man which have so often transcended his ability to communicate the

---

[1] III, 98–100. Cf. *Theologia Germanica*, ed. by T. S. Kepler (Cleveland, 1952), pp. 118–120.

[2] *Ibid.*, p. 146.

[3] IV, 191–192. Cf. Aug., *Conf.* i. 1.

[4] *Ibid.*, p. 437.

[5] *Ibid.*, p. 300. Cf. R. N. Flew, *The Idea of Perfection in Christian Theology* (London, 1934) pp. 275–312. This historical and theological study (according to the pages indicated) gives the context in which Whichcote developed his ethical thought.

real depth of his thought to us with all of its profundity. We are to remember, further, that Whichcote's thought is essentially a unity and the division we have made has only been necessary for our study. For this reason, therefore, we must look to the following three chapters for an enlargement and necessary supplement of much that has been introduced and it will only be after we have surveyed the whole sweep of his thought that we may justly and adequately estimate the merit or demerit of his thought.

CHAPTER SIX

RELIGION OF AFTER-REVELATION (I)

Saving Knowledge

Any discussion of Whichcote's thought begins logically with a consideration of his concept of the relation of natural to revealed theology. There seem to be at least two good reasons for this: first, as De Pauley says ,"Great thoughts were great things to him and he expresses them with directness as they come to him" [1] – thus the unsystematic nature of his discourse; and, second, there is such an interdependence of natural and revealed truth in his thought that the only justification for their separate discussion is that it leads to clarity and convenience of treatment. Revealed truth is super-imposed on natural truth and what we have is "more of the same thing." Thus we seem to have in Whichcote what John Baillie describes as the "traditional" concept of revelation. [2]

However, the "traditional" concept of revelation is only a half-truth when applied to Whichcote's view. Even when our author speaks of reason he does not refer to the unaided intellect, but, rather, reason divinely illuminated. In Whichcote we are closer to the *credo ut intelligam* of Augustine than the neat division of *theologia naturalis* and *theologia revelata* characteristic of Scholasticism. [3] Like Brunner, Whichcote cautions us against "the irrational arrogance of those who pride themselves on their intellect, and of the irrational self-sufficiency of reason." [4] And for Whichcote as for Brunner there is no question of revelation "or" reason, but of revelation "and" reason. [5] For Whichcote "the reason of man is the candle of the Lord, lighted by God and

---

[1] W. C. De Pauley, *The Candle of the Lord*, (London, 1937), p. 37.
[2] John Baillie, *The Idea of Revelation in Recent Thought*, (London, 1956), p. 18. Cf. Richard Baxter, *The Reasons of Christian Religion*, (London, 1667), p. 241. Baxter says: "... Grace is medicinal to nature.... Where natural light endeth, supernatural beginneth, and that superstructure which Christ hath built upon nature, is wonderfully adapted to its foundation".
[3] Cf. E. Gilson, *Reason and Revelation in the Middle Ages*, (New York, 1938), Chs. I, II.
[4] *Revelation and Reason*, tr. by Olive Wyon (Philadelphia, 1946), pp. 16–17.
[5] P. K. Jewett, *Emil Brunner's Concept of Revelation*, (London, 1954), p. 85.

lighting unto God." It follows that reason is in a real sense subsumed under the more comprehensive conception of revelation – it includes all that he calls truths of natural-inscription. It is likewise true that truths of after-revelation satisfy reason, they are at times *supra*-rational but never *infra-* or irrational. Any so-called truth that is contrary to reason cannot be revealed. C. C. J. Webb states this general position thus:

... "Reason" is the only possible judge of "Revelation" ... The judgment of the original credentials [of Revelation] ... at least cannot possibly be withdrawn from the tribunal of Reason; I must have some "reason" ... for accepting the Revelation as genuine. And so Reason cannot possibly be confined to a sphere distinct from that of Revelation.[1]

Yet of all the merit we may discern in Whichcote's attempt to harmonise faith and reason we cannot completely absolve him of Webb's observations and criticisms of the rational theologians of the seventeenth and eighteenth centuries who defended the necessity of revelation and likewise the impossibility of revealed truths having been found out by natural reason (fallen reason), but who conceived revealed religion mainly as a superstructure resting on foundations consisting of the truths which were apprehended by natural religion. According to Webb,

They must therefore have thought of the articles of Natural Religion in a sense in which the "revealed" doctrines were not; since what they called "the truths of natural religion" could be held and had been held without the "revealed" doctrines, while the latter could not be held without the former.[2]

When we turn to direct consideration of what Whichcote has to say concerning truth of "after-revelation," we find that he conceives this truth as coming with the same evidence and assurance as natural truth.[3] Divine truth, both natural and revealed, satisfies the mind. Revealed truth is "super-added" to natural truth and this revealed knowledge not only confirms the natural but restores reason to its original brilliance. Further, revealed truth does its own proper work; it teaches man to return to God.[4] All divine truth is distinguishable

1 *Problems in the Relations of God and Man*, (London, 1912), p. 25. Cf. *Supra*, chs., III, IV.
2 *Ibid.*, p. 52. This appears to be Whichcote's approach, but his more comprehensive view of revelation includes natural truth. We are reminded of John Baillie's observation that recently the concept of nature is swallowed up by revelation and nature is regarded as a more general kind of revelation and, therefore, there is no man and no nature apart from revelation. *Our Knowledge of God*, (London, 1939), pp. 37–39.
3 Whichcote, *Works*, III, 18–20.
4 *Ibid.*, pp. 49–50.

from the natural only as being a different "emanation."[1] Just as natural truths are the first emanation from God, even so truths of after-revelation, saving truths are the second emanation [2] from God and the proper supplement to the former.[3] We should not be confused by our author's phraseology, i.e., when he speaks of natural truth as truth of creation and of supernatural truth as truth of revelation.[4] This caution is necessary since Whichcote conceives all divine knowledge as revelation. John Baillie's conclusion seems to clarify his position as stated thus:

> ... Such moral and spiritual knowledge as may in any one period of human history seem to have become an inherent part of human nature, and so to be an "unaided" natural knowledge, is actually the blessed fruit of God's personal and historical dealings with man's soul, and so in the last resort also a revealed knowledge.[5]

All religion is intelligible, the moral part from creation and the purely revealed part from the time it was "given." Religion is knowable, it can be understood, for if it is revealed, it is made intelligible, and if not intelligible, it is not revealed.[6] The natural knowledge of religion is as spiritual as the revealed. The moral part of religion is the knowledge of God's nature, while the "positive" part is the knowledge of His will.[7] There are two things in religion, morals and institutions. Morals may be known by reason and they are "nineteen parts in twenty" of all religion. On the other hand, institutions depend upon Scripture, but never upon a single text; for an institution which has only one text of Scripture to support it, is actually unsupported.[8] Concerning these two approaches to divine knowledge, Whichcote says:

> God hath set up Two Lights; to enlighten us in our Way; the Light of Reason, which is the Light of his Creation; and the Light of Scripture, which is After-Revelation from him. Let us make use of these two Lights; and suffer neither to be put out.[9]

[1] *Ibid.*, p. 20.
[2] *Ibid.*, pp. 121–123. Elsewhere I have attempted to prove that Pascal's real contribution to religious thought is the concept of "saving knowledge." See my, *Faith and Reason: A Comparative Study of Pascal, Bergson and James*, (Boston, 1962), chs. II, III.
[3] *Ibid.*, pp. 29–30.
[4] Brunner's distinction between "general" and "special" revelation would lend clarity to our author's over-all view of revelation, allowing, of course, for Brunner's special use of the terms. It seems, also, that "saving knowledge" is what Whichcote implies by truths of "after-revelation." Cf. Baxter, *Ibid.*, pp. 192–193, 241–242, 445, 259.
[5] *Our Knowledge of God*, pp. 42–43.
[6] Whichcote, *Ibid.*, IV, 289–291; *Aph*, 889, 1168.
[7] *Aph*. 29.
[8] *Ibid.*, 586.
[9] *Ibid.*, 109. Cf. John Milton who while promising to rely on scripture alone as a religious authority, actually holds reason as well as scripture as authoritative. In his description of a

Divine wisdom, the knowledge of God, of divine things, of eternal life, is knowledge in the "scripture-sense." Such knowledge is not attainable by the efforts of the unaided intellect or by simple apprehension. Knowledge of God revealed in Scripture presupposes "concomitant affection" for God and this means that the pre-requisite for the knowledge of God is love of Him.[1] Divine wisdom is "given" and any want of perfection in our understanding of it may be attributed to our failure to awaken our faculties by meditation and careful study of Scripture. Thus real divine knowledge is not the result of a formal education, tradition and the like, but knowledge arrived at by the proper use of reason and the proper search of Scripture.[2]

It is Whichcote's view that purely revealed truth is recorded in Scripture and thus the authority of Scripture is of great importance to him. However, his interpretation of Scripture is rather critical for his day,[3] and in many ways he seems to anticipate modern Biblical criticism. Further, because for him truth is truth wherever it is found, he uses uncannonical sources, i.e., Wisdom of Solomon, and extra-Biblical writings freely. Nevertheless, Scripture has for him a special authority to which he gives full recognition. He asserts that God's "super-additions" to the law of creation are found in Scripture, but for him Scripture "contains" rather than "is" the revelation of God.[4] This latter assumption leaves him free to use reason even in his interpretation of Scripture. He opposes literalism in scriptural-interpretation: Scripture must be interpreted in relation to other Scripture and especially the context.

... If you will have divine authority, see what is said; and think it not enough that it is barely related in that book; neither is it enough to pretend to a single text, nor to anything accidentally spoken, that can amount either to matter of faith, or divine instructions: it must be express scripture in conjunction with scripture: for scripture as a rule of faith is not one scripture but all.[5]

In his estimation of various aspects of Scripture, Whichcote seems to anticipate the recent concept of "progressive revelation" in the

twofold scripture; external and internal, it is not difficult to see that what he calls "internal" scripture is close to Whichcote's definition of reason, see, De Doctrina Christiana, tr. by Charles Sumner (Cambridge, England, 1825), pp. 7, 89, 472–475.
   See also Douglas Bush, Paradise Lost In Our Time, (Ithaca, 1945), pp. 36–37.
1 Works, IV, 287–289; Cf. Aug. De Trin, xiv. 14.
2 Ibid., pp. 291–293; Cf. Aug., De Trin, vii, 3.
3 Supra, ch. III.
4 Aph., 542.
5 Ibid., III, 50–52. Ibid., III, 294; Aph. 422.

Bible.[1] Nevertheless he assures us that the Bible is "clear and full" concerning all things necessary for salvation.[2] Concerning non-essentials we are left to our prudence and fidelity of interpretation and thus we are as free as we should be and are not bound by words and phrases of Scripture where there is no necessity.[3]

We are all, whether we dissent or agree, one with another, in some matters, agreed that we ought to be guided by scripture. Scripture is clear, full, in all matters of life: and absolutely determining in all matters of necessary belief.[4]

From this point Whichcote makes a "leap of faith" which seems to go beyond his general position. He would leave room for "implicit faith" concerning things which have not been clearly revealed. These things may be contained in Scripture and yet transcend the reach of reason. In such cases, one can only refer oneself to God and "believe that that is true which God intended in those words." Then there are times when God only partly reveals Himself. When God at once reveals and hides Himself, we should know no more than God reveals. To know no more than God reveals is "learned ignorance" and to resign one's understanding to God is "implicit faith." We should be willing to be ignorant where God is silent and anxious to understand what God speaks.[5] Only the Spirit of God can declare the mind and will of God and for this reason we are greatly dependent upon the Spirit in the interpretation of Scripture.[6] Where we are unable to come to a meaningful conclusion after a diligent rational search of Scripture, it is safer to suspend judgment rather than to hasten to an erroneous conclusion.[7] We may be certain that if we are sincere and reverent in our search for

---

[1] *Ibid.*, I, 179–180. Cf. H. E. Fosdick, *Guide to Understanding The Bible*, (New York, 1938). This is Fosdick's general approach to the Bible. See also, John Owen, *Of The Divine Original, Authority, Self-evidencing Light, and Power of the Scriptures*, (Oxford, 1659), pp. 2–4. Owen, a Calvinist and independent represents those among Whichcote's contemporaries who believed that the penmen of the Bible were totally passive and received all immediately from God. The Scripture being the infallible word of God was to be literally interpreted. Owen insists upon direct study of scripture and distrusts the use of commentaries, see James Moffat, ed. *Golden Book of John Owen* (London, 1904), pp. 148–150. See also, C. H. Dodd, *The Authority of The Bible*, (London, 1955), pp. 269–285, 289–300, and Leroy Davis, "Typology in Barth's Doctrine of Scripture," A. R. R., Vol. XLVIII, No. 1 (January 1965), pp. 33–49.

[2] *Ibid.*, III, 56.

[3] *Ibid.*, IV, 183–185; *Aph.*, 1188.

[4] *Ibid.*, pp. 203–204. Cf. Jeremy Taylor, *Liberty of Prophesying*, (London, 1834), pp. 81–83, 102.

[5] *Ibid.*, I, 154–155. Cf. B. Pascal, *Pensées*, ed. by Stewart, (New York, 1947), *Pen.* 515; N. Cusa, *De Docta Ignorantia*, Eng. tr. (London, 1954), Whichcote's notion of "learned ignorance" reminds us of Cusa's work.

[6] *Ibid.*, p. 169.

[7] *Ibid.*, II, 3.

truth, that some organ of God's Spirit will tell us what we should do.[1] And if we see at this point an element of irrationality and therefore an inconsistency in Whichcote's thought, he would remind us of the advantages of this position. This reliance upon the Spirit for truth beyond the grasp of reason makes us receptive of all truth and protects us against error and intolerance.[2]

While this reliance upon the Spirit is good in one respect, our author conceives a danger here also. Being aware of the claims made by individuals and various religious sects of special spiritual gifts, he warns:

If you give leave, and listen to persons that now pretend to a private spirit of interpreting, and who do not give us assurance that their interpretation is warranted by the context; we set wanton wit at liberty to bring any fancy whatsoever, and lay a foundation for all manner of imaginary conceit; and so frustrate and enervate scripture, as a rule of faith.[3]

He adds:

If you only say, you have a Revelation from God: I must have a Revelation from God too, before I can believe you.[4]

Whichcote conceives the Bible as an instrument of God and since it contains saving knowledge, a man must read it in order to become a Christian. In the Bible, God has "committed his mind to writing" and sent His saving truth into the world thereby. When the Bible is properly read, it yields assurance of its sacred purpose as well as the knowledge of divine truth.[5] Concerning matters of revealed truth we are persuaded by the word of God as contained in the Scripture. Christianity cannot be forced, because it is a matter of supernatural revelation. Here we cannot be convinced by reason alone which is supreme in the reception of natural knowledge. This is true because Christianity involves the results of God's will which may be known only by revelation.[6] Articles of faith are resolutions of the divine will and are known only by God's voluntary revelation. To this end, the Bible is God's instrument in the

---

[1] *Ibid.*, pp. 17–18.
[2] *Ibid.*, p. 6.
[3] *Ibid.*, III, 116–117. Cf. G. F. Nuttall, *The Holy Spirit In Puritan Faith and Experience*, (Oxford, 1946), pp. 22, 42–45. Whichcote may have had in mind the early Quakers as well as other groups, see, Nuttall, *Studies in Christian Enthusiasm*. (Wallingford, Pa., 1948), pp. 23–24. See also, Hugh Barbour, *The Quakers in Puritan England*, (New Haven, 1964), pp. 124, 149–152, 241.
[4] *Aph.*, 443.
[5] *Works*, III, 58.
[6] *Ibid.*, I, 176.

world and we have the assurance that as far as revelation is necessary to convey anything by way of "super-addition" to the light of creation, God has "clearly, plainly, fully and satisfactorily laid [it] down in holy scripture." [1] Thus we may safely conclude that for Whichcote the revelation of God in Scripture is primarily saving knowledge.

... Concerning revealed truth, he that is not satisfied in the authority of revealing to us matters of faith, is not yet persuaded to become a christian. To make one religious in general, the principles of God's creation may suffice; to make one a christian, the receiving matters of faith are necessary: to the discerning of things of natural knowledge, the true, severe, impartial use of reason is needful to the knowing of things of revealed truth, the fair and ingenuous construction of words and phrases in scripture is needful.[2]

Looking more critically at Whichcote's view of Scripture, it appears that he has some insights which carry him beyond his time, but that others place him among his contemporaries. When he conceives the special revelation of the Bible as necessary for becoming a Christian, he thinks of Christianity primarily as a religion of the "Book" – of salvation as depending upon revealed truth as written down in the Bible. The more recent view, and one which the present writer finds more acceptable, is a more personal conception of revelation. As John Baillie puts it: "God does not give us information by communication; He gives us Himself in communion." [3] Whichcote provides himself with the thought-form to develop this more wholesome view when he speaks of the spirit of man as the candle of the Lord. But this more recent view which H. H. Farmer calls the "radical personalism" of Christian revelation escapes Whichcote when he treats Scripture as a religious authority. In this more recent view the Christian revelation

---

[1] Ibid., IC, 152. Cf. Baxter, Ibid., p. 240.

[2] Ibid., I, 386–387.

[3] The Idea of Revelation, p. 47. To be made aware of this new emphasis in the concept of revelation one only needs to be reminded of the "god-relationship" of Kierkegaard; the "I and Thou" relationship of Buber and the "divine-human encounter" of Brunner. We do not here have in mind the type of Personalism set forth by E. S. Brightman.
We can see the basis for Baillie's personal conception of revelation in Buber's I and Thou and Farmer's is rooted in John Oman's, Grace and Personality. But, we may observe the same tendency among hermeneutical scholars – they use the presuppositions of some philosopher. The philosophy of Buber radiates through G. E. Wright's Book of the Acts of God. The existentialism of Heidegger underlines Bultmann's demythologizing program. Karl Barth owes an infinite debt to Kierkegaard. The so-called Post-Bultmanians are no exception. Perhaps Paul Tillich assesses the situation correctly when he asserts that biblical theologians, no less than systematic theologians "use most of the terms created by the toil of philosophers and the ingenuity of the speculative mind." See, his Biblical Religion and the Search for Ultimate Reality, (Chicago, 1955), pp. 7–8. Cf. J. M. Robinson and J. B. Cobb, "The New Hermeneutic" New Frontiers in Theology, (New York, 1964), pp. 1–77. See also H. Richard Niebuhr, The Meaning of Revelation, (New York, 1941), pp. 109–137.

is conceived as communion of Person with person. Whichcote partly overcomes this criticism in his Christology, but it is worth remembering Brunner's worthy statement of the more personal view of divine revelation.

> Because, and in so far as, the Scripture testifies to Christ ... I can believe it. Faith in the message carries with it faith in the Book. ... It is not the Book which carries Christ, but Christ who carries the Book, and he carries it only so far as it bears witness to Him, the self-revelation of God.[1]

A proper approach to Whichcote's doctrine of sin must begin with a consideration of his view of the Fall. Though he relates the story of the Fall as recorded in Genesis,[2] he interprets it symbolically rather than literally. For him the story indicates man's rebellious nature, the refusal to use his reason and freedom to love God. Thus Adam is described by Whichcote as a "double" sinner: as immoral since he neither feared nor loved God; and as a rebel because of his wilful disobedience.[3]

The Fall for Whichcote implies that the *imago dei* has been marred. Since the *imago dei* includes the powers of reason and freedom, the Fall implies the fall of reason and perversion of freedom.[4] It follows that a careful consideration of the *imago dei* and the effect of the Fall upon it is desirable at this point.[5] It is to Augustine that we must go to find a historical reminder of our author's view. Augustine says:

> It is in the soul of man, that is, in his rational or intellectual soul, that we must find the image of the Creator which is immortally implanted in its immortality. ... Although reason or intellect be at one time dormant within it, at another appear to be small and at another great, yet the human soul is never anything but rational and intellectual. Hence if it is made after the image of God in respect to this, that it is able to use reason for the understanding and beholding of God, then from the very moment when that nature so marvellous and so great began to be almost none at all, whether it be obscure and defaced or bright and beautiful, assuredly it always is.[6]

---

[1] *Revelation and Reason*, pp. 175–176. According to Baillie, "Revelation consists neither in the dictation of writing nor in the communication of information, but in personal communion – the self-disclosure of Personality. *Our Knowledge of God*, pp. 36–37.

[2] Whichcote, *Ibid.*, II, 41–42.

[3] *Ibid.*, pp. 278–279. Cf. John Milton, *Ibid.*, pp. 262–264. *Paradise Lost*, bk. III.

[4] *Supra*, Ch., IV. Cf. Webb, *Ibid.*, pp. 127–129. Here original sin is described as the counterpart not of grace but of the image of God in man. It stands for the sollicitations of the lower nature, conceived of proleptically as sin, of which they constitute the potentiality, described from the point of view of one who has already turned away from evil to God.

[5] Reinhold Niebuhr has given a convenient summary of the *imago dei* in historical theology. He concludes that Augustine contributed the most satisfying concept of the *imago dei* of all early thought, and therefore, Augustine is the first theologian to comprehend the full implications of the Christian doctrine of man. *Nature and Destiny of Man*, (London, 1941–43), I, pp. 164–165. Cf. Brunner, *Man in Revolt*, tr. by Olive Wyon (London, 1939), pp. 82–205.

[6] *De Trin*, XIV. 4, 6; Cf. *Ibid.*, XV, 1 *passim*.

It would appear that Whichcote derived his view of the *imago dei* and its condition after the Fall almost directly from Augustine. What he means by the Fall is also implied in the above statement from Augustine. Calvin found Augustine's view praiseworthy [1] and according to T. F. Torrance, Calvin "refused to advance any doctrine of man, apart from God's original intention of grace in creating him in the image of God." [2] Unfortunately, Whichcote had to face the kind of Calvinist theology which in Torrance's own words "produced a doctrine of the fall and of human depravity apart from the context of grace, and interpreted grace as God's answer to human depravity." [3] Thus it will be best to recall Augustine's general position as we look more carefully at Whichcote's view.

Whichcote asserts that when a man fails to use his reason properly, he becomes an accessory to his own destruction.[4] Man is dependent upon God for his existence and when he asserts his independence he becomes vain, that is, vain in a "private" sense, for he deforms and defaces the image of God within. When a man by his disobedience to the divine will mars this high perfection, the *imago dei*, he loses more than all creation can repair. The result of the Fall leads to the impotency of reason and guilt of conscience. By this unnatural use of our faculties, they are spoiled; this is especially true of the mind and the consequence can be nothing less than unhappiness.[5] All men are born with a natural sympathy for the good life. However, by consent to evil, man develops a disposition contrary to virtue. By repetition this tendency increases until the habit of virtue is not only weakened but displaced by vice.[6] Our fallen condition is moral depravity, it is not natural but acquired. Whichcote asserts that nothing moral can be by generation, but by habit only. However, we are not born with habits,

---

[1] Niebuhr, *Ibid.*, p. 165 (n. 1).

[2] *Calvin's Doctrine of Man*, (London, 1945), p. 20.

[3] *Ibid.* Unfortunately, Luther's view of the *imago dei* is defined purely in terms of contrast to the present state of sin. *Commentary on Genesis*, referred to by Niebuhr, *Ibid.*, p. 171 (n. 2). Cf. Gerhard Von Rad, *Genesis*, tr. by J. H. Marks (Philadelphia, 1959), pp. 55–59. Von Rad says: "This basis work ("image") is more closely explained and made precise by *Demut* ("similarity"), with the simple meaning that this image is to correspond to the original image, that it is to resemble it.
See, *Ibid.*, p. 56. The whole man is created in God's image. Thus any anthropology which limits the "image to man's spiritual nature and ignores his corporeality is not true to the original intention of (Genesis 1:26–28).

[4] Whichcote, *Works*, I, 90. Cf. C. K. Robinson, "Philosophical Biblicism: The teaching of the Westminster Confession Concerning God, The Natural Man, and Revelation and Authority," S.J.T., vol. 18, no. 1. (March, 1965), pp. 23–39.

[5] *Ibid.*, pp. 114–116.

[6] *Aph.* 86.

but only with faculties. Any inclination which is not acquired is amoral and nothing is virtue or vice apart from a mind actually consenting to good or evil. We are as we have used ourselves and man's fallen condition may be explained by his self-abuse.[1] Thus "to neglect or abuse ourselves" is what Whichcote conceives as the true "Original of all sin." [2]

In this sunk, degenerate and apostate state of mankind, reason is much depressed and even enthralled to sense. Yet it is not completely bereft of all sense (at all times at least) of its noble pedigree; but is now and then awakened by God, stirred up at times to some generous motions in itself; touched with some deep remorse at the remembrance of its own ancient, pristine state and dignity. When it remembers, recollects and considers what it was or may be, it makes some faint efforts to recover that which was lost. The goodness and compassion of God directs and guides those notions that remind us of the height of our maker and... that we are His offsprings. The grace of God stirs up in us these motions that we may be restored. ... No man is good enough to his own satisfaction; the guilt that men have will make them tremble when they have been depraved, that they are short and imperfect and not as they should be.[3]

A few critical observations at this point will clarify Whichcote's general position concerning the Fall and point us to the next consideration, viz, sin and guilt. It seems good to look back upon his view from the position held by a select group of modern theologians, Brunner, Barth, J. Baillie and J. S. Whale. Barth who stands in the general Augustinian tradition, but who seeks to prove that revelation from God to man has practically no point of contact with man except that which it creates for itself, would find Whichcote's concept of the *imago dei* very inconvenient and would no doubt criticize it severely.[4] On the other hand, Brunner at certain points comes remarkably close to Whichcote on the subject. He refuses to depart from what he calls

[1] *Works*, III, 338–340. Whichcote indicates that the Platonists contribute to our understanding of man's fallen condition. Cf. *Ibid.*, II, 179.

[2] *Aph.* 31. Cf. Milton, *Ibid.*, pp. 194–196.

[3] *Works*, IV, 303–305 Whitcote describes the Devil as an "enemy extraordinary." God made no such enemy for man, but the Devil is the result of apostasy of the higher creation. God defends men from the Devil by His special providence, unless they wilfully betray or offend God and turn to the Devil by consent. However, if men will not accept their finitude and insist upon knowing more than God reveals by other means, even contrary to reason, this gives the Devil his opportunity to seize them. In such cases God removes his protection and suffers men to receive the effect of their choice.

If we remain under the protection of God's special providence, the power Satan has over us is limited and he is not able to do us much harm. Milton was greatly concerned with the problem of the Fall, see F. E. Hutchinson, *Milton and The English Mind* (London, 1946), p. 116; Cf. *Paradise Lost*, ed. by G. M. Davis (London, 1931), III, 372. We are here reminded of what Milton describes as God's "extra-ordinary providence," see, *De Doctrina*, pp. 215–216.

[4] Cf. Barth's "Nein!" in Barth and Brunner, *Natural Theology*, ed. by J. Baillie, tr. by P. Fraenkel (London, 1946), pp. 67–69.

Ansprechbarkeit, addressability in man, even sinful man. Thus he distinguishes between the formal and material *imago.* The formal *imago* is untouched by sin, while the material *imago* is lost. Brunner says:

> To formulate it differently: as before, man is a person, i.e., he is in a derived sense that which God is originally. Yet he is not a personal person but an anti-personal person; for the truly personal is existence in love, the submission of the self to the will of God and therefore an entering into communion with one's fellow creature because one enjoys communion with God. This *quid* of personality is negatived through sin, whereas the *quod* of personality constitutes the *humanum* of every man, also that of the sinner.[1]

Professor Baillie who gives a careful study and criticism of the position of Barth and Brunner alike seems to come closer to Whichcote than the other two theologians when he says that the doctrine of the *imago dei* has its basis in the fact that our existent human nature presents itself to us, not as a simply bad thing, but as "a good thing spoiled." [2] And Dr. J. S. Whale agrees that man's initial endowment is indestructible. He says: "...Man, just because he is man, is unable to destroy his endowment. God's image is not destroyed." [3]

When we turn to a direct consideration of Whichcote's concept of sin we face once again his "classical view" of man.[4] Niebuhr has significantly pointed out that wherever the classical view of man predominates, the tendency is to equate sin with sensuality, while the definition of sin as pride is consistently maintained in the strain of theology generally known as Augustinian.[5] Niebuhr concludes:

> Biblical and Christian thought has maintained with a fair degree of consistency that pride is more basic than sensuality and that the latter is, in some way, derived from the former.... The Pauline exposition of man's self-glorification ... is really an admirable summary of the whole Biblical doctrine of sin.[6]

---

[1] See Brunner' essay: "Nature and Grace," *Ibid.,* p. 24. Cf. Brunner, *Man in Revolt,* tr. Olive Wyon (London, 1939), p. 98 and Barth, *Christ and Adam,* tr. by T. A. Smail (Edinburgh, 1956), pp. 10–11.

[2] *Our Knowledge of God,* p. 23. The first section of this work is a valuable appraisal of Barth's and Brunner's controversy concerning nature and grace. Baillie's introduction to Barth and Brunner *Natural Theology* is also invaluable.

[3] *Christian Doctrine* (1956) p. 45.

[4] According to Niebuhr the classical view of man consists primarily of Platonic, Aristotelian and Stoic conceptions of human nature with varying emphasis upon man's capacity for thought and reason, *Ibid.,* p. 6. The Christian view, on the other hand, is determined by the ultimate presuppositions of the Christian faith and human nature in Christian thought allows for the unity of body and soul in human personality, *Ibid.,* pp. 12–13.

[5] Niebuhr, *Ibid.,* p. 199, (n. 1). Cf. Aug. *De Civ. Dei,* xii, 13, xiv, 13; Calvin, *Institutes,* Bk. I, Ch. 4.

[6] *Ibid.,* pp. 198–199.

If Niebuhr's general observations are correct and they seem to the present writer to be so, then Whichcote's concept of sin is, in emphasis at least, unAugustinian and what is more serious, unbiblical. To our author sin is always sin against the light, consent to known iniquity, or holding the truth in unrighteousness.[1] Further sin is moral evil, it is not only irrational, but immoral. By voluntary consent to known iniquity, a man parts, at once, with reason and conscience.[2] Sin is the result of a rational and free moral agent choosing evil in preference to the good.[3] Thus far the classical view of which Niebuhr speaks seems to apply to Whichcote's concept of sin – sin is irrationality and sensuality.

But to recognise this tendency in Whichcote's thought is only part of the picture, for to him sin is self-will as well as the lack of self-control. Whichcote asserts that self-will is the greatest idol in the world, it is anti-Christ or anti-God.[4] Even here, however, our attention is called back to the classical strand in his thought, for he insists that "ignorance" of our limitations is the basis of pride.[5] Thus instead of explaining man's fallen reason and sensuality by pride, Whichcote attempts to do just the opposite. It is because man has lost his self-control, because his passions have subdued his reason, that he has given himself over to self-will and pride. It is to the credit of Whichcote that he manages to give some significant emphasis to what he calls spiritual sins. Since true human behaviour is always for him intentional behaviour, he conceives hypocrisy as a serious spiritual sin. Concerning the hypocrite, he says "He, that is bad is worst of all; when he feigns himself to be good."[6] He also includes among spiritual sins: evil thoughts, sins of will and sins of passion.

Evil thoughts are first conceived in the mind and for this reason the mind of an evil man is his worst part just as the mind of a good man is his best part. An evil man cannot do all the evil he desires and it follows from this that evil thoughts are to be considered as the highest degree of wickedness. Sins of will occur when the will is undirected by reason, for it is like "wild-fire" for man in his finitude to set up will as

---

[1] *Whichcote*, Works, I, 41.

[2] *Ibid.*, pp. 96–98.

[3] *Ibid.*, pp. 81–83. Cf. Milton, *De Doctrina*, p. 277 and *Paradise Lost*, III, 103.

[4] *Aph.* 653.

[5] *Ibid.*, 747. J. S. Whale is in essential agreement with Niebuhr that pride is the basis of all sin. Whale uses Jung's apt definition of man's proud trust in himself as "his Godalmightiness," *Ibid.*, p. 45. I consider Whichcote's reflection on sin as self-will close to John Baillie's assertion that sin is self-centeredness including sensuality, pride, estrangement, disobedience, etc. See also D. Bonhoeffer, *Creation and Fall*, (London, 1962), pp. 77–78 and A. M. Dubarle, *The Biblical Doctrine of Original Sin*, tr. by E. M. Stewart (New York, 1964), p. 199.

[6] *Aph.* 1147.

a "light." Unless reason guides the will the order of nature is inverted and sins of the will are the result. Sins of passion are also among the spiritual sins, since it is in order for affections to follow judgment and choice. Our affections are only to quicken an action determined by reason and it is because passions are blind in themselves that they must always follow reason. Sins of passion always occur when the order is reversed or when reason is banished all together.[1] To sum up his general view of sin, Whichcote says:

> Here is a declaration of its filthiness and unworthiness, its odiousness in the sight of God, its ill demerit, its hurtfulness to the creature; for it destroys the subject, and is a pernicious example. ... It hath in it all impurity; there is no natural corruption hath in it that degree of naughtiness and impurity, that moral impurity hath; for in moral turpitude there is that that is spiritual impurity. ... It is loathsome, abominable, and detestable in the eyes of God; for it is contrary to his nature, and contrary to his mind and will. And then it is ill demerit; for whereas God delights to do his creatures good, this provokes God to turn from his creatures.[2]

Two important implications of Whichcote's concept of sin are that temptation is not sin and that there are degrees of sin. Since sin is the consent to known iniquity, the mere knowledge of evil is not evil. God is aware of evil or He could not punish it. "It is not what you know or think, but what you make choice of, and delight in" that is rightly conceived as sin.[3] F. R. Tennant puts it this way, "The thought of evil is not necessarily an evil thought." And Tennant adds that this view is consistent with the Christian belief that Christ was one tempted without sin.[4] The assertion of Whichcote that sin is "sin against the light" logically leads to the conclusion that the amount of light determines the degree of sin. If there is "clear light and full liberty," sin is great, but if sin results from "confusion of conscience" a man is not fully responsible, sin is of a lesser degree.[5] Tennant's agreement here is noteworthy.

> Not the highest that a given individual can conceive as the highest ideal to be known, but the highest that a given individual at a given time can know, must be the standard by which, at that time, that individual's acts and character are to be judged as sinful or sinless.[6]

---

[1] *Works*, IV, 429–435.

[2] *Ibid.*, II, 276–277.

[3] *Ibid.*, p. 368. *Aph.* 841, Whichcote does not take temptation lightly for he is aware of the prevalence and power of temptation, of the deceitfulness of sin and the tendency of sin to be self-perpetuating. Cf. *Works*, II, 353–354. I, 12.

[4] *Concept of Sin*, (Cambridge, England, 1912) p. 194.

[5] Whichcote, *Works*, I, 142–143.

[6] Tennant, *Ibid.*, p. 87. According to Tennant, the absolute or objective ideal of moral conduct, such as Christians find embodied in Christ, cannot be adopted as the standard or

Oddly enough the best statement of the rationalist-classical view of sin and the Biblical view, both of which are manifest in Whichcote's concept of sin, comes from Niebuhr who has taken his stand against the classical view. This observation by Niebuhr is also a worthy defense of Whichcote's view. Niebuhr says:

The Biblical view colours the definitions of the Christian rationalists so that, when they define sin primarily as sensuality, they recognise, at least, that this sensuality is not merely the expression of physical impulse but represents an inordinate quality made possible by the freedom of the spirit.[1]

We have seen that in our author's concept of the Fall, each man is the "Adam of his own soul" and in giving himself over to sensuality the candle of the Lord within burns so dim that he cannot see by it. Thus Whichcote's approach to the subject of the Fall and sin generally has the semblance of the classical view of man. It is not surprising that when he speaks of guilt, he does so in terms of self-condemnation.[2] He asserts that when God made man, He endowed him with "such principles that he was a law given to himself," and if he varied from this law of his creation, he must be self-condemned, and if self-condemned, unavoidably miserable. Thus to go against the way God made us is to contract guilt.[3]

Man knows what he ought to do both by reason and revelation. And he has put out both of his eyes, that does not see these things, that does not discern his obligation to them. He has put out the eye of natural light and the eye of divine revelation.[4]

We would expect from Whichcote's general position that once a man had deadened his conscience by sin, he would no longer feel the pangs of

criticism by which all sorts and conditions of men including heathen and children, for instance, are at once convicted of sin, without making sin a metaphysical necessity, a consequence of the limitations belonging to the finite as such: without making sin, in fact, precisely what it is not. *Ibid.*, p. 83. It is the form rather than the content of the standard that is constant; and the relativity of the content is not only compatible with the absoluteness of the form – the bare imperative – but constitutes an essential condition of its obligatoriness, *Ibid.*, p. 85. Tennant's concept of sin is a good supplement and commentary and in many ways a defence of Whichcote's view of sin. See Tennant's definition of sin, *Ibid.*, p. 245. Cf. *The Origin and Propagation of Sin*, (Cambridge, England), and *The Sources of the Doctrine of the Fall and Original Sin* (Cambridge, England, 1903) by the same author. Whale's criticism of Tennant's use of the evolutionary theory to explain the origin of sin, does not apply to Whichcote's view. Cf. Whale, *Ibid.*, pp. 47–49.

[1] *Niebuhr*, p. 200. Gregory of Nyssa is cited as an example as he says: "Thus the arising of anger in us is indeed akin to the impulses of brutes; but it grows by alliance of thought." *Ibid.*, (n. 1), from *On the Making of Men*, XVIII, 4.

[2] We have seen *Supra*, Ch. V. how he applies this notion to the function of conscience and in the next chapter he applies it in a special way to his concept of punishment. Cf. Cudworth, *A Sermon Preached Before The House of Commons*, (New York, 1930), pp. 72–73.

[3] Whichcote, *Works*, III, 347.

[4] *Ibid.*, IV, 437–438.

guilt. Our author sees the matter differently, for as sin multiplies we become more miserable. We must recall Whichcote's assertion that man's happiness is only in accordance with his relation to God,[1] and he is consistent when he argues that sin leads to unhappiness, because it alienates us from God. If follows that the more habitual sin becomes the more miserable a man becomes.

> The ground of man's misery is not the first fall but the second fault, that is, a lapse upon a lapse. A second sin is not another of the same kind, but the consummation of the first.[2]

In the lower degree of sin God is neglected, but in the higher degree of sin He is affronted,[3] and man comes to live entirely by sense and passion because of his violation of judgment, reason and conscience.[4] Guilt, then, is the normal consequence of sin. Because of sin God awakens such guilt in the sinner that he cannot escape it by various diversions. Even those who would sin themselves into senselessness, find that by sinning against the light they hurt themselves inwardly, and this wound within does not release them from guilt but adds to the torture of their souls. Nothing can bring inner peace to the man who voluntarily consents to known iniquity, for such a person is separated from God and in this state no man can be happy.[5] Whichcote concludes that in the state of guilt a sinner is self-condemned by conscience before he is judged by God, but he is finally condemned by both.

> There is no defence for that man who is in danger in respect of God; and the desperateness of the condition lies further in this; that this mischief is not alone: but a wounded conscience accompanies it: and this is a misery beyond all expression, to have almighty God, whose power no man can withstand, engaged against a person, and to have our own conscience accusing and condemning also; this is a state which causes astonishment both from without and from within: a man will be afraid to stay at home, or to enjoy his own thoughts, because of the troublesomeness and uneasiness of his own mind. And who can interpose in this case? Who can comfort, when God and conscience doth condemn and give testimony against a man? These are testimonies; against which there can be no objection; God's omniscience, and our own conscience.[6]

---

[1] See *Supra*, Ch. V.

[2] *Aph.* 525.

[3] *Ibid.*, 766.

[4] *Ibid.*, 985.

[5] *Works*, I, 94–95.

[6] *Ibid.*, pp. 129–130. According to Whichcote, a man is even more guilty when he enjoys the sins of others. It takes an extremely degenerate conscience and mind to get "pleasure and profit" from the sins of others. *Ibid.*, III, 286–288. See Tillich's profound treatment of anxiety and guilt in his, *Courage To Be* (New Haven, 1953), pp. 41, 51–54. Tillich combines the psycho-

In spite of all the emphasis Whichcote places upon the individual nature of sin and personal responsibility for it, he is also aware of social sins. Sin is destructive to oneself, but it goes deeper and is more far reaching than the effect upon a single life. Sin is a variation from the "reason of things," it is an attempt to over-rule the proper order of things "settled and established from eternity." [1] Sin is an attempt "to control the immutable and unalterable Laws of everlasting Righteousness, Goodness and Truth; upon which the Universe depends." [2] As J. S. Whale reminds us, all serious thought about the mystery of iniquity has had to grapple with its constitutional, as well as its volitional, aspect.[3] It is significant that Whichcote with all his emphasis upon the "volitional" aspect of sin also perceived what Tillich calls the "demonic" aspect of society, history, and the cosmos, as the result of sin. Whichcote states his view aptly thus: "Sin is such an ill-natured thing that a sinner is an Incendiary and sets the world on fire." [4] In a sermon before the House of commons, February 4, 1763, Whichcote says:

It shall be my business this day ... to press not only what is external ... but what is vital ... in the motion of repentance, which now this nation doth profess in this solemn application unto God. Our great and loud sins, they are the things that expose us to God's displeasure, indignation and wrath. And because generals do not affect, I shall instance in some particulars: our falseness and treachery to the true religion, in which this nation hath prospered above a hundred years: our affected atheism, and avowed profaneness, beyond what former times have had experience of: our wantonness and licentiousness, disgracefulto human nature: our own high immoralities and debaucheries in several ways. These have brought the judgment of God upon us, and turned God from us in displeasure. And none that is sober-minded can think otherwise, if he acknowledges God's government of the world, and doth consider that wickedness and unrighteousness are an abomination to him.[5]

---

analytic and theological approaches to the subject. His differentiation between existential and pathological anxiety is instructive and his notion that grace indicates God's acceptance of us though we are unacceptable is very meaningful. Generally he relates sin to estrangement, guilt to anxiety and forgiveness to acceptance. Cf. D. E. Roberts, *Psychotherapy and a Christian View of Man*, (New York, 1950), pp. 104–105, 110, 118–119, 129 and Dubarle, *Ibid.*, pp. 218–245. See also, Edith Weigert, "Psychotherapy and Existential Philosophy," J.R.T., Vol. XIX, no. 2 (1962–63), pp. 129–140. Cf. H. R. Mackintosh, *The Christian Experience of Forgiveness*, pp. 52–53.

[1] *Aph.* 646.
[2] *Ibid.*, 682.
[3] Whale, *Ibid.* Whale feels that some explanation for the universality of sin is necessary. He considers the concept of original sin which implies and means original guilt completely untenable especially on moral grounds. Thus he suggests that it is time to rethink the main implications attested to by the doctrine of original sin in face of the historical fact of universal moral imperfection. *Ibid.*, pp. 48–49.
[4] Whichcote, *Aph.* 730.
[5] *Works*, I, 123.

Indeed, when one reads the above sermon or Cudworth's famous sermon to the same assembly, one is reminded of the Old Testament prophets of social justice, i.e., Amos, Micah and Isaiah. On the other hand the same spirit is found in the writings of J. C. Bennett and Reinhold Niebuhr. But as Bennett reminds us it is not sufficient merely to distinguish between the two types of sin by definition, they must be overcome by different means. Bennett, in speaking of social sin, says:

> It can only be overcome by a variety of means which include knowledge of cause and effect and large scale changes in institutions and in external circumstances by social action.[1]

Whichcote now arrives at the central point of Christian theology. Between man's fallen and sinful condition and his redemption, Whichcote places the work of Christ. For him Christology continually merges into Soteriology,[2] and in his thought the Person of Christ can be discerned primarily from His work.[3] Nevertheless, he gives us some preliminary observations concerning the Person of Christ.

In the Incarnation Christ is made "like unto us" but this likeness requires qualification especially in the light of our imperfections. Thus Whichcote finds it necessary to distinguish between negative and privative imperfections in us. The former belong to our creatureliness, while the latter are the fruits of our apostasy. It is reasonable to assume that Christ shares the limitations of our creation with us, but He does not share our sins.[4] Brunner seems to capture our author's view when he asserts that Christ came "in" the flesh but not "after" the flesh. Whichcote insists, then, that our Saviour by partaking with us in our natures, partakes also in our weakness and infirmities and we, on our side, thus partake of the divine nature, which is free from

---

[1] *Social Salvation*, (London, 1935), pp. 8-9. That Whichcote meets this more active test is attested to by his life of general social concern. Cf. *Supra*, Ch. I. See my art. "Christian Conscience and Legal Discrimination," J.R.T., Vol. XIX, No. 2 (1962–63), pp. 157–161.

[2] D. M. Baillie, *God was in Christ*, (London, 1947) p. 160. Cf. C. E. Raven, *Natural Science and Christian Theology*, (Cambridge, England, 1953), II, 90.

[3] Brunner, *Dogmatics* tr. Olive Wyon, (London, 1949–52), II, 272. Dean Inge observes that Bishop Westcott "like all Hellenisers .... makes the Incarnation, rather than the Atonement, the central point of his theology." But according to Inge the Incarnation is the Atonement. *The Platonic Tradition in English Religious Thought*, (London, 1926), p. 102. Elsewhere the same author asserts that the religious philosophy to which Augustine was converted was the Platonism of Plotinus with the doctrine of the Incarnation added. *The Philosophy of Plotinus*, (London, 1918), II, 207; Cf. Aug., *Conf.*, VII, 9. Here, however, Inge's comprehensive notion of the Incarnation as the Atonement holds and only thus may we classify Whichcote among the Christian Platonists as Inge conceives them.

[4] Whichcote, *Works*, II, 247–248.

all want and imperfection.[1] To state it differently, the Word became flesh that flesh might become Word.

As a result of the Incarnation, the natural order can no longer be conceived as "base" for this is the real meaning of the Incarnation, that God reveals Himself as, at once, the Author of nature and the Giver of grace.[2] When our Saviour became embodied in flesh, the greatest honor was bestowed upon not only human nature but all nature. It is nevertheless true that God in the Incarnation assumes a special relation to man.

... Observe ... the great honour put upon human nature; when the son of God came into it; when divine goodness did take into consideration the rise and advance of created nature; and to recover and raise it to all possible perfection: he did take to himself a peculiar relation to human nature.... God united human nature to his own existence, and set it at his own right hand.... This ... is one of the greatest works of God. This, if possible, doth transcend the very creation of God, at first: for, there was nothing there to resist him: but, in the restoration, there was malignity and sin.[3]

Unfortunately, Whichcote's consideration of the way in which the Incarnation transcends creation appears inadequate. So important is this insight in relation to all his thought that John Baillie's observation is welcomed at this point.

What God does in Christ is a miracle not of omnipotence but of grace. Grace implies a self-limitation on the part of omnipotence, since there can only be grace where there is self-acceptance in the absence of coercion. The act of creation is an act of sheer omnipotence, but the act of recreation of God's image is essentially an act of grace – and to that extent different from an act of creation.[4]

The goodness of God, Whichcote conceives as the motivation of God's act of restoration in Christ.[5] Our Saviour came from God to do

---

[1] *Ibid.*, pp. 244–247.

[2] *Ibid.*, p. 76. William Temple, *Nature Man and God*, (London, 1951): "Christianity is the most materialistic of all religions." By which Temple refers to matter as a vehicle of spirit and as the sphere of the spirit's self-realization, p. 478.

[3] *Ibid.*, IV, 189. Cf. Athanasius' classic work *De Incarnatione Verbi Dei* might well have influenced Whichcote's notion of the incarnation. Though an Egyptian by birth, Athanasius was a Greek by training. He made the incarnation his special problem and theology since his time is in his debt. A modern classic on the incarnation is Father L. S. Thornton's, *The Incarnate Lord*, (London, 1928).

[4] *Our Knowledge of God*, p. 24. Since Whichcote's primary concern is with the work of Christ no detailed discussion concerning the person of Christ seems necessary. See also his, *Sense of the Presence of God*, (London, 1962), pp. 231–250; John Oman, *Grace and Personality*, (New York, 1925), pp. 80–90 an ecumenical discussion on grace in *The Doctrine of Grace*, ed. by W. T. Whitley, (London, 1932); and a comparison of grace in Christianity and Hinduism by Sabapathy Kulandran in *Grace: A Comparative Study of the Doctrine in Christianity and Hinduism*, (London, 1964), and Rudolf Otto, *Die Gnadenreligion Indias Und Das Christentum*, (Munich, 1930).

[5] Whichcote, *Works*, 77.

the work of God. While using the terminology of Aristotle he gives these terms Christian content: the First Mover or the Unmoved Mover becomes the Self-moving God, Who by His goodness moves in our direction in Christ to restore us from our lost condition. God takes the initiative in Christ to save us. This goodness of God moved him to have compassion for sinful man and was the "moving cause" of Christ's coming.[1] Here Whichcote breaks not only with the passionless God of Aristotle, but with the Neo-Platonic Absolute. To predicate motion on the part of the Absolute thus conceived is an intolerable contradiction, for movement means striving, and striving means to seek for something one does not possess, and this implies imperfection. It is often true that where Whichcote appears at first glance to be most Platonic, he is most Christian. Here the Platonic concept of the good is "baptised" into the concept of *Agape*. He uses the concept of the good in precisely the same way that Nygren [2] or Brunner employ *Agape*. Whichcote appears to anticipate Brunner's very words, allowing for the use of "love" instead of goodness, as Brunner says: "The God of the Christian faith... the living God, is in Himself motion, because in His very Nature He is Love." [3]

Let us compare Whichcote's own words:

> I will make the goodness of God's nature, which is his natural perfection, that that doth "inwardly" affect ... him to benevolence ... and compassion and to relieve lost creatures.[4]

God and the sinner, Whichcote asserts, come together only by means of a mediator.[5] The worst apostasy is the failure to accept Christ as the only Mediator between God and man. With this principle in mind, our author challenges the concept of "good works" held by Jews, Baptists and "mere" Naturalist, alike.[6] But he freely uses the ideas of the Jews and Platonists alike to illustrate his concept of mediation in Christ.

The Platonists, he recalls, had a notion of mediation between God and man which conceived Deity as being so transcendent as to be inaccessible to man in his meanness. They were aware of man's fallen condition and offered this as an explanation for the impossibility of

---

[1] *Ibid.*, pp. 96–97.

[2] Nygren's *Agape and Eros* is a monumental work on this subject. Insofar as Nels Ferré is an ardent exponent of the *Agape* motif he stands in the Lundensian tradition of theology with Nygren, Aulén and Wingren.

[3] Brunner, *The Mediator*, tr. Olive Wyon (London, 1934), p. 285; Cf. *Ibid.*, p. 287.

[4] Whichcote, *Works*, IV, 77–78.

[5] *Ibid.*, II, 334.

[6] *Ibid.*, pp. 320–321.

man's approach to supreme Deity. It was for this reason that they introduced a sort of "middle powers" called *Daemons* as intermediate between Deity and man. Now they were correct as to the idea, but they knew not the Person. But the real point is, that these heathen writers, outside the pale of the Church, without the light of Scripture, held such a high concept of mediation as to humble the proud within the Church, who attempt to embrace the Gospel without accepting Christ as their mediator.[1]

To illustrate the priestly function of Christ as mediator, Whichcote recalls the function of the Jewish high priest. He asserts that the Jewish high priest was an instrument of God, a "middle person" between God and the people and by God's appointment he made "reconciliation and atonement" for them. But the function of the Jewish high priest is superseded by our Great High Priest. We have in Christ a high priest in "substance and truth." Those who relied upon the Jewish high priest only touched the hem of His garment, they were acquainted only with His proxy, but we who accept Christ as our Mediator have the knowledge of His Person.[2] He conceives the priesthood of Christ as a fulfilment of what had only been foreshadowed by the Jewish high priest.

Christ, according to Whichcote, is the "middle person" in the order of being and is for this reason suitable as Mediator between God and man. It follows that all who are acceptable to God are accepted in Christ, and a fallen creature that is not accepted in Christ is rejected for ever. The fact that men may only be acceptable to God by Christ means that Christ is not merely a convenience but a sheer necessity. We are now, says Whichcote, at the center of "gospel-revelation" and though it is supra-rational, it is not irrational.[3] He reasons thus: there is no one more suitable for the office of mediator than Christ, that is, if we consider the height of His Person, the integrity of His nature, and His nearness to God and to man. In the height of His Person, He is equal to God; in the integrity of His nature, He is perfect; and, in His relation to God and man there is no one to compare with Him, for He

---

[1] *Ibid.*, pp. 302–304. Cf. Aug., *De Div. Dei*, viii, 4, 5. It was concerning their inadequate view of the mediation of Christ that Henry More attacked the Quakers of his day. See *The Grand Mystery of Godliness*, (London, 1660) bk. X Ch. XIII, pp. 533–534. Cf. Tallack, "Quakers and Cambridge Platonists," *F. Q. E.*, (1889), Vol. XXIII, p. 191. A comparison of Ficino's view of the mediation of Christ with that of Whichcote is instructive. See P. O. Kristeller, *The Philosophy of Ficino*, tr. by Virginia Conant (New York, 1943), Appendix, I, pp. 405–406.

[2] *Ibid.*, p. 254. Cf. A. Büchler, *Studies in Sin and Atonement: In The Rabbinic Literature of the First Century*, (London, 1928), pp. 441–456.

[3] *Ibid.*, pp. 300–302.

is the God-man.[1] To sum up his concept of the mediation of Christ, Whichcote says:

> I do observe in the history of all times, that those in all places, in all ages, that have been anything raised in their intellectuals, or refined in their morals, have expected some way from God whereby he should save sinners. If we were as real in matters of religion, as in other matters, we should find a necessity of some mediation with God, as they have done, and in answer to this, the scripture calls Christ the "desire of all nations.' . . . If he was not the voice of their souls, I am sure he was the voice of their necessity. . . . Let us make just use of him, and receive him for our justification. . . . Let us be willing to be as much beholden to Christ, as he is ready to gratify us.[2]

Christ is not only the Mediator in a general sense, but He is also the Reconciler. Thus our author asserts that Christ resigns Himself entirely to the will of God and is obedient unto death in order to move God to forgive fallen men.[3] Christ is the Reconciler of the offended God and the offending man. As Reconciler, Christ considers the right of both parties, that of God and man equally. God has a twofold right over man, the right of authority and of owner. In keeping with the former claim upon us, God has the right to expect our service and in keeping with the latter, our payment of debts. The creditor has the right to expect payment of a loan even if the debtor is non-solvent and it follows that God retains His demand upon us even if we have disabled ourselves by apostasy. However, if God meted out strict justice at this point, we should be eternally lost; but fortunately, it is at this point that Christ as Reconciler intercedes for us. Man as an apostate and rebel cannot render God satisfaction, but he may still do something, for however dim the light of God's candle within man may be, it is not extinguished. The Reconciler considers at once the creditor's right and the debtor's necessity. He asks man to do what he can, i.e., acknowledge God, repent and return to duty. If man does all he can, then the Reconciler "moves" God to "abate" His right and accept the "little but all" that the sinner can offer. The Reconciler does not "overbear" either party, but is completely governed by each party's rights and by the necessity of the case. But Whichcote adds that the Reconciler is most anxious to render God satisfaction and to protest His honor.

> He convinces the offender of his ingratitude and that he must offer something to the offended in exchange for forgiveness. There must be voluntary submission of the delinquent party, and voluntary remission of the offended party. There

---

[1] *Ibid.*, p. 335. Here we recall the similar argument of Anselm in *Cur Deus Homo?*
[2] *Ibid.*, pp. 331–332. Cf. Milton, *Paradise Lost*, bk. III, lines 160–182.
[3] *Ibid.*, pp. 263–265.

must be free forgiveness on God's part, and ingenuous submission on the sinner's part. Our Saviour takes care that God may come off with honour, and that that may be done that is safe and best, by the creature. By his sacrifice he doth persuade God to pardon; and thereby secures God's honour: for it is acknowledged "God hath right." The case is rightly stated for God's honour, and the creature is brought to rights again. Truth is acknowledged; and God is justified.[1]

Whichcote conceives the Cross as the crucial point in Christ's act of reconciliation of God and man. Reconciliation is by the act of atonement and as conceived by Whichcote it indicates the awfulness of sin. When Christ dies for sin He condemns sin in His death.[2] The Son of God upon coming to abolish sin finds it necessary to lay down His life. Christ is the second Adam who renders satisfaction to God for sin in the very nature that has transgressed.[3] God had prohibited sin under the penalty of death and Christ dies for sin overcoming death itself. In the death of Christ God's truthfulness and holiness are declared and vindicated according to the mind and will of God. And what makes the death of Christ more efficacious than all the passive sacrifices of Judaism was that His sacrifice was fully conscious, it was a true self-humiliation. Thus His sacrifice for sin is a "reasonable service" and for this reason highly acceptable to God.[4]

Now our Saviour being highly intelligent, and fully voluntary did in his understanding, design and aim at all these ends, which are so good for man as he was apprehensive of them, so he was free in all that he did; he did it with all his soul.[5]

Not only His conscious self-abasement, but His sinless nature enhances the efficacy of His sacrifice for sin. When the New Testament states that Christ "was made sin for us," it is using the language of the Hebrews. This being so, one word signifies sin, sacrifice for sin and expiation of sin. Christ, then, was a sacrifice for sin, for our Saviour was completely sinless or else He would have been unable to render

---

[1] *Ibid.*, pp. 266–268. Cf. Anselm, *Cur Deus Homo?* Bk. II. So close is Whichcote's doctrine of Atonement to Anselm's in its logical method and its emphasis upon rendering "satisfaction" and "honour" to God that Professor Mackintosh's criticism of Anselm's *Cur Deus Homo?* is applicable to our author's view. According to Mackintosh, "...This severely logical procedure provides no real guarantee of truth." *The Person of Christ*, (Edinburg, 1912), p. 408. It may be observed that Whichcote, in his conception of the complete self-abasement of Christ as Reconciler, seems to anticipate the Kenotic Theory of the Incarnation in recent thought. See a criticism of the theory by D. M. Baillie, *Ibid.*, pp. 94–96. Cf. A defence of the theory by Mackintosh, *Ibid.*, pp. 466–467. See also Duthie, pp. 29–31.

[2] *Ibid.*, p. 136.

[3] *Ibid.*, pp. 277–281.

[4] *Ibid.*, pp. 281–282. Here we are reminded of the Kenotic Theory.

[5] *Ibid.*, pp. 283–284. Cf. Milton, *De Doctrina*, pp. 295–316, 328.

satisfaction for sin. It is not His passion itself but the fact that it is a propitiation for sin that is the ground of our comfort. His passion is our justification because it leads to our reconciliation with God.[1]

A sacrifice suffers that which it does not deserve on behalf of others. Therefore Christ's suffering was vicarious, for he suffered in our stead. His suffering was above all others because of His unique and compassionate nature. Accordingly, His suffering was deeply in obedience to God and in compassion for us.[2] God is not responsible for His suffering since He suffered entirely of His own will. He identified Himself with us in His suffering being clothed with our nature and touched with our infirmities and tempted as we are. At the same time, His suffering was in accord with the will of His Father and by it the Father's honor is vindicated. By Christ's suffering, God is portrayed as One Who hates iniquity and Who governs with justice and righteousness. God might have pardoned sin by His power but did not consider this the best way. But He decided that sin should not be pardoned without atonement and that His displeasure concerning man's apostasy should be fully disclosed. Thus God chose Christ, the Person above all persons, One acceptable to Him as a proxy for sinful man as an offering for sin and Christ is permitted to suffer this evil for the establishment of the rule of righteousness.[3] And since Whichcote conceives Christ as equal with God, it would be consistent to add with Brunner:

... In the New Testament the Cross of Christ is conceived as the self-offering of God. It is God who does it, it is God Himself who suffers, it is God who takes the burden upon Himself.[4]

In our author's general conception of the work of Christ his purpose appears to be the wholesome one of demonstrating what he calls the goodness and compassion of God. But Dr. Whale's critical observation on the subject applies here.

Because the "objective" theories [of atonement] represent Christ's death as necessary, not only to man but to God; and because Western soteriology has

---

[1] *Ibid.*, pp. 267–270.

[2] *Ibid.*, p. 371. Cf. Milton, *Paradise Lost, III*, 183–212.

[3] *Ibid.*, pp. 371–374.

[4] *The Mediator*, pp. 482–483. One can only regret that Whichcote does not avail himself of more moving terms than the "goodness" or "compassion" of God in his concept of the Atonement. "Love" and what Anders Nygren calls the "Agape of the Cross" (*Amor crucis*) seems to capture and communicate the full meaning of the suffering love of God for "us men and our salvation" much better. See *Agape and Eros*, tr. by P. S. Watson, (Philadelphia, 1953), pp. 248–279.

used the legal word "Satisfaction" to affirm the holiness of God's love and the eternal oral realities which are implicit in his forgiveness, modern men protest that such a word makes God out to be a capricious Oriental Sultan, a cruel tyrant who arbitrarily demands the suffering and death of an innocent Victim, that the guilty man may be spared his avenging anger.[1]

God is the giver of grace and this grace is what Whichcote calls a "superaddition" to the creation.[2] God as the Author of nature is also the Giver of grace and bestows at once the gifts of nature and grace.[3] God's grace is truly a gift; it is not merited but flows naturally from God's intentions to do us good. Our Saviour came as the fulfilment of God's gracious purpose, to make even more evident the unmerited character of divine grace.[4] Our author defines grace in two ways which are complementary to each other. First, there is *gratia gratum faciens*, the favour of God through which He renders man acceptable to Himself. This is the usual meaning of the term in Scripture and in this sense, God is the Subject of grace while we are only objects. But, secondly, there is *grata gratis data*, or grace freely given by God. This latter concept of grace is the effect of the former and we are the subjects of it in such wise that the same thing which is virtue in us is grace in reference to God.[5] It is in agreement with the last usage of the word grace that the Gospel is often called the Gospel of grace, by virtue of the fact that it results from the goodness of God extended to us. It is significant that by his twofold employment of the concept of grace, Whichcote points to his views concerning justification by faith and by works as well as the agreement between them. Thus his assertion that the same thing which in man the subject, is virtue, is in God the Author, grace is central to his thought.

The work of grace is that of enabling us to do that which we could never do by reliance upon our own strength. With the help of grace, we are more than ourselves and, therefore, when God's grace is at hand

---

[1] Whale, *Ibid.*, pp. 92–94. A concise, yet a worthy view of the atonement is presented by Principal C. S. Duthie, *Ibid.*, p. 33. Anselm's doctrine of the Atonement was opposed by Abelard who offered his moral theory of atonement which is even less acceptable than Anselm's view, See Gustaf Aulén, *Christus Victor*, tr. by A. G. Herbert (London, 1931), pp. 112–113. Cf. E. R. E., I, 16–17. In his emphasis, at once, upon the rational and moral nature of the saving work of Christ, Whichcote combines in his view Anselmic and Abelardian elements. Whatever contradictions there are in this combination may be attributed to our author's anxiety to state a completely intelligible doctrine of the Atonement. Cf. De Pauley, *The Candle of the Lord*, (London, 1937), p. 33. Aulén's work is invaluable as a historical and theological study of the three main types of the idea of the atonement.

[2] Whichcote, *Works*, II, 74.

[3] *Ibid.*, pp. 75–76.

[4] *Ibid.*, pp. 86–88.

[5] *Ibid.*, pp. 204–206.

we should follow its impressions.[1] Grace fortifies and encourages us to come to God, to seek His mercy in spite of our offense. Grace goes before salvation and follows after it. We are here reminded of Pascal's famous assertion "Thou wouldst not be seeking Me hadst thou not found Me." [2] Grace, according to Whichcote, opens up a new and living approach to God which may be employed with great assurance since grace qualifies the subject to receive the benefits of the Gospel. It removes all hindrances such as the guilt contracted by sin.[3] Grace takes the initiative: it has the priority in that it first lays hold upon us without any merit on our part and it is efficacious and effective as it expresses itself in love.[4] And in the strength of grace received, we may fulfil its purpose, for all divine help is sufficient for the act for which it is given.[5] Nygren in his description of the idea of *Agape*, describes it as "groundless" to stress the absence of any extrinsic reason for it. He says

God's love is altogether "spontaneous." It does not look for anything in man that could be adduced as motivation for it. In relation to man, Divine love is "unmotivated." When it is said that God loves man, this is not a judgment on what man is like, but on what God is like.[6]

Indicative of the essentially rational character of Whichcote's thought is his assertion that knowledge of God's self-disclosure in Christ is saving knowledge. He says, "As Sin is a Vitiating the Reason of man! the Restauration must be by the Reason of God,...." [7] Christ becomes for us, wisdom to atone for our unreasonable consent to iniquity.[8] This means that the knowledge of Christ's saving work is of the greatest importance. Further, when one thinks seriously about Christ's atoning work, it brings mental satisfaction by virtue of its sheer reasonableness.

---

[1] *Ibid.*, I, 46–47.

[2] *Pensées* (Steward ed.), "Adversaria," 7.

[3] Whichcote, *Works*, I, 112–113. While Whichcote belongs to the "once-born," his contemporary, John Bunyan, belongs to the "twice-born." The struggle of Bunyan toward conversion, his lack of education, his impressionable temperament and the influence of Puritan Theology upon him make his *Grace Abounding* one of the most marvellous and dramatic accounts of conversion ever written. A comparison of Whichcote's doctrine of grace with Bunyan's is instructive; for much of a man's theology is recorded in his biography, i.e. St. Paul, St. Augustine, Luther, Pascal, Kierkegaard and many others. Cf. William James, *The Varieties of Religious Experience*, (London, 1911), pp. 78–126, 127–165, 189–258; A. D. Nock, *Conversion*, (Oxford, 1933), p. 7. See also M. Hiriyana, *The Essentials of Indian Philosophy* where the notion of salvation by the *prasāda* of *Iśvara* (the grace of God) through *prapatti*; (self-surrender) in the Vaishnava sect of Hinduism is explained (pp. 184–186).

[4] *Ibid.*, pp. 367–368.

[5] *Ibid.*, II, 347–349.

[6] Nygren, *Ibid.*, pp. 75–76.

[7] Whichcote, *Aph.* 1023.

[8] *Works*, II, 138.

The doctrine of the Gospel is a "vital principle." It gives satisfaction to the reason of our mind, removes fears and doubts, brings rest and peace, creates within quietness, composure and comfort. This is vital; for "to live is to be well." We can be sure that through Christ and by repentance, we are pardoned. This is "gospel-knowledge." In the intellectual nature a principle is vital.... We may call the doctrine of the gospel a vital principle, because it satisfies the reason of our mind and brings inner peace.[1]

Whichcote turns next to a consideration of repentance as a precondition of forgiveness. There is no promise of remission of sin without repentance, but we may be assured that repentance is effective if it is done sincerely.[2] But even if repentance were not effective this would not abolish God's claim upon us to humbly acknowledge and obey Him. God's first claim upon us is obedience and His second is repentance. Though the effect of repentance depends upon the Gospel of grace, the obligation to repent is natural and reasonable.[3]

"'Tis true, we are obliged to repent whether God will pardon or not; because we owe duty and obedience to God, as we are his creatures; and if we do not repent, we do, upon account, sin again. For ... whosoever hath done amiss, and doth not repent ... is in such a frame and disposition, that had he the like occasion and temptation offered him, he would do it again. So that both nature and grace do meet here, and shew the indispendable necessity of repentance, in the case of contracted guilt, and a wounded conscience.[4]

If Whichcote adheres to the notion of Total Corruption at all, it is in the sense "that the depravity which sin has produced in human nature 'extends to the whole of it.'" [5] He does not mean that we "are utterly indisposed, disabled and made opposite to all good, and wholly inclined to all evil." [6] Thus he is free, at once, to assert man's freedom and responsibility to repent and to deny that God out of His pleasure and by His irresistible power either elects the sinner to salvation or condemns him to eternal punishment. God made us free moral agents, therefore He does not force us to do anything against our will.[7] It follows that repentance is a free and rational act and it is not true

---

[1] *Ibid.*, III, 74–76. Cf. Aug. *De Trin.*, vii, 3, 5. Augustine says: "... When anything concerning wisdom is declared and narrated in the Scripture, the Son chiefly is intimated to us.
[2] *Ibid.*, I, 7–20.
[3] *Ibid.*, pp. 212–229.
[4] *Ibid.*, pp. 202–204.
[5] *Whale*, Ibid., p. 42.
[6] *Westminster Conf.*, vi, 4, (cited by Whale, *Ibid.*). Cf. Baxter, *Ibid.*, p. 195. Baxter, like Whichcote, while attributing great importance to reason, admits that reason is fallen as the result of sin.
[7] Whichcote, *Works*, I, 27–28. Cf. Milton *De Doctrina*, pp. 44–79.

repentance unless it takes place in this internal and vital sense. True repentance occurs only when a man "loathes sin out of a sense and judgment of the baseness and vileness of it and out of reverence for God." [1] And we have the assurance that through assisting our faculties, we may repent and obtain pardon.[2] There is the further reminder that repentance for sin committed in the past carries with it the resolve to avoid the same sin in the future and to develop a general attitude of obedience to God.

> ... The first motion towards repentance ... is lookt upon as if it were the ... remedy of repentance itself ... as if sorrow for sin were the whole product of repentance, whereas indeed, that which is true repentance must be accompanied with the forsaking of sin and bringing forth the fruits of righteousness.... My caution, therefore, is that you look towards God and your minds serve you to make any application to him; that you pursue that motion till you bring it into a settled state; for otherwise the first motion towards repentance may prove an aggravation of your sin, and heavier condemnation.[3]

Now repentance and faith go together and therefore "no man repents, who does not believe; nor can any believe, who does not repent." This is true by virtue of the fact that repentance is a prerequisite of faith. A man is never in the condition required for a vital act of faith until he repents of sin. Grace encourages our faith just as it leads us to repentance and, therefore, whoever believes and relies upon the goodness of God in Christ is set free from sin.[4] Repentance includes faith and it is impotent without it.[5] Speaking specifically of faith, Whichcote asserts that it includes obedience, in fact, belief and obedience are one.[6] Faith, then, is our free and rational assent to God in Christ. When a man receives any proposition upon God's authority, that is faith. And for this reason, natural knowledge is antecedent and fundamental to faith. His final point is that faith is accompanied and supported by obedience.[7] Here we recall the *credo ut intelligam* of Augustine and Anselm. Whichcote's faith is one seeking to know, to understand and he combines a faithful reason with a reasonable faith. The Gospel proclaims a "saving knowledge" when it states that God saves through

---

[1] *Ibid.*, pp. 262–268.
[2] *Ibid.*, p. 205. Cf. Milton, *Ibid.*, p. 333. See also Arthur Barker, *Milton and the Puritan Dilemma*, (Toronto, 1942), pp. 326–328.
[3] *Ibid.*, p. 190.
[4] *Ibid.*, III, 73–74.
[5] *Ibid.*, p. 83.
[6] *Aph.* 831.
[7] *Works*, III, 134–135.

Christ and that this is accomplished by repentance and faith through the grace of God.[1]

Our final concern in this chapter is to gather from our author's writings a workable understanding of his view of salvation. It is characteristic of Whichcote to be unsystematic and thus he presents ten terms which he conceives as implying alike the single state of salvation. He recognises a difference between these terms only in degree and insists that any attempt to impose an accurate distinction between them is superfluous since Scripture employs them with indifference. The words are: conversion, regeneration, adoption, vocation, sanctification, justification, reconciliation, redemption, salvation and glorification.

... "Regeneration" is used to distinguish the divine and heavenly life from the natural and animal. "Conversion," that imports a runnegate, one that had departed from God, and righteousness, and he is reduced from the practice of iniquity, to his duty to God, "Adoption," that intimates that a man hath broke with God, and parted from him; and here is again the renewal of the former relation to God, he is again made the son of God. "Vocation," that imports the taking a man off from ill usage, and guise of the world. "Sanctification," that imports the renewal of us in the spirit of our minds. "Justification" imports pardon of sin. "Redemption" imports rescuing us from the slavery of the devil. "Salvation" denotes holiness here and happiness hereafter. "Reconciliation" implies peace restored with God, and with our consciences. "Glorification" is a consummation and accomplishment of them all....[2]

It is indeed unfortunate that Whichcote does not give a definitive treatment of these important terms in a more acceptable and comprehensive manner. However, he has singled out a few of them for more detailed treatment and some other insights may be grasped by gathering some of his scattered reflections together. It is clear that conversion is understood by him as a mutual act of God and man. It is a serious

---

[1] *Ibid.*, I, 389. The soundness of Whichcote's view of repentance and faith, together with his assumptions concerning man as a free moral agent free to accept or reject God's offer of Salvation is supported by John Baillie as he opposes Barth's view that man is totally corrupted by sin. Barth adds that the revelation of God has to create its own capacity for reception when it is given. Dr. Baillie observes that what God does in Christ is a miracle not of omnipotence but of grace and that there can be grace only where there is self-acceptance. See *Our Knowledge of God*, p. 24.

We are also reminded of Brunner's concept of *Ansprechbarkeit*, though qualification is in order. See *Natural Theology*, Cf. Baillie, *Ibid.*, Ch. I and Nels F. S. Ferré who refers to the Augustinian–Anselmian *credo ut intelligam* as "revelational irrationalism." He points out that we can overstate the "believe" or the "know" of "I believe in order to know." In the first instance we turn faith into a thin fideism and rob reason of its rightful degree of functional autonomy within experience and in the latter case, we make out of faith a glorified philosophy. He suggests, therefore, that we place emphasis on both parts of the sentence with the stronger emphasis upon "I believe." *Faith and Reason* (London, 1946), pp. 244–245.

[2] *Ibid.*, II, 180–181.

and deliberate act and should not be delayed until sickness or death comes. It is important that conversion take place in the time of youth and health when one is capable of beginning a new way of life and acquiring religious knowledge.[1] We may be assured of the assistance of God's grace to draw us toward conversion and to empower us to carry this act through to its completion, for when one dares to begin a new life by means of grace received, God provides sustaining grace.[2]

Regeneration, or the new birth, is the transformation of the whole inner man. Fallen man is re-created by this act and he is brought to a new obedience to his created principles. This takes place by mental illumination and by man's willingness to be transformed by the grace of God.[3] Whichcote says: "The Regeneration of a Christian is by Superinducing the Divine Spirit upon the Rational; which makes him more than man." [4] Concerning regeneration, he concludes that by creation we are "earthly" but by regeneration we are "heavenly." [5]

Conversion and regeneration flow logically in the more comprehensive concept of reconciliation. God calls us to be reconciled in the name of Christ, according to Whichcote, and though God begins the act, He expects us to respond. God in Christ accomodates Himself to human principles, He addresses man as a person and gives man the capacity by His grace to be reconciled to Himself. God is the active party in the act of reconciliation and He seeks to arouse in us a favourable response to His offer of grace.[6] It follows that this act is acceptable both to God and man. On the one hand, God's honor is maintained, His infinite wisdom and goodness are employed; and on the other, man experiences the good and knows for the first time real blessedness.[7]

... Through this happy work of reconciliation, we come to savour and relish the things of God ... come to adhere to the rule of righteousness as God doth. ... We shall be, in our measure, in our understanding and will, suitable to God, judging as he judgeth.[8]

Any consideration of Whichcote's view of justification by faith must begin with his exegesis of (Phil. 2:12, 13). For Whichcote, imputed and inherent righteousness are of a piece and thus justification is conceived

[1] *Ibid.*, I, 48.
[2] *Ibid.*, pp. 236–238.
[3] *Ibid.*, III, 194.
[4] *Aph.* 855.
[5] *Ibid.*, 1192. Cf. Milton, *Ibid.*, p. 294.
[6] *Works*, II, 341–342.
[7] *Ibid.*, pp. 274–276.
[8] *Ibid.*, p. 362.

as a mutual act of God and man. He observes that the Greek text uses the participle "working." The verb would indicate a single act while the participle continual action. The passage thus interpreted implies that God "is" working in us both "to will and to do" and we are called upon to respond to God's activity. We are to act for God is acting, and where God is active there is sufficient grace to enable us to act.[1] Scripture is here concerned with what God does with us and what we do is ascribed to God. We work and God works, that is, we are awakened, assisted and directed by Him. But this does not imply that we merit salvation since it is impossible for any creature to merit anything from God.[2] Thus our author seeks a middle position between the radical assertion of the Reformers on one hand of justification by faith alone and the Roman Catholic concept of meritorious works.[3]

Whichcote asserts that to be righteous according to the Gospel is to be saved. This is true, notwithstanding certain limitations and imperfections found in the doctrine of the law. If a sinner truly repents and sincerely endeavours to imitate Christ's example, he has eternal life and shall be eternally saved.[4] Holiness could not denote absolute innocence since there is no such person among mortals, but it refers rather to a state of justification in which our sins are forgiven and we are accepted by God through Christ. And we are in this new relationship absolved of all necessity of punishment – that is we are made righteous.[5] Christ is made our righteousness, He is our sanctification and redemption, for by Him God has received satisfaction for our sins and through Him God bestows mercy upon us. It follows that we are justified not by works of righteousness but by the intercession of Christ.[6] Christ stood in our stead and we are looked upon as being in Him. It is appropriate that we should be in relation to Him since He was put in relation to us in His death. In this way we truly love and are accepted by God and righteousness is translated from Him to us. Holiness is bestowed upon us by God's gracious acceptance of us in Christ.

We must remember, however, the distinction between the righteous-

---

[1] *Ibid.*, I, 287–289. Cf. D. M. Baillie's classic statement of this fact in his discussion on what he calls the "paradox of grace," *God Was In Christ*, (New York, 1948), pp. 114–118. Cf. Benjamin Drewery, *Origin and the Doctrine of Grace*, (London, 1960), p. 21.

[2] *Ibid.*, pp. 312–313.

[3] Cf. *Supra*, Ch. III; Infra, Ch. VIII.

[4] Whichcote, *Works*, III, 112.

[5] *Ibid.*, pp. 60–62. Cf. H. R. Mackintosh, *The Christian Experience of Forgiveness*, (Edinburgh, 1912), p. 115.

[6] *Ibid.*, II, 138–139.

ness of Christ and that of a Christian. Though the righteousness of Christ belongs to the Christian, yet it is not the same. Christ is justified by works of righteousness, but the Christian is justified by pardon of sin. To state it differently, Christ is justified by the law of works, while the Christian is justified by faith. We are recommended to God by Christ and have the benefits of His passion and obedience. Christ is made our righteousness by virtue of the fact that he procures grace for us from the throne of grace and thus we are received as in Him and brought into a proper relation to God by Him. This takes place by communication as God communicates the gift of His grace of the Holy Spirit to us by Christ. It is of the greatest importance, then, that we should be found in Christ since our justification is the fruit of His grace in and through His saving work.[1]

The final note sounded here points to our concern in the next chapter. Whichcote assures us that righteousness in Christ does not interfere with but actually heightens our natural inherent righteousness. Reason and conscience, impaired by sin, are restored to their natural perfection. But even more important Whichcote comes remarkably close to the Pauline concept of union with Christ, that justification implies not only the assurance of forgiveness of sin, but as H. R. Mackintosh says:

It is through Christ that he [the Christian] has seen utter mercy in God's face; in Christ, therefore, he beholds fully and persuasively revealed the will of God which he is called to know and obey.[2]

---

[1] *Ibid.*, pp. 378–380. Whichcote comes closer to the notion of "communion" in his use of the word "participation" mainly in connection with his more natural theology than he does here when he speaks of God "communicating" grace to us in Christ. John Baillie rightly points out the inadequacy of the term "communication" in speaking of God's self-disclosure in Christ since God here gives Himself in communion. Cf. *The Idea of Revelation*, p. 47.

[2] Mackintosh, *Ibid.*, pp. 121–122. Cf. Whichcote, *Works*, II, 282–283. Howard in his introduction to Richard Ward's *Life of Henry More*, (London, 1911), p. 7, rightly observes: "Whichcote was suspected of preaching more Platonism than Christianity, but he did not mislead his followers, who strenuously maintained the doctrine of conversion, which implies Evangelicalism. This is indeed the very keynote of their (the Cambridge Platonists) system, death unto sin and a new birth unto righteousness....."

CHAPTER SEVEN

RELIGION OF AFTER-REVELATION (II)

Christian Morals

Whichcote states that social consciousness and responsibility are as much a part of revealed religion as of the natural. The death and resurrection of Christ must be verified in us and this means that we must die to the world, to selfishness and to sensuality.[1] When God calls us to salvation, He calls us from wickedness to holiness. The doctrines of the Gospel must become the "reason of our minds" and the "principles of our life." [2] Christ is a nature, a spirit and life in us, and His "design" is to advance the divine life in men. The fact that Christ condemned sin by His death means that none can be relieved by His death who would justify sin by their lives.[3] Dean Inge who quotes Whichcote in defence of his position asserts that "religion and ethics are, for a Christian, inseparable. There are unethical religions, and there are irreligious ethical schools or societies; but these are not Christian." [4] It appears that Inge has captured precisely Whichcote's position and thus we refer to Whichcote's views here as Christian morality.

Whichcote's favorite New Testament text (Tit. 2:11, 12) is con-

---

[1] Whichcote, *Works*, II, 143–144; I, 380. My use of "Christian morals" as the sub-topic of this chapter is deliberate. There is a rather confused distinction today between "Christian ethics," "Social Ethics" and Christian social ethics." I understand the first as that field of investigation which treats the biblical, theological, historical and philosophical foundations of ethics; the second deals with the physical, psychological and social aspects of Christian ethics; and the third combines all these approaches into one synoptic investigation. Whichcote's interest covers the scope of what we refer to as Christian social ethics, but we would be unjustified in attributing to him this technical point of view. Thus "Christian morals" appears to be a more appropriate caption for our discussion.

[2] *Ibid.*, II, 83; Aph. 94.

[3] *Aphs.* 355, 409, 689, 736.

[4] Inge, *Christian Ethics and Modern Problems*, (London, 1930), p. 379. It appears significant that Dr. C. E. Raven (in a conversation with the present writer) stated that one main influence behind his social concern was an early study of the Cambridge Platonists.

sidered by him as a summary of all "necessary divinity." [1] This text is the basis of his treatment of both natural and Christian morality. If the question is raised as to the difference between them, Whichcote's answer is that the difference is one of degree rather than kind.

That is to say, as a result of the "super-additions" of the Gospel, the principles of natural morality are "heightened" and developed. This answer can only be consistent, however, if we can conceive of a man as "naturally" attaining the height of his natural possibilities as Which-cote understands them. Thus Whichcote is forced to admit that man is a fallen and sinful creature, and for this reason the Gospel not only "adds" but "restores" and to this extent the notion of Christian morality does not only imply a quantitative but also a qualitative advance over mere natural morality as it stands. It is perhaps with this insight in mind that Whichcote seeks to root all his ethics in Scripture, using the ideas of Plato and other philosophers to illustrate what he finds there. The promise of God in Christ he considers to be a new principle of action in that it carries us beyond our natural possibilities. It restores the image of God in us and by it we partake of the divine nature. This new nature consists of knowledge first and then goodness, for without knowledge the heart cannot be good. It is "unnatural" to have this knowledge without obedience to Christ, for this is "holding the truth in unrighteousness" – "sin against the light." The very knowledge of Christ is saving knowledge bringing us to a holy life. His doctrine transcends all principles of natural morality and religion.[2] Christians are to remember that the "moral part" of Christianity is just as binding as the "instituted part." [3] Whichcote seems to believe that the moral part of Christianity is the more binding inasmuch as righteousness, equity and piety are the foundation of all religion.

These things are of certainty to all the world. Whereas ... other things in revealed religion (as these) the immortality of reasonable souls; future rewards and punishments; God pardoning sin to all those who repent; divine aid and assistance, as it is declared in the gospel .... these the famous philosophers did only hope they were true; but they were not assured of them. But of all the other things they were undoubtedly assured. We indeed have extraordinary assurance; because we have the gospel-revelation, they are certain to us Christians: but they were but hope, and fair persuasions, and belief to the philosophers, who had no scripture.... But in the other points, we have the happy harmony of the world; it is the language of every one's thoughts; it is nature's sense that these things are so.

---

[1] Whichcote, *Works*, II, 133–134.
[2] *Ibid.*, pp. 134–136.
[3] *Ibid.*, pp. 231–232, 236.

These are things of general obligation, and universal acknowledgement; for they bear a true and even proportion to the common reason of mankind.[1]

But lest we should as Christians, dismiss morals as mere "heathenish" virtues, Whichcote reminds us that they are "necessities." It is a serious mistake to oppose reason to faith and consequently morality to religion. Moral principles are an essential aspect of our Christian commitment. The Christian must seek to "know" as well as "believe" and this knowledge binds the Christian to all principles of religion, those "connatural" to our make and those that are final in Christ.[2] The man beginning the Christian life should not be led to despair by the moral responsibilities involved, for grace will always be at hand to aid him. We must be willing to begin well with the assurance that grace to promote and consummate our life will be added.[3]

A genuine Christian, by the grace of God, is enabled to excel in all natural virtues. A man becomes refined and reformed in nature as he advances in the Christian faith.[4] The Gospel inclines us toward a constant reverence for God, and an obedient and trustful attitude toward Him and through the assistance of grace, we are both able and willing to fulfill our moral and religious obligations. The principles of the Christian religion control, at once, external intemperance and inner motives, so that the Christ-like man seeks to do the will of God as it is made known in Christ.

Through his "participation" of Christ, his "temper" becomes meek, patient and gentle. It is by faith in Christ that we win a victory over the world and apprehend things invisible to reason and sense. Faith, which Whichcote implies to be supra-rational knowledge, illuminates the most important things of our Christian life, and for this reason we should resolve to allow faith to govern our lives. In this way, things of the future will become actual for us in the present.[5] The spirit of the Gospel transforms the Christian's attitude of life. He takes Christ as He is, as "king to rule and govern, as a prophet to instruct, and as a

---

[1] *Ibid.*, pp. 239–240. With this intense emphasis on the "moral part" of Christianity by Whichcote it is little wonder that the statesman-philosopher Shaftesbury, a luke-warm Christian, believing merely in "religion by state established," should find in Whichcote's writings the basis of a "benevolent" society without accepting Whichcote's deep spirituality.

[2] *Ibid.*, pp. 241–242.

[3] *Ibid.*, pp. 34–35; *Ibid.*, III, 66–71.

[4] *Ibid.*, III, 48.

[5] *Ibid.*, p. 79. Here Whichcote's Johannine position is manifest. The note sounded forth in the Fourth Gospel is that to know God in Christ is eternal life and eternal life conceived as qualitative rather than "temporal" begins when salvation begins. Cf. C. H. Dodd, *Gospel and Law*, (New York, 1951), pp. 31–32 and Joseph Fletcher, *William Temple: Twentieth-Century Christian* (New York, 1963), pp. 29, 302–303 (n. 75).

saviour to save." [1] In defence of his conception of Christian morality, Whichcote says:

.... We may gather how little they understand themselves, who in divinity, "decry morality," or that are impatient to hear it, and say that it doth not belong to "Christ." But I have the candor, as to think that they do not understand the terms, but that they mean some external ornament; that which is called "civility"; such a thing as doth not die....; such a thing as doth not establish a frame, and temper, a constitution of mind; such a thing as doth not make a man deiform, or restore a man to the image of God and make him really God-like. But now these principles of morality are those that do, and nothing else can do it; yea, these are final, and ultimate to all the doctrine of Christ to all matters of faith, and the principles thereof, if they do not finally end in all moral goodness and righteousness. For these do import the fullest "imitation of God," and the exactest "participation" of the divine nature.... This is the gospel obtaining in effect; and in the ultimate issue, this is to have "Christ formed in us"; and the gospel in its final accomplishment.... These are the principles of everlasting righteousness, of unchangeable truth and goodness: and of this I may say that it is not a law that is subject to any power whatsoever: it is a law of its "own nature"; it is that which is according to the nature of God; and that is the law of heaven.[2]

In order to put on Christ one must put off oneself since the image of Christ is self-denial. Christ became a servant for us and a servant is one who parts with his own will.

It is for this reason that one who imitates Christ must live in entire self-surrender. The true Christian is necessarily humble in view of his awareness of his imperfections and his dependence upon God. Where there is most of God, there is the least of self and in this way faith testifies to humility.[3] A truly religious man is humble in the face of his need for further growth.

He that is in a good state has still work to do to free his Understanding from Ignorance and Error, and to advance his knowledge of Truth to a just Height; to work-out perfectly the habit of sin and to work-in perfectly the habits of goodness.[4]

Reformation of life must begin within, by the renewal of the mind, before action may be redirected.[5] Intellectual calmness and proper

---

[1] *Ibid.*, p. 82.

[2] *Ibid.*, II, 60–62. This passage might well be Whichcote's answer to Tuckney's accusation that this view of Reconciliation consisted of "inherent righteousness" with a little of Christ added. Here Whichcote places Christian morality at the heart of his Christology. Cudworth's *Sermon before the House of Commons*, (New York, 1930) is almost a perfect copy of Whichcote's views on this subject. Cf. *Infra*, Ch. IX and see, Joseph Beyer's entire work, *Ralph Cudworth als Ethiker Staats-Philosoph und Aesthetiker und Grund der Bedruckten Schriften*, inaug. diss. (Bonn, 1935).

[3] *Ibid.*, I, 340–361.

[4] *Aph.* 564.

[5] *Works*, 1, 257.

self-control are of the greatest importance to the good life. The man who does not reverence himself, his own nature and dignity, will not have due honor for God and his fellows.[1] Reverence for self and God are so interrelated that Christian morals begin with the reformation of the inward man.[2] The heart is the principle of action, it is where life begins, it is the centre of motion. The greatest responsibility we have is that of regulating our mind and spirit in order to properly direct our actions and lives.[3] The actions of the good life proceed from the heart and only the "pure in heart shall see God." [4]

In his appeal to our "self-interest" as preceding the proper reverence for God and the proper attitude towards others, Whichcote appears somewhat to anticipate Butler's concept of "self-love." [5] But what seems more important is the insight he has that if a man does not have the proper reverence and respect for himself he readily perverts all ethical and religious ideals.

For example, the Golden Rule presupposes self-respect, for even this rule employed by one without reverence for his own nature and dignity, might easily prove more harmful than good. Whichcote, however, is aware that selfishness is at the root of sin and the danger for man is that he may become too fond of himself. What he calls for here is the wholesome love of self which is not turned in upon itself but finds its fulfillment in God and others. Butler's reflections on the subject of "self-love" would appear to be a valuable supplement to what is implied by Whichcote's notion of reverence for self. Knudson puts it this way, "it is the divine sanctity of the human soul that imposes the obligation of love upon us, and this obligation applies to ourselves as well as to others." [6]

Virtue, when used in reference to Christian morals implies what Whichcote describes as Christian "graces" or the "fruits" of the Spirit. Accordingly grace conferred upon us and the fruits of the Spirit constitute Christian virtue. The same thing which is called grace as proceeding from God is known as virtue in us. We are not to oppose virtue to grace since grace received in us becomes virtue or moral perfection.[7]

[1] *Ibid.*, p. 179, II, 398–399.
[2] *Ibid.*, I, 282.
[3] *Ibid.*, IV, 78–79.
[4] Cf. Matt. 5:8.
[5] See *Infra*, Ch. X; Cf. Joseph Butler, *Sermons*, 4th ed. (London, 1749), *Sers.* i, xi. See also, Baxter, *The Reasons of the Christian Religion*, (London 1667), pp. 90–92.
[6] *The Principles of Christian Ethics*, (New York, 1943), p. 178.
[7] Whichcote, *Works*, IV, 121–131. Cf. *Supra*, Ch. V.

Since we have dealt with Whichcote's concepts of justice and equality elsewhere,[1] we need mention them here only in relation to his view of mercy. He asserts that equity makes allowance in view of circumstances, but mercy goes beyond this. Mercy is manifest when a person does more than can reasonably be expected. As Christians we are called upon to "walk the second mile," to "love our enemies" and this implies that we are not only to "do justly" but to "love mercy" also.

The Gospel itself is a revelation of God's mercy to us sinful men.[2] A Christian, then, is to acknowledge the intrinsic and universal validity of justice and equity but he is at the same time to "love mercy." Mercifulness should normally and logically follow our acknowledgement of Christ's saving work. Because God extends His mercy to us in Christ and God in Christ speaks the words of forgiveness to us, we are to extend the same mercifulness to our fellows since Christ died as a sacrifice for all men.[3] This is part, at least, of the answer Whichcote gives to the searching question of our Lord to all Christians: "What do you more than others?" [4] This is one significant instance where Whichcote in his treatment of Christian morals takes us beyond the attainment of natural goodness.

By purity, Whichcote understands holiness. The holy life is a twofold obligation for Christians, for this demand is made upon us by the principles of creation and the purpose of Christ's redemption. His view of holiness is at the center of what Whichcote means by the very state of religion. Holiness involves the health of our minds as well as the divine life of the soul. It is the ultimate issue, the end of all institutions and ceremonies in religion. Holiness is a process of inwardly renewing, sanctifying and reconciling men to the nature, mind and will of God. A man receives the grace of God in vain if there is no evidence of holiness. In fact, the main objective of all religious acts is to produce holiness in us; for it is God's greatest concern to make us holy. Holiness is our resemblance to God and our participation in Him as far as we are capable. It is also in keeping with our status and dignity as men, our relation to God and our adoption by His grace. Holiness is the real truth and substance of our faith since beatitude belongs only to those who attain the real effects of holiness.[5] Only men with holy hearts and

---

[1] *Supra*, Ch. V.

[2] *Works*, IV, 14–31; Cf. Matt. 18:34, 35.

[3] *Ibid.*, pp. 31–47.

[4] Matt. 5:7.

[5] Works, *Ibid.*, pp. 77–83. Whichcote significantly distinguishes between "relative" and "real" holiness. The former is arbitrary and changeable; the latter is a participation of and

lives are capable of judging "holy doctrines and things." Holiness of life is even a pre-condition of clear revelation from God concerning His mind and will. But Whichcote does not imply by holy living a personal perfectionism. He is aware of the fallibility of man and the need for growth in goodness.[1]

Neither does he mean an ascetic life. The Christian is a pilgrim on earth, a citizen of heaven; yet he must live in the world though not of it. It follows that the holy life involves social concern. This is a necessary presupposition of the holy life. We are to deal with others with the same love with which God deals with us. If we have in our souls a true sense of God's goodness to us, it will form us into a like disposition of kindness towards men.[2] The Christian religion was given by God for the good of men, individually and socially. Whichcote says:

Did "Christians" live "according-to" their Religion; "They" would do nothing but what Truth, Righteousness and Goodness do; according to their Understanding and Ability: and then one man would be "God" unto another.[3]

Concerning the proper attitude toward material wealth, Whichcote has for us some valuable suggestions attested to by his own life. He asserts that it is neither a virtue to be poor nor a sin to be rich. It is sinful to use riches out of pride and for luxury rather than as an instrument of virtue. On the other hand, it is a mistake to think that poverty is a state of perfection or in any way meritorious; for we are not approved or disapproved by God either by poverty or riches. Since Whichcote was wealthy all his life, perhaps he has worked out an apology for the rich in view of the radical challenges to the rich in the ethics of Jesus. On the other hand, perhaps he has in mind the vow of poverty of the Roman Church with the claim of merit for those who take it. Whatever the motive behind his general position it appears to be a commendable view in intention.

Whichcote asks, how is it that some men are so rich, while others are extremely poor? His answer is that the distribution of worldly goods does not belong to the Kingdom of Christ. Possessions come by

resemblance to God. Relative holiness implies the use of things for holy or sacred purposes, but real holiness refers to "deiformity" or God-likeness in hearts and lives. Cf.*Ibid.*, pp. 57–58, 264; *Aph.* 285.

[1] Whichcote appears not to be bound by what Reinhold Niebuhr describes as the source of "perfectionist illusions," viz., the "Hellenic spirit," see *The Nature and Destiny of Man*, (London, 1941–43), II, 134–135. R. N. Flew, *The Idea of Perfection in Christian Theology*, (London, 1934) pp. 92–117, 151–157, 206, 244–257.

[2] *Ibid.*, pp. 174–176.

[3] Cf. J. C. Bennett, *Christian Ethics and Social Policy*, (New York, 1956) pp. 4–9.

inheritance and the like and thus the right of property is based on nature rather than grace.[1] It follows that there is no connection between a man's prosperity here and his happiness in the future life since the providence of God which governs the world and the Kingdom of Christ does not determine worldly prosperity. Happiness which comes from Christ has nothing to do with the distribution of earthly goods. Earthly goods tend to bring either happiness or misery according to their use. Thus a man should be a good steward of his earthly possessions, but he should never become a slave to them. His real concern should be to lay hold upon those things which bring true happiness.[2] Whichcote, however, appears to weaken and even contradict this position elsewhere. He asserts that there is a different "disposition" of providence as to "men's estate and affairs" which may be explained by God's sovereignty and "good pleasure." Further, he suggests that it is commendable to comply with the necessity of one's condition, in other words, to submit to the inevitable with complete resignation.[3] He cannot have it both ways, either providence is involved in the distribution of wealth or it is not. It appears that in this latter assertion, Whichcote without meaning to do so, gives a religious cloak to the oppressor of the poor and at the same time, deals a deadly blow to the disinherited. Being a wealthy man himself, it was quite easy for him to accept this "lot" with resignation. In view of his good-nature and wholesome life purpose, he easily found opportunities to do good. But it is more difficult with the same natural gifts and convictions to live the good life when one has not the means to procure even the necessities of life to say nothing of helping others. Such a poverty-ridden person is not likely to receive much comfort from Whichcote's assertion that his "lot" is the will of God. There is a real question as to whether Whichcote himself would have found this position acceptable had his condition been reversed. It appears that Whichcote's intention throughout is commendable, but I would consider his latter assertion untenable and dangerous by implication.

---

[1] *Ibid.*, p. 274.

[2] *Ibid.*, p. 322; Cf. *Ibid.*, pp. 275, 325–326.

[3] *Ibid.*, pp. 269–270. For an assessment of the impact of Stoicism upon Christian ethics, see W. L. Bradley, *The Meaning of Christian Values Today*, (Philadelphia, 1964), p. 82. Whichcote's advice, however, is difficult for a man without economic means. One needs a reasonable amount of wealth for self-respect and meaningful existence and service. The ancient Indian classic on Statescraft, Kauṭilya's *Arthaśāstra* while elevating wealth (*artha*) above enjoyment (*kama*) and duty (*dharma*) has considered an important matter. Without a reasonable amount of *artha*, conscience is seared and the moral imperative is paralyzed. For the Christian, however, earthly possessions may never be more than means - never the chief end of life, see my, "Majoring in Minors," *Link*, vol. 20, no. 9 (September, 1962), pp. 5–8.

The final statement concerning earthly wealth is essentially Christian. For Whichcote a man may be said to love all for Christ when he places loyalty to Christ above his estate. This means that we should put our ultimate trust in Christ rather than in our possessions and that we should retain them only so long as they do not interfere with our Christian commitment. We are to acknowledge God as the ultimate owner of all and act merely as stewards of our possession.[1]

> When we love less our estates, than our interest in God and his favor; less value the accommodations of this state, than the future; and subordinate all to the honor of God and to the public good, considering ourselves but stewards in respect to God, we have the proper attitude towards this world's goods.[2]

Those who acknowledge God and pray for help are not alone in the struggle for goodness, they are assisted by the Spirit and instructed concerning the good life. Accompanying this knowledge, the effects of holiness and goodness are experienced. Divine assistance is always available to those who are sincerely honest.

> The Spirit of God in us is a living law, Informing the Soul; not Constrained by a Law without, that enlivens not; but we act in the Power of an inward Principle of Life, which enables, inclines, facilitates, determines. Our Nature is reconciled to the Law of Heaven, the Rule of Everlasting Righteousness, Goodness and Truth.[3]

But it is important to have the correct view of the Holy Spirit; for He is not a "third rule" distinct from Reason and Scripture. The Spirit adds only assistance to Reason and Scripture which are together the "whole" Revelation of the Spirit.[4] The Spirit in us is Reason illuminated by the written Word and the Spirit now teaches by these Writings.[5] To assure us of the truth of the Scriptures we have "the inward work of the Holy Spirit, bearing witness by and with the word in our hearts," [6] but this witness is always "by and with," never independent of, the Word.[7] Thus having the Spirit, being guided by

---

[1] *Ibid.*, II, 149–150.
[2] *Ibid.*, pp. 151–153. When Shaftesbury speaks of a wholesome type of religion which supports and heightens man's natural benevolence, he might well have had in mind the religion envisioned by Whichcote, Cf. *Infra*, Ch. X. See also, V. G. Stanley "Shaftesbury's Philosophy of Religion and Morals." A study in Enthusiasm," unpub. diss. Columbia University, 1961; Alfred Sternbeck, "Shaftesbury *Über Natur, Gott und Religion*, inaug. diss. (Berlin, 1904).
[3] *Aph.* 625. Cf. *Works*, III, 57; II, 142.
[4] *Ibid.*, 920.
[5] *Ibid.*, 337.
[6] *The Westminster Confession*, Ch. i, 5, cited by John Baillie, *Idea of Revelation in Recent Thought* (London, 1956), p. 117.
[7] Baillie, *Ibid.*

the Spirit, led by the Spirit, and following the Spirit, all mean the same thing. These phrases imply the necessity of following the plain doctrine of the apostles who were inspired with and spoke by the Holy Spirit. The Spirit inspired them because they lived under His direction. It follows that we who receive words from those who were under the guidance of the Spirit are led by the Spirit speaking through them to us.[1] It seems obvious that Whichcote is attempting to counteract the irrationalism and even the immorality associated with the erroneous conception of the work of the Spirit.[2]

... God sends not his truth into the world alone and unaccompanied, but having done one thing, will also do another to make the former effectual. Now they that have not the divine spirit, want the great interpreter upon the words of God, the great commentator upon divine truth in the world; and therefore their minds are left unsatisfied and unresolved. And therefore let such men look after it. For this is a great and certain truth, that God, in his grace and goodness, will give his spirit to guide, and teach, and assure the minds of good men; tho' none know it but those that feel it. But they who have the spirit of God, know nothing more certain; for they have satisfaction, inward peace, and joy in believing; they perceive such operations of God in themselves, whereof the world cannot receive any account. The divine spirit doth open their understandings, as it did the apostles; brings things to their remembrance; makes them consider the inwards of things, and calls them to advertency and consideration. The great work of the divine spirit is to lead men in the right apprehensions, and stay a man's thoughts in consideration, till the principles do receive admittance, and become a temper and constitution; till they infuse and instill themselves, and make a lasting impression.[3]

Whichcote's doctrine of Christian morals is closely dependent on his doctrine of last things which leads us to a consideration of his view of the relation of time to eternity. He asserts that unused time is lost and that the virtue of time consists in the use of it. The best em-

---

[1] Whichcote, *Works*, II, 82–84. Cf. Baillie, *Ibid.*, p. iii. Baxter obviously has in mind the Quakers with other similar groups. See, G. F. Nuttall, *Studies in Christian Enthusiasm*, (Wallingford, Pa., 1948), pp. 23–24 and Hugh Barbour, *The Quakers in Puritan England*, (New Haven, 1964), pp. 94–99.

[2] Cf. Henry More, "Grand Mystery of Godliness," *Theological Works*, ed. by Joseph Downing (London, 1708) bl. X, Ch. xiii, p. 533. According to Richard Baxter, the Quakers made the "inner light" a sufficient rule. They made much of the "dwelling" and working of the Spirit in us, but little of justification and pardon of sin and our reconciliation with God through Jesus Christ. They pretended to depend on the Spirit's conduct, against set times of prayer and against sacraments, and against due esteem of Scripture and the ministry and would not have the Scripture called the Word of God. See *Autobiography*, ed. by J. M. L. Thomas (London, 1931), pp. 72–74. Against this background we can understand Whichcote's treatment of the Spirit in defence of "sober piety and rational religion." Baxter obviously has in mind the Quakers with other similar groups. See, G. F. Muttall, *Studies in Christian Enthusiasm*, (Wallingford, Pa., 1948), pp. 23–24 and Hugh Barbour, *The Quakers in Puritan England*, (New Haven, 1964), pp. 94–99.

[3] Whichcote, *Ibid.*, III, 55–56.

ployment of time is toward reconciliation with God.[1] The good life is
not attained at once but is the result of continual moral and spiritual
growth. It is for this reason that one should not wait until the time of
sickness, old age or death to seek reconciliation with God.[2] However,
if a person fails to turn to God early in life, he should seek to make
up for his previous negligence when he does turn. In view of the fact
that we cannot erase our past we should be the more anxious to
redeem the time that remains with the hope that this may compensate
for the whole span of life.[3] Time is conceived by Whichcote mainly as a
scene of good work for God and men, or a preparatory state for eternity.[4]

In the present state, we have every opportunity to achieve this end.
Youth is the time of our greatest physical strength which with divine
help may be directed to good ends and thus it is the best time to become
concerned about religion.[5] Time has considerable value as a "day of
grace" or a "probation state." It also follows that we may by the refusal or abuse of grace undo ourselves in time for eternity.[6]

We must always bear in mind the uncertainty of time upon which
the immortal soul depends.[7] We must be aware of the deceptive nature
of appearances, which parade as realities in the present life.[8] Time
according to Whichcote has no intrinsic value but derives its value
from its relation to eternity. It is in reference to eternity, to the immortal existence and welfare of the soul that every instance of time
takes upon itself a note of urgency. It would appear that Whichcote
is influenced by Plato's concept of time as "the moving image of
eternity" and thus eternity is what really matters. Time is subordinated to eternity just as body is to the soul and it follows that the
main work to be done in time is preparation for eternity.[9] Entrance
into eternal blessedness is based upon the proper temper of mind,

---

[1] *Ibid.*, I, 51–52.
[2] *Ibid.*, pp. 53–54.
[3] *Ibid.*, pp. 54–55. Cf. *Aph.* 1068, 1094.
[4] *Ibid.*, pp. 49–50.
[5] *Ibid.*, p. 51.
[6] *Ibid.*, pp. 262–270. Theologically Whichcote's view is rooted in the Fourth Gospel.
Philosophically we are reminded of Bergson's concept of time as "duration" rather than
"space-time" or time conceived as spiritualistic and qualitative rather than materialistic
and quantitative. Cf. Maritain, *Redeeming the Time*, (London, 1946), pp. 48–50 and my
article "Bergson as a Metaphysical, Epistemological and Religious Thinker," J. R. T., Vol.
XX, No. 2 (1963–1964), p. 108.
[7] *Ibid.*, p. 279.
[8] *Ibid.*, pp. 280–282.
[9] *Ibid.*, pp. 324–326. Cf. *Ibid.*, pp. 35–36. Muirhead, *The Platonic Tradition in Anglo-Saxon
Philosophy*, p. 418. See also Bishop Joseph Butler, "Analogy," *Works*, ed. by J. H. Bernard,
new ed. (London, 1900), vol. II. pt. I, chs. IV, V, pp. 68–99.

relation to temporal things and reconciliation with fundamental moral and religious truths.[1]

The Christian is called upon to behave as a citizen of heaven. He lives in this world under the law of heaven and though his body is present here, yet his soul is in heaven. Being a citizen of heaven, heaven becomes the purpose and rule of his life.[2] A Christian is to subordinate all things of this life to his preparation for heaven.[3] The rule of heaven is most suitable to be law here below and all things below should resemble things above. In Platonic language Whichcote asserts that things above are to be conceived as the "purest form" of which things here should be "a copy." The understanding when it becomes the thing understood, *modo spirituali*, is formed by the "images" of things represented and our souls become like that to which they are related. God made man in the "middle" between immortal and mortal nature. By motion upwards we contemplate God and are transformed into His image but by motion downwards we lose ourselves. These facts indicate our probation-state and point up the importance of our choice.[4]

Our "conversation" is in heaven, *analogice secundum materiam*, in regard to the quality of our actions and life. Our employment as well as our happiness are the same here and hereafter.[5] Heaven as an object to God, while heaven in the subject is our likeness to God. Thus to be happy we must enjoy God by vision and choice. We experience heaven when God becomes our all in all. If God is our all we are heavenly; for heaven is God's all and heaven and God are for us best of all. Thus the "state of grace" in the present and the "state of glory" in the future differ only in degree. The "Kingdom of grace" is the "kingdom of heaven" and the Kingdom of God is, indeed, within. It is

---

[1] *Ibid.*, p. 55. To use Ferré's convenient treatment of time appears valuable here. He understands the problems of "time" in terms of the *kronos*, or mere succession; *logos*, or meaning; and *kairos*, or concrete or filled time. For Whichcote time is conceived as *kronos*, but mainly as *logos* and *kairos*, as meaning and content. Cf. Ferré, *The Christian Understanding of God*, (London, 1952), pp. 79–81. See also, Cullman, *Christ and Time*, tr. by F. V. Filson (London, 1952), pp. 39–41. There appears to be no suggestion by Whichcote concerning Christ as the centre of time as presented by Cullmann. However, Whichcote's view is firmly rooted in the New Testament in spite of his Platonic leanings. He appears to anticipate, though faintly, something of the "realised" "eschatology" of C. H. Dodd, *Ibid.* For Tillich *chronos* is "formal time," while *kairos* is "the right time," the moment rich in content and significance, see *The Protestant Era*, tr. by J. L. Adams, (Chicago, 1951), p. 33.

[2] *Ibid.*, II, 154–155.

[3] *Ibid.*, p. 155, Cf. *Aph.* 818.

[4] *Ibid.*, pp. 160–161.

[5] *Ibid.*, p. 165.

within by virtue of the fact that it begins in grace and ends in glory.[1]

Heaven is known in two ways, as a state and as a place. Heaven as a state, Whichcote calls "heaven moral" or heaven in a moral sense, while heaven as place, is designated by him as "heaven local." The former may be experienced now, while the latter is "the .... place where all the blessed are entertained, and shall be entertained hereafter." By way of contrast, "hell moral" is a state of wickedness and impurity and "hell local" is a place of imprisonment, where "damned spirits" are confined. Thus both hell and heaven are states experienced in the present. Whichcote hesitates to seek further description of heaven or hell as places since they are "things we have not seen." It is for this reason that he lays stress on heaven and hell as states instead of places. We will have more to say concerning his view on this subject later, but now we are mainly concerned with his notion of heaven as a quality of life. As far as the place is concerned, he is of the opinion that the state of one's life necessarily determines the place. The real point is, we have here and now the opportunity to determine our state. To use Pauline language as Christians we are properly citizens of heaven and pilgrims and sojourners on earth.[2]

Our preparation for the state of heaven moral involves contempt for this world (understood as wickedness), but not for the created order, which is for Whichcote the medium of natural revelation. Heaven consists in the mortification of the body in the "state of humiliation" but not the body our souls shall be clothed with, namely a spiritual body. Whichcote is aware that he parts company with the philosophers at this point; for he is consciously Pauline.[3] He insists that Christian faith involves the assurance that the "form" of this earthly body shall be changed. This is a significant point where Whichcote's Christian convictions lead him beyond Platonism. But here we are mainly concerned with his assertion that in order to be capable of entering heaven, we must be born anew by regeneration and participate in the divine nature.

He asserts that there is a descent from above and an ascent from below by several degrees and every higher degree of perfection is "predominant" to that beneath it, includes the lower degree and rules over it.

[1] *Ibid.*, p. 167; Cf. Milton, *De Doctrina Christiana*, tr. by C. Summer, pp. 398–399. (Cambridge, England, 1825).

[2] *Ibid.*, pp. 156–157. Cf. *Aph.* 216 – "It is impossible for a man to be made Happy, by putting him in a Happy 'place'; unless he be in a Happy 'State'."

[3] Cor. 15:35–58. Cf. Krister Stendahl, ed. *Immortality and Resurrection*, (New York, 1965). Stendahl introduces the biblical approach of Oscar Cullman and Henry J. Cadbury in contradistinction to the Greek outlook of Harry A. Wolfson and Werner Jaeger on the future life. See also, Michael Fixler, *Milton and the Kingdoms of God*, (London, 1964), p. 219.

There are, then, four degrees of life, namely, the vegetative – the life of plants; the sensitive – the life of animals; the rational – the life of angels and men; and, the divine – the life of regeneration or the life of eternity. It is only by the life of eternity that we are prepared for heaven; for there can be no experience of heaven unless our wills are surrendered to God. There can be no citizenship in heaven as long as we contest with the Lord of heaven. Our wills are too feeble ultimately to prevail against the irresistible will of God. Of this act of self-surrender, essential to the heavenly state, our Saviour is a perfect example. He illustrates the truth of the creature-state, namely, that we are to be regulated by the will of God.[1]

Entrance into heaven is not at the hour of death, but at the moment of conversion. Salvation is not "wholly to come" but is already begun. Christ brought salvation with Him at His first coming, and, therefore, at His second coming, He will not begin a new thing, but will complete a thing of which the foundation has been laid in time. Here in this world is the "salvation of grace" which is the same thing as the "salvation of glory." In the world to come things are "carried on" which are "set on foot" here and thus a man is in a heavenly state when he comes to know, love and obey God.[2] No man who lives without God need expect to experience heaven. Heaven is where God is all in all. Those who live at present without God have no knowledge of His ways, no reconciliation with Him and no delight in Him.

God has no "negative" heaven for those interested only in escaping "torment" and who refuse the responsibility of the divine life.[3]

Heaven present is our resemblance and imitation of God; and holiness.... Heaven is rectitude, goodness of temper, health, strength of constitution, a God-like frame and temper of mind; consequently, it speaks of ease, pleasure, content and satisfaction....[4]

Whichcote's emphasis upon the future life as determining the course of the present gives religion a significant place in the ordering of life here and now. Religion for Whichcote is much more than a mere profession, it is reasonable, has transforming power and produces "fruits" in our experience. For Whichcote as for Bergson in his *Les Deux Sources de la Morale et de la Religion*, religion is dynamic rather

[1] Whichcote, *Ibid.*, pp. 173–185.
[2] *Ibid.*, pp. 194–195. Cf. *Aphs.* 368, 818.
[3] *Ibid.*, pp. 196–198. Cf. *Aph.* 290 – "We must now 'Naturalise' ourselves to the Employment of Eternity."
[4] *Ibid.*, p. 196; Cf. W. H. Rigg, *The Fourth Gospel and Its Message Today*, (London, 1952), Ch. III.

than static, it is the *élan vital* in man's earthly life. Although he refuses to give up the notion of heaven as a place, his obvious stress upon heaven as moral, as the divine life is of great value. This prepares the way for a vital and lasting view of eternal life even if his conception of the physical world in terms of three stories is no longer tenable. Perhaps the New Science with its modified view of the physical universe had begun to have a telling effect upon Whichcote and though he has faint hints concerning heaven as a place, he regards heaven as a quality of life.[1] Thus Whichcote's notion that salvation begins in the present and is consummated in the future is of tremendous importance for present Christian life and thought.

Whichcote appears to anticipate much modern theological discussion concerning the Now and the Not Yet or the fact that Christ has come and is to come.

This idea ran through the ecumenical meeting of the World Council of Churches at Evanston in 1954.[2] Whichcote anticipates Cullmann's position that the coming of Christ, His saving work, is decisive for the entire line of revelation henceforth.[3] For Whichcote time is Hebraic or linear rather than Greek or cyclical and eternity appears to be quite close to Cullmann's "endless time." [4] But Whichcote's main position, though making use of Pauline and Platonic concepts, is essentially Johannine. That is to say, his central purpose appears to be a description of the divine life or eternal life as a quality of life which is everlasting. In this sense a man becomes, by virtue of his relation to Christ, a permanent citizen of heaven and thus eternal life is for Whichcote relational rather than merely durational.

To live one's life against the background of eternity, meditation and prayer are necessities. Thus Whichcote reminded Tuckney that he had spent more time meditating than reading.[5] Whichcote cautions us

---

[1] We should bear in mind that Whichcote is most probably following the suggestion of the Fourth Gospel. Thus he has the advantage of having his view of eternal life grounded in the New Testament. A similar view is held by Westcott and Maurice, see W. R. Inge, *Platonic Tradition, in English Religious Thought* pp. 103–104. Cf. H. Richard Niebuhr, *Christ and Culture*, (London, 1952), pp. 197–199, 218–219, Westcott, *The Gospel According to St. John*, p. 87.

[2] Cf. Brunner, *Eternal Hope*, tr. H. Knight (London, 1954), pp. 90–92. "The Message of the Second Assembly of the World Council of Churches, Evanston, 1954," C.C., vol. lxxl, no. 38 (September 22, 1954), p. 1123. Evanston, 1954, C. C., vol. LXXI, No. 38, (September 22, 1954), p. 1123.

[3] Cullman, *Ibid.*, p. 59.

[4] *Ibid.*, p. 45–46.

[5] Cf. *Supra*, Ch. III. Georges Florovsky, "Saint Gregory Palamas and the Tradition of the Fathers," G.O.E.R. Vol. V, No. 2 (Winter, 1959–1960). There Florovsky presents the conviction of the Greek Fathers concerning the ultimate aim of human existence. Man remains

that unless we take ourselves out of the world, we are liable to lose ourselves in it. A man's spiritual capacities are rendered insensitive by our over-indulgence in the things of this life. At this point Whichcote's mysticism asserts itself. He points out that when the mind reflects upon God as object, it is fully occupied.[1] This is the way to put the soul into "holy ecstasy and rapture"; for the soul exercised by divine contemplations, inflamed with heavenly affections, is transported beyond the lower world and "sees and feels beyond all language." And thus it is by enquiring what God is in Himself and to us, that "we are swallowed up into heavenly exercise, experience and acquaintance with things that are excellent and transcendent." In order to have such an experience, purity of mind is necessary; for the mind can never contemplate God unless it be God-like.

There must be a suitable disposition of the faculty to the object and no faculty extends beyond its proper object, *nulla facultas extendit se extra rationem sui objecti*. Thus man must be in a spiritual "temper" to qualify him for spiritual-mindedness; otherwise he mars an action which would be good in itself. It is the business of genuine religion to render us capable of heaven as a state by making our hearts pure.[2] But the spiritual retreat suggested by Whichcote is not an end in itself; it is for the purpose of the divine life which involves a relationship of love to God and to one's fellows.

God as governor of the world, as the sustainer of righteousness and truth, controls and punishes sin. If we speak correctly of punishment, God only "chastises" sinners. A man is not punished by every evil that befalls him since he may not have done anything to deserve punishment. What appears to be punishment may be only the effects of God's absolute sovereignty. God in the use of His power may deal differently with several creatures; and yet where He "deals better," He does not reward, nor does He punish where He "deals worse." That is to say, He may make "a vessel of higher use," another of "inferior use" since this is His privilege. Furthermore, natural evil sometimes comes from God to test our "affections "for Him. These "harder conditions" are to lead to our moral growth. Or it may be that some evils are for "an evil neighbor's sake." [3] Whichcote's insistence that all evil that

---

a creature but he is promised and granted in Christ an intimate sharing in what is *divine* – life everlasting and incorruptible. The main characteristic of *theosis* is "immortality" or "incorruption" (pp. 126–127).

[1] Whichcote, *Works*, II, 201, 220–221.

[2] *Ibid.*, pp. 189–191.

[3] *Ibid.*, I, 78–80 ; C. *Aph.* 1003.

befalls man is not the result of sin is praiseworthy. Perhaps here he has learned from Job, one of his favorite Old Testament sources. One of the weaknesses of Whichcote's approach is his attempt, often very feeble, to explain everything rationally. In his explanation of evil that befalls good men as well as the good fortune that comes to evil men, he anticipates Butler.[1]

Butler's views are generally more pessimistic but are based primarily upon probable knowledge. Whichcote's views, on the other hand, appear unworthy of his more rational approach to religious knowledge. This seems to be one point at which he might well admit that he is dependent at least at some points, on probable knowledge – that he "believes where he cannot prove."

Punishment is required to maintain God's order in the world. We might easily forget that God governs the world if men could disregard the moral order of the universe without punishment. God does not love punishment, but uses it to maintain right and for the good of his creatures.[2] It follows that we, by our disobedience, incur our own punishment. God is not to blame for our punishment, the cause is in us and we should busy ourselves in removing it.[3] Guilt in the sinner is a form of punishment.[4] Every sinful action will eventually be punished and right shall finally prevail.[5] Thus Whichcote's clear statement that punishment, when correctly understood, is the result of sin is the key to all he has to say concerning this subject.

By considering the present state as a "probation-state" and "hell moral" as a present experience, Whichcote can make his point that punishment is now "remedial" rather than "punitive." God seeks the reformation of our lives and inflicts punishment to obtain an end which is better. Sometimes God brings about a small evil to prevent a greater or a present evil to prevent a future – suffering in time to prevent suffering in eternity. Basically Divine goodness aims to two things: first, the reformation of the sinner; and, second, the "information" of the onlooker. Punishment in human society should follow this pattern, that is, it should be remedial.

---

[1] Butler, *Ibid.*, Chs. II, IV, V, pp. 34–36. Whichcote, unlike Butler, has little sense of the "toughness" and perversity of the material world or of the difficulty of the moral struggle. It would be unfair to accuse him of otherworldliness or complacency; but his sense of sin and the experience of suffering seem defective. However, when one considers his good nature (without effort) and his wealth, his moral insights are commendable. Cf. D. E. Trueblood, *Philosophy of Religion*, (New York, 1957), pp. 235–256.

[2] Whichcote, *Ibid.*, pp. 83–85.

[3] *Ibid.*, pp. 85–86. Cf. *Ibid.*, III, 84.

[4] *Ibid.*, pp. 110–111. Cf. *Supra*, Ch. VI.

[5] *Ibid.*, pp. 201, 323.

We should always remember that God desires the salvation of a sinner rather than his death.[1] Without adopting the universalism of Origen, Whichcote reminds us of his Alexandrian predecessor as he speaks on the same subject. Whichcote points toward the future to Butler's *Analogy* and the theory behind modern social work, i.e. prison reforms.[2] Whichcote's view that God is moved by goodness to seek our good by means of punishment points to Nygren's treatment of *Agape* and his conclusion that "Whatever refuses to be won by.... self-giving love cannot be won at all." [3]

The cause of all our misery is rational, it arises from within us, and our relation with God is in no danger if we are innocent of sin. Hell according to Whichcote is not primarily a place, but a state. The guilt of conscience is the "fuel" of hell.[4] No greater "violence" is to be found in the "lower world" (among creatures below man in the order of creation), than the contradiction of the truth of judgment by will and practice. Further, there is no such condemnation in the state of the future as self-condemnation. The worst of hell is the inward torture of one's conscience. Whichcote describes the "worm of conscience as the life of hell." [5] With Butler, Whichcote assures us that every sin has its punishment regardless of the appearance of things. Sometimes *malum passionis*, the evil of suffering, follows after *malum actionis*, the evil of action, at some distance, but retribution will always follow unrepented sin.[6] Whichcote says:

> By contradiction to reason, men are challenged within themselves at present, and will be condemned hereafter at the day of judgment. It is the reason of man's mind that condemns, not God's power. Condemnation arises from man's own guilt. Without the condemnation of man's own reason, there is nothing in the world formidable: for God's power is directed by his wisdom, limited by his goodness, and never acts out of ways of justice or truth.
>
> But a man is confounded and broken, when he cannot approve himself to the reason of his mind. To go against the light of reason is to have a real experience of hell.[7]

---

[1] *Ibid.*, IV, 165–166. Cf. *Aphs.* 761, 1029.

[2] Cf. *Supra*, Ch. X; Origen, *De Princ.* ii. 10.

[3] Anders Nygren, *Agape and Eros* (London, 1953), p. 104.

[4] Whichcote, *Works*, III, 139–140. Cf. *Aphs.* 100, 824; Cudworth, *Ibid.*, p. 51.

[5] *Ibid.*, II, 140–141. Western societies like Eastern societies are rapidly moving from a "guilt" complex to a "shame" complex. Freudianism, nihilism, atheistic Existentialism and a host of other influences have converged to develop an ethic based upon expediency. But the "hell" that Whichcote speaks of is still with us in another form. Even Sartre speaks of "hell as other people." Cf. O. H. Mowrer, *The Crisis in Psychiatry and Religion*, (Princeton, 1961), pp. 81–102, 103–129.

[6] *Ibid.*, IV, 423–424; Cf. Butler, *Ibid.*, Ch. II. pp. 34–36.

[7] *Ibid.*, pp. 399–400. Cf. *Aph.* 129, 311. Whichcote's confidence in reason and conscience (both are for him the "voice of God"), anticipates Butler's trust in the accuracy of conscience.

If God punishes sin, it is no more than just, Justice in God does not require that a penitent man should be punished, but goodness requires that impenitence be controlled. However, sin committed may be unpunished without injustice. Scripture does not show God necessarily punishing repented sin. All acts of justice and forgiveness are subject to wisdom. Actual punishment is not necessary to uphold government, but the power to punish and pardon is becoming to wisdom.[1]

Punishments and Judgments are, 1. to Remind those who are within the Compass of Religions that they may not lose themselves; 2. to Awaken those who are Devoid of Religion; that they may come to themselves; 3. to Discover those, who are Hypocrites in Religion; that they not Prejudice their Neighbor; 4. to bear Testimony to those, who Renounce Religion; that they may not Misrepresent God; as not maintaining Righteousness.[2]

The judgment of God is based upon His infallible understanding and unerring will.[3] Thus God judges us according to the general course of our life rather than by occasional acts; by what we do by choice rather than what we do with reluctance; by what we do in the full use of reason than in confusion; by what we do through resolution, rather than in moments of weakness.[4] What Whichcote wishes to say is that God's goodness punishes the impenitent, while His justice and righteousness compassionate the penitent.[5] We have the assurance, therefore, that things finally "will be as they should be." Concerning the future we have now a "fore-sight" from what we are and feel. However, things which are perfectly new are beyond our "fore-knowledge" and concerning these we must have faith and patience at present.[6]

It is his belief that for the committed Christian the future life will be one of blessedness and this we now know in part; for the knowledge of God in Christ is eternal life. The business of this life is to be Christlike

---

The weakness in the views of both men appears to be in the failure to make sufficient allowance for the degeneration of these facilities, i.e. in the case of Whichcote, the perversion of reason and the searing of conscience. Kant upon observing that so many evil men appear to go unpunished in the present life infers necessarily the existence of God as well as the immortality of the soul in support of the moral order. Paul L. Lehmann in *Ethics in a Christian Context*, (London, 1963), presents a worthy safeguard. For the Christian, according to Lehmann, the church as *Koinonia* – "the fellowship creating reality of Christ's presence in the world" is the context of ethical reflection. A contextual ethic is indicative rather than imperative and acquires meaning and authority not from demands, but from specific ethical relationships. The latter constitute the context out of which demands emerge and are shaped. (pp. 45–49, 150).

1 *Aph.* 1108.
2 *Ibid.*, 317; Cf. *Ibid.*, 760.
3 *Ibid.*, 380).
4 *Ibid.*, 1077.
5 *Works*, IV, 48–50.
6 *Ibid.*, I, 330.

and heaven will be, at once, a present and future experience – a proper relation to God which is man's true end and happiness. The God of Creation and Redemption are one – the Author of Nature is the Giver of Grace. If we seek God in His work and follow Him in His ways and if He has disclosed Himself to us by His saving work in Christ – His self-disclosure and fullest revelation to us, then we know assuredly that unrepented sin is punished and that the divine life – the life hid in Christ-in-God, is rewarded. As Whichcote says:

> ....As God in the world of nature hath fitted one thing to another...., so will he also in the intellectual world of souls and spirits finally proportion capacities and states.... and fit moral actions and dispositions with recompense and reward that no challenge may befall his superintendency and government.[1]

It is significant that in speaking of death, Whichcote refers to the death of Socrates. Socrates was pleased to be free from his body for the benefit of the future growth of his soul. Although his disciple Plato and other friends mourned for him, Socrates was full of resolution and courage for in his own way he had conquered death. Death for him was the gateway to a richer and fuller life.[2] Thus Whichcote conceives the best proof of the immortality of our souls before the Gospel as being philosophical. Philosophically speaking, arguments offered for the immortality of the soul are of two types, namely, natural and moral. Natural arguments may be based on the immateriality of soul, its independent action apart from the body and the separate existence of the soul.[3]

On the other hand, moral arguments are often based on the unequal distribution of worldly goods by providence and likewise upon the fact that many wrongs are not set right in the present life. Whichcote is of the opinion that these rational arguments made the idea of immortality

---

[1] *Ibid.*, I, 331–332. Cf. Butler, *Ibid.*

[2] *Ibid.*, II, 110–112. Whichcote's views on life as well as on death are an example to us. Tillotson's account of Whichcote's death is remarkably similar to Plato's account of Socrates' death in the *Apology*. However, just as his teaching concerning death takes us beyond the most admirable philosophical view of death, even so his acceptance of the Sacrament of the Lord's Supper as a declaration of his communion with the "Church of Christ all the world over" is an invaluable Christian example. Cf. John Tillotson, *Funeral Sermon of ..... Whichcote*, (London, 1673), pp. 28–29.

[3] Cf. John Smith, "Of the Immortality of the Soul," *Select Discourses*, ed. by H. G. Williams, 4th ed., (London, 1859), pp. 62–63. I am not sure that Whichcote appreciated the fundamental difference between the Greek and biblical views of the body. To Plato, the body is a tomb or prison; to St. Paul, it is a temple. Therefore, he could not give a worthy statement to the affirmation in the Creed, "I believe in the resurrection of the body." Recent historical study of the Bible enables us to appreciate the essentially unique conception of the after life of the Christian faith while taking into consideration the manner in which Greek philosophy has aided us in the statement of this belief.

credible to philosophers while they were under the spell of their notions, but in their less thoughtful moments, doubts arose in their minds. It follows that even though they were convinced of the fact of immortality, they had not the assurance we have in Christ.

Christ has brought meaning to life and immortality and in this He has fulfilled God's purpose. He has abolished death and He has brought life and immortality to light. These words include the fullness of perfection, our ultimate accomplishments, all the happiness that created nature is capable of. Death may be understood in three ways, as external, internal and eternal. The worst effects of external death are removed. The "sting" of death conceived as the "wages of sin" is removed from those who "die in the Lord." The fear of external death is abolished. The apprehension of death is the greatest fear of this world, but without such apprehensions, a man may die as securely as he may fall asleep. By the Gospel and through faith in Christ, Who is Lord, our apprehensions are removed. Internal death is death by sin as it affects us within, the difficulty of the mind, overcome by inferior faculties, to embrace pure virtue. It implies the tendency to allow sense to rule one's life rather than reason and virtue. This inevitably leads to internal death or death within. This death has been abolished by Christ through His grace and the assistance of the Holy Spirit. Sin has no dominion over the regenerate who partake of the spirit of Christ and the power of His resurrection.

Finally, eternal death is no longer a menace to the redeemed. Christ has removed eternal death by taking away the "fewel of Tophet," namely, guilt. The fire of hell will go out if fuel is removed and this is precisely what Christ has done. He has removed our guilt and over against guilt He has offered justification. We are relieved from eternal death by justification just as we are relieved from internal death by sanctification. In this belief, death is but a passage into another life, for death to the Christian means to be with Christ. And the only reason why a Christian should hesitate to die is for the purpose of further service to God and His Church. Christians have expectations of good by death – it is the passage to life, to a better state. The very notion and nature of death is changed.[1]

The death of the righteous, or of those that partake of the grace of the Gospel puts an end to their sorrow. Henceforth they are out of the Devil's reach either as a tempter or tormentor. They are rid of sin, the

1 *Ibid.*, pp. 105–112.

basis of death. Death for the righteous is not only the death of life, but the death of death, the death of sin, which is the death of the soul. By the death of sin, the soul is restored to life, and it is thus that death (which ends the present life) "takes away" but does not "destroy" life. It takes it away from time to be restored "after awhile" to last beyond time. Death carries the righteous out of this world, but for them it is a "happy passage" from labor to rest; from expectation to fulfillment; from faith to knowledge; form the world to God; from death to life. Such death is not corruption but the occasion of a new and better life.[1]

On the other hand, the wicked find death dreadful and terrible. Those who are unprepared, who are without faith have no ground for expectation, no foundation for hope. They are beset by fears from within and from without.

> On the one hand, sin rises up to accuse them; on the other, the righteousness of God terrifies them. As they look downward, there is nothing but the open mouth of that vast chaos, the bottomless pit, that gaps upon them; upward, God, an angry judge; within, a tormenting, burning, accusing, condemning conscience; abroad the world a-fire about their ears.[2]

Christ brings life and immortality. These two abstractions signify the excellency of the future life of the righteous. The present life has the mixture of death in it, it is dependent upon sleep, the "image of death" and upon food and health. The present life is contingent, indeed, the most uncertain thing about life is life itself. But the future life is different, it is all good and we have it in full possession without interruption. It involves complete communion with God and total reconciliation with the whole creation of God. As we grow to years of maturity we transcend ourselves as infants. How much better we shall be when we are born to eternity! [3] The "good estate" of the righteous lies in the fact that they possess life and immortality or immortal life and that they are free from and have security against all contrary evils. All evils that befall us center in death. By the abolition of death, by our Saviour, Who is Lord over death, all things leading to death are removed. Death does us no harm but rather a great courtesy; for it saves our life and makes it secure. It lets the soul out of the body to our benefit and advantage. The death of the righteous is not "a going out

---

[1] *Ibid.*, pp. 117–118.

[2] *Ibid.*, pp. 125–126. This passage reveals Whichcote's Puritan background perhaps as much as any passage to be found in his writings.

[3] *Ibid.*, pp. 119–120.

of being" but "an entrance into life," a departure from the world to be with the Lord. The death of the righteous is a great kindness.[1]

The final note of victory for the Christian is sounded by the Resurrection of our Lord. It is because He lives that we may live also. Whichcote's reflections upon this subject show that Paul's influence is greater than Plato's on him. He insists that the body which we now have is to be remarkably changed, that it shall be a "spiritual body," an incorruptible body like unto our Saviour's "glorified body." This change shall be effected by almighty power. This will be for the Christian "a house not made with hands " a fit instrument for our soul throughout endless ages.[2] By His Resurrection, we know that Christ has brought life and immortality to the redeemed. He only can effectively absolve men from their sins and death by sin, who can lose the "Bonds of Death." [3] This is exactly what Christ achieves by His death and resurrection – victory over sin and death.

As J. A. T. Robinson puts it:

By His death Christ, as it were, "died out on" the forces of evil without their being able to defeat or kill Him, thereby exhibiting their importance and gaining victory over them.... The Resurrection is the inevitable consequence of this defeat; death could have no grip on Him, since sin obtained no foothold in Him. It was impossible that He should be holden of it.[4]

From the point of view of dogmatic theology, the weakness of Whichcote's views concerning last things will appear to be his refusal to speak significantly beyond the present. He deliberately makes a distinction between heaven and hell as states and as places, between these states in the present and future in order to place his emphasis within the range of present experience and knowledge. Where he points beyond the present he does so by inference from the present to the

---

[1] *Ibid.*, pp. 124–125.
[2] *Ibid.*, I, 292.
[3] *Aph.* 986; Cf. Rev. 1:18.
[4] *The Body*, (London, 1955), p. 40. In this work, (pp. 11–13) and in Cullmann, *Ibid.*, pp. 61–63., the tendency appears to be to make a radical distinction between the Greek views of the relation of soul and body and time and eternity and the New Testament ideas on the same subjects.

In Cullmann this is carried over in his reflections upon the immortality of the soul and the resurrection of the body. Cullmann finds complete contrast between the death of Socrates and the death of Christ. Whichcote appears to be on safer ground. He can see a similarity between New Testament and Greek thought on these subjects, but always points out where Christianity takes us beyond the wisdom of the Greeks. I am reminded of John Baillie's helpful suggestion that the Christian doctrine of last things is essentially a doctrine of resurrection not of flesh, but spiritual body though it includes insights from the Greek conception of immortality of the soul as well as the notion of survival after death in primitive religions. The same view is advocated by H. H. Farmer.

future and he does even this with caution. He places his conviction in the fact that the God of creation and redemption are one and that eternal life and heavenly citizenship are present possibilities.

Thus through the Incarnation the Kingdom of God has come and is to come. His message is more distinctly Johannine than Platonic. He accepts the good in the notion of the survival of the soul in primitive religions and the concept of the immortality of the soul in Greek philosophy; but for him the Christian belief in the resurrection of the body, while including a doctrine of survival and one of the immortality of the soul, goes beyond them. The Christian message is that God has both raised up Christ and will raise us up. The Christian doctrine of resurrection implies that the living and saving God holds man in being. God is always actively encountering and claiming man and man only exists as God's man. God might withdraw His creative love from a man and that person would be annihilated, but God's love will not let man go. In Christ shall all be made alive, He brings life and immortality through His saving work. Men cannot vanish into "nothingness" because of Christ. Whichcote is consistent with the scheme of his thought since his doctrine of resurrection and his doctrine of man are grounded in man's personal relation to God. A proper God-relation is the basis of man's happiness in His life and the life to come and this relation is possible only by the saving work of Christ.

As we have followed Whichcote through his reflections on Christian morals, it is easy to understand why in 1821, his *Aphorisms* were published to "inculcate moral conduct on Christian principles," [1] and in 1930, Dean W. R. Inge expressed a similar purpose in presenting Whichcote's *Aphorisms* to this century.[2] Certainly for Whichcote, Christianity and morality are united in what we have treated here as Christian morals.

He presents a religion of real effects, a religion that is dynamic rather than static, a religion of life rather than ceremony and throughout his writings and, indeed, his life he echoes the words of Jesus "by their fruits ye shall know them."[3]

---

[1] Whichcote, *Select Aphorisms*, The Christian Tract Society, No. XXVIII, Vol. III, cited from the title page.

[2] *Ibid.*, Preface.

[3] Matt. 7:20.

CHAPTER EIGHT

RELIGION OF AFTER-REVELATION (III)

The Universal Church

It appears significant that Bishop Westcott who has so much in common with Whichcote should accuse him of an inadequate doctrine of the Church [1] and even attributes the transitoriness of Whichcote's influence to this. We must admit together with Westcott that Whichcote has not spoken definitively concerning the nature of the Church. The reason seems to be that he has spoken mainly against popery and in defence of Christian tolerance. Thus, while accepting B. F. Westcott's criticism, we must, in all fairness to Whichcote, portray him as a loyal member of the Church of England, but as one who deserves to be remembered most for his protest against religious intolerance among Roman Catholics and Protestants alike. Whichcote is true to his purpose and the contribution he makes to this aspect of Church life lives till this day.

Any observation of Whichcote's notion of the "universal Church" rightly begins with his reaction against Romanism. [2] Whichcote says:

> It had been better for the Christian Church; if that, which calls itself Catholic, had been less employed in creating pretended "Faith," and more employed in maintaining universal "Charity." [3]

Whichcote dislikes the credulity of the Roman Church, which calls its adherents to blind obedience.

He is just as opposed, however, to the same tendency among Protestants. [4] Whichcote raises the question, what is the true Church? Instead of giving us, as we would expect, a definitive answer, he pro-

---

[1] *Religious Thought in the West* (London, 1891), pp. 393–394.

[2] In order to understand fully the reason why Whichcote's negative attitude toward Romanism was so passionate, one must take a look at the policy of the Roman Church at this time and pay special attention to its effects upon England. See Arthur Galton, *Our Outlook Towards English Roman Catholics, and the Papal Court* (London, 1902), pp. 104–124.

[3] Whichcote, *Aph.* 68.

[4] *Works*, I, 156–157.

ceeds to state the Roman claim to be the only true Church and his denial of the same. The Roman Church pretends to be the only true church and asserts that there is no salvation outside of it. Many reasons can be brought forward to illustrate the pretence of the Roman claim: for instance, they attempt to propagate religion by fire and sword; and, also, they do not consider themselves bound to keep faith with heretics, for they insist that heretics lose all their right to truth. In both instances their methods are unworthy of Christians. They try to sanctify by their religion many evils in order to bring men into their Church. But if we observe their practices, we would never think their intention to be religious.[1]

Whichcote puts a series of questions to point up his protest against Romanism. Was this spirit of popery learned of the meek and lowly Jesus? Is it not rather the spirit of him who "goeth about like a roaring lion, seeking whom he may devour?" Is not this the work of him who was a murderer from the beginning? Is this the fruit of that religion which allows no evil and which requires patient bearing of wrongs and doing good for evil? The answers to these questions seem obvious to Whichcote. Christianity is the best principle of kindness that there is, but often the corruption of the best proves to be the worst.

The more false a man is in his religion, the more fierce he becomes; the more mistaken, the more imposing. The more a man's religion is his own, the more he is concerned for it, and shows coolness and indifference to that which belongs to God.[2]

It is far better to rely on nature alone than upon an insincere and false religion. Whichcote here recognizes nature to be debased, abused and neglected, in a word "fallen," but even this is better than false religion. He recalls Aristotle's assertion that man is by nature a "mild and gentle creature." Thus Whichcote concludes that if the only estimate of Christianity were popery, or any similar superstition, he would return to philosophy again and leave Christianity alone. Philosophy, as far as it goes, is sincere and attains "good effects," It is true that it falls short of the saving knowledge revealed in Christ, but philosophy is free of the corruption of the Word of God under the spell of Popery. The Roman Church has made "merchandise" out of the Word of God and the "ingredients" of its religion are power, pomp and wealth.[3]

---

[1] *Ibid.*, pp. 160–164.
[2] *Ibid.*, pp. 165–167.
[3] *Ibid.*, pp. 168–169. Whichcote's general position here is reflected in Shaftesbury's "luke-

Whichcote speaks of certain notorious errors of the Roman Church as being extremely dangerous. They impose upon the Christian faith things contrary to reason. A good example of this is the doctrine of *transubstantiation*. If we accept this doctrine, we may no longer trust our senses and if we concede that our senses are unreliable, how shall we hold that God made our faculties true?

If God did not make them true, then we are released from all duty to God because we cannot know that God is God. If we cannot trust the reason of our mind in relation to three or four of our senses, how can we know anything to be good or true? Thus for Whichcote this doctrine is completely absurd.[1] Whichcote states that even when the Romanists acknowledge truth, they render it invalid by qualifications. A good example of this is their doctrine of probability. According to this doctrine if any doctor among them held a certain view it made it probable. However, they also put up a mental reservation that what they say may be only half what they mean. They direct the intention, that is, they may declare what is false and deny the truth in the interest of their Church. By equivocation they mean that a thing is self-explanatory, or by evasion a thing is believed to have a double meaning. And they employ "hypocritical prolucation,," that is, they intone words in such a way as to deceive the naive.[2] In their endeavour to "superadd" to religion things which are false, inhuman, and ungodly, and in their attempt to frustrate the effects of real religion by their

warm" attitude toward religion, see *Infra*, ch. X. Cf. John Smith, "Superstition," *Select Discourses* ed. H. G. Williams, 4th ed. (Cambridge, England, 1859), pp. 28–30.

[1] *Ibid.*, p. 170. Cf. Aulén, *The Faith of the Christian Church*, tr. by Whalstrom-Arden (Philadelphia, 1948), pp. 394–397. Aulén's position is more tenable and convincing than Whichcote's. While Whichcote is true here to his general rational position, Aulén's argument is more fundamental for he goes back to the Biblical record and the history of the early Church and points out that the Roman doctrine of *trans-substantiation* has substituted a "realism" for the original "symbolism" of the doctrine of the Lord's Supper. See also "Eucharist," *Catholic Encyclopaedia* (New York, 1913), V, pp. 572–590.

Whichcote is confused by the Roman distinction between "substance" and "accident" which makes it possible for bread and wine in the Eucharistic Celebration to be transformed *substantially* into the body and blood of Christ while the chemical properties of these elements remain unchanged. I share his like of comprehension, but, at the same time, I am impressed by the *fact* of Christ's presence in the Eucharistic Feast. All basic Christian doctrines of the Eucharist are concerned with His *presence*; whether *total* or *actual* (Roman), *real* (Lutheran), *mystical* or *spiritual* (Calvinist), or *symbolical* (Zwinglian). The *manner* of His presence remains a mystery to all. If all Chistians, therefore, should center more of their attention on our common experience of the *presence* of the risen Lord in the celebration of Holy Communion greater progress could be made in the ecumenical dialogue and fellowship among Christians at the Lord's Table. Observe the bitter conflict between Luther and Zwingli over the *manner* of Christ's presence in the Eucharist, see, Oskar Farmer, *Zwingli: The Reformer*, tr. by D. G. Sear (New York, 1952), pp. 113–114. Cf. Hubert Jedin, *A History of the Council of Trent*, tr. by D. E. Graf (Edinburgh, 1961), pp. 370–395.

[2] *Ibid.*, pp. 171–172, 189. Cf. "Probabilism," *Catholic Encyclopaedia*, III, 441–446.

pretence to power and privilege, they deserve the greatest condemnation.[1] The Romanists add things to the Christian faith unlikely to be true and dishonor God by these. They exalt image-worship and veneration of relics, and by these frustrate the effects of real religion. They pretend to make lawful what is unlawful. Whichcote refers to Ballarmine who claimed for the Pope the power to declare virtue to be vice and *vice versa*, and thereby turning attrition into contrition.

They often substitute a bodily penance for an inward change of heart, by use of holy water and the cross. They pretend that indulgences are efficacious for the pardon of sin or absolution from oaths or obligations. The design of Popery, as Whichcote sees it, is clearly to keep the magistrate in awe, maintain the clergy in a state of submission and keep the people in ignorance, enslave them and disable them from seeing or knowing. If a man is willing to accept these three things, then he should turn to Romanism.[2] But Whichcote conceives Romanism as the arch-enemy of his entire scheme of religion and morality, for its tenets are opposed to any rational and moral view of religion whatsoever.

The Church of Rome holds the doctrine of implicit faith which asserts that masses ought to be said to relieve souls in purgatory. Implicit faith, then, is a part of the notion of "merit" as held by the Roman Church.[3] Thus Whichcote aims his attack upon the doctrine of merit. By merit, *meritum*, the Roman Church means the following:

.... That property of a good work which entitles the doer to receive a reward (*proemium, merces*) from him in whose service the work is done. By antonomasia, the word has come to designate also the good work itself, in so far as it deserves a reward from the person in whose service it was performed. In the theological sense, a supernatural merit can only be a salutary act (*actus salutaris*), to which God in consequence of his infallible promise owes a supernatural reward, consisting ultimately in eternal life, which is the beatific vision in heaven.[4]

According to Whichcote there is no such thing as the "creature's merit with God." It is above the capacity of any creature to merit anything at the hand of God.

---

[1] *Ibid.*, p. 170.

[2] *Ibid.*, pp. 173–174. Cf. *Ibid.*, II, 316; *Aph.* 502. See also, Henry More, "An antidote Against Idolatry," *Theological Works* ed. Joseph Downing (London, 1708), pp. 773–775. All the Cambridge Platonists oppose Romanism since it threatens the very foundation of their ethical and religious structure.

[3] *Ibid.*, p. 180. Whichcote's view of "implicit faith" is entirely different. By this concept, Whichcote refers to faith in God concerning things not yet revealed and concerning things revealed in Scripture which are beyond the comprehension of the unaided reason. Cf. *Supra*, ch. VI. See art. on "Faith," *Catholic Encyclopaedia*, V, 752–754.

[4] Art. "Merit," *Catholic Encyclopedia*, X, 202.

He condems forthright the Roman notion of a "treasure of grace" or merit, out of which the grace of departed saints may be bestowed upon the undeserving.[1] The Papists place undue stress upon the states of obedience, single life and poverty as perfections.[2] These "popish vows" are denounced by Whichcote as folly and superstition. There is nothing in these states automatically to recommend a man to God, for only virtue understood as obedience to the will of God, can do that. It is not genuine mortification merely to abuse the body for the sake of the soul. A serious attempt to bring the lower appetites under the control of the higher faculties, involves a denial of the self, and keeping ourselves within the bounds of reason. But to pretend perfection by making a distinction between flesh and fish, by abstaining from flesh and drinking wine, is nothing but hypocrisy, and there is no true religion in it.[3]

Then Whichcote directs his attack at the Pope, the one person in the Christian world who pretends to be an infallible visible judge of the will of God for man. Whichcote satirically adds that if God had set him up a great deal of labour would have been saved, and all controversies would have ceased. There is no justification of this claim either by reason or revelation. It follows that the Pope is an imposter, having usurped upon God's authority and thereby making his sin the more detestable.[4] It would be becoming to the Roman Church, with its pretence to apostolic succession to show by evidence of reason what it claims to be true.[5]

The Pope is rather concerned with the infinite gain that comes from this one doctrine in terms of power and privilege, and because the cheat is greater, the consequences are greater.[6]

Let these from whom we are departed, give an account to the world why they make use of such mediations as they do. But I would here distinguish between means that upright persons use as helps and means that may operate

[1] Whichcote, *Ibid.*, pp. 312–313.

[2] *Ibid.*, p. 276.

[3] *Ibid.*, IV, 271–272.

[4] *Ibid.*, II, 255. Cf. *Ibid.*, I, pp. iii–iv. Whichcote's Latin poem commemorating the death of Oliver Cromwell is mostly a protest against the Papacy. He describes the Lord Protector as his great ally in this cause. This is easily understood in view of the plea of Cromwell and Whichcote alike for religious toleration. It is worth remembering that Cromwell called Whichcote to his conference concerning toleration for the Jews. William Chillingworth, in many ways, a predecessor of Whichcote, devotes his work, *The Religion of Protestants* (London, 1886), to a position quite similar to Whichcote's.

[5] *Ibid.*, III, 161; Cf. *The Apostolic Ministry* ed. by K. E. Kirk (London, 1946), pp. 40–41. Here a similar claim is made for the episcopal ministry or Essential Ministry which alone is considered valid.

[6] *Ibid.*, p. 387.

upon God. If any one doth better dispose his mind to prayer, or meditations, by fasting, separation for a while from company; he may use it, I see no danger in it. But the danger is, when we fancy such a thing will recommend us to God, when God hath not said so....[1]

Whichcote's protest against Papacy is based mainly upon rational and moral grounds. The reason for this is obvious since the Roman Church appealed to blind obedience on the part of its adherents and by theory and practice upheld a relative standard of moral principles in regard to convenience. Since for Whichcote, reason and the immutable principles of morality are the essence of all true religion, and especially of Christianity, his position is completely irreconcilable with that of Rome. Whichcote's case appears reasonable as it stands, but his appeal to reason in his protest against popery overshadows any appeal to Scripture or to the early Church in support of his views. His arguments against Romanism would have been far more convincing if he could have indicated where the Roman Church departed from the message of the New Testament and the Primitive Christian Church as well as from reason and morality. In this way he would have uprooted the traditional claims of the Roman Church and made his protest more convincing.

Whichcote asserts, however, that there is "but one Church (one Religion) in all ages." [2] To make clear his opposition to the Roman view, we prefer to use the term "universal" rather than "catholic"

---

[1] *Ibid.*, II, 327. Cf. Whichcote, *The Malignity of Popery*, ed. by John Jeffery, (London-1717). For an account of "apostolic succession," see, Roman view: Art. "Apostolic Succession," *Catholic Encyclopaedia*, I, 641–643; other views, K. E. Kirk, *Ibid.*, pp. 1-2, and A. G. Herbert, "Ministerial Episcopacy," *Ibid.*, pp. 493–494. Whichcote is quite modern here and anticipates though dimly the dialogue now in vogue between various branches of Christendom. One of the most decisive factors between Roman Catholicism and all other Christian bodies is "papal infallibility." Likewise one of the most serious considerations between Anglicans and most Protestant bodies is "apostolic succession." For a discussion between Roman Catholicism and Eastern Orthodoxy on the primacy of the Bishop of Rome, see Yves Conger, *After Nine Hundred Years* (New York, 1959), pp. 59–67 for the Roman view and John Mayendorff, *The Orthodox Church* (New York, 1962), pp. 208–31, for an Orthodox view. Those involved in discussions between Anglicans and Presbyterians in Great Britain as well as between Methodists, Presbyterians, Episcopalians, Disciples of Christ and others in the United States must grapple with this problem if there is to be an ecumenical breakthrough. I am impressed with Bishop J. A. Pike's suggestion that we get to the essentials of church structure.

He distinguishes between various forms of episcopal ordination as follows: The first type is for the well-being of the church (*de bene esse*); the second type is for the fullness of the church (*de plene esse*), and the third is essential for valid ministry and sacraments (*de esse*), His views are similar to Whichcote's, see Pike, *A Time For Christian Candor* (New York, 1964) ch. X. Cf. J. F. H. New *Anglican and Puritan: The Basis of Their Opposition, 1558–1640* (Stanford, 1964), p. 107 and Dietrich Bonhoeffer, *The Communion of Saints* (New York, 1963). pp. 72–85.

[2] *Aph.* 1107.

to express Whichcote's view of one Church for all times and places. Whichcote insists that our Saviour accepts no other separation of His Church from the world than is required by "Truth, Virtue and Holiness of Life." [1] God rejects our institutions when we make them compensations for morals.

.... Institutes have their foundation, in the "will" of God; and the matter of them is alterable: Morals have their foundation, in the "nature" of God, and the matter of them is necessary and unalterable.[2]

The Reformed Church meets Whichcote's approval. Some parties break the policy of this Church, but this cannot be held against the Church. According to Whichcote, the Reformed Church holds to the following principles: (1) All worship is performed in the vulgar tongue so that knowledge and devotion may be united; (2) free use of Scripture in public and private; (3) the Scripture is the only rule of faith. Traditions, Councils and Fathers and the like are to be used only for better understanding of Scriptures; (4) everyone has the right of private judgment, that is, to distinguish between good and evil, truth and falsehood; they make themselves capable of this right by prayer and meditation and other helps to knowledge; (5) teachers of the Church are to be helpers rather than dictators and masters of men's faith: they are not to make religion, but to show it, and their purpose is not to take away the key of knowledge from the people, but out of compassion they are to lead people in the way of truth and recover them out of error and mistake; (6) the people are told that Scripture is full and clear in all things necessary to life and practice; (7) the Reformed Church does not deceive men by fraud; it deals honestly with men and informs them that without personal holiness they cannot see the face of God; and (8) it asserts that all who agree in the main points of religion may look upon themselves as members of the same Church notwithstanding any differences of apprehension in other matters. These principles, according to Whichcote, enable Christians to live together in peace and charity. It is his firm belief that these are the fundamental affirmations of Protestantism and if a man believes differently, although he may be a professed Protestant; yet he is actually a Papist.[3] Whichcote's statement of the principles of the Reformed Church, which refer primarily to the Church of England, show that he is not a member of an established party in that Church. He is not a Laudian or Puritan

[1] *Ibid.*, 138.
[2] *Ibid.*, 1121.
[3] *Works*, I, 175–192.

and certainly he is not related to the Dissenters or Papists. There is a group in the Church of England aptly described by Fowler as "moderate divines, abusively called Latitudinarians," of which Whichcote's position is representative.[1] When Whichcote is at the peak of his career in the middle of the seventeenth century, this group does not appear to be a strong "party," but to consist of isolated individuals of a liberal stamp, i.e. Chillingworth, Hales, Mead, Taylor and others. But by the inspiration of his predecessors and contemporaries, Whichcote develops Cambridge Platonism.

It is easy to discern even in Whichcote's statement of the Reformed Faith his own presuppositions concerning a rational and moral religion. But he is honest, he admits that he "takes the reformed faith in latitude." As a matter of fact, this possibility for "liberty of comprehension" of religious knowledge makes this faith most desirable. He considers this religious liberty as a fundamental justification for the Reformation. This may well be a hint to those Protestant groups, such as the Puritans, whose policy had become as dogmatic as the Papists. He is also aware of the many divisions within Protestantism, which have challenged the integrity of the Reformation. To a certain degree, these dissensions are the price of religious liberty.

It appears in order to give here such further explanation as Whichcote provides us of his conception of the Reformed Faith. It professes to do all things in a reasonable manner. Reasonable worship and service are according to the mind of God and are worthy of us. The Reformed Faith requires us to do what Scripture demands. For instance, we have in Scripture a "superaddition" to rational worship and we go to God by the mediation of Christ. We receive the sacraments and the preaching of the Word as "means of grace," and this implies that we are to lead a holy life in keeping with our profession.[2] There is nothing in the Reformed Church which infringes upon Christ's priestly office or which is a "superaddition" to God's institution. What we do is justified either by reason or Scripture and in most cases the beliefs and practices of the Reformed Church are attested to by both. Anything beyond what can be supported by reason and/or Scripture is to be considered circumstantial and therefore unnecessary for salvation. Since these surface

---

[1] Edward Fowler, *A Free Discourse Between Two Intimate Friends*, 2nd ed. (London, 1671). See the title page. Cf. John Hales, "Schism and Schismatics," (1642), in *Several Tracts* (London, 1677), Jeremy Taylor, *Liberty of Prophesying*, (London, 1834) first appeared, 1646.
[2] Whichcote, *Works*, II, 324–325.

matters do not recommend us to God, we should maintain love and agree to differ concerning them.[1]

> The Sense of the "Church" is not a "Rule"; but a thing "Ruled." The Church is bound unto Reason and Scripture, and governed by them as much as any "particular" Person.[2]

Whichcote describes ministers of the Church as "rational instruments" of God. Ministers are helpers of men's faith, preachers of righteousness and interpreters of Scripture. To use H. H. Farmer's suggestive title, they are "servants of the Word." They are to seek the edification of the congregation, to administer the sacraments and in every way to lead man in the proper worship of God and holy living. These persons by virtue of their functions are used by God for a holy purpose, and, therefore, they may be said to be relatively holy. This appellation of relative holiness may be ascribed in like manner to the Lord's day and the Sacraments since these are set apart for supernatural purposes. Whichcote appears to be saying what J. S. Whale has emphasized, "The Sacraments are efficacious, only because Christ Himself uses the minister as his instrument." [3] On the whole, then, Whichcote does not give us a definitive statement of the nature of the Church in terms of Scripture or the thirty-nine Articles, but he implies most that is worthy in both. What he has to say concerning the Reformed Church can be understood only against a background of intense desire for a rational and moral faith based upon the best concepts derived from the theological and philosophical traditions up to his time.

There seems to be every reason to believe that Whichcote was a loyal member of the Church of England and that he accepted willingly its liturgy, ceremonies, government and doctrine as one of his contemporaries testifies.[4] Above all, we must remember his passion for religious liberty which accounts for his negative reaction to all religious intolerance, whether Papist, Laudian, Puritan or Sectarian. The Church is for Whichcote universal and in a real sense invisible including only those persons who by thought, commitment and life acknowledge Christ as the Lord of the Church.

> God looking upon us, not as we are in ourselves, but as we are gathered together in Christ, as a head. In the "mystical body" the head is a truly influ-

---

[1] *Ibid.,* p. 329. Cf. Fowler, *Ibid.,* pp. 228–230. *passim.*
[2] *Aph.* 921.
[3] *Christian Doctrine* (Cambridge, 1956), pp. 160–161. Cf. Whichcote, *Works,* IV, 68.
[4] S. P. (Simon Patrick), "A Brief Account of the Sect of Latitude-Men," (1662) in *The Phenix,* (London, 1707), pp. 504–506.

ential as the natural head is influential and beneficial to the members of the natural body.[1]

For Whichcote, as for the Old Testament prophets of social justice and for Jesus, worship is best when we resemble God most.[2] What Whichcote has to say about worship has its basis in the exegesis of a passage of Scripture (Jn. 4:24). The statement "God is a Spirit" in the King James Version [3] of the Bible is understood by Whichcote as "Spirit is God." The question is, where is the place of worship? Jesus answers that the place of worship is neither in Jerusalem, nor in the mountain, for worship is spiritual. Worship is elevated above our space-time conceptions. Spirit is God and, therefore, spiritual worship alone is acceptable to God. If we use the traditional statement, God is a Spirit, there is no purpose for our Lord's argument.

God had always been known as a spiritual substance according to Whichcote, therefore, there would have been little purpose for Jesus' re-statement of this accepted fact – that "God is a Spirit." But to say that "Spirit is God" has a special significance for worship. Only spirit can meet with spirit, and therefore any communion between ourselves and God must be by a spiritual and intellectual approach. What Jesus means here is that God has been approached all along by figures, types, rites, ceremonies and the like, but God had been to a great extent hidden. It is only by spiritual worship that man may have a full encounter with Spirit. Jesus' definition of worship as spiritual communion stripped of all unnecessary ceremonialism shows the real essence and purpose of all that is implied by the words "Spirit is God."[4] This is the point at which the worship of the New Israel envisaged by Jesus is in a vital sense a "new thing" from that of the Old Israel. Whether we grant Whichcote his rendering of the text or not, it seems most probable that the meaning he had derived from the text is invaluable for the proper understanding of what is genuine Christian worship.

If we worship God with sincerity, we may do so with cheerfulness and clear understanding. True worship is rational and moral. The profane have confusion in their worship, and the superstitious look

---

[1] Whichcote, Works, II, 330; Cf. W. L. Bradley, P. T. Forsyth: The Man and His Work (London, 1952), pp. 226–228. The most comprehensive study of the "images" of the church in the New Testament known to the writer is Paul S. Minear, Images of the Church in the New Testament (Philadelphia, 1960), see especially, pp. 11–27, pp. 173–220. See also, Vladimir Lossky, The Mystical Theology of the Eastern Church (London, 1957), pp. 174–195.

[2] Aph. 248.

[3] The Authorized Version for Whichcote.

[4] Works, II, 123–124.

upon God as the enemy of their nature. These worship God in "dread and horror," but true worshippers worship God with delight.[1]

As John Smith so aptly puts it:

> Superstition is such an apprehension of God in the thoughts of men, as renders Him grievous and burdensome to them, and so destroys all free converse with Him; begetting, in the stead thereof, a forced and jejune devotion, void of inward life and love.[2]

Acts of worship and devotion must be intellectual as well as external otherwise they are not piety but hypocrisy. Outward formality without inward loyalty to Christ is useless. The body should be observant but one should not depend upon external acts as the essence of worship. God as Spirit cannot be duly worshipped without the Spirit's presence.[3] This is the point at which idolatry so often emerges. Idolatry consists in the attempt to confine the Deity to a material thing or act and likewise in the endeavour to raise some material thing to a divine status by the mere fiat of our wills.[4] Thankfulness and obedience are the true sacrifices, they are worthy of the creature and the Creator, and those which God will certainly accept. But it is certain that the zeal of any institution, though it be a divine institution, is unacceptable to God, if it is in conjunction with immorality.[5] In view of the formal nature of the accepted liturgy of the Church of England, a prophetic reminder of the true nature and purpose of worship in the spirit of Whichcote's observations is quite necessary. As a matter of fact, all Christians, even in "free churches," need to be reminded that worship is rational, moral and spiritual if it is not to degenerate to the level of magic or at best to a shell of ritualism with no spiritual substance.

Whichcote also significantly reminds us that every deed, word and attitude of life is a part of our worship. We enter the Church (the institution) to worship once or twice each week, but we depart to serve in our daily life. Worship is for him "reasonable service" and holy living. Thus in a real sense worship begins at the close of the formal service of worship. Finally, he cautions us to refrain from substituting the "instrumental part" of religion, i.e. prayer, hearing sermons, receiving sacraments, for the "end" of religion. The instruments "are

---

[1] *Ibid.*, p. 356.
[2] Smith, *Ibid.*, p. 37.
[3] Whichcote, *Ibid.*, IV 79; Cf. *Ibid.*, III, 316–317.
[4] *Ibid.*, II, 101–103.
[5] *Ibid.*, III, 207; Cf. Henry More, "The True Grounds of the Certainty of Faith," *Ibid.*, pp. 765–770. Whichcote describes worship in the following *Aphorisms*: 474, 762, 806, 936, 961, 1009, 1013, 1116, 142, 143, 970, 1082, *passim*.

valuable in respect to an end and are crowned when they attain their purpose." [1] He adds:

> They, who mistake the Means for the End, may be reproved; without prejudice to the Means; for the Use of "Means" is nothing, if there be not "thereby" an Attainment of the End.[2]

Preaching is for Whichcote an indispensable part of worship. He appears to have been at his best in the pulpit proclaiming the Gospel. In a broad sense preaching was for him sacramental – "a means of grace." Preaching is a solemn and necessary responsibility arising out of the nature of the Gospel itself. Preaching is in a superlative degree the encounter of one person with another by means of which God takes this human encounter up into a personal encounter with Himself. God makes the human word the "instrument" of the Divine Word. To Whichcote preaching is not always strictly Scriptural, the testimony of truth from other areas of human knowledge and experience is also valid as long as it witnesses to Christ. The use of Scripture related to the message which God reveals in Christ is desirable, but to twist a text changes it into a pretext – this is to use Scripture merely as a perch for one's own ideas.

One should read Scripture as one would a letter from a friend to discern the "mind and will" of that friend. Preaching consists in making the mind and will of God as contained in the Scripture and as revealed in Christ, known to men with all its moral and rational claims. He says: "I have always found that such 'Preaching' of Others hath most commanded my 'Heart'; which hath most illuminated my Head." [3]

To be employed by God to preach His Gospel is the noblest calling in the world. There is no earthly vocation to be compared with the privilege and responsibility of declaring the Gospel of redemption. The preacher is sent on God's "errand," he bears a message from God to man and this is the highest honour God has bestowed upon mortal men. God does not direct the affairs of the visible Church by the ministry of angels, but by men whom he appoints as "stewards of the mysteries" of the Gospel.[4] Preaching is to have a moral content and purpose.

---

[1] *Ibid.*, IV, 116–117.

[2] *Aph.* 976.

[3] *Ibid.*, 393. Whichcote's general attitude concerning preaching is quite similar to that presented by H. H. Farmer in his *Servant of the Word* (London, 1941), pp. 14–15, 24–25.

Cf. Dietrich Ritschl, *A Theology of the Proclamation* (Richmond, Va., 1960), pp. 67–78 and St. Francis de Sales, *On the Preacher and Preaching*, tr. by J. K. Ryan (New York, 1964), pp. 23, 32.

[4] *Works*, III, 65; Cf. Whale, *Ibid.*, p. 161.

.... Men are not wanting to preach the doctrine of the gospel, or to preach Christ, tho' they do not name Christ in every sentence or period of words; who contend for all effects of real goodness and decry every wickedness .... If men contend for the effects of real goodness, and decry wickedness, they do truly and properly preach Christ. And this is the reason; for this is the effect of Christ, and this is Christ's business.[1]

Thus Christ is preached if His business is done and if His work is carried on. It follows that Christ is not effectively preached, even if His name is mentioned constantly, where there is no serious attempt to be Christ-like.

Therefore talk no more against moral preachers: for they who call upon men to live godly, righteously, soberly, they carry on the work of Christ, and these men preach Christ.[2]

A contemporary estimation of the preaching of Whichcote and his disciples by Fowler is invaluable. Fowler says:

They preached the whole duty of man to God, his Neighbour, and to Himself. These insisted upon true holiness, the divine life of virtue, the righteousness which is of God by faith in Jesus Christ, inward rectitude and integrity and doing all the good we can from the best and most divine motives. They preached that divine and heavenly life whose root is faith in God and our Saviour Christ; and the branches or parts of it are humility, purity and charity.[3]

It would be difficult to point to an individual who has in greater measure lived up to this worthy view of what we may call the "total Gospel" than Whichcote. He shows us by word and deed the real privilege and responsibility of all "servants of the Word."

Whichcote's observations on prayer are just as worthy as what he has to say concerning preaching.

All is not done when we have spoken to God by "Prayer": our Petitions are to be pursued with real Endeavours; and our Prayers are to be Means and Instruments of Piety and Virtue, must be subservient to a Holy Life. If they are not the former, they are worth nothing; if they are not the latter, we but deceive ourselves.[4]

Oddly enough Whichcote appears to exalt prayer above the Sacraments because of its "purely mental" character. While the Sacraments (baptism and communion) are temporary acts and are accommodated to this state of imperfection, prayer is a purely spiritual act, and, therefore, "continues to Eternity." [5] Here Whichcote is consistent

---

[1] *Ibid.*, p. 262.

[2] *Ibid.*, p. 263.

[3] Fowler, *Ibid.*, pp. 117–118. Cf. Tillotson, *The Funeral Sermon of* ..... *Whichcote* (London, 1683), pp. 214–216.

[4] Whichcote, *Aph.* 201. Cf. *Ibid.* 1120.

[5] *Ibid.*, 1082. Cf. *Ibid.* 970.

with his mental, or spiritual view of worship and he is likewise true to his insistence that worship is moral, but this tendency to subordinate the Sacraments in his scheme would appear unjustified. We will, however, suspend our judgment until we examine his observations on the subject.

In spite of his appreciation of a spiritual retreat when one is "alone with God," he views prayer as essentially social. This stems logically from the "social concern" which is fundamental to his total message.

The Right to "Pray" is a Trust; from those, who are to pray "with" us: therefore nothing doubtful and uncertain, or peculiar and singular shou'd be put into our Prayer: or be matter of it.[1]

If we will remember that Whichcote has in mind here public prayer, we will find his suggestion quite helpful. Too often public prayers degenerate to the mere suggestive imposition of one's own interests upon others and the sense of mutual concern and divine communion is absent.

Whichcote regards prayer in the Reformed Church as both formal and conceived. Formal prayers are aids for wandering minds and they are proper and succinct; whereas spontaneous prayers are not always "purely prayer matter." Genuine prayer consists of these aspects: confession; thanksgiving; adoration; and petition. Anything that does not refer to these four aspects of prayer is to be omitted.[2]

In prayer we should be sure that we are in a "praying temper" and that we offer to God in sacrifice "prayer-matter." We should be concerned at once with the proper attitude in which we approach God in prayer and with the nature of our thoughts. Attitude and intention are united in prayer and we are to remember that "truth of the matter may be false for the manner." [3] If men would confine their prayers to what is necessary and essential, all undue repetitions would be removed and none would be too long. Above all, men should not in prayer take the liberty to tell God stories. If we confess our sins in prayer, we should do so with a desire for pardon. Those who make a serious attempt to live as they pray, will not have the same sins to confess a second time. The Christian religion is not designed in order that we may sin and pray, and pray and sin. One may acknowledge that he has done something be-

---

[1] *Ibid.*, 1074.

[2] *Works*, II, 327. Cf. Friedrich Heiler's psychological and phenomenological study of prayer. It is odd that Whichcote should have overlooked dedication and communion as vital to Prayer, see *Prayer*, tr. by S. Mc Comb and J. E. Park (New York, 1958), pp. 353–363. See also, W. N. Pittenger, *Christian Affirmations* (New York, 1954), pp. 52–63.

[3] *Ibid.*, I, 15–16. See Whichcote's own prayers appended to Salter's ed. of his *Aphorisms* and to Vol. IV of his *Works*. These prayers are a concise statement of his theology.

fore which by some weakness he has done again; but to take confession lightly and to practice a sin again and again willfully is not religious but profane. When we pray in adoration of God, His perfections, superiority and greatness, we should be aware of our "unworthiness" in His presence, our dependence upon Him. We should be filled with a sense of our insufficiency and weakness and desire the assistance of His grace. And as we reflect upon God's goodness and faithfulness to us, we should render to Him most hearty and sincere thanks.[1] For Whichcote, as for H. H. Farmer, prayer is man's sincere response to God's self-disclosure. Farmer says:

> In the thought of revelation there is expressed the sense of God's active approach as personal to the spirit of man; in prayer there is expressed the answering activity of man, as self-conscious personality towards God.[2]

We receive bread and wine in memory of Christ's passion and death and we use water in baptism to acknowledge Father, Son and Holy Ghost. The Sacraments are required by Scripture as "means of grace" and these are the "superadditions" to rational worship.[3] Whichcote reminds us that no specific instructions are given concerning the institution of the Lord's Supper save the action and its interpretation.

But men are divided on such questions as the following in regard to the Sacrament of Holy Communion: In what company? What prepatation? At what time? How often? In what posture? Such men seek "determinations beyond Scripture." All these questions are unanswered in Scripture.[4] But our Lord clearly commands that we should celebrate this Feast in remembrance of Him. This alone is fundamental however we may answer the series of questions just stated. There was no concern of our Lord about the company or Judas would have been excluded. All laws are rigorously obeyed when they are first made. Thus if the lawgiver did not insist upon the rule regarding a

---

[1] *Ibid.*, III, 207–209.

[2] *The World and God* (London, 1955), p. 128. Cf. Heiler, *Ibid.*, p. 362. "Prayer is a living communion of man with God."

[3] Whichcote, *Works*, II, 325.

[4] Some recent studies on the Lord's supper are worth studying. Norman Hook attempts to present the scriptural basis of the doctrine for the sake of Christian unity in his, *The Eucharist in the New Testament* (London, 1964), p. lx. Joachim Jeremias relates the Lord's Supper to the background of the Jewish Passover and to Christology in his *The Eucharistic Words of Jesus*, tr. by A. Ehrhardt (New York, 1955), pp. 152, 159. B. J. Kidd discusses the concept of *ex opere operato* in his *The Later Medieval Doctrine of Eucharistic Sacrifice* (London, 1958), p. 44. G. H. Williams in his *Anselm: Communion and Atonement* (St. Louis, Missouri, 1960) links Anselm's conceptions of incarnation and atonement with Holy Communion, see p. 64. Robert S. Paul in his *The Atonement and The Sacraments* (New York, 1960) attempts the more comprehensive task of relating historically and theologically the various views of atonement with the two sacraments recognized by reformation Christianity, viz., Baptism and Holy Communion.

special company neither should we. No time was given for the Supper,
for it was instituted when our Lord and His intimate disciples were
met upon another occasion – in preparation for the Passover. At the
Passover there were four eatings and two drinkings. Our Lord gave a
new significance to one of the cups and one of the breads. It was a
religious exercise that they had met to observe and it may be assumed
that they were in a worshipful mood. Those who live Christian lives
and follow the Saviour's doctrine may freely and indifferently enter
into all religious exercises. Some men, who make no preparation for
prayer or other Christian acts of worship pretend to make serious
and special preparation for Holy Communion. Is not the object of
worship the same in all cases? It appears that such people conceive
the Sacrament as possessing some "magical power" or their lives are
so corrupt that they fear the literal meaning of the words of Paul
that "they eat and drink damnation to themselves" (I Cor. 11:29).

Surely the sacrifice of the wicked is an abomination unto the Lord,
but this is to point up the fact that it is not safe to "lay all the weight
upon one piece of religion and be trifling and neglective in others." [1]
Whichcote observes:

> Whosoever lives according to the difference of good and evil, and governs
> himself so that he may make application to God, either by prayer, reading
> meditation, or Christian conference, or any other Christian duty, is in a prepa-
> ration and disposition, wherein he may come safely to the table of the Lord. [2]

Our Lord does not tell us how often we should observe the Feast, but
He did say "as often as you do it," apparently implying frequency.
As a matter of fact its importance implies frequency because it is in
remembrance of the saving work of our Lord for us. It is reasonable
that this Sacrament should be observed frequently and with sincerity
of heart and life. As for the posture we should assume while observing
the Feast, there is no instruction, for apparently our Lord "took them
as he found them." The danger is that by our superstititions we may
make rules which harden into dogmas and then seek to impose these
on others.

> It is to be feared, that so much of curiosity as a man bestows about any piece
> of religion and devotion that is of his own formation, so much will he abate in
> his conscientious observance of that which is of God's institution. [3]

---

[1] *Ibid.*, IV, pp. 179–180.

[2] *Ibid.*, p. 180.

[3] *Ibid.*, pp. 181–182. Cf. Cudworth, "The True Notion of the Lord's Supper," *Works*, 1st
American ed. (Andover, 1837), II, 499–542. See also, Farmer, *Ibid.*, pp. 72–74.

Whichcote has not given us a definitive account of the Lord's Supper, but his position is consistent with his purpose to defend the principles of Christian liberty and charity.

However, what he has to say is most vital, for he has called our attention from the surface matters surrounding the Holy Communion to the attitude of worship and life which are conditions of its meaning and effectiveness in our experience. He tells us how we are to live and worship if in this Sacrament God is to come to us and if God is to sacramentally unite the symbolic action and the grace it conveys for our growth in holy living.[1] He tells us what the dogmatic theologians omit for all their careful statements of Christian dogmas, namely, that if we are to commune together across barriers of incidental differences, we must not seek to "determine beyond Scripture." For those of us who are involved in the present ecumenical movement, he reminds us that we are not truly ecumenical until we can "keep the Feast" together and this we are not prepared to do as yet.[2] And for those of us who exclude others from partaking of this Sacrament with us, he reminds us that the essential fact in the Eucharist is not man's remembrance and commemoration of Christ's death alone, but that Christ here gives Himself to man. It is Christ Himself Who administers this Sacrament. It is His, not mine, or yours, and He alone invites us to His table. He is at once, the Giver of the Feast and the Feast itself. It follows that no mortal man is worthy or has the power to exclude any one from the Lord's Table. Whichcote correctly cautions us that determinations beyond Scripture may enlarge faith, but lessen charity.

Whichcote's treatment of Baptism is likewise casual. He assumes that we have sufficient knowledge concerning the doctrine of Baptism and seeks to rid the celebration of this Sacrament from all adulterations and false dogmas which are the basis of so much contention among Christians.

After he completes his discussion on Holy Communion, Whichcote says:

I might also show you the very same thing in the other institution. For, there you have only the material action, and the acknowledgement.... Now, how hath the world been troubled about the circumstances of time, and several other things about this Sacrament? and all without foundation.... Charity hath

---

[1] Whale, *Ibid.*, p. 160.

[2] It is encouraging to note the successful Protestant-Anglican-Orthodox-Roman Catholic worship service during the Faith and Order meeting of the World Council of Churches at Montreal during the summer of 1963. Perhaps this is an important step on the way to inter-Communion.

been wanting, when men have gone about to make out Scripture further than what hath been plainly declared.[1]

Whichcote's attention is focused upon tolerance in religion. "Tolerance" as used by Whichcote does not imply being "put up with" or as we say "merely tolerated," but in the more wholesome sense of sympathetic understanding, positive good-will and mutual helpfulness in spite of doctrinal differences. Further, "charity" as used by Whichcote here should be purged of all accretions. He means essentially what St. Paul means in his famous "Love Poem" (I Cor. 13), by the term translated in the King James Version of the Bible as "charity," but for which J. B. Phillips and other translators substitute the word "love." [2]

For Whichcote religion is not a system of doctrines, "observance of modes," a "heat of affections," a "form of words," or a "spirit of censoriousness." [3] While it is necessary to know what God has revealed creatively in the natural order and redemptively in Christ; it is impossible to know more than he has revealed. It follows that if men would refrain from going beyond God's revelation, in nature and by grace, there would be less controversy.[4] Thus his reaction against dogmatism is as marked as that against passion, false zeal, enthusiasm, superstition and the like.

He says concerning all these "disturbers of peace" among Christians:

Curious "Determinations" beyond Scripture, are thought to be improvement of Faith; and inconsiderate "Dullness," to be the denial of our Reason; "Fierceness" in a Sect, to be Zeal for Religion; and speaking "without sense," to be the Simplicity of the Spirit.[5]

But as for him such things may have enlarged faith, they have certainly lessened charity, and increased divisions in Christendom. John Smith appropriately captures his master's meaning when he describes theology as a "divine life rather than a divine science." [6]

[1] Whichcote, *Works*, IV, 182. Cf. T. F. Torrance and John Heron, eds., *The Biblical Doctrine of Baptism: A Study Document issued by The Special Commission on Baptism of The Church of Scotland* (Edinburgh, 1958). It states: "The heart of the New Testament teaching ... is that in Baptism the person baptised enters into a vital personal relationship with the living Lord, and so has made available to him all that his Lord accomplished for men in his incarnation, life, death, resurrection, ascension, and the bestowing of the Holy Spirit," p. 55. See also, A. H. Legg, "Christian Baptism," *The Sacraments*, a report prepared by the Joint Theological Commission of the Church of South India and The Federation of Evangelical Lutheran Churches in India (Bangalore, India, 1956), pp. 99–127; Joachim Jeremias, *The Origins of Infant Baptism*, tr. by David Cairns (London, 1960), pp. 19–42. J. de Baciocchi, *La Vie Sacramentaire De L'Église* (Paris, 1958), pp. 63–96.

[2] *Letters to Young Churches* (London, 1951), pp. 79–80.

[3] Whichcote, *Aph.* 1127.

[4] *Ibid.*, 1054.

[5] *Ibid.*, 505.

[6] Smith, *Ibid.*, p. 1.

Over against Whichcote's reaction to these disturbers of peace among Christians, he presents his view of Christian tolerance and thus it is to his positive suggestions toward Christian understanding and cooperation in spite of surface differences that we now turn.

Whichcote makes clear his awareness of the difficulty of calling in question treasured beliefs, but, nevertheless, he insists that no wise, nor truly good man, should be so fond of an opinion that he will not give it up if he finds it to be false. The very nature of our creaturehood, as "finite and fallible" beings, indicates that we should always be inquirers after truth, that we should keep an open mind for the examination of new information, and that we should be willing to follow truth wherever it leads.[1] We should also remember that there are some things in religion that are not absolutely clear to any of us about which others may be "otherwise minded," and yet not be necessarily opposed to truth.

Fortunately these obscure matters do not involve things "necessary to salvation," for these are clearly revealed. And, furthermore, God will "bring out of particular mistakes, him that is right in the main," It follows that those who differ in some particulars, but who agree on essential points of doctrine and policy, should "hold together" as if they were agreed in all things. The principle things of religion, which include the honor of God, form the foundation of Christian union and all matters of particular apprehension ought not to make for differences or separation. If the fundamentals of religion were digested and duly considered, there would be a solid ground for peace and unity in the Church. The normal result would be agreement in "hearty love and good-will" and mutual helpfulness.[2] That is to say Christians are of "one spirit" and all enmity between them is to be "subdued and vanquished." Being fellow citizens of heaven, it is to be expected that Christians should be in essential accord upon earth, for men from the same country are normally elated to meet each other abroad, and are faithful and kind to each other.[3]

It is a scandal to the world when professors of religion do not agree. Disagreements among Christians are hindrances to missionary work among the unsaved.[4] It is easy to understand, therefore, in view

---

[1] Whichcote, *Works*, I, 355; II, 8; IV, 103.

[2] *Ibid.*, pp. 377–378; Cf. *Ibid.*, IV, 403.

[3] *Ibid.*, II, 23; Cf. *Ibid.*, IV, 183.

[4] It is necessary to point out that by disagreement, or difference among Christians, Whichcote means an unwholesome and odious division on non-essentials.

He leaves ample room for a wholesome divergence of opinion in the Christian spirit. It is, indeed, unfortunate that various denominations within Protestantism were so belated in practicing this principle on the foreign mission field. It is regrettable that many "enthusi-

of the divisions within the Church why those who stand outside refuse to come in, and why they look upon Christians with derision. Truth, nevertheless, is single and all who are joined in it are united.

It follows that agreement between Christians would be of mutual benefit: for their spiritual edification, for their subsistence in an evil world, for their peace of mind, and for the general effectiveness of the Christian Church. Competition between parties can only lead to envious comparisons, while there should be but one division, that between the Church and the world. For the good of the Cause, those who profess faith in Christ should be one in heart, as to all issues and purposes.[1]

Whichcote reminds us of Socrates as he raises questions and makes us aware of our ignorance and limitations. Why should not agreement in the fundamentals of the faith be more conducive to concord than differences on non-essentials are to separation? All that are in accord on essentials are informed by the same spirit and the things agreed upon are more numerous and more important than the things upon which they differ. Why should men differ concerning religion which is the greatest bond of union? Religion has two things "final" in it, namely, reconciliation with God as Creator and Redeemer, and reconciliation with each other. Why should one be aggrieved because every one uses his own right? There is no greater right than that of worshipping God with all our mind. Every one has the right to judge what he should believe and it is not within a man's power to judge as he wills, but only according to reason. As a matter of fact, if a man could believe as he wills, the

---

astic" religious sects still prefer to "go it alone" in their missionary program to the detriment of the entire Christian cause. My recent visit to Asia has enabled me to observe the situation firsthand. This situation, it appears to me, is being corrected more by the rise of nationalism in these areas than by Christian good-will. The fact is that many governments in Asia (i.e. Japanese, India) group most Christian bodies together under a Ministry of Religious Affairs. If the religious bodies want to remain in these countries to witness at all, they must, as a minority religion, do so along with other Christian bodies. In some cases the Roman Catholic Church has been granted a measure of autonomy because of its excellent contribution to education in underdeveloped countries. This I understand as a pragmatic rather than a religious concession. It is unfortunate that we have not worked out our internal differences as Christians; for now we must brace ourselves for an encounter with non-Christian religions which have now become aggressive in the propagation of their own beliefs not only in the East but in the West also.

E. G. Parrinder compares the present impact of Eastern thought on the West with that of classical thought on Europe at the Renaissance. See his, "A Contribution to the Honest to God Debate," W. F., No. 62 (March, 1965), p. 10. One of his concerns is that the scholars who entered into the debate with Bishop Robinson all but ignored all non-Christian religions making one slight reference to one other religion (p. 9).

[1] Whichcote, *Works*, II, 25–26. The originality and courage of Whichcote's views on Christian tolerance may be appreciated only against a background of a full realization of the religious situation in seventeenth century England. His tolerant spirit is thrown into a higher relief when we recall the fanaticisms and extravagances of almost every type of Christianity and the unwholesome effects of the bitterness thus produced.

sinner would never be self-condemned, for the guilt or self-condemnation of the sinner implies the unnaturalness and irrationality of sin. Why over-emphasize the questionable matters of faith? In view of our finitude, is it wise to over-value our opinions while at the same time we undervalue the opinions of others? Why not make the same favorable interpretation on behalf of another which one desires for oneself? Is it not possible to lessen differences by fair debate, which may be increased by jealousy and suspicion. When persons with supposed differences talk together, they often find that they are not as far apart as they imagined. Is it fair to reject one from Christian conversation whom God in Christ has not rejected? Why condemn others on points which we are not willing to stake our eternal destiny? Why blame others for not knowing what we have arrived at by much effort over a long period of time? As long as there is a possibility of wisdom and experience, of growing in faith and knowledge, there is still hope for those who seek religious truth.[1] This series of questions by Whichcote is suggestive of the answers he gives to them. Indeed, this intention runs through his inquiries. Both his questions and answers are of the deepest significance to all who are seriously seeking grounds for Christian understanding.

Whichcote offers an apology for all who are honest in their search for truth, all who are of a "modest and teachable" spirit. He asserts that even if a man is mistaken, he need not be heretical and it is easy to perceive if a man is either a hypocrite or heretic. He is not a hypocrite if he means well, and he is not a heretic if he is sincere and ready to be informed

But Whichcote is also aware of the danger of this position if carried to the extreme. Those who are less competent to judge for want of education should rely upon qualified guides. Here he conceives the role of religious teachers not as the mere transmitters of dogma but as those who appeal to the mind and experience of others as dignified and autonomous persons. Great respect is due "superiors" in the government of the Church if disturbances arising out of pretense to private judgment are to be averted. Here he implies his loyalty to an ecclesiastical hierarchy in the Church and there is every reason to believe that he subscribed to the episcopal organization and polity of the Church of England. But episcopacy for him as for the liberal Churchmen, i.e. Chillingworth, Taylor and Stillingfleet, was to be understood as the *bene esse* rather than the *esse* of the Church. Thus Whichcote seeks a balance between the complete religious liberty of the individual on the one

---

[1] *Ibid.*, pp. 29–36; Cf. *Aph.* 136.

hand and a secure control by those invested with religious authority on the other. Whether we accept his solution or not we must envisage his problem and the necessity of some constructive thought and action regarding it.

Whichcote desires to see the principle of democracy rule in the Church as elsewhere. He insists that a person should not consider his private judgment as superior to all others, and he considers it safer to err in a matter that is common than in one that is personal.[1]

One who asserts his personal judgment as final regardless of all other opinions should ask himself: "How went the spirit of God from the generality of worshippers, and determined itself to me?" By sincerely raising this question, one is led to cautious and diligent inquiry, to a desire for further information. Before becoming certain of one's beliefs, one should submit them to impartial examination by others more competent to judge, weigh what others have to say, and suspend judgment until the matter has been repeatedly reflected upon. After this process our decisions are more reliable, for nothing is more certain than that which we have arrived at after honest doubt. Without these considerations we are likely to be easily persuaded and therefore credulous or "light of faith." It is essential that such modesty as becomes a Christian should always accompany our private judgments. Such judgments should be allied with good behavior so as to prevent any unrest in the family of God, the Church. Private judgment is important but should be preceded by education, meditation and discussion. In this sense, private judgment is a fundamental right of intellectual nature; but the fact that we are born only with faculties or possibilities for acts and habits, means that we are responsible for the proper development and use of these potentialities.[2] This is just as important from the religious view point as it is from the moral, and by adherence to this principle greater understanding would be possible among Christians.

Apart from Scripture and the Sacraments, all other things in Christianity are circumstantial.

---

[1] Here we are reminded of recent church theologies (i.e. Aulén, John Knox, Wingren, Barth) which are seen as correctives for the more individualistic approaches to theology. In Whichcote's day most Puritans depended on the Holy Spirit to understand scripture. This was especially true of the Quakers and other similar groups. John Goodwin and Richard Baxter were exceptions among the Puritans – they considered reason as a criterion. Another possible criterion was the Church, provided it was not papist (Anglo-Catholic).

See G. F. Nutall, *The Holy Spirit In Puritan Faith and Experience* (Oxford, 1946), pp. 22, 42–43, 45. Cf. Howard Watkin-Jones, *The Holy Spirit From Arminius to Wesley* (London, 1929), pp. 223–229.

[2] *Ibid.*, II, 36–38. Cf. *Aph.* 570, 637, *passim.*

There are, then, "circumstantials" in religion which are changeable as the security of the Church may require and the maintenance of charity among Christians demands. God intends that the Christian Church should have the protection of a sound government, but liberty among Christians concerning indifferent matters is also allowed. There is, then, a very great latitude within the framework of the Church especially concerning liturgy. We should, however, manifest obedience to those in authority and in order to attain brotherly love and charity, we should "live in love" among the members of the Church. Nothing is more prejudicial to charity than unnecessary separation. Therefore, it is advisable to "affect to differ" on merely circumstantial questions of religion since "every degree of separation begets an alienation." A valid distinction may be made in religion between those things which are good in themselves, and those that are good only in relation to other things. The former are immutable, for instance, love of God, faith in Him, truth and goodness. These things sanctify by their very presence. On the other hand, matters in religion "good in order to these" are not important enough to cause a breach of peace in the Church. For example, the manner of worship is not "necessary to salvation," and, therefore, is to be valued only as required by saving truths.[1]

Not only do men separate upon what they consider to be essential to the faith, but they divide over what they consider not to be of God; i.e., the "moral part" of religion. These are those who insist that the very knowledge of our Lord is opposed to moral responsibility. This is for Whichcote the "strangest mistake" of all, since the very purpose of the saving work of Christ is to restore and reinforce the moral principles of creation, in other words, to "re-establish" the moral part of religion impaired by man's fallen and sinful condition. This being so, the fact that men should separate by setting morality over against religion is indeed difficult to understand. It follows that in this case, there is a serious mistake as well as a deviation from Christian love.[2]

Whichcote observes that most great differences in Christendom are not based on necessary and indispensable truth or Scripture, but on points of "curious" and "nice" speculation or on arbitrary modes of worship. Such surface differences should not make it impossible for men to live in peace, "with a safe conscience" and in "full communion" in

---

[1] *Ibid.*, pp. 325–326.
[2] *Ibid.*, pp. 390–391. Cf. *Supra*, ch. VII, for a detailed account of Whichcote's view of Christian morality.

the Church of God and to submit to its government. It appears that if Whichcote had to choose between the liturgy and government of the Church of England, he would give preference to the government. But most important, he would insist upon the acknowledgment of Christ as the Head of the Church. He is greatly disturbed because Christendom is "scattered into particular ways," multiplied into sects and parties, divided over non-essentials of the faith and what is worst, disagreed upon the great and bright truths of reason and Christianity.[1] In view of this state of affairs, he makes the following suggestion:

... All that are serious in religion, do agree in the main; so may hold communion. If they have the love of truth in their hearts, if they mean by religion, to prepare themselves for happiness, all these do agree in main and principle things; therefore they may hold communion; and if they may they ought, if they ought and do not, they sin.[2]

We turn now to Whichcote's more constructive suggestions concerning Christian tolerance. We should not confuse the certainties of the faith with uncertainties. All uncertainties should be by themselves among matters requiring further enquiry; while the certainties of religion should issue into life and practice. That is to say, a man should never admit anything among his settled beliefs which is not in itself rational and self-consistent.[3] Where the light of Scripture does not direct, God refers us to the light of creation.[4]

Differences in a wholesome sense are natural and are to be expected. The persecution of a brother out of zeal for truth is unwarrantable and any such pretense deserves careful examination; for men must think as they find cause; they have the freedom of their own thoughts; and, sincere believers do not greatly differ about saving truths. It is better for men to make mistakes about religion than to neglect it completely since the mere interest in it indicates that they are awake and are seeking truth even where they have not attained it. This emphasizes the necessity for patience and love among Christians.[5]

---

[1] *Ibid.*, III, 33; *Aphs.* 588, 1036.

[2] *Ibid.*, p. 59. Whichcote's contemporary John Milton was one of the greatest exponents of Christian liberty in seventeenth century England, *De Doctrina Christiana*, tr. by Charles Sumner (Cambridge, England, 1825), p. 424. This conception is set forth in Milton's *De Doctrina* and briefly near the end of *Paradise Lost* ed. by G. M. Davis (London, 1931). Cf. Douglas Bush, *Paradise Lost in Our Time* (Ithaca, 1945), pp. 35–36.

[3] *Ibid.*, p. 60; Cf. More, *Ibid.*

[4] *Ibid.*, p. 269.

[5] *Ibid.*, IV, 201–203. Whichcote has sounded a significant warning for our age characterized so much by indifference to religion. Professor Matthew Spinka, of Hartford Seminary, used to say, "There are no more holy wars because no one cares enough for religion to fight about it." On the other hand, one wonders if all the variations on the theme of the death of

One should not expect unity in all opinions, and divergences in comprehension may be no one's fault. Things appear different to people of different temperaments and backgrounds.[1]

For all his intellectualism, Whichcote realizes that it is impossible to render such a conclusive reason for an opinion that another may not offer an even greater in contradiction. There is "reason against reason" in most cases and differences of opinion are, therefore, inevitable. We are naturally different, in temperament, education, employment, presuppositions, early prejudices, and the like. Moreover there is difficulty in judging many "uncertainties" partly from the nature of the things themselves, and partly because our understanding is fallible. Even those who are sincerely religious, who are diligent to be informed, arrive at different conclusions. They find cause to suspend judgment, to rethink their tentative conclusions and to "compare notes" with others. Thus understanding for those who differ from us is a Christian responsibility.[2] Whichcote's point is that all saving truths are certain and clear and thus the things concerning which it is safe to differ and upon which sincere Christians often do differ, are the uncertain and incidental matters of faith. This being so, we should have sympathy and understanding for those who differ from us in their sincere search for truth. His suggestion, in brief, is that it is essential for the maintenance of the spirit of love for Christians to "agree to differ."

It is better for us that there shou'd be "Difference" of Judgment: if we keep "Charity": but it is unmanly to "Quarrel," because we Differ.[3]

Whichcote is concerned with what may best be described as "unity in diversity."

"Why should not they," he asks, "who meet in the regenerate nature, who agree in the great articles of the faith, and principles of the good life, over-look subordinate differences?" As a matter of fact, if there is love and good-will, we come to a more rational and better grounded faith as a result of our different apprehensions. Without differences, any conversation concerning faith would end as soon as it had begun, for it is only by disagreement and new insight that one's faith is examined. Without this give and take in discussion, truth will be lost for

God, the fascination for Zen and Atheistic Existentialism is not a reflection of a deep spiritual hunger.

[1] Cf. Heiler, *Ibid.*, pp. 103, 136–170 where he discusses various psychological types of devotees – the philosophical, the mystical and prophetic.

[2] *Ibid.*, pp. 378–380.

[3] *Aph.* 569.

want of critical examination.[1] Our position should be one of implicit faith in God, that is, belief in the Holy Spirit's meaning. If this is so we meet in "the rule of truth" even though we differ in the particular explanation of it. If there were no contradiction in the several apprehensions of men, we might never be awakened to search into things and if we were mistaken, we would never be delivered from it. But is it not possible that such discussion may lead to dangerous error? It is Whichcote's belief that this is God's "charge" and He will not allow a sincere "seeker" after truth to err in anything saving. This being so, our task is to put forward what we believe to be true, together with the reason for it. To say what is reasonable and make this clear to others by appealing to their minds and hearts, is the most we can do and the rest is up to God. Saving knowledge is available to all, it is clear and self-evident.

Since all things that are necessary to salvation are delivered plainly in the holy scriptures; we may resolve that none but those who are gross neglecters, do err, "dangerously." There is no need of curiosity since the appearance of Christ... The points of Christian faith are clearly intelligible to all capacities, as they are clearly necessary to be believed by all men. God accepts alike the faith that results from dark mists of the ignorant, and from the clearest intelligence of the learned. The holy scriptures are so written, that they are sooner understood by an unlearned man that is pious and modest, than by a philosopher who is arrogant and proud.[2]

If the question is raised, as to the place of zeal for God and truth, Whichcote's answer is that this has its principal operation on oneself in improving one's judgment and practice. Towards others it shows itself in strength of argument, a well-governed spirit and a Christian love and patience for those not yet satisfied.[3] Religion is a "bond of union" and obliges us at once to God and one another and should never be the basis of displeasure.[4] The charitable spirit is essential to Christianity [5] and, therefore, Christians must be peacemakers and reconcilers.[6] It is indeed difficult to understand why some people are worse for their religion, who are otherwise good-natured. Some are moved by their religion to do things unnatural and unreasonable; while "common good-nature makes men innocent, harmless and friendly." [7] Whichcote attested to these precepts by his example. Tillotson says concerning

1 *Works*, II, 26–27.
2 *Ibid.*, pp. 27–28.
3 *Ibid.*, p. 28.
4 *Ibid.*, IV, 205.
5 *Ibid.*, p. 211.
6 *Ibid.*, 212.
7 *Ibid.*, p. 214.

his work at Milton:

... He preached constantly; and relieved the poor, and had their children taught to read at his own charge; and made up differences among neighbors...[1]

In matters of religion, we are to maintain "unity of verity" in faith and "unity of charity" in communion, notwithstanding all differences in apprehension.

This is possible of a perfect rule of faith and practice in Scripture. It follows that all other differences should lessen daily, and if not, we may turn these into an advantage, making them matters of friendly debate.[2] Some surface differences are wholesome since they offer a challenge to the faith without which it may become "shallow and remiss" in practice. Those who profess faith in Christ are to be united in a common loyalty to Him in thought and life and be in loving fellowship one with another since our Lord, the Head of the Church, is the ground of our faith.

We must maintain good behavior towards one another, love and goodwill, notwithstanding any difference whatever, as a material point of righteousness between man and man. If it be a difference concerning religion, it must be so upon account of religion; and religion requires concord. Religion is a bond of union between man and God and between man and man. You cannot imagine that which is the principle of union should be the occasion of disaffection. We cannot pretend to do that for religion, which is unnatural to religion, contrary to religion, and which religion forbids. Religion excludes all dissention, misbehavior, everything contrary to peace, love and goodwill.[3]

This principle of unity in diversity is not only upheld by Scripture, but is duly supported by reason. We are only finite beings and, therefore, we naturally differ in many things. Furthermore, there is "misrepresentation" by our senses. By reason we are able to rectify the errors of sense. But the truth is that neither by the truths of creation or redemption can we secure an absolute exemption from all error. The Reformed Church makes no such claim to infallibility.

What we shall be in the future life we only "know in part," but we do know that the nearer we draw to God, the more we shall be exempt from error and our approach to Him is by imitation and participation of His nature, by becoming like Him in holiness, purity and righteousness.[4] Since reason is our highest perfection it should be recognized as what indeed it is – "the voice of God" Who is the Highest Intelligence. We must use reason, then, in seeking understanding one with another, for it is a uniform principle, that is, it is always constant and self-

[1] Tillotson, *Ibid.*, p. 25.
[2] Whichcote, *Works, Ibid.*, pp. 380–382.
[3] *Ibid.*, pp. 284–286.
[4] *Ibid.*, I, 392.

identical. Reason in one man accords with reason in another and, therefore, cannot be refused, it must be acknowledged and accepted. Reason is the rule of all men's mind, it leads to moderation of opinions and even where there is disagreement it renders men more reconcilable. In a fair debate where reason directs, neither person will stray far from the truth or from each other. And, furthermore, men thus divided will be more satisfied with each other and less fierce.[1] Thus by the authority of Reason and Scripture, we may agree to differ, since all things "saving" are made plain by Nature and Grace.

All objects affect; and all Faculties incline: God and Nature have appointed a "directing" Principle... that there might be, in multiplicity, a reduction to Unity; Harmony and Uniformity, in Variety.[2]

But it appears obvious that in his suggestions for Christian tolerance, the authority of Scripture has first place.

Nothing is "of Faith," that is not in Scripture; nothing is "necessary," as otherwise expressed; nothing is "certain," as farther made out. We may live in Christian love and Union; without Consent and Agreement in nonscriptural expressions and forms of words.[3]

To conclude our observations upon Whichcote's views concerning the Church, it is fair to say that he believed in a universal Church in the sense that all true Christians belong to it in spite of minor differences. As long as Christians are united on things necessary for salvation, surface differences should occasion no breach in the universal fellowship. Tillotson's sermon at Whichcote's funeral is an invaluable estimate of the life which Whichcote set forth as a witness to his teaching. Here, however, it is sufficient to recall once again the scene at the death of Whichcote at the home of Cudworth. Whichcote took the Sacrament of Holy Communion and spoke highly of it as a symbol of the Universal Church.[4] If a man's last words have any special importance it is clear that the Church and Sacraments have a central place in Whichcote's thought. However, it was not his purpose to present a doctrine of the Church or the Sacraments, but to plead for Christian tolerance. He remained loyal to the Church of England to the end and his protest against what he regards as unwholesome tendencies within the Church of England, i.e., Laudian, Puritan and Sectarian, makes this loyalty more evident. But loyal as he was to the Church of England, he could envisage the need for a purging from the inside. In

---

[1] Ibid., IV, 401.
[2] Aph. 1042.
[3] Ibid.
[4] Tillotson, Ibid., pp. 28–29.

Whichcote and his successors, extremely interested as they were in the moral transformation of clergy and members alike, the Church of England reaches its highest peak of self-criticism in the seventeenth century.

What is most amazing and significant is Whichcote's anticipation of the ecumenical spirit and the sound manner in which he worked out his view. We repeat again his concise statement of his view:

> Determinations, "beyond" Scripture, have indeed "enlarged" Faith; but lessened "Charity" and multiplied divisions.[1]

Indeed a statement on unity by the World Council of Churches at Evanston might easily be a summary of Whichcote's reflections on Christian tolerance. The statement reads:

> Only in the light of the oneness of the church of Christ can we understand the difference between diversity and division in the church, and their relation to sin. There is diversity which is not sinful but good because it reflects both the diversities of gifts of the Spirit in the one body and diversities of creation by the one Creator. But when diversity disrupts the manifest unity of the body then it changes its quality and becomes a sinful division. It is sinful because it obscures from men the sufficiency of Christ's atonement, inasmuch as the gospel of reconciliation is denied in the very lives of those who proclaim it.[2]

This being the final chapter in the presentation of Whichcote's thought, it seems appropriate to sum up what he means by true religion. Natural religion or religion of creation requires us to deal fairly, equally and righteously with our neighbour; and soberly or temperately as to ourselves.[3] The Gospel as a "superaddition" to the law of creation involves the acceptance of the mediatorship of Christ and the two sacraments.[4] Religion of Creation and Redemption complete his total concept of revelation as follows:

> I would superadd one thing more, that is the harmony and consistency that is between true reason, and Christianity. There is the greatest correspondence between the principles of reason, and Christianity.... For the latter, Christianity doth wholly acknowledge the former; and Christianity coming in upon the apostacy from God's creation, it restores, and calls men back again: Christianity reinforceth, recovereth, establisheth, yes doth advance and highly improves every one of the principles of God's creation; which are the principles of reason.... Christianity doth not only recover human nature, but carries it on to a higher perfection; secures the common instincts of good and just; and

---

1 Whichcote, *Aph.* 981. Richard Baxter resembles Whichcote as a prophet of Christian tolerance, see F. J. Powicke, *Richard Baxter Under the Cross* (1662–1691) (London, 1927), pp. 231–260.

2 "Our Oneness in Christ and Our Disunity as Churches," Report of Sect. I – Faith and Order, C. C., Vol. LXXI, No. 38, (Sept. 22, 1954), p. 1137.

3 Whichcote, *Works*, III, 252–253.

4 *Ibid.*, p. 283.

polishes human nature.... The principles of reason, the principles of God's creation, and Christ's restoration, do the self-same thing, and if they are considered, nothing would give so great a satisfaction to the mind of man as they; nothing would better carry him on to that perfection, of which he is capable.[1]

Having brought to focus what Whichcote has said in his writing concerning truths of "first-inscription" and "after-revelation," we turn next to a reflection of his thought in the writings of his disciples and successors.

[1] *Ibid.*, pp. 254–255.

CHAPTER NINE

THE FATHER OF
THE CHRISTIAN PLATONISTS OF CAMBRIDGE

Before we can discuss realistically Whichcote's relation to the so-called Cambridge Platonists, we must decide if, in fact, he was a Platonist. In order to have a standard of judgment, we must first arrive at a definition of Platonism.

Dean W. R. Inge's observations are helpful here, for he points out that Plato is unintelligible until we read him as a prophet or prose-poet and cease to hunt for a system in his writings. Further, Inge draws a distinction between personal and traditional Platonism. Traditional Platonism is the intellectual system based on the implicit philosophy of the personal Platonist. Personal Platonism is the mood of one who regards the endless variety of this visible and temporal world with an inquisitiveness, and at the same time is haunted by the presence of an invisible and eternal world, sustaining both the temporal world and men – a world not perceived as external to himself, but inwardly lived by him. But Platonism, then understood, is more than a "mood"; it is a sustained attitude towards life founded on deep convictions – a practical philosophy or religion.[1]

Some reflections by C. E. Raven help us to carry this discussion further. According to him, the Platonic attitude toward life at least from Origen onwards bequeathed to the Church the importance of nature as a medium of divine revelation.[2] Raven does not hesitate to assert that Whichcote profoundly affected the naturalist, John Ray,

---

[1] *The Platonic Tradition in English Religious Thought*, (London, 1926), pp. 65–67. Inge derives most of his insights here from Professor J. A. Stewart's essay, "Platonism in English Poets." J. S. Harrison in his *Platonism in English Poetry of the 16th and 17th Centuries*, (New York, 1903) considers Henry More's *Song of the Soul* as the boldest attempt to blend Platonism and Christianity in the poetry of the day. J. H. Overton in his *William Law*, (London, 1881) p. 413, points out the unsystematic nature of Plato's thought and the danger of quoting him in support of any doctrine.

[2] *Natural Religion and Christian Theology*, (Cambridge, England, 1953), I, 46–48. Cf. Whichcote, *Works*, III, 176. "... Every grass in the field declares God."

by his Sunday lectures. Raven continues by asserting that one cannot study Ray's immensely influential book, *The Wisdom of God in the Works of Creation*, without seeing how much he and the whole scientific movement owed to the wise, liberal and reverent teaching of Whichcote and his followers. It follows that the indirect influence of the Cambridge Platonists can hardly be overstated since they encouraged an attitude toward nature radically different from that which had prevailed in Christendom since the death of Origen. Hence, nature and the natural order for them are not only God's creation but the foundation of the true religion both moral and philosophical and there is no contradiction between nature and grace. For Whichcote the same God is the Author of nature and the Giver of grace. Under this influence Ray conceived communion with nature as real worship and even as a matter of particular religious obligation.[1] Raven sums up his general position as follows:

...The scholars, who appealed to antiquity, to the Greek and Latin Classics, to the Greek New Testament, and to the example and teaching of the earliest Church, actually found in the writings of the Greek Apologists and Christian Platonists of Alexandria an attitude towards nature, a concept of progressive revelation, and an insistence upon education and intellectual effort wholly appropriate to the new insistence upon observation and experiment. The naturalists, striving to develop hypotheses consistent with fresh data disclosed by astronomy and geology, botany and zoology, found themselves anticipated by thinkers, who had drawn their conclusions not from the study of the physical world, but from the ancient Logos-theology of Justin, Clement and Origen.[2]

We are assured that this appreciation of nature was by no means irreligious. Raven says:

Not that the philosophy of Ray and his contemporaries was naturalistic or irreligious: for almost everyone of the pioneers of science this is certainly far from the case. They were in fact men of deep and genuine Christianity sharing in the large and reasonable faith which Joseph Mead... had pioneered, which Benjamin Whichcote at Emmanuel and later in his remarkable preaching at Holy Trinity had proclaimed, and which More and Cudworth, John Smith and Nathaniel Culverwel and John Worthington had expounded. It was this group of men (whom John Wilkins joined for a brief space in 1659) that created the "latitude" or Cambridge Platonist school. They were men who repudiated the two antitheses both that between the secular and sacred characteristic of the Protestant Reformers; men who insisted that creation and redemption were alike manifestations of God; men who set themselves to welcome all truth, to study it reverently, and to interpret it so far as they could reasonably and Christianly.[3]

---

[1] Raven, *Ibid.*, pp. 110–111. Cf. Whichcote, *Ibid.*, I, 370; *Aph.* 109. See also John Smith, "Divine Knowledge," *Select Discourses*, ed. by H. G. Williams (Cambridge, England, 1859).
[2] *English Naturalistic from Neckham to Ray, etc.* ...... (Cambridge, England, 1947), p. 356.
[3] *Synthetic Philosophy in the Seventeenth Century*, (Oxford, 1945), pp. 21–22. Wilkins deserves a brief tribute since he is not usually mentioned with the Cambridge Platonists. He befriended Whichcote after his ejection from the Provostship of King's College, recom-

From the observations of Inge and Raven, Whichcote's status as a Platonist is unquestioned. To Inge, our author is a Platonist of the natural or personal type and even of the traditional type since there is sufficient evidence that he did study ancient philosophy and his thought reveals a casual acquaintance with the history of Platonism. Similarly Raven has attributed to Whichcote a Platonic attitude toward all experience. But it is to be remembered that these two writers are somewhat partial toward the Cambridge Platonists and this is indicated by their frequent and favourable references to them in their several writings. Further, we must take into account the opinions of other writers who have attributed great religious and ethical importance to Whichcote's thought but who state that he made no contribution to philosophy or natural science.[1]

It is characteristic of writers who approach the study of the Cambridge Platonists from a purely philosophical point of view to disregard any acquaintance Whichcote may have had with Platonic thought, though they admit that Smith, Cudworth and More were all Platonists.[2] But if the school was founded by Whichcote, then it would

mending Whichcote to succeed himself as Vicar of St. Lawrence Jewry, London. Wilkins' views are quite similar to Whichcote's. Cf. John Wilkins, *Of the Principles and Duties of Natural Religion*, 5th ed. (London, 1704), pp. 19, 39–61, 125–135, 410 and *passim*. See also Burnet, *History of My Own Time*, ed. by Swift (Oxford, 1933), I, 340; *Supra*, Ch. I.

[1] This view is held to a certain degree by J. A. Passmore, *Ralph Cudworth*, (Cambridge, England, 1951), Ch. I. and by Cassirer, *The Platonic Renaissance in England*, tr. Pettegrove, (New York, 1953), Ch. V. According to Cassirer, only Cudworth and More of the four main members of the school undertook to develop a philosophy of nature and they were totally unequipped for the task. He concludes that whereas in its philosophy of religion, the Cambridge School was ahead of its time, in its philosophy of science, it was far behind, see *Ibid.*, pp. 130–131. It should be remembered that Cassirer approaches this school from the viewpoint of its relationship to philosophic systems and the history of ideas, see *Ibid.*, p. 25 (n. 1). In the opinion of the present writer this approach is inadequate for the simple reason that the Cambridge Platonists were philosophers in the service of Christianity. Thus the purely philosophical approach can reveal only "half-truths" concerning the real significance of their thought.

[2] Henry More, *Philosophical Writings*, ed. by F. I. MacKinnon (New York, 1925), p. 246. J. B. Mullinger, *A History of the University of Cambridge*, (London, 1888), pp. 123–124; *The University of Cambridge*, (Cambridge, England, 1911), III, 596–597; and his article in *Cambridge History of English Literature*, (Cambridge, England, 1917), Vol. VIII, pp. 273–275. This is true of the most recent research in English, French and German. For example, see the following: Anderson, *Science in Defense of Liberal Religion: A Study of Henry More's Attempt to Link Seventeenth Century Religion With Science*, (New York, 1933); E. M. Austin, *Ethics of the Cambridge Platonists*, (Philadelphia, 1935); Gunnar Aspelin, "Ralph Cudworth's Interpretation of Greek Philosophy," tr. by Martin Allwood in *Goteborgs Hogskolas Arsskrift*, vol. XLIX (Goteborg, 1943); Joseph Beyer, *Ralph Cudworth als Ethiker, Staats-Philosoph und Aesthetiker auf Grund der Gedruckten Schriften*, (Bonn, 1935); Lydia Gysi, *Platonism and Cartesianism in the Philosophy of Ralph Cudworth*, (Bern, 1962); D. A. Huebsch, *Ralph Cudworth, ein englischer Religionsphilosoph des siebzehnten Jahrhunderts*, (Jena, 1904); Charles Huit, "L'école de Cambridge," *Annales de Philosophie*, (Nouvelle Serie, 1899, v. 40., pp. 285–304); Marlyn Meyer, "Ralph Cudworth's Philosophical System," unpub. Ph. D. diss., Columbia University (1952); K. J. Schmitz, *Cudworth und der Platonismus*, (Bonn, 1919);

appear impossible for him to be completely ignorant of Platonic thought. It is my belief that he did found this school, however, this will be our next problem. Concerning the present issue, there seems to be ample contemporary evidence that Whichcote was both acquainted with Platonic thought and that he taught it to others.[1] We should give special attention to Tuckney's insistence that quite early in his teaching career, Whichcote embarked upon an intensive study of "Philosophie and Metaphysicks" and especially "Plato and his schollars." [2] Whichcote himself affirms his admiration for Platonic thought.

> In some Philosophers especially Plato and his scholars I must need acknowledge from the little insight I have ... I find many excellent and divine expressions.[3]

We may add to this the internal evidence of Whichcote's own writings. Mullinger asserts that Whichcote does not use either Plato or Plotinus as authorities and that he does not mention Plotinus. He states that Burnet's comment that Whichcote taught "Plato, Tully and Plotinus" was "the inaccurate impression derived by a young man of twenty during a hurried visit to the University." Burnet's observation actually referred to Henry More who was then at the height of his reputation at Christ's.[4]

One needs only to read Whichcote carefully to disprove Mullinger's

J. J. De Boer, *The Theory of the Cambridge Platonists*, (Madras, 1931); Aharon Lichtenstein, *Henry More: The Rational Theology of a Cambridge Platonist.* (Cambridge, Massachusetts, 1962) is an exception; and Rosalie L. Colie, *Light and Enlightenment*, (Cambridge, England, 1957). cf. general works: W. R. Sorley, *A History of English Philosophy*, (Cambridge, 1920); Ueberweg in his *Grundriss der Geschichte der Philosophie*, (1868) and Windelband in his *Lehrbuch der Philosophie* (1892) make a passing reference to Cudworth in relation to Descartes and Hobbes. On the contrary, it may be that Inge is over- zealous for Whichcote and his disciples. They represent for him the "high-water mark in English religious history, especially in its rational and mystical development, see his *Christian Mysticism*, 3rd ed. (London, 1913), pp. 285–286; *The Platonic Tradition in English Religious Thought*, pp. 36–38; *Christian Ethics and Modern Problems*, (London, 1930), p. 379. Inge also published the most recent edition of Whichcote's *Aphorisms* in 1930 and in his preface to this volume his admiration for Whichcote is evident. George Santayana is generally critical of Inge's interpretation of Platonism, see *Platonism and the Spiritual Life*, (New York, 1927), pp. 83–91.

[1] Burnet, *Ibid.*, pp. 339–340. Cf. Samuel Parker, *A Free and Impartial Censure of the Platonick Philosophie*, (2nd. ed. Oxford, 1667), Edward Fowler, *The Principles of Practices of Certain Moderate Divines of the Church of England, etc.* .... 2nd ed. (London, 1671) and, Simon Patrick, "A Brief Account of the New Sect of Latitude-Men, etc. ...," (1662), in the *Phenix*, (London, 1707). The dating of these contemporary sources places them at the period when Cambridge Platonists rather than the Latitudinarians, i.e. Tillotson, who reached their peak toward the end of the century. There is, then, no explanation for the "censure" of Parker, or for the "apologies" of Fowler and Simon Patrick apart from the existence of a real Platonic movement in England in the mid-seventeenth century, viz., the Cambridge Platonists.

[2] Whichcote and Tuckney, *Letters*, pp. 36–40. See, *supra*, Ch. III.

[3] "Reflections," "Sloane," (MS.), 2716.4; (n.p.).

[4] *Cambridge History of English Literature, Ibid.*, Hereafter, C.H.E.L.

observations. Whichcote does mention Plotinus by name at least once,[1] and Plato and Tully are frequent and significant authorities for him throughout his writings.[2] While Mullinger may be correct in asserting the inaccuracy of Burnet's observation there remains sufficient evidence that Whichcote had direct knowledge of "Plato and his schollers." This is not to ignore the fact that such acquaintance as he had with this philosophical tradition was inadequate and uncritical and that he was excelled in many ways by Smith, Cudworth and More. Whichcote belongs to the class Inge has described as a "natural" Platonist, that is, he seems to find a natural affinity between his own general outlook and the Platonic spirit. F. J. Powicke's conclusion that in Whichcote's writings, Platonic writers are used to illustrate rather than to establish his doctrines seems reasonable.[3]

Whichcote appears to be just as much impressed by Jewish Wisdom Literature and the Johannine and Pauline absorption of this same tendency. A careful study of the Scriptural references of Whichcote to illustrate points of doctrine indicates this. His use of passages from Job, the Psalms, Ecclesiastes, the Wisdom of Solomon and Proverbs is incessant. His use of Johannine and Pauline writings is also frequent. The maxim of the movement he founded is from Proverbs 20:27 and the basis of his natural theology is essentially Romans, Chapters 1 and 2 (also Genesis 1:26–27) and the basis of his natural ethics is Titus 2:12. His concept of Christian morals is based on Philippians 4:8.[4]

When Raven says that Whichcote was more "Johannine" than Platonic, he is true to the spirit of the man. This is another way of saying that though Whichcote was free to acknowledge all truth and was particularly influenced by Platonic thought he was even more insistent that all his thought should be firmly rooted in Scripture. His thought is too deeply rooted in the Judaeo-Christian tradition to ignore the possibility of the Wisdom Literature of Israel together with its reflection in Johannine and Pauline thought as a direct influence upon him.[5] Thus we conclude with De Boer concerning Whichcote and his disciples:

---

[1] *Works*, II, 160. This one reference to Plotinus is too important to be ignored, see *Supra*, Ch. II.

[2] See *Supra*, Ch. II, Cf. John Tulloch, *Rational Theology and Christian Philosophy in England in the Seventeenth Century*, (Edinburgh, 1872), II, 119–120.

[3] *The Cambridge Platonists*, (London, 1926), pp. 193–194.

[4] Inge finds a Platonic strain in St. Paul as well as in St. John. He conceives the Fourth Gospel as a further development and Explication of Paulinism, with the help of Philo's Platonised Judaism, see *Platonic Tradition*, pp. 10–13. Elsewhere, we asserted that although Hellenic-Judaism is manifest in the Fourth Gospel, the extent of Philo's influence is in question, see *Supra*, Ch. II. Cf. Raven, "Note of Greek and Jew," *The Theological Basis of Christian Pacifism*, (London, 1952), pp. 17–18.

[5] For an excellent account of the impact of Jewish Wisdom Literature on future moral and

Their Platonism was a Platonism in the broad sense in which it had become a part of the Christian tradition through Augustine and more directly through the Platonic Academy at Florence.[1]

Finally, one must not allow Whichcote's frequent reference to Aristotle to obscure the extent of his indebtedness to Plato. Whichcote's starting-point, that truth is truth wherever it is found, leaves him free of course to derive his ideas from all sources. He read Calvin, and as W. C. De Pauley points out, was more of a true Calvinist than the Puritans of his day.[2] Similarly, he read the original Aristotle and was perhaps more true to what is central in his ethics and theology than many of the Scholastics who knew Aristotle only through St. Thomas. But there is a sense in which Aristotle is the student and disciple of Plato as well as the independent logician and scientific philosopher. It is most probably in the former sense that Whichcote knew Aristotle and admired him most.

Although Whichcote refers directly to Aristotle more than to Plato, either by name or as "the Philosopher," there is a great deal more of the spirit of Plato in his writings. It is through the eyes of Plato that he views reality, especially the moral and religious life of man and where he goes beyond Plato it is as a Christian.[3]

Having arrived at the conclusion that Whichcote was a Platonist in the broad sense of the word, we now examine his status as founder of the Cambridge Platonist School. Although Whichcote is named as the founder of the movement by common consent, at least two other persons have been offered as deserving the same honour. These are Joseph Mead and John Sherman and a third person, Henry More, has been sometimes suggested. Since Whichcote's status as founder is

religious thought, see O. S. Rankin, *Israel's Wisdom Literature*, (Edinburgh, 1936). Rankin considers the literature as the source of all worthy "humanism" in Judaism and Christianity. Cf. *Ibid.*, pp. viii–ix, 1–2, 9, 14, 17. See also Howard's introduction to Ward's *Life of* . . . . . *Henry More*, (London, 1912), pp. 3–4.

[1] De Boer, *Ibid.*, pp. 129–131, 98. Cf. Tulloch, *Ibid.*, pp. 117–119; C. E. Lowry, *The Philosophy of Ralph Cudworth*, (New York, 1884), pp. 59–60; Inge, *Christian Mysticism*, p. 287; G. P. Pawson, *The Cambridge Platonists and Their Places in Religious Thought*, (London, 1930), pp. 9–18; Charles de Rémusat, *Histoire de la Philosophie en Angleterre depuis Bacon jusqu'à Locke* (Paris, 1875), II, 9–10; G. F. von Hertling, *John Locke und die Schule von Cambridge*, (Strassburg, 1892), p. 134; S. P. Lamprecht, "Innate Ideas," P.R., vol. XXV (1926), pp. 553–571; G. P. Fisher, *History of Christian Doctrine* (Edinburgh, 1896), pp. 368–369; *Encyclopedia of Religion and Ethics*, III, 167–168; Basil Willey, *The Seventeenth Century Background* (London, 1934), pp. 134–138; Douglas Bush, *English Literature in the Earlier Seventeenth Century (1600–1660)* (Oxford, 1945), pp. 342–345.

[2] *The Candle of the Lord*, (London, 1937), pp. 231–232. This is especially true in regard to Calvin's Alexandrine background, his appreciation of Platonic thought and his version of the *imago dei*.

[3] De Pauley, *Ibid.*, pp. 35–36.

contested by these claims we must carefully examine the evidence.

Joseph Mead [1] (1586–1638) was educated at Christ's College, Cambridge. He was not a party man, but had an open mind, and expressed this by his maxim, "I cannot believe that truth can be prejudiced by the discovery of truth." Against the Presbyterian discipline, the institution of "lay-elders," and the use of the term "minister" in place of presbyter, he argues learnedly in his *Discourses*. In the same strain are his historical arguments for reverence due to sacred places, and for the view of the Eucharist as a sacrifice. With the Puritans he held the Pope to be anti-Christ; with the high Churchmen he admitted that the Roman Church teaches the fundamentals of the faith. He was lecturer in Greek and fellow of Christ's College for many years.

Henry More came under the direct influence of Mead.[2] It is little wonder that he has been referred to as the father of the Cambridge movement in some respects.[3] Dr. Raven holds that Mead was the forerunner of this new movement, but that Whichcote was its leader. That is to say, Mead had in many respects prepared the way, especially by his opposition to Calvinists and Laudians alike, opposing the former by moderation and the latter by his Greek outlook in contrast to the strict Latin view. Mead appealed to reason and insisted upon morality as manifesting the presence of the Spirit of God. He refused to place nature and grace in antithesis. He emphasized the need for loyalty to truth and took his stand against traditionalism and enthusiasm.[4]

Mullinger maintained that the real originator of the Platonist movement at Cambridge was John Sherman through his "commonplaces" of 1641. The title of Sherman's volume, *A Greek in the Temple*, indicates that his appeal is from the traditions of the Latin Church to that pagan philosophy from which he, and those with whom he was in sympathy, derived their inspiration. He was slightly Whichcote's senior in academic status and for this reason may have contributed

---

[1] The alternative spelling is "Mede," but we shall use "Mead" throughout this study.

[2] Article on "Joseph Mead," *Dictionary of National Biography*, ed. by Sidney Lee (London, 1909), XIII, 178–180.

[3] *Ibid.*, XXI, 957.

[4] *John Ray, Naturalist* (Cambridge, 1942), p. 37. Cf. Raven, *English Naturalists*, p. 356; *Natural Religion and Christian Theology*, I, 107–108. J. H. B. Masterman, *The Age of Milton*, (London, 1873), pp. 221–222. E. Gilson observes that the notion of "image" is central in Greek theology as "grace" is in Latin theology, see *History of Christian Philosophy in the Middle Ages* (London, 1955), p. 94. It is significant that both these tendencies are manifest in Whichcote's thought, yet in his case as in that of Mead's, the emphasis is more Greek than Latin.

more to the origin of this movement through the publication of his
work than has been generally attributed to him.[1]

Finally, Nicolson argues that in spite of the early association
of Whichcote and Cudworth with Emmanuel College, Christ's College
has always been considered the real home of Cambridge Platonism
and the philosophical latitudinarianism synonymous with that term.

That it should have been so considered was due largely to the
presence there of Henry More. The history of the movement until at
least 1654 must be read in his biography. More's importance is explained by his early association at Eton with Falkland and Hales and
at Christ's with Mead.[2] Mullinger seems to lend support to this general
position by insisting that Whichcote's claim to rank as the founder of
a school or the leader of a party in the University would not have
survived had not his efforts been seconded, his learning surpassed, and
the range of his "intellectual survey" greatly transcended by More.
Mullinger's emphasis on More's contribution is mainly based on his
assumption that Whichcote was not a Platonist and that Burnet's
statement in support of this claim really applied to More.[3]

The justification for the statement of these various views is that
all of them contain some truth. With Raven we would necessarily agree
that Whichcote had been preceded by "fore-runners" and Mead is
no doubt one of them. Falkland, Hales, Chillingworth, Taylor and
even Hooker deserve this honour. The present writer would agree
that many came before Whichcote in the general trend of his thought.
However, he would hasten to add that Whichcote is the leader of the
new movement in the special sense that he was the first to give
life and power to it. Mullinger's contention that Sherman's work,
A Greek in the Temple is the basis of the movement misses the
point since Whichcote's status is not based upon his writings.

And Mullinger's contention that Whichcote was not a Platonist has
been considered earlier. While I would agree with him that Whichcote's
scholarship was surpassed by More, I am likewise reminded of the
fantastic extremes to which More's brilliance led him. We need only
add that Whichcote's status is not based on his scholarship. Nicolson's
conclusion appears to be totally unfounded. Without denying the
importance of More to the movement, one may still maintain Whichcote's right as the leader. It is true that More came under the direct

[1] G.H.E.L., *Ibid.*
[2] H.P., Vol. 27, (1929–30), p. 36.
[3] *The History of the University of Cambridge* (London, 1888), *Ibid.*, pp. 595–596.

influence of liberal thinkers at Eton and Christ's and it is true that by virtue of the presence of Mead, More and later Cudworth at Christ's, this institution as well as Emmanuel may be considered as a center of Cambridge Platonism. The close association between the two colleges is a historical fact. Emmanuel College came out of Christ's and not only are they near to each other but there has been also a close fellowship and exchange of ideas between them throughout their history.Apart from the history of Emmanuel, the seat of Puritanism, founded to perpetuate Puritanism, one can never explain the new movement. To explain any movement of thought one must know what is denied as well as what is affirmed. Although More's reaction to Puritanism from early childhood is well-known, it is my contention that the most effective reaction is made not by More but by Whichcote. It is Whichcote, trained in the "nursery of Puritanism," rejecting and to a great extent defying the Puritan system for a more liberal approach to Christian thought who gives birth to the new movement and has the right to be called the "father" of it.

Since Whichcote's place at the fountain-head of Cambridge Platonism is unrivalled not because of his writings or his scholarship, but by virtue of his personal influence, the reference to him as father of the movement is suggestive. If we make this claim for him, then we are free to admit that others contributed their share by preparing the way for its advance and that even his disciples excel him in scholarship. Socrates' status as father of Greek philosophy is uncontested by pre-Socratic thought or by the more elaborate philosophical system of Plato. Socrates' marvellous personal influence upon the youth of Athens is in a real sense echoed by the unusual influence of Whichcote in the University of Cambridge. In fact, we should remember that publications and unusual scholarship do not necessarily make a man the founder of a movement. Personal influence is of primary importance and thus it is Luther rather than Erasmus who heads the Reformation. It follows that Whichcote is the father of the Cambridge Platonists by virtue of the incarnation and communication of truth through his powerful personality. It was thus that he drew his contemporaries to him and through his teaching, preaching and personal example, gave life to the Cambridge School. We agree with De Boer's observation as follows:

Whichcote may be called the father of the School, not because of his scholarly research of the classical sources of Platonism, for he has less claim to scholarship than any of the other members of the group; nor because of the systematic presentation of Platonism on his part. Rather it is because of the suggestive character of his tutoring and preaching, which inspired in his students an interest in the study of ancient philosophers, chiefly Plato, Tully and Plotinus.[1]

Having presented our defence of Whichcote's position as a Platonist and as the father of the Christian Platonists of Cambridge, we are now concerned with the reflection of his thought in the writings of the other members of the school. These observations should further confirm what has gone before, for his thought is the real foundation upon which his followers build their system. This is true notwithstanding the fact that differences also appear. Where there are differences they should be indicated, for one of the unwholesome tendencies in most treatments of the thought of the school is the failure to point out the unique contribution of each member of the group. Thus we shall be concerned with the point at which Whichcote's disciples disagree with him and where they go beyond him.

Dr. Raven considers Worthington as being personally the closest member of the group to our author and a careful study of Worthington's *Diary and Correspondence* appears to substantiate this claim.[2] Though Worthington holds the basic presuppositions of the school he contributes more to the literary advance of the movement than to its thought. Since our primary concern here is with thought, John Smith may be considered the disciple closest to Whichcote. In order to compare the thought of Whichcote and his disciples, their personal fellowship will need to be taken into account, but only as a means of illuminating the relation of their thought. We shall consider only the inner circle, namely, Smith, Cudworth and More.[3]

Concerning Smith's close association with Whichcote we have spoken earlier.[4] For this reason, we may proceed at once to point out the

---

[1] De Boer, *Ibid.*, p. 2. Cf. Tulloch, *Ibid.*, pp. 83–85; Rémuset, *Ibid.*, pp. 9–10; Barry, *Ibid.*, p. xvi; Sorley, *Ibid.*, p. 76. Fisher, *Ibid.*, pp. 367–368; W. K. Jordan, *The Development of Toleration in England* (London, 1939), IV, 94–96; Austin, *Ibid.*, p. 8; MacKinnon, *Ibid.*, p. 246; Henry More, *Philosophical Poems*, ed. G. Bullough (Manchester, 1931), p. xviii.

[2] He published Mead's *Works* and Smith's *Discourses*. It is of interest that Tillotson preached the funeral sermon of both Whichcote and Worthington. Whichcote married Worthington to Mary, daughter of his brother Christopher. Cudworth was a wedding guest. Cf. Tulloch, *Ibid.* From Worthington's *Diary*, it is obvious that he, Whichcote and Cudworth were the best of friends.

[3] Tulloch, *Ibid.*, adds to the four main members of the group Culverwel, Worthington, Rust, Patrick, Fowler, Glanvill, Norris, and Browne. De Pauley, *Ibid.*, adds to this list Cumberland and Stillingfleet, while Powicke adds Sterry not listed by the other writers. Most other works on the Cambridge school hold to Whichcote, Smith, Cudworth and More. However, there is the undesirable tendency in some cases to omit Whichcote and replace him by Culverwel, i.e. De Boer, *Ibid.* In my opinion this attempt is self-defeating since Whichcote's contribution is so central to the school that apart from him no adequate account of the movement can be given.

[4] *Supra*, ch. I.

relation between his thought and that of Whichcote. In Smith the speculative character of the movement started by Whichcote increases.[1] Smith is a true Platonist and from the very beginning he takes his line of thought either from Plato or the Neo-Platonists. The questions which occupy him are more directly philosophical than the more specifically religious concern of Whichcote. In his *Discourses*, Smith is concerned with such questions as the essence of divine knowledge, the ultimate springs of our rational and spiritual life, the nature of revelation and the true idea of righteousness. Though these discourses are religious in the highest sense, yet they involve in their statement the primary data of all philosophy. According to Tulloch, these discourses "were intended for oral delivery by the preacher and yet they are handled with a freedom, elevation and amplitude of grasp, which stamps him pre-eminently as a Christian philosopher." [2]

To say that Smith was a Platonist is enough to settle the general character of his method. All knowledge to him, especially all higher divine knowledge, springs from the soul within. It is the reflection of our souls – the interpretation of our spiritual life.[3] The picture Smith draws, both of the Gospel and its effects, corresponds in the main to that drawn by Whichcote – with here and there a fuller insight and comprehension, greater wealth of spiritual allusion, and a deeper grasp of evangelical principles.

For example, where Whichcote sketches the ethical and outwardly harmonious relations of the divine life, Smith gets more to the root and vitalizing center. His mind appears both more creative in conceptions and more largely philosophic in survey. The elevation of Smith's thought marks both a certain intellectual and spiritual advance over Whichcote. The breadth and freedom of mind we trace in Whichcote still lies, in some degree, on a polemical and scholastic background. Whichcote was in a sense a Platonist because he found in Platonic writings certain principles coincident with his own enlarged Christian thoughtfulness. But Smith drank deep of the "Platonic spring"

---

[1] Tulloch, *Ibid.*, pp. 120–121. Smith, among the main numbers of the Cambridge school, has suffered the same neglect as Whichcote. So far as I have been able to determine, no major study has been made of Smith in recent years. Cudworth and More have been overworked in comparison, both in English and in German. The explanation appears to be that More and Cudworth were not only more profound, but they reacted to the systems of Hobbes, Descartes and others and entered readily into the philosophical and scientific controversies of the day. Philosophers, therefore, have adopted Cudworth and More. It is up to theologians to do the same for Smith and Whichcote. Any proper assessment of the religious climate of seventeenth century England cannot ignore their contribution.

[2] *Ibid.*, pp. 121, 129, 186. Cf. Smith, *Ibid.*, pp. 1–2, 62–64, 128–130.

[3] *Ibid.*, pp. 121. Cf. Smith, "Of the Immortality of the Soul," pp. 82–83.

and if as Pawson asserts, Platonism was allied in his day with the attitude of protest,[1] Smith makes this claim good by setting himself free from all scholastic trappings which, in some degree, still clung to his master.[2]

Smith made a clear advance upon the theological spirit of his age, having pushed the lines of his thought manfully forward, till they touched all the diverse aspects of speculative and moral culture. He thus redeemed religion from the dogmatism and faction which were alike preying upon it and taught men to see in it something higher than any mere profession of opinions or attachment to a side. But this, which may be said to form the summit of Whichcote's thought, attained through meditative struggle and prolonged converse with Platonic speculation, was the starting point of Smith. He began easily on this level, and never needed to work out for himself the rational conception of religion. This was given to him by his teacher and thus he began, so to speak, on Whichcote's shoulder.

Religion for Smith was inconceivable under any other form than the idealization and crown of our spiritual nature. The Divine represented to him from the first the compliment of the human. The assimilation of man to God was consequently the one comprehensive function of Christianity. But Smith saw what Whichcote perhaps has not made apparent, that the Divine, while being linked to human reason, and finding its first and essential utterance in it, is yet a living power, something which human nature itself could never elaborate. According to Smith, mere philosophy or moralism can never transmute itself into evangelical righteousness. This has its rise from within the heart, no doubt, but not as a spontaneous product. It can only come from the original fount of Divinity – a new divine force within us springing up into eternal life.[3] No better statement can be made of Smith's Platonism, his religious depth and indebtedness to Whichcote than his own words as follows:

Were I .... to define divinity, I should rather call it a "divine life," than a "divine science" ...[4]

And

True religion is a vigorous efflux and emanation of the "first truth and primitive goodness" upon the spirits of men and is for this reason called a participation of the divine nature.[5]

[1] Pawson, *Ibid.*, p. 11.
[2] Tulloch, *Ibid.*, p. 180.
[3] *Ibid.*, pp. 187–191. Cf. John Smith, *The Excellency and Nobleness of True Religion*, (Glasgow, 1745), p. 16.
[4] Smith, *Select Discourses*, ed. by H. G. Williams, 4th ed. (Cambridge, England, 1859), p. 1.
[5] Smith, *True Religion*, pp. 4–5. In addition to Tulloch's account of Smith as well as the

Cudworth was a year older than Smith and entered Emmanuel a few years earlier.

It is most probable that Smith was Cudworth's pupil though the fact is not mentioned in the scanty biography of either. Between them may be traced not merely the common type of mind belonging to the members of the school, but certain special affinities and ways of looking at the religious questions of their time. This is especially true of the earlier and more generalized phase of Cudworth's thought. A special bond of association between these two men is more likely when we remember that Whichcote, the lifelong friend of Cudworth, was the patron and friend of Smith also.[1]

Cudworth is the most celebrated, systematic and formal writer of the school. While tutor in his college, he was presented to the rectory of North Cadbury. Whichcote at a different time held the same position.[2] Cudworth was appointed master of Clare Hall by the Parliamentary Visitors. The Puritan authorities confided in him as they did in Whichcote, yet he was not a religious partisan and his theological spirit was very unlike that of the Westminister Assembly.[3] Along with Whichcote he had been bred at Emmanuel and to have been a student there seems to have formed a sufficient passport to promotion in the eyes of Parliament. Apparently Cudworth accepted the appointment without the scruples which Whichcote had in replacing Collins.[4] As a matter of fact Cudworth appears to have been generally free of conscience in the midst of all the changes around him. He was even retained at his post at the Restoration while Whichcote was ejected. The comparatively active character of Whichcote as a leader of opinion may account partly for his change of fortune, or it may be that Cudworth was protected by some special influence.[5]

Cudworth was a Platonist, although his Platonism was that of the Renaissance, innocent of modern scholarship. The religious outlook

---

other members of the school, see De Pauley, *Ibid.*, and Powicke, *Ibid.* So close is Smith to Whichcote that in order to understand either, one should read the other.

[1] Tulloch, *Ibid.*, p. 194. We have mentioned earlier the personal friendship of Whichcote and Cudworth. Cf. *Supra*, ch. I. See also Passmore, *Cudworth*, pp. 15–16. Passmore believes that Cudworth may have learned from Smith even if the latter's indebtedness to Cudworth is more certain.

[2] See *Supra*, ch. I. Cf. Tulloch, *Ibid.*, pp. 194–195.

[3] See *Supra*, ch. III. Both Cudworth and Whichcote were absent from the Assembly and yet both were appointed by its representatives (through Parliament) to key positions in the University of Cambridge.

[4] Cf. *Supra*, ch. I.

[5] Tulloch, *Ibid.*, pp. 203–204. Cf. Leslie Paul, *The English Philosophers*, (London, 1953), p. 101. According to Paul, Cudworth made his peace with the new regime at the Restoration in the form of congratulatory verses addressed to King Charles II.

which colours all his writings, with its emphasis on moral goodness and its distrust of all mechanical rules, was the common faith of all who fell under the influence of Whichcote. Whichcote was not in any professional sense a philosopher but it is obvious that Cudworth was profoundly influenced by him.[1] Cudworth has been described as a Plotinist rather than a Platonist in view of the extensive use he makes of the teachings of the Neo-Platonists (in its broadest sense, including Christian Platonism of writers like Clement and Ficino). All the same, Cudworth made a close study of the Platonic texts, particularly of the later dialogues. His Platonism is neo-Platonically tinged but it is not merely second-hand.[2] Whichcote had no real interest in many of the questions which Cudworth was later to ask and attempt to answer. Whichcote takes for granted a Christian world-view; atheism is not for him, as it is for Cudworth, a "living option." [3] What Whichcote sets out to do is to develop a liberal and humanistic version of Christian ethics. This liberal ethics had a very great influence on Cudworth's main problem – how is it possible to live the god-like life, as Whichcote conceived it? [4]

Cudworth raises the question, how is knowledge possible? This is also Kant's problem.[5] Cudworth set out to treat the metaphysical problems connected with the existence of God and the soul, the fixity of moral standards, and the spontaneity of the practical reason.

The first question is dealt with in *The True Intellectual System of the Universe*, while his projected ethical work, which was never published, was intended to treat the two remaining problems. Fortunately, another of his works, *The Treatise Concerning Eternal and Immutable Morality*, discusses explicitly the second problem and answers the third by implication, while it is also a critique of the

---

[1] Passmore, *Ibid.*, p. 1, 7–8.

[2] *Ibid.*, pp. 14–15. Gysi, *Ibid.*, pp. 9–11. Cf. J. K. Feibleman, *Religious Platonism* (London, 1959), pp. 211–212.

[3] Cf. *Supra*, ch. IV. We gave detailed attention to this difference when we treated Whichcote's observations on atheism. The Renaissance brought with it into England a wave of atheism which became to Cudworth an arch-enemy as manifest in the materialism of Hobbes, see G. T. Buckley, *Atheism in the English Renaissance* (Chicago, 1932). According to Buckley atheism was well established in England by the end of the sixteenth century (pp. 43–44).

S. I. Mintz describes Hobbes as the opponent *sine qua non* of all the Cambridge Platonists though only Cudworth and More launched a direct attack against Hobbes, see *The Hunting of Leviathan: Seventeenth Century Reactions to the Materialism and Moral Philosophy of Thomas Hobbes* (Cambridge, England, 1962), p. 80.

[4] Passmore, *Ibid.*, pp. 15–16.

[5] For a comparative study of the thought of Cudworth and Kant, see James Martineau, *Types of Ethical Theory* (Oxford, 1885), II, 410–411. Martineau's account of Cudworth's thought is quite valuable, see *Ibid.*, pp. 396–424.

faculties of cognition, since the problems of knowledge and moral action, according to Cudworth are related. However the last question is discussed in *A Treatise Concerning Free-Will* published posthumously.

But it is in Cudworth's *Sermon .... Before the House of Commons* that he makes his greatest reflection of the thought of Whichcote. It is an early work of Cudworth thus implying that he may have been still under the more direct influence of Whichcote.[1] Furthermore, it is a sermon rather than a treatise as his most celebrated works are. Most of Whichcote's thought comes to us in Sermons, even his aphorisms are mainly insights scattered throughout his sermons. This observation may, in part at least, explain the unusual similarity of this work of Cudworth to Whichcote's writings. Thus the early date of this work and its homiletical purpose most probably account for its likeness to Whichcote's thought. Whatever the explanation, Cudworth's moral theory,[2] notion of Providence,[3] reaction to Calvinism [4] and his general view of the "god-like" life is almost a copy of Whichcote's thought.[5]

We are reminded of Whichcote's own sermon to the same body as Cudworth says:

... If we desire a true Reformation, as we seem to; Let us begin here in reforming our hearts and lives, in keeping of Christ's Commandments. All outward Formes and Models of Reformation, though they be never so good in their kind; yet they are of little worth for us, without this inward Reformation of the heart.[6]

Notwithstanding the similarity of Cudworth's thought as viewed above with Whichcote's, there are differences between them. As Passmore points out, "for all that Whichcote taught to Cudworth, even though Whichcote made him the sort of Christian he was, their moral psychology lies poles apart." [7] Whichcote distrusts all enthusiasm, while Cudworth takes the view that there is a kind of enthusiasm which is wholesome. To Whichcote anything that disturbs the deliberation or reason is suspect, but Cudworth asserts that reason without

---

[1] Powicke, *Ibid.*, p. 112.

[2] Cudworth, *Sermon ..... Before the House of Commons*, (1647), Preface [n.p.]; Cf. *Ibid.*, pp. 18–20, 61–63.

[3] *Ibid.*, Preface; Cf. *Ibid.*, pp. 26–27.

[4] *Ibid.*, Cf. *Ibid.*, pp. 11–12.

[5] *Ibid.*, pp. 28–30. *passim.*

[6] *Ibid.*, pp. 81–82. Cf. *Ibid.*, pp. 79–80, 82. Cf. Whichcote, "Sermon ..... Before the House of Commons," *Works*, Vol. I, pp. 119–120. It is clear from the dates of the sermons that Cudworth's sermon could not be based on Whichcote's since Whichcote's sermon was delivered in 1673, but what we are suggesting is that Cudworth was most probably influenced here as elsewhere by the general trend of Whichcote's thought.

[7] *Ralph Cudworth: An Interpretation* (Cambridge, England, 1951), p. 53. Cf. Whichcote, *Works*, IV, 432 with Cudworth's MS., "On Liberty and Necessity," No. 4942, 9, cited by Passmore, *Ibid.*

enthusiasm is impotent, as much for good as for evil. Whichcote finds no goodness in irrational obedience; Cudworth finds none in obedience without enthusiasm.[1] As a result of this difference between Whichcote and Cudworth, the latter stands closer to the Puritans than the former. However, Cudworth's religion and ethics still remain in intention that of Whichcote. The real difference emerged mainly because Cudworth tried to work out systematically what Whichcote was satisfied to state as self-evident.[2] Furthermore, this moral psychology of Cudworth appears to contradict his own position in a line of rational thinkers as well as his own logic and epistemology.[3]

In this matter, Whichcote appears to anticipate the eighteenth century Enlightenment, but his position is best explained by a total reaction against the Sectaries. Henry More's *Antidote Against Enthusiasm*, an intense reaction against enthusiasm, appears to be similar.[4] However, in all fairness to Cudworth, we must remember that he admits that there is a bad sort of enthusiasm. But his insistence is for the kind of enthusiasm without which nothing worthwhile can be accomplished. Cudworth's emphasis upon spontaneity does not ignore the role of knowledge in the good life. Whichcote had asserted that knowledge alone does not amount to virtue, but there is no virtue without knowledge. Whichcote leaves room for passion which follows reason and judgment. It appears that Whichcote's position is a modified version of the Socratic dictum such as Cudworth would accept. Cudworth would agree that the good life is rational by virtue of the fact that it implies a goodness which sees things as they are rather than a mere application of rules.[5] Thus what first appears to be a fundamental disagreement between the two men turns out to be a matter of emphasis since what Whichcote is really opposing is "irrational obedience"[6] and therefore an emotive quality of the good life is approved as long as it follows rather than precedes reason.

Any further variance by Cudworth from Whichcote appears to be related either to the more systematic approach of Cudworth or his variety of interests, i.e. natural science. There is a very signifi-

---

[1] *Ibid.*, pp. 69–70.

[2] *Ibid.*, p. 81. Cf. Whichcote, *Ibid.*, p. 387.

[3] *Ibid.*, p. 52. This may be only apparent if we take seriously Lichtenstein's distinction between modern and seventeenth century psychology. Modern psychology thinks in terms of a trichotomy of intellect, will and emotion, while the earlier psychology relates both affection and volition to will. The tripartite division rightly begins with Moses Mendelssohn though some wrongly attempt to push it back to Spinoza and Descartes, see *Henry More*, p. 20 (n. 30).

[4] Cf. More's *Enchiridion Ethicum*, (Eng. tr., 1690), pp. 31, 33–35, 79–81.

[5] *Ibid.*, pp. 69–71.

[6] Whichcote, *Ibid.*, I, 258.

cant point at which the more systematic mind of Cudworth has drawn out and developed a fundamental assumption of Whichcote's.

Cudworth derived the basis of his notion of free-will from Whichcote. To Cudworth, free-will is a power in such beings as are not essentially good but yet are capable of being holy.[1] Free-will is not the same thing as freedom according to Cudworth, for a perfectly free being would not possess will. To talk of us as possessing the power to choose the good life implies that we are not perfect: a perfect being does not choose the good life, it is never to him an end, he lives the good life by nature. Thus, free-will is a mixture of perfection and imperfection. It is perfection in so far as it shows us capable of preferring goodness, it is imperfection in that it testifies to the heteronomy in our souls. Freedom and free-will must not be identified, but "free" in both cases has a similar significance: the "freedom" of free-will is nothing but the capacity for preferring the spiritual to the animal. Free-will is the power of choosing to be free. But how can it be our capacity for free-will which is the source of our sin, if free-will consists, simply, in our power to choose the good life? Cudworth's answer is that we do not sin through our exercise of free-will but rather through our failure to exercise it. Sin is privation in the positive sense of failing to live up to one's possibilities. Sin is not the willful opposing of the arbitrary command of another person, but it is falling short of natural perfection.[2] However unsatisfactory Cudworth's conclusions are, there is no doubt concerning his "attempt to grapple with a serious problem, seriously envisaged." [3]

It appears that he gives careful consideration to a problem introduced by Whichcote.

In Cudworth Christian Platonism is in active conflict with the

[1] "Cudworth," MS. 4082, 20, cited by Passmore, *Ibid.*, p. 61, (n. 4); Cf. Whichcote, *Aph.* 13. See Austin Farrer's scholarly treatment of this problem in his, *The Freedom of the Will* (London, 1958). It was my good fortune to hear Dr. Farrer deliver the Gifford Lectures at New College, University of Edinburgh in 1957. The author is as moving in his speech as he is brilliant in his writings.

[2] Passmore, *Ibid.*, pp. 62–67. Cf. *Ibid.*, his references to Cudworth's MS. 4982, 40. Cf. Farrer, *Ibid.*, pp. 106–125. But, is the will really free that cannot choose evil? Sin is moral evil, but more. It is willful disobedience – a perversion of freedom. For a comparison of free-will in More with that in Cudworth and Whichcote, see Lichtenstein, *Ibid.*, pp. 181–182.

[3] Passmore, *Ibid.*, p. 65. Cf. *Supra*, chs. IV, V. To my knowledge, Passmore's *Ralph Cudworth: An Interpretation* is the most valuable analysis of Cudworth's thought, while Muirhead's treatment of Cudworth's thought in his *Platonic Tradition in Anglo-Saxon Philosophy* (London, 1930), Chs. II, III, remains noteworthy. See also Martineau, *Ibid.*; Lowrey, *The Philosophy of Ralph Cudworth* and Aspelin, *Ralph Cudworth's Interpretation of Greek Philosophy*; Selby-Bigge, *British Moralists*, II, 247–249. Consult (n. 2, p. 203) of this chapter for other sources.

materialism of Hobbes and the mechanism of Descartes. Although he accepts in principle the position of Whichcote, his master's confident self-evident approach does not satisfy him. Cudworth sees the necessity for a clear and logical statement of the Christian position not merely as an apology but rather as a challenge to atheism, materialism and dogmatism.

To establish a direct personal relation between Whichcote and More is more difficult than in the cases of Smith and Cudworth. It appears most probable that they were personal friends. However, one has to be careful not to assume too much by virtue of the general agreement of their thought, both because of the marked differences of thought at certain points and the possibility that More by his early reaction to Puritanism and the influence of the Liberal Churchmen at Eton and the teaching of Mead at Christ's may have arrived at his points of agreement with Whichcote independently. But when we consider the close ties between Christ's and Emmanuel, it is difficult to imagine that two men with so much in common failed to have any personal association especially in view of their mutual friends, i.e. Worthington and Cudworth.

We are on safer ground when we attempt to establish Whichcote's relation to More through Cudworth. More was four years older than Cudworth. His main works were written before Cudworth had published anything but brief essays and sermons.

It is logical to conclude that when More and Cudworth agree on a point of doctrine, More is the originator. But there is evidence against this conclusion. Cudworth was the first to graduate and was very likely More's teacher. The dispute between More and Cudworth over who would publish an ethical work is scarcely intelligible unless More was Cudworth's disciple. That is to say, Cudworth's indignation and More's apologetic response is quite unintelligible unless Cudworth was the master and More the disciple. More expresses his indebtedness to Cudworth in his apology. It is significant that the protest to More from Cudworth and the response are passed through their mutual friend Worthington, Worthington we know also as a close friend of Smith and Whichcote.[1] A further testimony to the intimate association between

---

[1] *Ibid.*, p. 18. Cf. John Worthington, *Diary, and Correspondence*, ed. J. Crossley (Manchester, 1886), vol. II, pt. I, p. 116. The account of this incident between More and Cudworth is as follows: Cudworth began an ethical treatise concerning moral good and evil. This work was to cover most of the great ethical problems, such as an explanation of the true notion of morality, of the *Summum Bonum*, and liberty. But at the same time, More had been ap-

More and Cudworth concerns the appointment of Cudworth to the mastership of Christ's in 1654. More was preferred for the position but most probably declined in favour of his friend Cudworth.[1] From these observations it appears in order to conclude that there was a mutual influence and personal respect between More and Cudworth and for this reason a personal relation between More and Whichcote seems most probable since Whichcote was the oldest member of the group and the acknowledged leader.[2]

The Cambridge movement ripened into its finest personal and religious development in More.[3] Cudworth and More have more in common than Whichcote and More, that is, beyond the main concern of the Cambridge School.

For example, the supposition that all higher wisdom and specu- lation were derived originally from Moses and the Hebrew Scriptures, and that this traditional connection confirmed both the truth of Scripture and the results of philosophy, was widely prevalent in the seventeenth century. Both Cudworth and More believed in this con- nection. Cudworth and More had a similar interest in the development of natural science in their time.[4]

In his general method and the avowed basis of his thought, More

proached by friends to write a treatise on morality. When More told Cudworth of his plans it became apparent that their plans were in conflict and More withheld his treatise for a time.
  This was in 1665, but two years later (1667) More published his work in Latin (the *Enchiridion Ethicum*) so that he would not interfere with Cudworth's plans. However, Cudworth's work never appeared.
  [1] Tulloch, *Ibid.*, p. 324.
  [2] Passmore, *Ibid.*, p. 324.
  [3] Tulloch, *Ibid.*, p. 303.
  [4] *Ibid.*, p. 352. Cf. C. E. Raven, *Natural Religion and Christian Theology* (Cambridge, England, 1953), I, 110–114. More was a member of the Royal Society, thus indicating his interest in natural science. Concerning his attempt to prove that the early Greeks received their wisdom from the Jews, see his *Grand Mystery of Godliness*, (1660), bk. I, ch. IV, p. 9. More and Whichcote are close at one point, viz., where More contends that John in his Gospel used the word (λογος) in the Jewish sense, although Platonism helped to prepare the way for Christianity, see *Ibid.*, ch. V., pp. 11–12. Whichcote would agree that this is true, but he does not get involved as More and Cudworth do in Cabbalistical studies. See S. T. Coleridge's criticism in *Notes on English Divines* ed. by Derwent Coleridge (London, 1853), I, 532.
  For a further account of More and Cudworth on their scientific interests, see Raven, *Ibid.*, pp. 113–114, 110; More, *Antidote Against Atheism*, (1662); Cudworth, *Works*, (I st American Ed., 1837), pp. 213–215; E. Cassirer, *The Platonic Renaissance in England*. Ch. V, pp. 129–156. Concerning the celebrated controversy between Bayle and Le Clerc on Cudworth's concept of the "plastic medium," see Passmore, *Ibid.* pp. 22–24. Leo Pierre Courtines, *Bayle's Relation with England and the English*, (New York, 1938), pp. 47–48. For a good statement of More and Cudworth's philosophical and scientific interests at home and abroad, see Colie, *Ibid.* – the entire work. Cf. D. A. Huebsch, *Ibid.*, pp. 37–41; Cf. Herbert Butterfield, *The Origins of Modern Science 1300–1800* (New York, 1959), p. 125; E. A. Burtt, *The Metaphysical Foundations of Modern Science*, revised ed. (London, 1932), pp. 127–144. Robert Hoopes' contention that Smith and Whichcote were pre-scientific is unsupported, see his *Right Reason in the English Renaissance* (Cambridge, Mass., 1962), p. 175.

occupies the common ground of the Cambridge school. He is a vigorous advocate of the rights of reason, and believed it to be one of his chief missions to show how the "Christian and Philosophic genius" should "mix together." He asserted that the Christian religion rightly understood is the deepest and choicest piece of philosophy. His doctrine of reason is eminently Alexandrine.[1] More was more withdrawn from society than Cudworth or Whichcote and thus it is little wonder that when we read More's writings we feel that we are conversing with a mind too little embraced by active discipline in society.[2]

In More's early days at Cambridge, three factions flourished at Christ's, nicknamed "Powritans," "Puritans" and "Medians." The Powritans, so called after their leader, William Power, were of the High Church Party suspected of popery. The Puritans have been considered elsewhere.[3] The "Medians" were moderates between Powritans and Puritans, and were lead by Mead. Until his death in 1638, Mead was one of the most popular figures in the college, and undoubtedly exercised some influence on More who was of his party.

As Lecturer in Greek, Mead guided More's classical reading, his theory of the Bible and, as a moderate in religious observances, fostered More's general liberalism. Mead is at one with the Cambridge Platonists in his insistence upon the necessity of good works as an aid to salvation, and he declared that none may be saved by faith alone.

If ever there was a time when Christians thus deceived themselves, that time is now ... because we look not to be saved by the merit of works.... but by faith in Christ alone; as though faith in Christ excluded works and not rather included them; ... or as if works could no way conduce unto the attaining of salvation, but by way of merit and desert, and not by way of the grace and favour of God in Christ.[4]

In Bullough's opinion the vigilant tolerance and moral emphasis of Mead anticipated More's views in many ways and prepared More's mind for the influence of Whichcote.[5] But this influence of Mead upon More in no way undermines the role of Whichcote on the father of the Cambridge Movement. There seems to be no way of linking the direct influence of Mead with the other members of the group; it may be

---

[1] *Ibid.*, pp. 353–355.

[2] *Ibid.*, pp. 336–337.

[3] Cf. *Supra*, ch. III.

[4] Joseph Mead, *Works*, ed. by J. Worthington, 3rd ed. (London, 1672), p. 265; Cf. *Ibid.*, pp. 270, 280–282. All cited by Bullough, in his introduction to More's *Philosophical Poems*, pp. xiv. It is significant that Worthington, friend of the Cambridge Platonists, edited Mead's *Works*.

[5] Bullough, *Ibid.*, p. xv.

traced only indirectly through More. On the other hand, Whichcote's direct and personal influence upon the group is unquestioned except in the case of More where it is most probable.

There is a remarkable resemblance between Whichcote's general position and More's *Psychozois* which makes More's debt to Whichcote almost a certainty. In describing his conversion More hints that 1637, the year after Whichcote's appointment as University Preacher, marked the beginning of his return to serenity. Although their close association probably did not come about until after 1639, when More received his Fellowship, it appears that by this time More had already assimilated Whichcote's attitude to the philosophers, his tolerance, and the stress on subjectivity in religious experience which added new force to his own moral proclivities. Whichcote's influence upon More was pervasive rather than systematic. It was natural, therefore, that More, in recollecting the sources of his intellectual conversion, should mention only recognized authorities and the ultimate sources of their common views. In addition More differed from Whichcote in several ways, notably in his enthusiastic acceptance for imaginative purposes of the Plotinian system of the universe, and in the detail through which he followed the mystical process.[1]

More's approach to Platonism, like that of most Renaissance scholars, was unhistorical. He recognized no difference between Platonism, Neo-Platonism, Alexandrian mysticism, theurgy, Cabbalism and modern Italian commentary. Consequently, Pythagores, Plato, Philo, Hermas, Trismegistus, Plotinus, Clement, Origen, Dionysius the Areopagite, and Ficino appeared to him equally Platonic and authoritative and each contributed something to his eclectic creed.[2] This is more or less true of all the Cambridge Platonists, though the list of authors and variety of subjects with which More was concerned relates him closer to Cudworth than to Whichcote or Smith.

It is safe to say, however, that in most of his interests More was associated with some or all of the Cambridge Platonists. He was related to them by personal friendship, by academic association, by common philosophical interests and by his opposition to dogmatism and intolerance in religion. But More is to a certain extent differentiated from the others by the variety of his interests,[3] especially by his belief in witchcraft.

[1] *Ibid.*, pp. xxi–xxii. Lichtenstein, *Ibid.*, refers to the similarity between More and Whichcote on several important matters; i.e. deiformity (pp. 46, 56–57); God (p. 178).

[2] *Ibid.*, p. xxii. J. H. MacCracken correctly refers to Cudworth's *Intellectual System* with its nine hundred pages "as a mine of philosophical knowledge," P. R. vol. XI, no. 1 (1902), p.35.

[3] MacKinnon, *Ibid.*, pp. xvi–xvii, MacKinnon's treatment of More's philosophy is invaluable. Tulloch's analysis of More's life and thought is uncontested, see, *Ibid.*, ch. V.

In More's *Discourse of the True Grounds of the Certainty of Faith*, etc., he sets forth the moral and rational basis of faith like a true disciple of Whichcote. The following statement might well have been spoken by Whichcote as More says:

> No Revelation is from God that contradicts plain natural Truths.... If Reason where it is clearest is false, we have no Assurance it is ever true and therefore no "Certainty of Faith" which presupposes Reason.... That which is contradictory to certain Truth is certainly false: But Divine Revelation is true: Therefore there can be no Revelation from God that bears with it such a Contradiction. ...No Revelation that enforces, countenances, or abets "Immorality" or Dishonesty can be from God.... For it is repugnant to God's attributes, his Justice, Fidelity, Goodness, and Purity.... The image of God is Righteousness and true Holiness....[1]

More's notions of the harmony of faith and reason, and morality and religion, and the relative importance of reason and scripture as religious authorities appear to be in essential agreement with Whichcote's view on these subjects.[2]

Having compared the thought of Whichcote with that of his followers, we come finally to an observation of the general characteristics of Cambridge Platonism.

We are here concerned only with the main members of the group,

---

[1] *Theological Works*, ed. by Joseph Downing (London, 1708), pp. 766–767; Cf. *Ibid.*, pp. 765–770.

[2] By the "Boniform Faculty," More seems to imply a moral sense or faculty which immediately apprehends the morally good. One wonders if this insight is already implicit in Whichcote's view of conscience, see *Supra*, ch. V. Cf. More, *Ethicum*, p. 31. Furthermore, More's notions of the *imago dei*, body-soul relationship, orders of creation and related concepts are similar to Whichcote's views, see More, *Complete Poems*, ed. by A. B. Grosart (Edinburgh, 1876–78), p. 48.

Cf. Lichtenstein, *Ibid.*, where he asserts that the emphasis of the Cambridge Platonists upon the kinship of God and men, the identity of the ethical and the rational natures and upon their equal subjection to the objective moral law without adequate stress on man's unworthiness and God's otherness led to the decline of the "numinous." He describes this tendency as reaching its highest point in Whichcote who in his obsession for reason in all things denounces "mystery" as imperfect in comparison to knowledge (*Aph.* 1014).

Lichtenstein further suggests that Whichcote's dread of the substitution of theological dogmas for moral principles may have created the very situation he would have avoided – a moralism torn loose from its divine roots (see, pp. 117, 204). My reply is: (1) No one starts a movement by speaking in mild terms – he must "shout" in order to be heard. In his attack upon what he viewed as the wrong type of enthusiasm, Whichcote is overstating his case; and (2) A careful examination of Whichcote's own words, as we have shown in chs. IV–VIII would have resolved these doubts. Whichcote has a remarkably well articulated doctrine of sin, revelation and grace. These have a central place in his thought and his ethics are essentially theocentric rather than anthropocentric.

Karl Barth, under the spell of Kierkegaard's "infinite distinction between eternity and time" and in reaction against the humanistic emphasis in theology, ethics and biblical studies initiated his "theology of crisis" on the note of the "otherness of God." Having made his mark, after almost a half century, he now speaks of the *Humanity of God, God Here and Now* and a *God Who Acts*.

Whichcote, Smith, Cudworth and More, a fellowship consisting of academic, personal and intellectual kinship.

For these men the power of reason is more than a purely psychological fact. It is the "candle of the Lord," which, though sometimes immersed in affairs of time and sense, never fails to reflect the eternal realities.[1] For all these men activity is the most general attribute of spirit. Whichcote revises Descartes' *cogito ergo sum* to read "I act, therefore I am." [2] More and Cudworth hold that spirit is of its own nature active but only certain grades of spirit are possessed of consciousness.[3] Smith argues the existence of spirit from the inactivity of matter (since the power of producing motion or rest is inconsistent with body), and from the nature of consciousness.[4] We note that even More is a real part of the fellowship. His personal and intellectual relation to Cudworth is unquestioned. He resembles Smith on the point just mentioned and he also resembles Whichcote and Smith in his discussion of the *imago dei*.

The characteristic Platonic or Neo-Platonic doctrines which the Christian Platonists of Cambridge held in common, and which are touched at one point or another by all of them, i.e., the doctrines of the world-soul, the reality of innate knowledge, the substantiality and immortality of the human soul, while forming the basis on which they were Platonists, are less important, as bonds of connection between them, than their common feeling for the unity of the natural and spiritual world and their sense of the intimate nearness of the spirit of God to the mind of men. Their aim was to combine the new knowledge of the Renaissance with the teachings of the Church Fathers and the wisdom of the Greeks, to reconstruct theology on the basis of reason, to separate scientific fact from materialistic implication, and to show forth a unity of faith and reason which should be indeed a "candle of the Lord." [5]

It was the purpose of these Christian Platonists to marry philosophy

---

[1] MacKinnon, *Ibid.*, p. 276.

[2] Whichcote, *Works*, III, 241.

[3] More, *Divine Dialogues* (London, 1668), p. 98; Cudworth, *The True Intellectual System of the Universe*, 2nd ed. (London, 1743), pt. I, p. 844.

[4] Smith, "Of the Immortality of the Soul," *Ibid.*, pp. 69–70; Cf. Cudworth, *Eternal and Immutable Morality* ed. by Edward Duresne (London, 1731), bk. II, ch. VIII, sect. II; bk. IV, ch. I, sect. II.

[5] MacKinnon, *Ibid.*, pp. 246–247, 296–300. A comparative study of the life and thought of Nathaniel Culverwel and the Cambridge Platonists is invaluable. Although such a treatment is beyond the scope of the present study, it appears safe to say that Culverwel was one of the most constructive contemporary critics of Whichcote and his school. Cf. N. Culverwel, *Discourse of the Light of Nature* ed. by J. Brown (Edinburgh, 1857), see especially the Introduction. See also, Tulloch, *Ibid.*, pp. 41–44.

and religion; and to confirm the union on the basis of our humanity. Negatively, they differed from the dogmatic systems of their times: (1) In the interpretation they gave of what was essential in religious experience; (2) In the direction in which the foundation of belief in God as the object of religious experience was to be sought; and (3) In their view of the relation between faith and reason. Positively, they asserted that: (1) Religion is communion with God in Neo-Platonic fashion; (2) It is from the nature of the soul and its experience that we can learn of the existence, nature and operation of God; and (3) Reason is a reality transcending our existence, and therewith a belief in a Providence in nature and history. As a corollary, fundamental to morality and religion, they asserted that there is no antagonism between freedom and determinism. Man is free because he can choose and determine himself by the idea of the good; he is more fully free according to the fullness of his knowledge of it. It follows that this antithesis between freedom and determinism is solved as well as that between faith and reason. Religion is committed to the honoring of reason.[1]

Muirhead significantly sums up their position as follows:

> ... They were also bound to recognize in the name of reason that its own was a derived light, and that it might have to trust in the source of that light where it could not see. But this was entirely a different thing from declaring the object of faith wholly beyond knowledge (in a sense they were ready to hold that the Infinite Source was the more known); *a fortiori* from declaring that it was contrary to knowledge.[2]

In this chapter we have been concerned with the sense in which Whichcote may be called a Platonist, his role as father of the Christian Platonists of Cambridge and the reflection of his thought in the writings of the members of this movement. In the next chapter we shall be concerned with our author's influence down to the present.

[1] Muirhead, *Ibid.*, pp. 28–31.

[2] *Ibid.* p. 31. Cf. H. J. C. Grierson, *Cross Currents in English Literature* (London, 1929), pp. 222–223; John Worthington, *Diary and Correspondence*, ed. by James Crossley (Manchester, 1886), see Crossley's note, vol. I, p. iii; John Hunt, *Religious Thought in England* (London, 1870), I, 410; E. A. George, *Seventeenth Century Men of Lattitude* (London, 1909), pp. 197–198; W. H. Hutton, *The English Church From the Accession of Charles I to the Death of Anne (1625–1714)* (London, 1903), pp. 291–292; F. D. Maurice, *Moral and Metaphysical Philosophy*, new ed. (London, 1873), vol. II, 349–51; F. L. Nussbaum, *The Triumph of Science and Reason, 1660–1685* (New York, 1953), pp. 187–188; Marilyn Meyer, *Ibid.*, pp. 33–35, 39–40.

CHAPTER TEN

WHICHCOTE AND THE INTELLECTUAL TRADITION

There is no satisfactory measure of the relative importance of religious writers, but the extent of their influence at least indicates to what degree they mould later thought. In this respect Whichcote and his disciples occupy a peculiar position since they profoundly affect their successors. Because of their distinctive qualities, they seem slightly isolated from contemporary thought, and yet subsequent developments in theology are unintelligible if we ignore their influence. The record of those who acknowledge a debt to them in itself suggests their importance.[1] F. J. Powicke's statement of the case is so significant that it deserves repeating here. He says:

The direct influence of individual members of the [Cambridge Platonist] School is easier to trace than its collective influence. Thus, Whichcote's influence on

[1] The thought of Glanvill and Norris was so colored by the writings of the Cambridge men that they are sometimes treated as members of the group, see Joseph Glanvill, *The Vanity of Dogmatizing* (London, 1661), and J. H. Muirhead, *The Platonic Tradition in Anglo-Saxon Philosophy* (London, 1931), pp. 72–74. Cumberland also stood on the vague frontier between the Latitudinarians and the Cambridge Platonists, see W. C. De Pauley, *Candle of the Lord* (London, 1937), pp. 149–150; D.N.B., V, 289–290. art. by Leslie Stephen; James Seth, *English Philosophers and Schools of Philosophy* (London, 1912), pp. 91–92; Cumberland, *De Legibus Naturae*, pp. 39, 165, 189, cited by Seth, *Ibid.* Stillingfleet, Tillotson, Patrick, Fowler and Burnet – the so-called Latitudinarians in fact – might modify the teachings of the Cambridge Platonists, but the imprint of the older men was upon them to the end. For an account of Patrick's and Fowler's relation to them, see Tulloch, *Rational Theology and Christian Philosophy in England in the Seventeenth Century* (Edinburgh, 1872), II, 437–439. Edward Fowler, *Free Discourses Between Two Intimate Friends*, 2nd ed. (London, 1671). Stillingfleet, *Origines Sacrae*, 3rd ed. (London, 1666), and *Irenicum* (London, 1681); Cf. De Pauley, *Ibid.*, pp. 187–189. Tillotson will be discussed later in this chapter to show the relationship between the Latitudinarians and Whichcote. G. Burnet as one of the Latitudinarians and a memoir writer makes this link between the Platonists and the Latitudinarians unquestioned when he testifies thus: "The most eminent of those, who were formed under those men the Cambridge Platonists ..... were Tillotson, Stillingfleet and Patrick." Cf. *History of My Own Time* ed. by Dean Swift, 2nd ed. (Oxford, 1933), I, 343. See also G. R. Cragg, *From Puritanism to the Age of Reason* (Cambridge, 1950) pp. 59–60. In addition to the positive agreement between the Platonists and their successors, Hobbes appears as the negative influence or "common enemy" of them all, see Laird, *Hobbes* (London, 1934), pp. 258–285.

John Smith, and Smith's on Simon Patrick (1626–1707) and John Worthington (1618–1671); More's on Joseph Glanvill (1636–1680) and Peter Sterry and John Morris (1657–1711); Cudworth's on John Locke (1632–1704); Whichcote's again, on John Wilkins (1614–1672), and John Tillotson (1630–1694), and (through Tillotson) on Burnet (1643–1715), and (by means of his published Sermons) on the third Lord of Shaftesbury (1671–1713) ... All this, and more of the kind, is traceable. In this way, no doubt, the collective influence of the School was transmitted and circulated. But, inasmuch as it necessarily mingled with other streams of tendency which might be flowing in the same direction, we cannot mark off its source and range with precision. Bearing this in mind, we may say, nevertheless, that some of the most salient developments of the eighteenth century – Rationalism, Deism, Scripturalism, Moralism, Tolerance – went the way and took the form they did, because directed more or less, by the principles or spirit of the Cambridge men.[1]

The term "Latitudinarian" was first applied to the Cambridge Platonists, but was soon found to be more appropriate for the liberalism of the latter part of the seventeenth century. The Latitudinarians understood the mentality of their time and before the Revolution they were the most influential preachers in London and after 1688 their ascendancy on the bishops' bench was unchallenged.[2]

By the term "Latitudinarian" we refer to a more inclusive group than the Cambridge Platonists, in fact, to the progressive theologians of the Restoration and Revolutionary periods.[3] But even though the Latitudinarians may be distinguished from the Platonists, their relation is close.[4] Apparently most of this latter group were tutored by Smith, Cudworth or More, and doubtless listened to Whichcote preach in Trinity Church. Tillotson we know to have been Whichcote's assistant

---

[1] *The Cambridge Platonists* (London, 1926), p. 198. While agreeing in the main with Powicke's excellent statement above, the present writer would contend that Whichcote's individual influence is difficult to separate from the collective influence of the School by virtue of his being the leader. Whichcote is in a real sense the personal symbol of the movement not merely by his own contribution, but by the fact that he directly influenced all the members of the school as well as others outside it. Thus at times we shall speak of Whichcote individually, but where his views are reflected in the collective influence of the school, we shall feel justified to speak of Whichcote and his disciples or simply, the Cambridge Platonists.

Cf. Howard's introduction to Richard Ward, *The Life of ..... Henry More* (London, 1911), pp. 6–8; E. T. Campagnac, *The Cambridge Platonists* (Oxford, 1901), pp. xxx–xxxi.

Cf. E. R. Dodds, *The Greeks and the Irrational* (Berkeley, Cal., 1956), pp. 185, 213.

[2] Cragg, *Ibid.*, p. 62. Cf. Burnet, *Ibid.*, pp. 347–348. John Tillotson became Archbishop, see, H. G. Plum, *Restoration Puritanism* (Chapel Hill, N. C., 1943), p. 74.

[3] Cf. M. Kaufmann, "Latitudinarianism and Pietism," *Cambridge Modern History*, ed. by A. W. Ward (New York, 1908), V, 742–763; W. von Leyden, "Cambridge Platonists," *The New Cambridge Modern History*, ed. by F. L. Carston (Cambridge, England, 1961), V, 90–91. See also, J. B. Mullinger, "Platonists and Latitudinarians," *Cambridge History of English Literature* (Cambridge, England, 1917), VIII, 273–275.

[4] Cf. Simon Patrick's funeral sermon of Smith included in Smith, *Select Discourses* 4th ed., ed. by H. G. Williams (Cambridge, England, 1859), John Tillotson, *Funeral Sermon of ..... Whichcote* (London, 1683).

at St. Lawrence Jewry, London. Burnet, one of the Latitudinarians, assures us of the influence of the Platonists upon the younger man [1] and this influence may be traced in the writings of the Latitudinarians.[2]

But their differences are as marked as their similarities. In the Platonists there is a vein of genius lacking in the Latitudinarians. There is a depth missing – rationalism can be transmitted but mysticism is more elusive. The Latitudinarians stressed reason in religion and reacted against "fanaticism" and "enthusiasm." The threat of Romanism was for them a more formidable foe than Puritanism or Sectarianism when they were at the height of their influence.

Against Romanism they asserted reason as an authority.[3] Against atheism also they appeal to reason and here Cudworth's *Intellectual System* serves as a pointer. But the Latitudinarians were more ready to praise reason than to define it. To them it signifies in a general way all the mental faculties and their purpose was to eliminate the irrational from religion.[4]

Stillingfleet and Tillotson were more cautious than most of their party, but all of them willingly accepted the testimony of reason to natural religion. From the witness of reason they drew three important inferences: (1) that the concept of immortality has the greatest practical and speculative importance; (2) that reason, by recognizing the limitations in our knowledge, is the corrective of dogma; and (3) that in the light of reason, superstitious beliefs and practices, whether in religion or elsewhere, are utterly indefensible. The Latitudinarians sought first to frame a reasonable system of belief and then demonstrate that it accorded with the traditional faith.[5] They were interested, however, in vindicating the claims, at once, of reason and revelation. Against the fanatic they maintained with Whichcote the essential congruity between reason and revelation; against the pure rationalists, called by Whichcote, the "mere naturalists," they insisted on the supreme importance of the truths which, because they were beyond the reach of reason, God had disclosed. But because they were more conscious of the challenge from the fanatics than from the rationalists, Christian doctrine was generally overlaid by them with a veneer of natural morality.[6]

---

[1] Burnet, *Ibid.*
[2] Cragg, *Ibid.*,63.
[3] Cf. Whichcote, *The Malignity of Popery* ed. by John Jeffery (London, 1717). Also in *Works*, I, 160–162.
[4] Cragg, *Ibid.*, pp. 63–65.
[5] De Pauley, *Ibid.*, p. 200.
[6] Cragg, *Ibid.*, pp. 66–70.

The Latitudinarians endorsed new scientific developments and concluded that any divorce between science and religion would be to the detriment of both. Thus, Wilkins, Glanvill, Burnet and other kindred minds were either directly or indirectly connected with the Royal Society.[1] For the spirit of moderation to Non-Conformists expressed by Tillotson and Stillingfleet, they were bitterly criticized, and dubbed as Socinians and the like.[2] The doctrinal vagueness and indifference of the Latitudinarians were readily pointed out by their opponents. The fact is they avoided certain theological issues because they were sure that these topics had no vital purpose, they were concerned to teach men to live the good life. Here they appear to be the true successors of Whichcote.[3]

Tillotson was not an original genius. He was the heir of the Puritans on the one hand and of the Cambridge Platonists on the other. He had his upbringing among them both. He was influenced by Chillingworth and formed acquaintance at Cambridge with Whichcote, Smith, Cudworth and More. He accepted from the Platonists the axiom that human reason is capable of understanding the principles of natural and revealed religion. From the Puritans he retained a simplicity of life, a natural and familiar method of expression and perhaps his manner of preaching from a manuscript and not extempore.[4] Tillotson was among the most outstanding preachers of his day. His homiletics represent a popular and effective protest against smothering sermons with quotations. Here Tillotson goes beyond the Platonists generally, though Whichcote's sermons are freer of excessive classical quotations than the writings of his disciples. The Platonists, like Tillotson, rebelled against the use to which classics had been put, nevertheless they believed there was a legitimate authority in them which should be carefully observed, especially in Christian antiquity and Scripture.[5]

[1] *Ibid.*, pp. 72–73.

[2] Cf. Tuckney's criticism of Whichcote, *Letters*, No. 1. Cf. *Supra*, ch. III.

[3] Cf. G. Burnet, *A Sermon Preached at the Funeral of ..... Tillotson......* cited by Cragg, *Ibid.*, p. 78. Both Bishop J. A. T. Robinson in his *Honest to God* (London, 1963) and Bishop J. A. Pike in his *A Time for Christian Candor* (New York, 1964) have identified themselves with the latitudinarian tradition in Anglican theology.

[4] Charles Smyth, *The Art of Preaching, 1749–1939* (London, 1940), p. 102. For a further account of Tillotson's relation with Whichcote and disciples, see Thomas Birch, *Life of Tillotson*, 2nd ed. (London, 1753), p. 101.

[5] Cragg, *Ibid.*, pp. 72–73. For a contemporary account of Tillotson's homiletical method, see Burnet, *Ibid.* To compare his method with the Puritan preachers, see William Haller, *The Rise of Puritanism* (New York, 1938), pp. 19–23, 86–87. Among the Platonists, Whichcote was the most outstanding preacher. Henry More wrote sermons, but it is doubtful whether he delivered them. Cudworth and Smith apparently preached with effectiveness. Whichcote appears to have engaged in what R. E. Sleeth has called "life-situation" preaching, see his, *Proclaiming The Word* (New York, 1964), pp. 93–104.

According to Tillotson, Scripture is plain in all things necessary to faith and the good life. He asserts that emotionalism is not the fundamental thing in religion, for reason plays a greater part. He is against intolerance and false zeal. In essential agreement with Whichcote, Tillotson conceives faith as rational and as supported by good works.[1] Tillotson's essential agreement with Whichcote is reflected in the following passage:

All revealed religion, says Tillotson, does suppose and take for granted the clear and undoubted principles and precepts of natural religion, and builds upon them. By natural religion I mean obedience to the natural law and the performance of such duties as natural light, without any express and supernatural revelation, doth dictate.... These and such like are those which we call moral duties; and they are of eternal obligation, because they naturally oblige, without any particular and express revelation from God. And these are the foundation of revealed and instituted religion, and all revealed religion does suppose them and build upon them; for revelation from God supposeth us to be men, and alters nothing of those duties to which we were naturally obliged before... The great design of the Christian religion is to restore and reinforce the practice of the natural law, or, which is all one, moral duties.[2]

The convenient description of what Whichcote calls truths of "first inscription" and "after-revelation' is clearly reflected in Tillotson's thought. However, in spite of the fact that Whichcote's framework is left intact by Tillotson, much of the essential content is missing. This fact is especially evident in Tillotson's conception of Christianity. Here the vital message of Whichcote concerning grace, saving knowledge, the work of Christ and the guidance of the Spirit, are overshadowed by Tillotson's rationalism and moralism.[3] It appears, than, that for all the personal contact and influence which Tillotson may have had with Whichcote, he is not Whichcote's disciple.[4] Tillotson was Whichcote's successor, nevertheless, in a vital sense. It was part of Tillotson's service to the seventeenth century that he stated from the pulpit a number of diffused ideas about religion and reason which had been growing in the minds of ordinary people and by his simple and clear statement reinforced their hold upon the age. His excellency lay in seeing that reasonable Christianity involved moral requirements as well as mental. His attack upon enthusiasm was based not merely upon its denial of reason, but also because it often took moral standards lightly. He was very

---

[1] Tillotson, *Works* (London, 1757), I, 315–316, 430; II, 12, 213–214; III, 20–21, 249 *passim*.
[2] *Ibid.*, II, 307–308; Cf. *Ibid.*, III, 442–443.
[3] Cf. *Ibid.*, II, 405 with *Supra*, ch. VI.
[4] Cf. James Moffatt, ed., *The Golden Book of Tillotson* (London, 1904), pp. 2–3, 12, 32–34. See also, Leslie Stephen, *English Thought in the Eighteenth Century*, (London, 1876), I, 79.

close to Whichcote in the variety and concern of his preaching as well as in the general trend of his thought.[1]

From the available evidence we may conclude that the Latitudinarians carry on the spirit of the Cambridge Platonists by their emphasis upon the relation of reason and faith, morality and religion and in their general contribution to philanthropy and toleration.

On the other hand, Christian doctrines are diluted by the Latitudinarians in anticipation of much of the Rationalism and Moralism of the Age of Reason. But although their trend appears to be away from the more balanced position of Whichcote, most of their presuppositions are traceable in his writings.

It is most probable that Whichcote had contact with the Friends on many deep questions.[2] Cambridge Platonism and early Quakerism are related both historically and theologically. Before George Fox drew attention to "the Light within," the importance of this doctrine had been stressed by Whichcote and his disciples. To Whichcote "the Inward Voice" was a practical and prized reality.[3] Whichcote often speaks of the "superintendency of the Spirit." It was precisely this belief of Whichcote and his disciples, in the reality of "innate ideas" and of "Divine intuitions," which obtained for them the name of "Platonists." [4]

In comparison with the Calvinistic Puritans, the early Friends were "Broad Church" but even these were not so "broad" either in a Scriptural or philosophical sense as Whichcote.[5] Whichcote strikes a

---

[1] Moffatt, *Ibid.*, pp. 35–38. The Latitudinarians resemble the Platonists in their charitable thought and work. Cf. Cragg, *Ibid.*, pp. 79–80. Norman Sykes, *The English Religious Tradition* (London, 1953), pp. 53–54. For an account of Whichcote's charitable work, see *Supra*, ch. I, and Tillotson, *Funeral Sermon of . . . . Whichcote* (London, 1683), p. 27. It would be difficult to overestimate the effect of Whichcote's personal example upon Tillotson. For an account of the general relationship between the Cambridge Platonists and the Latitudinarians, see Kaufman, *Ibid.*, pp. 742-753. Richard Baxter's account of the "Latitudinarians" is valuable, see *Autobiography*, ed. by J. M. L. Thomas (London, 1931), p. 185.

[2] Cf. Tallack, "Quakers and Cambridge Platonists," F. Q. E., Vol. XXIII, (1889), p. 187.

[3] Prov. 20:27. We need only recall the maxim of Cambridge Platonism: "the reason of man is the Candle of the Lord."

[4] Plato's philosophy has for one of its characteristic features the prevalence of a similar doctrine. We need only to be reminded of Plato's notions concerning "pre-existence" and "reminiscence."

Cf. Leif Egg-Olofsson, *The Conception of the Inner Light in Robert Barclay's Theology* (Lund, 1954), pp. 20–22. Here the concept of the "inner light" has been traced from early Greek through the writings of the Cambridge Platonists and Quakers.

[5] My reference to Whichcote here instead of the Cambridge Platonists is deliberate since he appears to be free of the excesses traceable in the writings of his disciples, i.e. Cudworth and More. More's views on witchcraft in his own treatise on the subject and his co-operation with Glanvill in presenting the subject, deserves the same severe criticism that is due the fanaticism of the early Quakers, i.e. George Fox, Cf. Joseph Glanvill, *Sadducismus Trium-*

balance which appears difficult for the Quakers of his day. For instance, many of the early Friends, i.e. Naylor, Barclay, Sewel and others, attached somewhat too subordinate a position to the authority of the Scripture and to the Incarnation.[1]

Whichcote and Smith, in particular, resemble the early Quakers in their minor estimate of dogmas as compared with their emphasis upon living obedience to Christ and of the love of God and man.

But Whichcote and Smith are portrayed as great Gospel preachers and to them Jesus Christ, the "Word made flesh" is in a unique sense "the Bearer of God's Spirit."[2] The Cambridge Platonists regarded the Holy Spirit mainly as the worker of holy dispositions and godly lives, rather than as operating even by orthodox intellectual influences. God's laws were written on the affections in this Christian Dispensation. The special object and function of God's human sympathies and condescending experiences, in the Incarnation, is to draw out, awaken and sustain this affection and loving obedience of the heart. The pre-Incarnation anointings had failed to do this, and only the Anointed Humanity of Jesus was able to do this, as brought home to the soul, by His own Holy Spirit, and the preaching of His own historic Gospel.[3] Yet for all their emphasis upon the Inward Teacher, they were careful to avoid discarding the "means of grace" instituted by Christ and the

---

phatus, 4th ed. (London, 1724), including More's "Supplementary Collection of .... Stories of Apparitions and Witchcraft," pp. 403–404.

[1] Tallack, *Ibid.*, p. 190. Henry More among the Cambridge Platonists gives praise to the Quaker doctrine of "Divine immanence" and points out the inadequate notion of the Quakers concerning the historic Incarnation. Cf. *Ibid.*, pp. 191–192. See also, More, *Theological Works*, ed. by J. Downing (London, 1708), pp. 533–534. Whichcote would appear to be in complete agreement with More in his worthy defense of the Incarnation.

[2] This expression, "the Bearer of God's Spirit," is used often by C. K. Barrett in his *The Holy Spirit and the Gospel Tradition* (London, 1935), pp. 68, 92.
He alternatively refers to Jesus, the Messiah as a "pneumatic" person. Cf. H. Daniel-Rops, *The Church of Apostles and Martyrs*, tr. by Audrey Butler (London, 1960), pp. 70–75 and J. Robert Nelson, *The Realm of Redemption* (Greenwich, 1951), pp. 37–66.

[3] E. G. Selwyn points out that the root of practical religion for the New Testament writers lies in the indwelling of the Spirit of Christ in the spirit of man rather than a merely natural affinity between the divine and human spirit, for that natural affinity has been marred by sin. Thus for the bridging of the chasm so caused there is needed on God's side redemption, and on man's side repentance and for this reason the New Testament teaching about the Holy Spirit is "historically conditioned," that is in relation to the Incarnation. This is precisely the note sounded by Whichcote and More. Yet in a footnote concerning his statement above Selwyn adds this unjustified assertion, "It is, I think, because the ... Cambridge Platonists ... tended to obscure this side of New Testament teaching that their influence has not been widespread." See *The First Epistle of St. Peter*, (London, 1946), p. 285 *Ibid.*, (n.). More challenges the Quakers and Familists alike for dwelling upon the Word of Logos revealed to man before the Incarnation and speaks of the "Logos, in conjunction with the Divine Soul of the Messiah" as the special object of Christian faith. Thus for the Cambridge Platonists the deepest spirituality is always in relation to Christ. See More, *Ibid.*

Holy Spirit.[1] The Cambridge men insist that the chief proof and test of the possession of genuine spirituality consists in the faith "that Jesus Christ is come in the flesh" [2] and this was their real issue with the Quakers. This warning of the Platonists is significant, for Quakerism has been barren, repulsive, and dividing wherever it has divorced the Inward Voice from the Incarnate Word.[3]

We may compare Whichcote and his disciples with the early Quakers on several points. Both appealed from Scripture to the authority that is within us. To the Platonists, "the spirit of man is the candle of the Lord"; for the Quakers it is the indwelling Spirit which lights our darkened understanding.

The Platonists start from human reason quickened by the Spirit, the Quakers from the Spirit, quickening human intuition. The Platonists tell us of the divine spark of the image of God within which judges of God's truth without; the Quakers discourse more like the Puritans of the strivings of the Spirit. Both have links with Puritanism. The Platonists, however, shade off into Latitudinarianism, while Quakerism often tends toward false zeal and divisiveness among Christians. But when the two movements are true to their original intentions, they bear spiritual, moral and theological resemblance.[4]

John Locke, though an empiricist, may be said in some sense to be the successor of Whichcote. Even Maurice in his critical appraisal of the Cambridge Platonists considers them as "preparing to make [the] ascendency [of Locke] for a while more complete and absolute." [5] Professor Sykes asserts that "what they [the Cambridge Platonists] had taught in the academy, Locke and his disciples proclaimed in the market place." [6] Locke himself admits his appreciation for the sermons of Whichcote and Tillotson implying his moral and religious affinity

---

[1] In keeping with his Christological argument, More wrote William Penn defending the Lord's Supper, on the ground of its being designed as an "abiding, visible monument" of the Incarnation. See Tallack, *Ibid.*, p. 192.

[2] I John 4:2. Cf. Joseph Fletcher, *William Temple: Twentieth-Century Christian* (New York, 1963), pp. 29. 392–303 (n. 75) and Vincent Taylor, *Forgiveness and Reconciliation* (London, 1948), p. 225.

[3] Tallack, *Ibid.*, pp. 196–198.

[4] Cf. H. M. Gwatkin, *Church and State in England* (London, 1917), pp. 340–341.

[5] F. D. Maurice, *Moral and Metaphysical Philosophy*, new ed. (London, 1873), II, 350–351.

[6] Sykes, *Ibid.*, p. 55. H. W. Richardson, of Harvard Divinity Faculty, in his "The Glory of God in the Theology of Jonathan Edwards," unpub. Ph. D. diss., Harvard University (1962) has stated well the influence of Locke on Jonathan Edwards (pp. 50–97). In his discussion on "innate ideas," he believes the position of Edwards to be closer to the Platonists than to Locke (pp. 81–82). I consider his association of the Cambridge Platonists with Ramist logic unfounded (pp. 50–52). I will return to this at the end of this chapter.

with the Platonists and Latitudinarians.[1] Powicke asserts that Locke was personally acquainted with Cudworth, Tillotson and Whichcote. Locke is said by this author to have been a good friend of Tillotson. Further Locke most probably met Whichcote often in personal fellowship as well as heard him preach from his pulpit at St. Lawrence Jewry, London, between 1667–75 when Locke lived in London.[2]

It appears that Locke became less rather than more of a Puritan under Puritan rule at Oxford and in this sense his reaction to Puritanism can be said to be similar to Whichcote's. Many, if not most of Locke's friends, as far as we know, were churchmen. There is nothing to show that he ever shared the extreme views of the Puritans; but there is also nothing to show that he ever had much sympathy with the High Church party, as apart from political matters. His sympathy was rather with those Latitudinarian members of the church who were rising in importance under the living and posthumous influence of such men as Chillingworth, Whichcote and Tillotson.[3] Locke was exiled in Holland and became acquainted with Limborch, grand-nephew of Episcopius. Limborch was busy when he made Locke's acquaintance, upon his *Theologia Christiana* – an unsectarian and undogmatic work. It seems to follow that Locke was a friend of liberal-minded theologians at home and abroad.[4] Fraser makes the following observation concerning Locke:

> His religion as well as his metaphysical disposition always attracted him to theology. His revulsion from Presbyterian dogmatism and congregationalist fanaticism favoured friendly connection with latitudinarian Churchmen. Soon after the Restoration, Whichcote, the Cambridge divine, was his favorite preacher. [5]

Cudworth's daughter, Lady Masham, was inbued with her father's philosophical and religious spirit, modified by the newer principles of Locke. She appears to have been Locke's pupil at Oxford and a friend and admirer of his for life. Locke died as a guest in her home in 1704.

A little book which she anonymously published in 1696 *A Discourse*

---

[1] Salter, "Testimonies," p. xxxiv, in Whichcote, *Aphorisms*, (1753). Salter here refers to Locke's letter to the Rev. Richard King.

[2] Powicke, *Ibid.*, p. 20.

[3] H. R. F. Bourne, *Life of John Locke*, (London, 1876), I, 77; Cf. G. F. von Hertling, *John Locke und die Schule von Cambridge*, (Strassburg, 1892), p. 160.

[4] Bourne, *Ibid.*, II, 228, 8, 212–214.

[5] A. C. Fraser, *Locke*, (Edinburgh, 1890), p. 16. Cf. P. Lord King, *The Life and Letters of John Locke*, new ed. (London, 1858), I, 337, 344. For an account of the personal relation of Cudworth's daughter, Demaris (later Lady Masham, Sir Francis' second wife) and Cudworth's widow to Locke, see Bourne, *Ibid.*, I, 77, 170, 310; James Martineau, *Types of Ethical Theory*, (Oxford, 1885), II, 403.

Concerning the Love of God, marks a middle position between the spiritual fervour of the Cambridge Platonists and the "common sense" position of Locke's conception of duty and religion. In this pamphlet she sets the example of deprecating the demand for enthusiasm in devotion, and of discouraging any claim, in the name of God, beyond the one true end, of "a good life." At this point of contact between the Platonists and Locke it is interesting to observe the vain attempt to maintain a balance between the ideal and material interpretations of the world, the intuitive and the empirical.[1] Lady Masham's reflections are important in indicating this point of continuity and discontinuity between Whichcote, Cudworth and others, and Locke.

Locke sets out to refute the doctrine of Innate Ideas – or to refute the claim of any elements in our so-called knowledge to be exempt from criticism. He opposes the insistence that a principle may be made the "principle of principles" and therefore unquestioned. Locke vindicates the right to examine critically all the so-called principles of human knowledge.[2] The materials of knowledge are called by Locke "ideas," an idea being the object of the understanding when a man thinks. In one sense, therefore, the measure of our knowledge is found in the extent and clearness of our ideas. What we actually know, we must have an idea of: that of which we have no idea, or only an obscure and inadequate idea, we cannot know, or can know only inadequately. The limitation of our knowledge will be found in the limitation of our ideas.

The common source of our ideas is found by Locke in experience, in one or other of its two forms, sensation and reflection, or external and internal sense. It appears that Locke is building his epistemology upon the ruins of that of Whichcote and especially that presented by Smith in his *Discourse* – "Of the Immortality of the Soul" and Cudworth in *Eternal and Immutable Morality.*[3]

---

[1] Martineau, *Ibid.*, p. 404.

[2] John Locke, *An Essay Concerning Human Understanding*, 31st ed. (London, 1853), I, iii, 25. Cf. James Gibson, *Locke's Theory of Knowledge and its Historical Relations* (Cambridge, England, 1917), pp. 29–44.

[3] For an account of Whichcote's epistemology see *Supra*, Ch. IV. For a full discussion concerning "innate ideas" in Cambridge Platonism, see Lamprecht, "Innate Ideas," P.R., Vol. XXV, (1926), pp. 553–73. It is the opinion of Seth, *Ibid.*, p. 92–93, that Locke is reacting negatively to Descartes' confidence in the "clearness and distinctness" of ideas as a criterion of truth. Even if we should accept this view, we would still need to consider his reaction to Cambridge Platonism.

Ernest Cassirer points out in his *The Platonic Renaissance in England*, tr. by Pettegrove (New York, 1953), p. 59 (n. 1), that in their defense of the *a priori*, most of the thinkers of the Cambridge School do not distinguish between the "logical" and the "temporal" sense of the *a priori* concept. Hence they argue not only for the *a priori* validity of theoretical and ethical principles, but also for the "innateness" of these principles. In this respect they

But if it is true that Locke opposed the concept of "innate ideas" held by Whichcote and disciples, it is just as true that they opposed empiricism which is most characteristic of Locke's thought. Of the two outstanding English empiricists who preceded Locke, namely, Bacon and Hobbes, Locke is closer to Bacon. Like Bacon, Locke is a critic of human knowledge and a surveyor of the foundations of knowledge. The difference between Locke and Bacon, epistemologically speaking, is that while Bacon sought to formulate the true method of scientific investigation, Locke is concerned with the previous question of the possibility of knowledge itself; how far it extends, and where the line must be drawn between certain knowledge and probable opinion. While Bacon sought to formulate the methods of scientific knowledge, or to construct a system of inductive logic, Locke concludes that there is no certain knowledge of the real world and that the needs of practice are sufficiently met by probabilities of opinion, or belief. Thus, Locke appears to have been the first in British philosophy to state the problem in this form; his is the criticism of human knowledge, or epistemology. His philosophy is epoch-making in influence especially in the subsequent development of the thought of Hume and Kant.[1]

Thus even in his theory of knowledge, Locke's empiricism is an empiricism radically different from Hobbes' and to a lesser degree from Bacon's.

It is more significant for our purpose that Locke differs in his moral and religious thought from Bacon. According to Bacon, "sacred theology ... is grounded only upon the word and oracle of God, and not upon the light of nature ... This holdeth not only in those points of faith which concern the mysteries of the Deity, of the Creation, of the Redemption, but likewise those which concern the moral law truly interpreted." [2] At this point Locke parts with Bacon and is manifest

advocate essentially the position which Locke assails in the first book of his *Essay*. And it is quite probable that Locke, in formulating his arguments, was aiming largely at the philosophers of Cambridge as his real opponents. It is significant that Culverwel, closely associated with the Platonists, rejects the temporal and psychological interpretation of the *a priori* and to this extent anticipates Locke's criticism. Cf. *Of the Light of Nature*, ed. by John Brown (Edinburgh, 1857), pp. 123–124. It seems reasonable to the present writer that Locke's criticism of "innate ideas" may be a reaction, at once, against Descartes and the Platonists. For a comparison of "innate ideas" as conceived by Descartes and the Platonists, see Lamprecht, *Ibid.*, pp. 571–73. Cf. Robert McRae, "'Idea' as a Philosophical Term in the Seventeenth Century," J. H. I., vol. XXVI, no. 2 (April-June, 1965), pp. 175–190.

[1] Seth, *Ibid.*; Apparently Locke by his concept of probable Knowledge anticipates this aspect of Butler's thought. This position of Locke also explains why Shaftesbury, his pupil, reacted negatively against his Master's epistemology and found a greater affinity with his own views in the sermons of Whichcote. Aesthetics appealed to Shaftesbury more than epistemology, see Richardson, *Ibid.*, p. 292.

[2] Francis Bacon, *Advancement of Learning*, ed. by G. W. Kitchin (London, [n.d.]), p. 209.

as a disciple of Whichcote. Locke disagrees with Bacon and at the same time agrees with Whichcote that there is no divorce between reason and revelation.[1] Lowery considers Hertling's tendency to distinguish sharply between an empirical and rationalistic tendency in Locke's thought and to attribute the rationalistic tendency exclusively to the influence of Whichcote and his disciples as an exaggeration. However, Lowery would agree that the rationalistic aspect of Locke's theory come to be more definitely conceived and more sharply emphasized, as his reflection proceeded.[2] Austin asserts that the rationalistic element in Locke's thought is definitely related to the Cambridge Platonists. In the little that Locke has to say about ethics this rationalistic element appears most frequently.

In this domain there is a constant wavering between a moral positivism with the consequent stress upon the sensualistic and the utilitarian motifs, and on the other hand, a recognition of an objective, rational moral law, with the underlying theological motive constantly in evidence. The empirical element by which Locke's system has come to be characterized most frequently, was never able to submerge completely the strain of rationalism which was constantly appearing in his writings. As a result there is a constant conflict wherever Locke turns his mind to the problem of morality. Had he written a book on ethics, we might have had his solution to the antinomy; in the absence thereof, we have no alternative but to accept the rationalistic element for what it is. And for the explanation of its presence in Locke's philosophy we must turn to the Cambridge Platonists.[3]

Locke was in complete sympathy with the outlook of Whichcote concerning theology and ecclesiastical politics. Like him, he dreaded equally the arrogant claims of authority and the warm fancies of enthusiasm; like Whichcote, he sought in reason the basis of a simplified theology, the acceptance of which would lead to toleration in non-essentials.[4] Locke summed up an attitude to religious issues which was steadily gaining ground as the seventeenth century ended, and his influence was even greater in the eighteenth century. Even in his philosophical work religion occupied an important place. He did more than affirm the importance of reason in religion; he explained

---

[1] Cf. Cassirer, *Ibid.*, pp. 59–60; Hertling, *Ibid.*, pp. 100–157, 161–180, 293, 314–315; J. J. De Boer, *The Theory of Knowledge of the Cambridge Platonists* (Madras, 1931), pp. 4–6.

[2] Gibson, *Ibid.*, p. 237.

[3] E. M. Austin, *The Ethics of the Cambridge Platonists*, (Philadelphia, 1935), pp. 78–80. Cf. Laird, *Hobbes*, pp. 280–281, 290.

[4] Lowery, *Ibid.*, pp. 236–237.

how it worked, and made it seem both necessary and inevitable.[1] One passage written by Locke appears to make his affinity with Whichcote clear. Locke says:

> Reason is natural revelation, whereby the eternal Father of light, and Fountain of all knowledge, communicates to mankind that portion of truth which he has laid within the reach of their natural faculties. Revelation is natural reason enlarged by a new set of discoveries communicated by God immediately, which reason vouches the truth of by the testimony and proofs it gives that they come from God. So that he that takes away reason to make way for revelation, puts out the light of both.... [2]

Locke is in essential agreement with Whichcote on the necessity for toleration in Church and State. Whichcote is considered as the real apostle of toleration among the Cambridge Platonists and thus, at this point, Locke is his successor in a special way. Concerning the relation of Church and State, Locke presupposes that a government will be entitled to demand conformity to a simple form of religious belief, but will not undertake to force its subjects to accept any particular doctrinal system. It is the responsibility of the citizen to live up to the ideals of the Christian life, as set forth in the Bible; it is the duty of the State to make that possible. Locke was very much concerned with the question of religious toleration and liberty of conscience. Toleration followed naturally both from his conception of the nature of knowledge and from his view of the true character of the Christian faith.[3]

From what we have pointed out above, Locke's affinity with Whichcote appears obvious. But, on the other hand, if Locke can be credited with handing on the moral and religious insights of Whichcote as well as

---

[1] Cragg, *Ibid.*, pp. 114–117. This writer conceives Locke's treatise, *The Reasonableness of Christianity*, (London, 1695), as a standard work in Christian theology in England for the greater part of a century. See *Ibid.*, pp. 117–118.

[2] Locke, *Essay*, IV. 19. 4. Locke appears to be in an essential agreement with Whichcote on several points: (1) Opposition to enthusiasm, *Ibid.*, IV. 19. 3. (2) The role of revelation, *Ibid.*, IV. 16. 14; 18. 3, 5, 7, 8, 10. Cf. *Reasonableness of Christianity*, p. 14. (3) Scripture, its authority and interpretation, *Reasonableness*, pp. 1, 4., 43, 292–293 and (4) The relation of morality and religion, *Ibid.*, pp. 15, 19, 24–25, 260–261, 243–244. Cf. *Essay*, IV; 12. 11

[3] One can hardly read Whichcote's *Sermons* and *Aphorisms* and compare them with Locke's *Letters of Toleration* without admitting the probability of Whichcote as a direct influence towards Locke's tolerant spirit. See *Supra*, ch. VIII, Cf. Locke, *Four Letters on Toleration*, (London, 1876), esp. the 1st Letter, (1689), *Ibid.*, pp. 2–4. Cf. W. K. Jordan, *The Development of Religious Toleration in England* (London, 1939), IV, 111–116; Cragg, *Ibid.*, pp. 230, 190, 213–17. Locke's minimum faith, viz., the confession that Jesus is the Messiah is well known, see *Reasonableness of Christianity*, pp. 1, 4–5, 43 *passim*. Locke in spite of his affinity with the Cambridge Platonists and the Latitudinarians in simplifying the faith, goes beyond both in his doctrinal vagueness and indicates the suppositions which tend to overthrow the accepted systems of theology. Cf. Plum, *Ibid.*, pp. 80–93; Otto Gierke, *Natural Law and the Theory of Society* ed. by Ernest Barker (Boston, 1957), II, i, 16 and see my "A Theological Conception of the State" J. C. S. vol. IV, no. I (May, 1962), pp. 66–75.

others in the same tradition, there is a sense in which he betrays them.

Locke sets forth his argument as a corrective for the irrationality of "enthusiasm," but those who followed him used it to challenge affirmations which Locke never questioned. The intellectual atmosphere of the period fixed men's attention on one half of Locke's argument. He had asserted that religious knowledge discoverable by reason is supplemented by revelation; but revelation is subject to the scrutiny of reason. Given the mental outlook of the age, it was natural that the part played by reason should gradually eclipse the place given to revelation.[1] It is clear that Locke's contribution to the rationalism of the following century is to a great extent derived from Whichcote, his disciples and successors. It follows that if Whichcote is to be credited with contributing to the notions modified and transmitted by Locke's superior genius, Whichcote must share the blame with Locke for overshadowing revelation by reason. Whichcote's unusual personal influence helped to create an atmosphere for the reception of Locke's rationalism. The intellectualism in Whichcote appears more intense than that in any of his disciples and to this extent he is closer to the Age of Reason than they. This tendency in Whichcote as in Locke may be partly explained by their common, but radical reaction against enthusiasm and their common desire for toleration.

Liberal theologians like Chillingworth, Whichcote and Tillotson, accustomed to trust in reason and to practice toleration asserted that since men differ hopelessly on many points, let us take that in which all agree.

That surely must be the essence of religion and the teaching of universal reason. Thus we should be able to found a reasonable Christianity. But others were willing to forgo a reasonable Christianity to found a religion of reason.[2] The vigour of English theology during the latter part of the seventeenth century was due to the fact that for a time, reason and Christian theology were in spontaneous alliance. Theologians like Taylor, Whichcote, Tillotson and others were anxious to construct a philosophical religion, but were not alive to the possibility that such a religion might cease to be Christian. If the Cambridge Platonists rationalize, it is with a sincere belief that they are bringing out the full meaning of the doctrine which they expound; purifying it from

---

[1] Cragg, *Ibid.*, pp. 124–125. Cf. Bourne, *Ibid.*, II, 87; John Omam, *The Problem of Faith and Freedom in the Last Two Centuries* (London, 1906), p. 105.

Locke's intention and dedication to truth is remarkably similar to Whichcote's. Cf. Lady Masham's tribute to Locke in a letter of Jean Le Clerc cited by Cragg, *Ibid.*, p. 135, with Tillotson's tribute to Whichcote in his *Funeral Sermon of . . . . Whichcote.*

[2] Stephen, *Ibid.*, I, 85.

human accretions. This process had not yet developed far enough to imply any insincerity in the reasoners. But when their approach was later developed and employed by certain sceptics, it ran counter to their original intention. A change was inevitably approaching, and philosophy, hitherto in alliance with Christianity, began to show indications of a divorce. Though these latter philosophers might use the old language, it became increasingly difficult to identify the God of philosophy with the God of Christianity.[1] Passing from the original intention of Whichcote to develop a philosophical theology or a Christian philosophy to the Deists and the more comprehensive Rationalism of the Age of Reason, Pascal's famous distinction between the "God of Christians" and the "God of philosophers" becomes a truism.[2]

For our purpose, John Toland's assertion that there is not only nothing in Christianity "contrary" to reason, but that there is nothing in it "above" reason indicates the extreme tendency of this new rationalism. Thus Toland says:

... We hold that "Reason" is the only Foundation of all Certitude; and that nothing reveal'd, whether as to its "Manner" or "Existence" is more exempted from its Disquisitions, than the ordinary Phenomena of Nature.... There is nothing in the Gospel contrary to Reason, nor above it; and that no Christian Doctrine can be properly called a Mystery.[3]

This refusal to accept the supra-rational element in religion clearly goes beyond anything to be found in the religious thought of Which-cote or Locke. As Leslie Stephen reminds us, to expel mystery is to expel theology; for there is no religion and no God without mystery. This rejection of mystery even plucks at the roots of natural religion. It is fortunate that Toland's extreme view encouraged later writers to attempt a more constructive theory especially with regard to the Divine Nature.[4] Furthermore, it was fortunate that the most eminent of the

---

[1] *Ibid.*, pp. 77–81.

[2] Pascal, *Pensées*, ed. by Stewart (New York, 1947) "Apology," *Pen.* 12. Lord Herbert of Cherbury is considered the true father of Deism, see Oman, *Ibid.*, pp. 81–82. Stephen, *Ibid.*, 83–84; F. L. Nussbaum, *The Triumph of Science and Reason*, (New York, 1953), pp. 186–187; C. C. J. Webb, *Studies in the History of Natural Theology*, (Oxford, 1915), pp. 89–90; Seth, *Ibid.*, pp. 89–90; Cf. Cragg, *Ibid.*, pp. 137–139. Locke, *Essay*, I, ii, 3. For an account of the manner in which John Toland builds his deistic theory upon Locke's general position, see Toland, *Christianity Not Mysterious* (London, 1696), pp. 6, 37, 42, 127–134, 139–155 *passim*. Cf. Cragg, *Ibid.*, Oman, *Ibid.*, pp. 107–110; Stephan, *Ibid.*, pp. 93–94. For an account of Stillingfleet's protest against Locke and Toland alike, see Stephen, *Ibid.*, pp. 112–113. For Locke's defense, see Locke, *Works*, 12th ed. (London, 1824), III, 108, 42. Stillingfleet may be said to represent the Cambridge Platonists and Latitudinarians in this controversy. Unfortunately, however, he blamed Locke for the inferences which Toland had derived from Locke's epistemology and this most assuredly against Locke's consent.

[3] Toland, *Ibid.*, p. 6.

[4] Stephen, *Ibid.*, pp. 110–112. Cf. Cragg, *Ibid.*, pp. 139–155.

early English religious thinkers, of the Age of Reason, were generally on the orthodox side. They could find liberty enough to satisfy their logical instincts within the old lines; and were not led to embrace Deism. Among the champions of the faith were such men as Locke, Berkeley, Clarke, Butler and others of similar rank. The Deists had the further disadvantage of limited toleration. Toleration was still limited primarily to adherents of the Church of England and for this reason there was little toleration for the outright Deists.[1]

The Deists, then, are not to be considered Whichcote's true successors inasmuch as they are not true to his purpose to wed reason and revelation rather than to divorce them.

Samuel Clarke reveals his interest in Whichcote's thought by publishing anonymously a fourth volume of Whichcote's sermons in 1707 in spite of the protest of Jeffery who had been instructed by the Whichcote family to publish Dr. Whichcote's writings.[2] This would seem to imply either that Clarke saw in Whichcote's thought the basis of his own or that he was impressed by the similarity of Whichcote's thought with his own. At any rate, his anxiety to make Whichcote's thought public is of interest here.

Clarke is described by Leslie Stephen as the founder of the so-called "intellectual school." [3] Clarke was a great representative of the *a priori* method of constructing a system of theology. His approach to religion and morality is mathematical. He clothes his arguments in quasi-mathematical phraseology, common to Descartes, Leibnitz and Spinoza. He names Spinoza as an adversary but appears to follow his argument up to the point where it conflicts with ordinary theism.[4]

In Clarke's *Discourse Concerning the Being and Attributes of God*, he does not abandon revelation, but the center of gravity has shifted, and revelation becomes an adjunct rather than the first consideration. Clarke goes to the limit in his attempt to derive good

---

[1] *Ibid.*, p. 85.

[2] Whichcote, *Aphorisms* (1753), see Salter's preface, pp. xviii-xix.

[3] *D.N.B.*, IV, 443–445. Martineau in the second volume of his *Types of Ethical Theory* treats Cudworth and Clarke as Dianoetic ethicists. Martineau's term was used by Aristotle in describing intellectual virtues. We have seen *Supra*, chs. II, V, that Whichcote leans heavily upon Aristotle's *Ethics*. Furthermore, the essential "intellectual" element in Whichcote's ethics is more marked than in Cudworth. We have seen *Supra*, ch. IX, that Cudworth's moral psychology is in part a reaction against the intense intellectualism of Whichcote's ethics. Clarke in his mathematical deduction of moral law from logical necessity appears to be closer to Whichcote than to Cudworth.

[4] Stephen, *Ibid.*, I, 119–121. Cassirer finds a remarkable affinity between the rationalism of Whichcote and Leibnitz. If this observation is correct, there is little wonder that Clarke, an admirer of Leibnitz, should prize similar notions in Whichcote, a British predecessor of his, see Cassirer, *Ibid.*, p. 39.

and evil from "the Eternal Fitness and Relation of Things."

The very language and spirit of Clarke's writings is found in Whichcote's sermons. God, Clarke declares, has chosen these "fitnesses," not thereby constituting them "good" *ex arbitrio*, but choosing them because they were antecedently "best," and the ground of morality lies in these. We ought to act in accordance with the "Fitness and Reason of Things." [1] Clarke asserts that that which is truly the "law of Nature" or the "Reason of Things" is in like manner the "Will of God." [2] Thus the will of God takes second place, as if its function were merely to ratify the enactments of the natural legislature. Clarke conceives "Moral Virtue [as] .... the Foundation and Summ, the Essence and Life of all true Religion." [3]

Clarke, however, does find a place for revelation in his system. There is cause to believe from right reason and the light of nature that God would seek a way to assist man toward his salvation. Whichcote also considers revealed truth as being implied by the natural and he appears to be in agreement with Clarke that the purpose of this revealed addition to natural light is primarily for the purpose of man's salvation.[4] In his view of revelation as opposed to the Deists, Clarke anticipates Butler. Clarke is driven to abandon the high *a priori* view and only seek to demonstrate that some revelation or other is probable. That any given revelation is the true one can only be proved by evidence applicable to it alone, and consequently of the ordinary *a posteriori* kind.[5] Clarke then points back to Whichcote and forward to the Deists.

He adopts almost entirely the deist method, but applies it on behalf of Christianity. If the description is permissible, he may be called a Christian Deist. He was not an originator of thought but represented a modification of current opinions. As a result he influenced a number of younger men, including Butler and plainly exerted a powerful influence upon the moral thinkers of the day.[6] He appears to transmit the

---

[1] Samuel Clarke, *Being and Attributes of God*, 6th ed. (London, 1725), pp. 256–257; Cf. *Discourse Concerning the Unchangeable Obligations of Natural Religion*, (1705), p. 86, (cited by Willey, *The Eighteenth Century Background*, (London, 1940), p. 60.).

[2] Clarke, *Unchangeable Obligations*, pp. 147–148, (cited by Willey, *Ibid.*).

[3] *Ibid.*, p. 141, (cited by Willey, *Ibid.*). Allowing for the scientific and philosophical advancement between the Cambridge Platonists and Clarke, most of his ethical theory is anticipated in the writings of Whichcote and Cudworth and to a lesser degree in More's work on ethics. See Martineau, *Ibid.*, pp. 425–38.

[4] See *Supra*, ch. VI.

[5] Stephen, *Ibid.*, pp. 127–29.

[6] *Ibid.*, pp. 129–130. Austin, *Ibid.*, p. 70, observes that the Cambridge Platonists have been considered the founders of an "intellectual" school in English ethics which extends from them through Clarke, Wollaston, Balguy and Price, to Reid and Stewart of the Scottish School and, finally, to Martineau and others.

liberal religious and moral tradition, begun by Whichcote and his disciples, into the eighteenth century.

Whichcote influenced the third Earl of Shaftesbury, but it is not easy to determine the extent of this influence.[1] It is significant that the first publication of Shaftesbury was a volume of Whichcote's sermons.[2] According to Shaftesbury's preface to this volume he was generally impressed by Whichcote's moral and religious outlook. He considers Whichcote as a philosopher of good-nature as well as a common opponent with himself against Hobbes.[3] Maurice's designation of Shaftesbury as a "philosopher of sunshine" is suggestive, for there can be little doubt that he was impressed with the kind disposition of Whichcote together with the emphasis in his writings upon natural "sympathy" toward virtue and benevolence.[4]

Shaftesbury fixes his attention mainly upon man as a member of a good society and not upon theological subjects. He feels that religion of a proper sort plays an important part in furthering the realization of his social ideal. According to Shaftesbury there are two affections which make us candidates for happiness or virtue.

They are the "natural" or "public" affections, and the "self" or "private" affections, and when the two sets do not combine in comfortable alliance, this is because their subject has not understood the meaning of good as it attains to rational beings. The balance between public and private affection is arrived at by "right reason." The morally good is beautiful, and the morally bad is ugly and this awareness is immediate to our minds. The heart of man must be involved in a decision and it knows the "difference" between beauty and ugliness. All the higher faculties of man are involved in moral decisions.[5]

Whichcote's sermons throw much light upon the thought of

----

[1] Whichcote's influence upon the "common sense" school of English ethicists may be traced through Shaftesbury, who was under a more direct influence of the Cambridge Platonists. Butler is an outstanding representative of the same ethical school. Cf. Stephen, *Ibid.*, II, 15.

[2] See *Supra*, Appendix I.

[3] *Select Sermons* (London, 1698), preface. Cf. *Characteristics* (London, 1723), II, 80, 110, 311–313 *passim*. In these passages Shaftesbury attacks Hobbes.

Cf. P. R. Anderson, "Science in Defense of Liberal Religion: A Study of Henry More's Attempt to Link Seventeenth Century Religion with Science" (New York, 1933), pp. 200–202. Two research works are invaluable for a general knowledge of Shaftesbury's moral and religious outlook. They are: Alfred Sternbeck, *Shaftesbury Über Natur, Gott und Religion* (Berlin, 1904) and V. G. Stanley, "Shaftesbury's Philosophy of Religion and Morals: A Study in Enthusiasm," unpub. diss. Columbia University, 1961.

[4] Maurice, *Ibid.*, II, 449–451.

[5] *Characteristics*, (London, 1732), vol. II, bk. I, pt. II, sect. I; bk. II, pt. I, sect. I; pt. II, sect. I *passim*. Cf. L. A. Selby-Bigge, *British Moralists*, (Oxford, 1897), I, pp. 4–85; De Pauley, *Ibid.*, pp. 18–20.

Shaftesbury and the "moral sense" school of ethicists. Whichcote distinguishes clearly between affections as such and the role of reason. He is more careful than Shaftesbury to reserve the office of making judgments in moral matters to reason. In Whichcote's analysis of moral action, it is reason that deliberates and the affections follow reason's decision.[1]

Shaftesbury's divergence from Whichcote is more extreme than appears from a first comparison. However, it is not in psychological analysis but in theological principle that the real difference lies – in the question of the relation of morality and religion. To Whichcote morality and religion are interdependent. Shaftesbury's conclusion is favorable on the whole to religion, by which he means communion with God, he maintains that it is of value primarily because it helps to sustain the moral stability of the community.

On the whole Shaftesbury seems to attempt to separate what Whichcote has conjoined since for Shaftesbury morality and religion are not necessarily united. According to Shaftesbury, if he must choose between religion and morality, he would take morality.

> If we are told a Man is religious; we still ask "What are his morals?" But if we hear at first that he has honest moral Principles, and is a Man of natural Justice and good Temper, we seldom think of the other Question, whether he be religious and devout? [2]

Shaftesbury's influence can be seen in Alexander Pope's poetry and in Butler's theology. Most British ethical writers since his time are related to him either by sympathy or opposition. He was profoundly influenced by Whichcote and disciples and for all his sceptical tendencies, which prevented him from being a true disciple to the school, their spirit permeates his pages.[3] In spite of his being Locke's pupil, he has more in common, morally speaking, with Whichcote than with Locke.[4] In a real sense, Shaftesbury is a bridge between Whichcote's

---

[1] Cudworth's moral psychology is closer to Shaftesbury's than Whichcote's, see *Supra*, ch. IX. Cf. De Pauley, *Ibid.*, pp. 20–22; Whichcote, *Works*, II, 395, for Whichcote's view of the beauty of the good life.

[2] "An Inquiry Concerning Virtue," *Characteristics* (1723), vol. II, bk. I, pt. I, sect. I, p. 6; Cf. De Pauley, *Ibid.*, pp. 22–24. For an account of Shaftesbury's notion of the value of religious belief to the good life, see Shaftesbury, *Ibid.*, pt. III, sect. III, pp. 52–76 *passim*. For a comparison of Whichcote and Shaftesbury's view concerning the nature of happiness here and hereafter, see De Pauley, *Ibid.*, pp. 23–26; Cf. Shaftesbury, "The Moralists," *Ibid.*, pt. II, sect. I, pp. 221-245.

[3] Stephen, *Ibid.*, II, 24; Cf. Oman, *Ibid.*, pp. 99–100.

[4] Maurice, *Ibid.*, II, 449. Cf. Austin, *Ibid.*, pp. 81–82; Laird, *Hobbes*, p. 283; Willey, *Ibid.*, pp. 61–75; Martineau, *Ibid.*, II, 448–473; Whichcote, *Select Aphorisms*, (1822), p. 22. Cassirer who stresses the influence of the Cambridge Platonists not only upon German rationalism and aesthetics, conceives this influence as being transmitted mainly by Shaftesbury, see *Ibid.*, pp. 160–162.

thought, especially his moral theory, and the future British moralists.

The thought of Butler is in many ways a continuation of Shaftesbury's thought.[1] But there are ways in which Butler is Whichcote's successor more than Clarke or Shaftesbury. This is particularly true of Butler's views concerning the relation of nature and grace and morality and religion.[2] Butler in his age as Whichcote in his, had the serious intention of developing an apology for Christianity.[3]

The agreement between Whichcote and Butler may be explained in part by the common source of their inspiration and their similar apologetic intention, while their differences appear to stem from the different circumstances giving rise to their systems as well as by the intervening development of thought.

The main thesis of the *Analogy* is summed up in Butler's quotation from Origen, that "he who believes the Scripture to have proceeded from him who is the author of Nature, may well expect to find the same sort of difficulties in it, as are found in the constitution of nature." [4] Thus Butler is concerned with the God of Revelation as being identical with the God of Nature in the same way in which Whichcote speaks of the same God as Creator and Redeemer – "the God of Nature is the Giver of Grace." [5] But whereas Whichcote is confident that God may be known in both instances as moral perfection and the highest Intelligence, Butler attempts to show that Nature and Revelation are both baffling and that as such they appear to be the product of the same mind. Butler, then, finds a place for revelation, but only by showing it to be as perplexing as nature.[6] Passing from Whichcote through Locke, Clarke and Shaftesbury to Butler, we move from an optimistic to a relatively pessimistic theory of the world. Many of the self-evident truths of Whichcote have become for Butler probabilities only.

Although in his theological views, Butler in many ways resembles Whichcote, it is in Butler's ethical thought that he resembles Whichcote most.

As a matter of fact, Butler seems best known by his ethical

---

[1] For an account of their agreements and differences, see Stephen, *Ibid.*, II, pp. 16, 28, 46–47.

[2] According to W. R. Scott, there is a close connection between Cudworth, Clarke and Butler, see *An Introduction to Cudworth's Treatise Concerning Eternal and Immutable Morality*, (London, 1891), pp. 59–61. Whichcote certainly belongs to the same moral and religious tradition and is in many ways the founder of it.

[3] Cf. Willey, *Ibid.*, pp. 76–77.

[4] Quoted by Butler, *Analogy* 6th ed. (Glasgow, 1764), p.v.

[5] *Supra*, ch. VI.

[6] Willey, *Ibid.*, Cf. Butler, *Analogy*, pt. I, ch. VII, Con.

views [1] and it is in this area that he appears as a real successor of Whichcote. He raises the question as to the real nature of man. Like Whichcote he finds man to be the crown of creation. Butler discovers in man a reflective faculty which he calls conscience and this faculty for him as for Whichcote is the final authority in all moral decisions, it is the "very voice of God." [2] As far as Butler's concepts of the nature and role of conscience, the subordination of passions and human moral responsibility are concerned, he appears to have been anticipated by Whichcote. But Butler has obviously given reason a subordinate position to his concept of conscience. It appears that the function of reason as conceived by Whichcote has been given over to the "Faculty of Conscience" by Butler.[3]

In his view of a natural principle of benevolence in man,[4] Butler reminds us of Whichcote and Shaftesbury. Butler conceives the disposition to friendship, compassion and filial affection as benevolence. And wherever this tendency is present, even in a very low degree, the possibility of growth in mutual helpfulness is present.[5] Butler like Whichcote and Shaftesbury conceives the possession of this natural spirit of benevolence a responsibility to contribute to the "public good."[6]

Conscience is enthroned by Butler above natural self-love and benevolence. He exalts conscience and thus illustrates the dogma of the common sense school of moralists. Butler remains, however, in a practical sense the deepest moralist of the century. But he attempts to absorb nature in God as revealed in conscience, instead of absorbing God in nature.

Butler and Whichcote are agreed that each man is a law unto himself – a little kingdom in himself, with a constitution of divine origin.[7] In spite of Butler's concealment of his religion as a moralist, it appears that he has succeeded in building morality upon a supernatural principle in the make-up of human nature. Thus for Butler no less than for Whichcote, religion and ethics are a unity. The reverence Butler expects us to pay to conscience is the kind that most men will only

[1] *Ibid.*, pp. 76–94.
[2] Butler, *Sermons* 4th ed. (London, 1749), Ser. i–iii, See esp. *Ser.* i, p. 13.
[3] Butler, *Works* (Oxford, 1836), II, Preface, p. xiv; *Ser.* vi, p. 80; *Ser. ii*, pp. 33, 34 *passim*.
[4] Butler, *Sermons*, *Ser.* i, pp. 6–7.
[5] *Ibid.*, pp. 9–11.
[6] *Ibid.*, p. 10. Cf. Whichcote's reflections on the same subject, *Supra*, chs. V, VII. However, Butler's views concerning "self-love" have no parallel in Whichcote's writings, see Butler, *Ibid.*, pp. 12–13; Cf. *Ser.* xi, p. 203. The closest Whichcote approaches Butler on this subject is when he asserts that immortality is unnatural and self-destructive. The positive corollary to this would be very close to Butler's appeal to self-interest or "self-love."
[7] Stephen, *Ibid.*, II, 54–56.

accord to something other than themselves.[1] We conclude that on many fundamentals in religion and ethics, Butler and Whichcote are in essential accord, but that much of the self-confident intellectualism of Whichcote is absent from Butler's thought.

Since Whichcote was just as anxious to assert the authority of Scripture concerning truths of after-revelation as the authority of reason concerning truths of first-inscription, he contributes to the Scripturalism as well as the Rationalism of the eighteenth century. By the middle of the eighteenth century, reaction against dogmatic theology was partly occasioned by a growing desire to base religious belief on Scripture alone; and to keep strictly to its literal teaching. It is obvious that there is a perversion of the original intention of men like Chillingworth and Whichcote, by taking one side of their teaching and over-emphasizing it. In the case of Chillingworth and Whichcote, the role of reason is emphasized even in the interpretation of Scripture.

Whichcote points out that "Determinations beyond Scripture have.... enlarged faith, but lessened Charity, and multiplied Divisions," [2] but in his writing, quotations from Scripture and the Platonists stand side by side. Whichcote was not a "mere Scripturalist," this is the basis of much of Tuckney's dissatisfaction with Whichcote's views. Thus, by including the unquestioned authority of Scripture in his concept of reason Whichcote may be said to have contributed to the Scripturalism of the following century, but the movement drifts far from his original intention.

Our final concern in this chapter is with Whichcote's contribution to subsequent Christian Platonism. In this tradition the work of Norris appears of great importance.[3]

---

[1] Willey, *Ibid.*, pp. 93–94. Cf. Butler's epitaph (in Bristol Cathedral), cited by Willey, *Ibid.*, p. 76; Cf. Stephen, *Ibid.*, I, 281–307; II, 47–56; Oman, *Ibid.*, pp. 118–127; Butler, "Of the Nature of Virtue," *Dissertation*, II in *Analogy*, (1764), pp. 344–356. Butler, together with the Cambridge Platonists, conceived Hobbes as his opponent, see Laird, *Ibid.*, pp. 283–284.

[2] Whichcote, *Aph.* 981; Cf. *Ibid.* 1161. For a fuller discussion of the Cambridge Platonists upon Scripturalism in the eighteenth century see Powicke, *Ibid.*, pp. 206–208. Powicke is no doubt correct when he asserts that Whichcote and his school would have been driven to similar conclusions to those of the Scripturalists if they had tried to work out their reading of the New Testament into a system.

[3] Norris' basic agreement with the Cambridge Platonists was as follows: (1) Platonic love; (2) Reverence for reason; (3) The use of reason in the service of religion; (4) His dislike of Calvinism; (5) His insistence upon the ethical side of religion; (6) His view that orthodoxy of judgment is necessary only in fundamentals; (7) His attachment to the Church of England; and (8) His general indifference to politics. Powicke, *Ibid.*, pp. 126–32.

Concerning the work of John Sergeant of Cambridge and Arthur Collier of Oxford, see Muirhead, *Ibid.*, pp. 72–73. Although there appears to be no direct relation between Berkeley and the Cambridge Platonists, his work entitled *Siris*, places him in the Christian Platonic tradition with them. All we can say is that Berkeley like the Cambridge Platonists is a great

Norris shows no acquaintance with Whichcote or Smith. He quotes from Cudworth once or twice, but there is nothing to prove his indebtedness to him, though Norris appears to have corresponded with Cudworth's daughter. More was the one member of the school he corresponded with and greatly admired. Through his correspondence with More his points of agreement with the Cambridge School are seen.

In his spirit of tolerance and his use of reason Norris resembles Whichcote most. He is in essential agreement with Whichcote as to the basis and scope of religious toleration. Like Whichcote, Norris condemned Papists and Dissenters alike. Norris did not consider differences important enough to justify separation and at the same time he asserted that men should have the freedom to think freely unless they disturb the public.[1] But his tolerant spirit, as also Whichcote's, is based upon his belief that religion is rational and that all things saving are evident to reason.

Norris says:

> Since our Religion is so Reasonable a Service, 'twill follow hence, in the first place, that there may be a due exercise and use of reason in Divine matters; and that whatsoever is apparently (i.e. clearly) contrary to Reason ought not to be observed as of Divine Authority, not to be accounted as any part of the Christian Religion..... 'Twill follow, secondly, that no man ought to be Persecuted, or have external violence done him for his Religion, supposing that by overt acts he gives no disturbance to the public. For, since God has required nothing of us but what is agreeable to our Reason, why should man?[2]

This entire passage might well have been extracted from Whichcote's writings. This appears to be explained by Norris' indebtedness to More. In 1684, Norris confessed that he had read all More's works – thus More was one medium through which Plato's influence reached Norris.[3] It

foe of scepticism, atheism and materialism, and in so far as he goes to Plato for his inspiration, he uses a common source with the Cambridge man. Cf. Seth, *Ibid.*, pp. 123–128 and John Wild, *George Berkeley* (New York, 1962), pp. 71–77.

[1] *Ibid.*, pp. 131–132.

[2] Quoted by Powicke, *Ibid.*

[3] *Ibid.*, pp. 126–127. Lovejoy's essay in which he compares the thought of Cudworth, Norris and Collier with the so-called Neo-Kantians, i.e., T. H. Green, J. Royce, F. H. Bradley and others, is interesting.

He dares to suggest that Cudworth anticipated Kant and much of the material which they claim to have received from Kant might well have been derived from the English idealists of the seventeenth century. See O. Lovejoy, "Kant and the English Platonists," *Essays Philosophical and Psychological in Honor of William James* (London, 1908), pp. 265–302. A similar position is taken by James Mackintosh, *Discourse on the Progress of Ethical Philosophy* (Edinburgh, 1872), p. 142. The same position is implied in Muirhead, *Ibid.* The work begins with the Cambridge Platonists and ends with American idealism, i.e. Royce. Muirhead dares to refer to Cudworth as the founder of British Idealism, see *Ibid.*, p. 35. This tendency to imply the influence of the Cambridge Platonists upon Neo-Kantianism and even upon Kant himself has been convincingly criticized by Austin, *Ibid.*, pp. 83–84; Scott, *Ibid.*,

is obvious that the version of Platonism absorbed in Norris' writings is that set forth by the Christian Platonists of Cambridge under the leadership of Whichcote.

This consideration of the thought of Norris as a Christian Platonist is sufficient for our purpose, and we may pass at once to the thought of S. T. Coleridge. At Jesus College, Cambridge, in 1791, Coleridge encountered Platonic philosophy. It was revived by Thomas Taylor at the time of Coleridge's sojourn there. Coleridge became acquainted with the writings of Whichcote and his disciples and found an affinity in their writings with what he had learned from Plato and Plotinus and this helped to deepen his mystic strain.[1]

The distinction between Understanding and Reason was applied by him to all subjects of philosophical enquiry. Plato and the Cambridge Platonists greatly influenced him though Kant confirmed and gave more definite form to his distinction between discursive reason and the intuitive exercise of the faculty.[2] Seth observes that even though Coleridge derived his distinction between Reason and Understanding from Kant, his debt to Kant seems to include primarily a means of stating scientifically convictions previously attained. Further, as he applies Kant's theory he does not distinguish clearly between the speculative and practical reason, it is, however, the latter rather than the former that he regards as the organ of spiritual vision. God, the soul, and eternal truths are for Coleridge the objects of reason and are themselves reason. Practical reason becomes synonymous with faith – fidelity to our being so far as such being is not and cannot become an object of the senses.[3]

pp. 62–64; Martineau, *Ibid.*, II, pp. 396–399. The evidence is practically balanced on both sides. However, since Whichcote was not a systematic philosopher, the problem does not deserve further consideration. Whichcote is involved only indirectly in so far as he contributes to the idealism of Cudworth.

[1] Muirhead, *Coleridge as Philosopher* (London, 1930) pp. 38–39, 97. See Coleridge's lecture on "Plato and Platonism" in Kathleen Coburn, ed., *The Philosophical lectures of Samuel Taylor Coleridge* (London, 1949), pp. 144–169.

[2] *Ibid.*, pp. 65–67, 83, 95, 97, 113–115, 116–118, 234.

[3] Seth, *Ibid.*, pp. 320–27. Cf. Coleridge, *Aids to Reflection* ed. by Thomas Fenby, revised (*London*, n.d.), *Aphorisms*, X, II, VII. Though Coleridge's two main doctrines, viz. the distinction between Imagination and Fancy in *Biographia Literaria* and between Reason and Understanding in *Aids to Reflection* are interrelated, we are only concerned with the latter distinction here. Cf. J. D. Boulger, *Coleridge As Religious Thinker* (New Haven, 1961), pp. 3, 65–93. In his discussion on Coleridge's concept of "higher reason," Boulger is correct, I believe, in recognizing the influence of Kant as well as the Cambridge Platonists. In addition to Kant's critical philosophy, Coleridge had also passed through the enlightenment. He had witnessed the breakdown of the unity between reason and revelation. It can readily be understood, therefore, why his circumstance called forth a more profound and critical concept than that provided by the Cambridge Platonists.

According to Coleridge, knowing in terms of togetherness is what is meant by reason in religion and ethics. Reason is the organ of the supersensuous while Understanding is the faculty by which we generalize and arrange the phenomena of perception. Reason is the law of the whole considered as one, Understanding is the science of phenomena. Reason seeks ultimate ends, Understanding studies means. Reason is the source and substance of truth above sense; Understanding judges according to sense. Reason is the eye of the spirit, the faculty whereby spiritual reality is spiritually discerned; Understanding is the mind of the flesh.

Understanding is necessarily used for measurement, analysis, classification and the other processes of natural science, and it controls our lives on the practical routine level. It begins to err when it encroaches on the sphere where Reason alone is valid, that is, when it pretends to erect its limited theories into absolute laws, mistaking a technique of experiment or method of classification for an exhaustive account of reality. This happened in the eighteenth century in the "godless revolution" of materialism, determinism, atheism and utilitarianism.[1]

Coleridge uses the certainties of Plato, of Christianity and German idealism (together with his own insights) to oppose the eighteenth century tradition, just as Whichote and his disciples use Platonism and Christianity against Hobbes. Coleridge sought to combine the Platonic theory of the world and a voluntaristic theory of being and of knowledge, largely Kantian, with a psychology essentially his own. By shifting the emphasis from God as Being or Substance to God as Will, he was able to vindicate the practical nature of religion, which was later to become the keynote of the treatment of it by British and American idealists, i.e., F. H. Bradley, Josiah Royce, and to identify

---

[1] Basil Willey, *Nineteenth Century Studies* (London, 1949), pp. 28–29. Cf. Seth, *Ibid.*, pp. 320–321. William Whewell, *Lectures on the History of Moral Philosophy*, new ed. (Cambridge, England, 1862), p. 122. According to Whewell, Coleridge's distinction in kind between Reason and Understanding is untenable. He asserts that the verb to reason is always employed to designate the discursive or ratiocinative operations of the mind while the verb to understand implies a fixed contemplation.

Thus Coleridge's view is neither good English nor good philosophy, for Coleridge describes the understanding as the faculty which judges according to sense obtaining truth by generalizing from experience, while he conceives Reason as observing Truth by intuition. Cf. Whewell, *Ibid.*, pp. 119–130; Coleridge, *Ibid.*, *Aphorism* VIII. It seems fair to conclude that however confusing Coleridge's language may be, his intention is clear. He desires to purify the term Reason as applied to the supreme spiritual and moral faculty of man. Thus in intention he is perhaps closer to Whichote than to any other member of the Cambridge Platonists school.

faith and fidelity with conscience and the indications of the will of God upon earth as rationally interpreted, instead of with belief in any system or doctrine. In a real sense, both Plato and Kant were his masters.[1]

For Coleridge as for Whichcote, theology and ethics belong to the sphere of reason. Reason according to Coleridge discerns the necessary laws and postulates of the moral life, for it includes the conscience or moral sense, which is the chief witness of spiritual realities. By means of this distinction, Coleridge is able, at once, to attack the so-called "rationalists" (a word, he thinks, has been debased in meaning) and to refer approvingly to the "rational theologians" of the seventeenth century. Their Reason according to Coleridge was Reason indeed, for it was a faculty independent of sense, and linked with the Will; in the eighteenth century *"raison"* had invaded regions beyond its competence.[2] Coleridge seems to deserve the position of a reviver of many of the same insights in the nineteenth century which were revived by Whichcote in the seventeenth. The insights were eclipsed during the Age of Reason and thus Coleridge's significance in tracing the subsequent influence of Whichcote and his school is the more important.[3]

From Coleridge we may pass to F. D. Maurice. In a statement by Maurice we perceive, at once, the contribution of Coleridge to the forward advance of Christian Platonism and the trend of Maurice's own thought. Maurice gives Coleridge credit for "the power of perceiving that by the very law of Reason the knowledge of God must be "given" to it; that the moment it attempts to create its Maker, it denies itself. . . ." [4] Maurice constantly protested against being identi-

---

[1] Muirhead, *Ibid.*, pp. 254–255; Cf. J. H. Rigg, *Modern Anglican Theology* 2nd and revised ed. (London, 1859), pp. 8–32.

[2] Willey, *Ibid.*, pp. 33–34. It is of interest that Coleridge chose to call his insights in *Aids to Reflection* "aphorisms," the very term made famous by Whichcote in the seventeenth century. This implies literary as well as thought affinity between them. One wonders if in fact Coleridge conceived this term by a study of Whichcote's writings.

[3] Cf. Muirhead, *Ibid.*, p. 125. Muirhead calls Coleridge the reviver of the Platonic tradition and the founder of nineteenth century Idealism in England. Earlier in the same work (p. 35) he claims for Cudworth the position of the real founder of British Idealism.
If this observation is correct, the relation between Cudworth and Coleridge is obvious. This would mean also that the relation between Whichcote and Coleridge is unquestioned since that which, idealistically speaking, is explicit in Cudworth's writings is implicit in Whichcote's. On the question of Justification by faith, Coleridge takes his stand against both Arminians and Catholics in defence of the Lutheran view. Thus on his view of saving faith, he differs somewhat with Whichcote who holds out for considerable Arminian influence, see, Boulger, *Ibid.*, pp. 58–64.

[4] *The Kingdom of Christ* 3rd ed. (London, 1883), I, xxv.

fied with any party. He stood in a relation to the parties of the Church of his day in a position analogous to that of the Cambridge Platonists in relation to the Laudians, Puritans and Sectaries.[1]

Maurice, by virtue of his affinity with his master, Coleridge, was a Platonist as opposed to an Aristotelian and has been regarded by his opponents as a Neo-Platonist.[2] He was kept from a strictly mystical view by his strong conviction of the necessity of an historical element in theology.[3] This position is akin to the Cambridge Platonists, for Whichcote insisted on the fact of the Incarnation and More, the most mystical member of the school, defends the Incarnation against its subordination in early Quakerism.

Dr. C. E. Raven refers to Maurice as one of the most important and prophetic English Christians in the nineteenth century. He lived and thought against an eternal background and all his thought and experience was conditioned by his conviction of the universality of Christ and of the unity of all men. His faith is vindicated by social action and noteworthy philanthropy. He was haunted by a desire for unity in Church and State all his days. While he appeared to those who liked logical statements of dogma as heretical, yet as a prophet his work lives.[4] Maurice was deprived of his chair at King's College, London, nominally on theological grounds but actually because of his Christian Socialism.[5] It appears that it was the social implications of his theology that led to his dismissal. He maintained the Johannine view of eternal life, that is, he conceived judgment as a process working here and now and immortality in relationship rather than duration.[6] As a corollary he conceived salvation as beginning in the present life and Christian social action as a duty.

A close observation of the life and thought of Maurice reminds us of Whichcote: his moderate theological position, desire for toleration in Church and State, Platonic sympathies, deep spirituality, social

---

[1] Leslie Stephen's art. in *D.N.B.*, Vol. XIII, pp. 104–105.

[2] Bigg, *Ibid.*, pp. 115–214. Cf. Candlish, "Professor Maurice and His Writings," L.Q.R., Vol. III, No. VI, (1855) pp. 393–436; C. R. Sanders, *Coleridge and the Broad Church Movement* (Durham, N. C., 1942), pp. 14–15.

[3] Cf. C. E. Raven, *Natural Religion and Christian Theology* (Cambridge, England, 1953), II, 214. See also A. M. Ramsey, *F. D. Maurice and the Conflicts of Modern Theology* (Cambridge, England, 1951), pp. 58–71.

[4] *Ibid.*, p. 213. This tribute to Maurice might almost be applied to Whichcote as it stands.

[5] *Ibid.*, p. 2.

[6] *Ibid.*, pp. 187–188. Cf. Jn. 3:19, 17. Cf. W. M. Davies, *An Introduction to F. D. Maurice's Theology* (London, 1964), pp. 16, 118, 153 and R. N. Flew, *The Idea of Perfection in Christian Theology* (London, 1934), p. 116.

consciousness, Johannine view of salvation and eternal life and "dynamic" application of the doctrine of the atonement in the experience of mankind. Especially in his zeal for Christian social action Maurice appears to carry forward the implications of Whichcote's life and thought. This notion of justifying faith by works is a mark of Cambridge Platonism. Even Henry More, the most introverted and mystical member of the school, extended a helping hand to the "poor and needy" who sought him out in his academic retreat. For Maurice, as for John Smith, Whichcote's closest disciple, theology is a "divine life" rather than a "divine science." [1] Inge says:

> There was at Cambridge a hundred years ago, a society of Platonists, not very unlike the group gathered around Whichcote. F. D. Maurice came under the influence of these men, and through them was led to study Coleridge.

He continues:

> Maurice is perhaps at his best as an interpreter of St. John though he is chiefly remembered as the leader of a Christian Socialist movement. These interests led him back from the religious and mystical Platonism which had mainly interested the Cambridge group in the seventeenth century, to the practical and political philosophy of Plato himself...[2]

In some ways Bishop Westcott may be considered a follower of Maurice. Westcott had a natural sympathy for Johannine theology, and wrote a well-known commentary on the Fourth Gospel. But what concerns us most is Westcott's collected volume of essays called *The History of Religious Thought in the West*. This work is described by Inge as "an excellent treatise on orthodox Christian Platonism." [3] It

---

[1] Smith, "Of Divine Knowledge," *Ibid.*, p. 1. Cf. Maurice, *Moral and Metaphysical Philosophy* new ed. (London, 1873), II, 350; *The Kingdom of Christ*, II, 6–8, 193–195; Raven, *Christian Socialism, 1848–1854* (London, 1920), pp. 78–82.

[2] W. R. Inge, *The Platonic Tradition in English Religious Thought* (London, 1926), pp. 96–97. It is obvious I believe, that even the social consciousness and action of Maurice is present in Whichcote's life and thought though not in the same degree. Inge numbers Wordsworth, Shelley, Coleridge and Ruskin among what he calls the "personal Platonists." Willey, *Ibid.*, pp. 53–54, considers Thomas Arnold as a successor of Whichcote and one who echoed in his whole life the exclamation of Whichcote: "Give me a religion that doth attain real effects." Arnold stands in a succession which descends from Hooker, through the Cambridge Platonists to Coleridge, and leads through Maurice to William Temple. Cf. Stanley's *Life of Arnold*, (1835) II, 13, cited by Willey, *Ibid.*, p. 53. In Arnold's concept of the "end" of the Church as that of "putting down of moral evil" and its "nature," a loving society of all Christians, he reflected in his life and thought the spirit of Whichcote. Matthew Arnold, according to Willey, is akin in spirit to the same succession as his father, Thomas Arnold. Matthew Arnold, in fact, was trying to do for the nineteenth century what Whichcote attempted to do in the seventeenth, viz. "to preserve a spirit of piety and rational religion" in opposition to the "fanatic enthusiasm and senseless canting then in vogue."
Cf. Willey, *Ibid.*, pp. 266–267. It is understandable that Matthew Arnold should have written an introduction to a work edited by W. M. Metcalfe, entitled *The Cambridge Platonists*, (1885).

[3] Inge, *Ibid.*, pp. 97–98.

begins with the myths of Plato and ends with an essay on Whichcote. After one reads this work there can be little doubt concerning Westcott's relation to Whichcote, for they clearly stand in the same stream of Christian Platonism.[1]

In Westcott's book, *The Historic Faith*, his view of eternal life is Johannine recalling similar statements in the writings of Whichcote. Whichcote considers the future life different only in degree from the present. Eternal life is for Whichcote a "quality" of life beginning with the first stages of salvation and progressing henceforth so that the life hereafter is simply "more of the same thing." Westcott says:

> Eternal life then is that knowledge of God which is communion with Him; it "is" not something future but absolute; it is in realization: It answers to a divine fellowship which issues in perfect unity.... Eternal life is not something future: it "is," it is now. It lies in a relation to God through Christ. The manifestation of the life is confined and veiled by the circumstances of our present condition, but the life is actual. It does not depend for its essence upon any external change.[2]

Archbishop William Temple, it seems to me, deserves brief attention as standing in the Christian Platonic succession with Whichcote. When Temple asserts that the God who reveals Himself in the most exceptional occurrences, is revealed as the ultimate Lord of all occurrences, we are reminded of Whichcote's doctrine of revelation.[3] Temple says:

> Unless all existence is a medium of revelation, no particular revelation is possible.... Either all occurrences are in some degree revelation of God, or else there is no such revelation at all; for the conditions of the possibility of any revelation require that there should be nothing which is not revelation. Only if God is revealed in the rising of the sun in the sky can He be revealed in the rising of the son of man from the dead.[4]

Temple's general assertion that God reveals Himself in nature but that the main field of revelation must always be in the history of men [5] reminds us of Whichcote's notion that the "reason of men is the candle of the Lord" as well as his view of providential history. Further Temple reminds us of Whichcote when he insists that "faith is not the holding of correct doctrines, but personal fellowship with God.[6]

---

[1] B. F. Westcott, *Essays in the History of Religious Thought in the West* (London, 1891), p. 357.

[2] Cited by Inge, *Ibid.*, pp. 103–104. Inge comments that this language about eternal life, as a higher plane of existence into which we may pass here and now, is so much the hallmark of Platonism that it is needless to expatiate upon it. *Ibid.*, p. 109. Cf. Henry Chadwick, *The Vindication of Christianity in Westcott's Thought* (Cambridge, England, 1960), pp. 8, 10.

[3] Cf. Temple, *Nature, Man and God* (London, 1943), pp. 304–305, 314. See *Supra*, ch. VI.

[4] *Ibid.*, p. 306.

[5] *Ibid.*, p. 305; Cf. *Supra*, chs. IV–VI.

[6] *Ibid.*, pp. 321–322. Temple places himself in the Christian Platonic tradition by his work

As we pass on to Dean Inge, the name of Charles Bigg deserves to be mentioned.[1] Inge's own affinity with Christian Platonism which flows through Whichcote, his disciples and successors is obvious. Inge's tolerant spirit is evident in his quotation from Ignatius as follows: "Christ Himself levelled almost all barriers by ignoring them." [2] Inge praises Christian Platonic thought, sometimes referred to by him as "Johannine" for the following reasons: first, in it the center of gravity shifts from authority to experience,[3] and secondly, it is a faith which need not be afraid of scientific progress. This school has no need of the dualism of the natural and supernatural which is wholly unacceptable to science.[4]

Inge conceives the Platonic tradition in the Church as an influence for good in its moral and spiritual life. All his commitment to this type of Christianity is unwavering.[5] He commends highly the works of Whichcote, Smith, Cudworth and Culverwel, and is convinced that anyone who reads the works of the first two named will "gain a lasting benefit in the deepening of his spiritual life and the heightening of his faith." [6] Inge's introduction to his 1930 edition of Whichcote's *Aphorisms* is instructive. What Inge says in this introduction indicates, at once, his indebtedness to Whichcote and his high estimation of the value of his thought for modern readers. Inge traces for us the influence of the Cambridge Platonists as follows:

Plato and Christianity (London, 1916). It appears obvious that he stands in the same tradition with the Cambridge Platonists and receives his inspiration from a common source. See, W. D. Geoghegan, *Platonism in Recent Religious Thought* (New York, 1938), pp. 82–109. Cf. Joseph Fletcher, *Ibid.*, pp. 295–296 (n. 51).

This relation between nature and grace in Raven led him to write a book on Father Pierre Teilhard de Chardin, the noted scientist-theologian, see His *Teilhard de Chardin Scientist and Seer* (New York, 1962), pp. 17–29. It is interesting that John MacQuarrie relates the theologies of William Temple and Teilhard de Chardin in his *Twentieth-Century Religious Thought* (New York, 1963), pp. 269–273.

[1] Inge says, *Ibid.*, p. 104, that Bigg belongs to the Christian Platonic tradition and in his Bampton Lectures on the Alexandrian Fathers he did much to awake the public interest in this type of theology. His sermons and addresses show that his personal religion belonged to the same type as that of Bishop Westcott.

[2] Inge, *Ibid.*

[3] *Ibid.*, pp. 113–114.

[4] *Ibid.*, pp. 115–116. This seems to be the main point at which Dr. C. E. Raven aligns himself with the Christian Platonic tradition, i.e. early Logos-theology, the Cambridge Platonists and others. His volume "Science and Religion," *Natural Religion and Christian Theology*, Vol. I, is a noteworthy attempt to prove that there is no conflict between nature and grace. Here he devotes a chapter to Cudworth and kindred minds who had a constructive influence upon modern scientific advance. Cf. *Supra*, ch. IV. For Raven as for Whichcote the God of Nature is the Giver of Grace.

[5] *Ibid.*, pp. 116–117. Cf. W. D. Geoghegan, *Ibid.*, pp. 5–33 and George Santayana, *Platonism and the Spiritual Life* (New York, 1927), pp. 83–91.

[6] *Christian Mysticism* 3rd ed. (London, 1913), p. 287.

The influence of the Cambridge School did not die with them. Although the
18th Century was very unfavorable to Platonic mysticism, William Law ... was
a kindred spirit.... A little later, no one can doubt that Coleridge and Wordsworth were in the line of succession from the Platonists of the Renaissance, nor
that Maurice and Westcott ... were of the same brotherhood.[1]

Concerning the relevance of their thought for the present, Inge says:

I believe our age has much to learn from this Cambridge group.... This type
of Churchmanship may, I think, be a reconciling Principle between Catholics
and Protestants, going back to the Alexandrian and Cappadocian Fathers, and
further still to St. Paul and St. John, is catholic without being Latin.... It may
also be a vitalizing principle, for we are in need of a spiritual and idealistic
revival.[2]

Taking all the facts into account, Dr. C. E. Raven appears to be the
most recent exponent of the total view of Whichcote and his school. It
is important that we should quote a statement from him which
significantly designates Whichcote, his disciples and immediate successors as the founders of British "liberalism." Raven says:

In Britain theological liberalism derives not from the "enlightenment" of the
eighteenth century, from Voltaire and his disciples, but from an older and more
august ancestry, the Cambridge Platonists or "Latitude-men" of the seventeenth
century, who broke away from the Calvinism of the Puritans and the Catholicism
of Archbishop Laud and appealed to the Fourth Gospel and the Greek theologians of Alexandria on behalf of a reasonable faith. S. T. Coleridge, Thomas
Erskine of Linlathen, F. D. Maurice and the liberal or broad–church movement
in England and Scotland carried on this tradition which has always been
independent of Continental liberalism, even when it has owed much to it.[3]

[1] Whichcote, *Aphorisms* (1930), Intro. by Inge, pp. ix–x.

[2] *Ibid.*, p. x. Cf. *Christian Mysticism, Ibid., The Philosophy of Plotinus*, II, 227–228. By
comparison Inge appears more mystical than Whichcote though they have much in common.
Inge's mysticism like Whichcote's is a "practical" mysticism. Raven considers W. R. Inge
as a representative of British "modernism." Raven, *Ibid.*, II, 6. It would appear, then, that
the roots of this modernism might reach back to Whichcote and his disciples. Willey, *Ibid.*,
pp. 226–267, calls Matthew Arnold the "founder" of English modernism but insists that
Arnold gets his inspiration from the Cambridge Platonists.

[3] Raven, *Ibid.*, p. 6. The scope of this book does not take us into New England religious
thought. There has been, however, a number of hints that the influence of the Cambridge
Platonists passed to Jonathan Edwards. But the theory that the Cambridge Platonists were
greatly influenced by Ramus and that it was through this common source that Edwards and
the Platonists are linked, appears unfounded. There is also a real question as to whether
Edwards read even Cudworth's *Intellectual System*, see J. H. McCracken, "The Sources of
Jonathan Edward's Idealism," P. R. vol. XI, no. 1 (January, 1902), p. 35.

Most authors rely on two sources: Perry Miller, *The New England Mind: The Seventeenth
Century* (New York 1939) and H. W. Schneider, *History of American Philosophy* (New York,
1947). Both authors appear to be very knowledgeable concerning both Edwards and Ramus,
but reveal slight insight into Cambridge Platonism. Thus I would question the conclusions
of D. J. Elwood, *The Philosophical Theology of Jonathan Edwards* (New York, 1960), see
pp. 168 (n. 47), 183 (n. 46). His assumption that Ramus influenced the Cambridge Platonists
more than Renaissance Platonism cannot be supported. It may be true that Ramus' influence
was more important on Congregational Puritanism than Renaissance Platonism, but this is
not true of the Cambridge school. There is, however, evidence that Ramus made a greater

It appears fair to conclude that the spirit of Whichcote, one of the foremost rational theologians of his day, whom Shaftesbury described as "a philosopher of good-nature," lives to this day in British modernism and liberalism. His spirit may be said to have its effect wherever there is liberty of comprehension of religious knowledge and where religion has "real effects" being, conceived as a "divine life" rather than merely a "divine science."

impact at Cambridge than at Oxford, but there is no way of establishing such a strong tie to Whichcote and his school. Their writings indicate no excitement over Ramus. There are two key factors to remember: (1) The Cambridge men were Puritans who did not leave the Church of England to become Congregational Puritans; therefore their theology was a reaction against the Calvinism of the Westminster Assembly; and (2) They were against the claims of papacy, but they were not Aristotelian in the Ramistic sense; they were rather pro-Platonic. For example, Whichcote used much of Aristotle and referred to him as the Philosopher indicating his admiration for him. There may be a tie between some Puritans in England with others in New England through Ramus, but this does not seem true regarding the Cambridge Platonists. What can be established, I think, is that Edwards was influenced by John Locke and Locke in turn was influenced directly by Whichcote and his school. This point we have already discussed earlier in this chapter. Cf. Richardson, *Ibid.*; H. G. Townsend ed., *The Philosophy of Jonathan Edwards* (Eugene, Oregon, 1955), p. vi–vii; Paul Ransey's introduction *The Works of Jonathan Edwards* (New Haven, 1957), pp. 47–65. Concerning Ramus see the following: W. J. Ong, *Ramus and Talon Inventory* (Cambridge, Mass., 1958), Pierre De La Ramée, *Dialectique* (1555) (Edition critique avec introduction, notes et commentaires de Michel Dassonville) (Geneva, 1964), pp. 7–46; F. P. Graves, *Peter Ramus* (New York, 1912), pp. 212–213; Charles Waddington, *Ramus, Sa Vie, Ses Écrits Et Ses Opinions* (Paris, 1855), pp. 364–380, 396–397. For an account of the continuing influence of Platonism on religious thought in England and America, see, W. D. Geoghegan, *Ibid.*, the entire work.

CHAPTER ELEVEN

EPILEGOMENA

In conclusion we shall consider Whichcote's lasting contribution to theology: the preservation and development of the characteristic Greek and Platonic ideas which figured largely in the formulation of early Christian theology and which have been so seriously misunderstood by Neo-Orthodox theologians.[1] Inge and Raven, I believe, are right in

[1] *The Candle of the Lord*, p. 37.
It seems to me that for the first time in the history of Western thought, we have a radical replacement of the primacy of essence by the primacy of existence, see M. M. Madison, "Primacy of Existence: The Existential Protest Against The Logos," *The Personalist*, vol. XLVI, no. 1 (January, 1965), pp. 5–17. In addition we have a basic conflict with depth psychology, Marxism, and other anthropological theories with the Christian faith regarding the nature of man to say nothing of the existence of God, see Erich Fromm, "Limitations and Dangers in Psychology" *Religion and Culture: Essays in Honor of Paul Tillich*, ed. by Walter Leibrecht (New York, 1959), pp. 31–36; Cf. O. H. Mowrer, *The Crisis in Psychiatry and Religion* (Princeton, 1961), pp. 81–221. The existence of God in essentialist terms has been under such attack by atheistic Existentialism and various approaches to the "death of God" theme in modern literature that even many theologians have abandoned the traditional theistic arguments for a novel approach, see John MacQuarrie, "How is Theology Possible?" *New Theology*, ed. by M. E. Marty and D. G. Peerman (New York, 1964), pp. 21–33. Mac-Quarrie merely intends to move from man to God; while Bishop J. A. T. Robinson's *Honest to God* cuts away at the roots of theism and the morality supported by it.
Thus we have a "new morality" as well as a "New Theology." Bishop J. A. Pike has contributed to ecumenical dialogue in his *A Time for Christian Candor* (New York, 1964), but at the same time he has cast a shadow over the "trinity" which is not a matter of indifference for millions of Christians as it is for him. Much more could be said about the current theological ferment. Theology and morality today are more like "fads" than stable guides to purposeful living. Against this unsettled background Christian Platonism stands for the "unchanging" in the midst of "change." We have seen, in our study, how the Platonism that passed through Whichcote and his school has prevailed and continues to give stability to man's moral and spiritual pilgrimage. A. N. Whitehead makes a classic statement in the preface to his *Process and Reality*, "all Western Philosophy," he says, "is but a footnote to the philosophy of Plato." Cf. Anthony Flew and Alasdair MacIntyre ed., *New Essays in Philosophical Theology*, (London, 1963), pp. 28–75; W. R. Hepburn, *Christianity and Paradox: Critical Studies in Twentieth Century Theology* (London, 1958), pp. 24–59; C. A. Mace, *British Philosophy in the Mid-Century* (London, 1957), pp. 195–264, 267–357; John MacQuarrie, *Twentieth-Century Religious Thought* (New York, 1963), pp. 318–338, 351–370; Roger Hazelton, *New Accents in Contemporary Theology* (New York, 1960), pp. 33–58; J. B. Cobb, Jr. *Living Options in Protestant Theology* (Philadelphia, 1962), pp. 17–119, 199–311; N. E. S. Ferré, *Searchlights on Contemporary Theology* (New York, 1961), pp. 3–40, 79–93, 145–183; Richard R. Niebuhr, *Resurrection and Historical Reason* (New York, 1957), pp. 32–104; and,

insisting upon the permanent value of this element in Christian thinking.[1] Raven believes Neo-Orthodoxy to be in error both historically and theologically in contrasting Hebrew and Greek and disregarding the latter.[2] Whichcote finds a complementary relationship between these strands and transmits the best of both.

H. H. Farmer calls our attention to the criticisms which any Christian philosopher may expect. He is exposed to criticism from two flanks: on the one hand, he is attacked by dogmatic theologians who question his use and interpretation of some Christian dogma, and even may assert that he has surrendered its essential import altogether, on the other hand, he exposes himself to attacks from philosophers, who with a different set of presuppositions, will be quick to discern the insufficiencies of his argument.[3] Whichcote has always been under attack from these two flanks. For instance, Tuckney questioned the authenticity of his theology and Locke built his epistemology on the ruins of Whichcote's concept of *a priori*. One main reason, it seems to me, why Whichcote's thought has not received the treatment it deserves either by his contemporaries or successors, is that neither philosophers of the first rank nor orthodox theologians have been willing to consider his thought as valid.

Thus, it is our purpose to bring to focus the real merit of his thought in the light of this study. In this chapter we present a critical examination of three notions central to Whichcote's message as a rational theologian. They are: (1) The harmony of faith and reason; (2) The inseparability of religion and morality; and (3) Christian tolerance.

Whichcote's attempt to harmonise faith and reason is a significant milestone in the history of religious thought. For him, reason is above rationalism: it includes intellectual effort, but it is mainly an inner experience of the whole man acting in harmony.[4] But he has no illusions concerning man's excellency or infallibility; on the contrary, he insists on the frequent degeneracy of reason as well as will. Yet he is far from any assertion of total depravity or the complete helplessness of man's judgment, and he is eager to urge the use of whatever degree of reason man possesses or still retains. Although he exalts the power of reason, he does not show the slightest tendency towards naturalism.

for general background; D. D. Williams, *What Present-Day Theologians are Thinking* (New York, 1959) and John Passmore, *A Hundred Years of Philosophy* (London, 1957).

[1] W. R. Inge, *The Platonic Tradition in English Religious Thought* (London, 1926), Preface.
[2] Cf. E. Gilson, *Reason and Revelation in the Middle Ages* (London, 1955), Chs. I, II.
[3] *Revelation and Reason*, tr. by Wyon (London, 1946), pp. 16–17.
[4] J. P. K. Jewett, *Emil Brunner's Concept of Revelation* (London, 1954), p. 85.

Reason is for him the power of the human mind, but it is not merely a natural power, it is also in some sense supernatural; it is a divine revelation, not simply the means by which man reaches forward to the knowledge of God; reason is also the means by which God comes down into the life of man; it is a direct seizure by the mind of the truth of certain supreme principles; it is not merely a discursive, but also an intuitive, faculty; its intuitions have authority more final than the arguments of the discursive reason and need no experimental verification; it is the gift of God and His very voice[1]; it discovers the natural and receives the supernatural; that is, it passively receives revealed truth, but it actively assimilates and transmits this truth. The reason of man is the candle of the Lord, lighted by God and lighting unto God.

Involved in what Whichcote has to say concerning reason are his doctrines of God and man: God is man's Creator and Redeemer: man is made in the image of God. The theological importance of Whichcote's concept of reason is increased in the light of Augustine's doctrine of illumination. He illustrates his view by references to Platonic and Stoic philosophy. But it is in Jewish Wisdom Literature, and especially as it is reflected in the Fourth Gospel, that he finds his sure position. John unites believing and knowing, and attributes a saving significance to knowledge. Thus for all his praise of the philosophers, Whichcote has not purchased his synthesis between faith and reason by the subordination of scriptural authority. In the development of his concept of reason he has used what has appeared to him to be good and true from Platonism, Stoicism and Renaissance Humanism, but throughout his treatment of the subject he stands securely within the Christian camp. Apart from the actual importance of his notion of reason in contemporary discussion, he teaches us how to recognize and accept truths from all quarters and use them for the enrichment of our Christian faith.[2]

The weakness in Whichcote's intellectualism appears to be in the fact that it makes too much sense. Without hesitation he attempts to explain the unexplainable and many of his conclusions will not stand the test of critical examination. His confidence in the rationality of religion leads in some instances to an over-simplification of many perplexing problems.

---

[1] C. C. J. Webb, *Problems in the Relations of God and Man* (London, 1915), p. 25. Cf. *Supra*, Chs. III, IV.

[2] *Ibid.*, p. 52. This appears to be Whichcote's approach, but his more comprehensive view of revelation includes natural truth. We are reminded of Prof. J. Baillie's observation that recently the concept of nature is swallowed up by revelation and nature is regarded as a more general kind of revelation and, therefore, there is no man and no nature apart from revelation, see, *Our Knowledge of God* (London, 1939), pp. 37–38.

His treatment of the problem of evil and his reflections on atheism are good examples.

With due appreciation for his balanced position concerning the harmony of faith and reason, it appears that his intellectualism led him to ignore or evade many serious problems in theology. This insufficiency was apparently discerned by Cudworth who struggled honestly to give due consideration to many problems envisaged by Whichcote but which were inadequately treated by him. There are occasions when one wonders if Whichcote was unaware of the full implications of some questions raised in his writings. In such instances there seems to be no other worthy explanation for his naive confidence in the self-evident nature of his rather superficial conclusions. One wonders if he was, in fact, misled by his confidence in reason. He often appears more willing to contradict himself than to admit in a forthright manner the necessity "to believe where we cannot prove." It is essentially this tendency toward an over-emphasis upon the role of reason and a failure to give this an ample counter-balance with the claims of revelation that places Whichcote closer to the Age of Reason than any of his disciples. His purpose is sound, namely, "to overcome" religious fanaticism by a rational faith, but without knowing it, he passes on the instrument with which opponents of Christianity were soon to undermine it. Whereas Whichcote was a Christian apologist employing reason to develop a Christian philosophy, many who admired his rationalism preferred to use it to construct a religion of reason which ceased to be Christian.

Notwithstanding the many criticisms which may be offered against Whichcote's intellectualism there remains much in his reflections of great value. This is especially true in view of the outstanding revolt against reason in religious circles for the last twenty-five years.

It is seen in the revival of the thought of Kierkegaard, and the general "existentialist" approach to biblical and theological studies; it is characteristic of the "crisis" theology of Barth and explains many of the inconsistencies in the thought of Brunner [1]; it is also evident in the anti-intellectualism characteristic of the systems of Henri Bergson and William James.[2]

With this trend toward irrationalism in mind, we may appreciate more fully Whichcote's contribution. He attacks logical as well as

[1] Whichcote, *Works*, III, 18.

[2] *Ibid.*, pp. 49–51. I have presented a counter- argument in my *Faith and Reason: A Comparative Study of Pascal, Bergson and James* (Boston, 1962), Ch. II.

theological dogmatics, and suggests that if we wish to penetrate to the very source of religious certainty, we must diligently avoid both extreme judgments.[1] Whichcote observes that religion contains suprarational knowledge, but there is nothing in it irrational. He adds that since reason in man is the candle of the Lord, it is the medium of revelation and, therefore, when God declares His mind and will to us, He does so by an appeal to our reason. It is thus that Whichcote points us to "sober piety and rational religion" and this is of great contemporary importance as Inge observes:

> His robust faith in the rationality of being a Christian is extremely stimulating in our day, when sentimentality, emotionalism, and sheer superstition are conspiring to eject Reason from her throne.[2]

For Whichcote, religion is the rational basis of ethics. Whether he speaks of religion of first-inscription or religion of after-revelation morality is central. His purpose is distinctly religious, and therefore, morality is conceived as a part of religion.[3] In his over-all view of revelation, the moral principles of religion are disclosed either by the light of creation or by biblical revelation. For the Christian moral responsibility is revealed in nature and by grace.

Further, he unites reason and morality in the interest of religion. He tells us that without knowledge the heart cannot be good; that knowledge without obedience is not virtue but that there is no virtue without knowledge. Religion is the standard by which reason and morality are to be judged and it is in the interest of true piety that they are to be employed.

The union Whichcote proposes between religion and morality is praiseworthy, but we may legitimately ask if he were too optimistic concerning man's natural goodness. Like most platonists and especially those influenced by the Renaissance, he appears to overrate man's sympathy for the good and under-estimate the fact of sin and the power of evil. We cannot accuse Whichcote of ignoring these forces – he does describe man as fallen. However, a greater stress upon the tragedy of evil in human experience and upon the way in which we

---

[1] *Ibid.*, p. 20.

[2] *Ibid.*, pp. 121–22. Elsewhere I have attempted to prove that Pascal's real contribution to religious thought is the concept of "saving knowledge," see, Roberts, *Ibid.*

[3] *Ibid.*, pp. 29–31. The attack against metaphysics and theism is, at present, also an attack against ethics. If man's nature and destiny are tied to his relation to God, the denial of God is also the death of ethics. A "New Theology" requires a "new morality." Whichcote was by no means conservative in his outlook, but for him a dynamic ethic must evolve out of the content of a faith rooted in the "reason in things" and the "goodness of God." Paul Tillich, I believe, has attempted an apology for the Christian faith (with a different thought – structure, yet similar to Whichcote and his disciples).

are enabled to overcome it by strength from beyond ourselves, by the Grace of God, seems desirable. But against the background of the general moral indifference of his age, the separation of religion and morality, faith and works, by some Puritans and Sectaries, Whichcote's social consciousness is remarkable in insight and courage. His combination of salvation by faith and works is one of the most substantial contributions he bequeathed to theology and ethics. Thus if he appears to lean too far in the direction of inherent righteousness and justification by works it is reasonable to assume that he does so because it is necessary to shout in order to be heard.

Whichcote reminds us that it is better to live up to the moral principles that are known to all men than in the name of a new liberty in Christ claim eternal salvation, not by virtue of our moral efforts but in spite of our immorality.

By placing the moral part of religion among things "necessary for salvation" Whichcote calls us to a serious concern for sobriety, equity and thus piety. His message is vital for those who are socially conscious but only against a background of humanitarianism. It is indispensable to unite faith and ethics. Whichcote refuses to contrast nature and grace and his doctrine of salvation includes not only additions to nature but he asserts that by grace the natural moral faculties are restored and heightened. Man is the crown of the creation, but he is also a fallen creature and totally depraved, in the sense that there is a sinful perversion running through his whole being including his reason. God is good, but He is also just; God as Saviour is also Judge. Thus Whichcote's doctrines of God and man, of sin and salvation, of sanctification and last things are a unity.

We might in a general way consider Whichcote as a representative of the Johannine view of Christian Ethics. According to this view history is the story of God's mighty deeds and man's responses to them. Man lives somewhat less "between the times" and more in the divine "Now." The eschatological future has become for him less the action of God before time and less the life with God after time, and more the presence of God in time. Eternal life is a quality of existence in the here and now.[1] Westcott, himself a Johannine scholar, has made Whichcote's contribution to Christian morality clear and has pointed out the relevance of his message to Christian moral responsibility for all time.

[1] Brunner's distinction between "general" and "special" revelation would lend clarity to our author's over-all view of revelation, allowing, of course, for Brunner's special use of the terms. It seems, also, that "saving knowledge" is what Whichcote implies by truths of "after-revelation." Cf. Baxter, *Ibid.*, pp. 192–193, 241, 259, 445.

Westcott says:

Anyone who has followed this outline of Whichcote's teaching [Westcott's own essay] .... will, I think, have been struck by its modern type. It represents much that is most generous and noblest in the modern divinity of today. It rightly affirms in the name of Christianity much that is said to be in antagonism with it.

It brings faith into harmony with moral law, both in its object and in its issues. It enables us to understand how all that we can learn of the true, the beautiful, the good, the holy, through observation and thought and revelation, is contributory to the right fulfillment of the duties of life.[1]

---

[1] B. F. Westcott, *History of Religious Thought in the West* (London, 1891), p. 379. Cf. *Our Knowledge of God*, pp. 42–43. I am in essential agreement with Westcott on this point. On the three points we have selected from his thought, viz. the relation of faith to reason, faith to ethics and religious tolerance, there is no question in my mind as to the importance of these matters.

There is a need for what Westcott has suggested: a wider application of these principles. There is a need to add other concerns, however, and the crucial relation of religion to science, which was outstanding in the work of More and Cudworth, but almost ignored by Whichcote, is an example. We have been frequently concerned in our discussion with the first two of Whichcote's interests. Here we would like to put his plea for religious tolerance in contemporary perspective. Whichcote limited his concern for tolerance to the members of the Establis-Church, primarily, though his affection for individuals in the Congregational branch of Puritanism has been indicated in this study (i.e. his relation to Tuckney). He was also influenced by what John MacMurray describes as "stoic cosmopolitanism" which, on the basis of universal reason, advocates the oneness of humanity. His admiration for non-Christian religions, except the Moslems, illustrates this point. But inherent in his thought is the possibility for conversation between Orthodox, Roman Catholic and Protestant communions within Christendom as well as with non-Christian religions. His is a mediating theology – a theology of dialogue with philosophy, culture, ethics, literature and Eastern religions. Thus he points in the direction we should travel in an age when the world has become one.

Fortunately this theme has been treated by any number of persons within and without the Church – in both East and West. The one reservation I have, and I believe the thought of Whichcote illustrates this, is that those who enter into dialogue with others should first have an adequate understanding of their own religious and moral background. For works that enter the ecumenical discussion on the theological level see: Thomas Satory, *The Oecumenical Movement and The Unity of the Church*, tr. by H. C. Graaf (Oxford, 1963); Norman Goodall, *The Ecumenical Movement* (Oxford, 1961); W. M. Horton, *Christian Theology: An Ecumenical Approach*, revised and enlarged (New York, 1958), S. H. Miller and G. E. Wright, eds., *Ecumenical Dialogue at Harvard: The Roman Catholic – Protestant Colloquium* (Cambridge, Mass., 1964); Wilhelm Niesel, *The Gospel and the Churches: A Comparison of Catholicism, Orthodoxy, and Protestantism*, tr. by David Lewis (Philadelphia, 1962). Rock Caporale's study is an excellent sociological study of Vatican Council II, *Vatican II: Last of The Councils* (Baltimore, 1964) and Nicolas Zernov presents an invaluable account of the history and theology of Eastern Orthodoxy in his, *Eastern Christendom* (New York, 1961). Hans Küng, *Justification: The Doctrine of Karl Barth and a Catholic Reflection*, tr. by Thomas Collins, E. E. Tolk, and David Granskow (New York, 1964) and Yves Conger, *After Nine Hundred Years* (New York, 1959) represent the kind of deep understanding of another tradition needed for a real ecumenical break- through. Ecumenical social action projects must eventually be underlined by theological understanding. Life and Work and Faith and Order must develop together.

In the area of dialogue between religions the following are invaluable: N. F. S. Ferré, *The Finality of Faith and Christianity Among the World Religions* (New York, 1963); R. L. Slater, *World Religions and World Community* (New York, 1963); Arnold Toynbee, *Christianity Among the Religions* (Oxford, 1958); W. E. Hocking, *Living Religions and a World Faith* (New York, 1940); Rudolf Otto, *Mysticism East and West*, tr. by B. L. Bracy and R. C. Payne

The significance of Whichcote's concept of Christian tolerance is not to be overlooked. He observes that in the last analysis the basis of agreement between Christians is something which it is impossible to define in a series of statements. A theological statement is necessary only to guard from distortion what is essential to our "being in Christ." This is not to cut short the process of theological synthesis by accepting an easy common factor. It is to secure the conditions under which alone real progress in the task of theological synthesis can be made. It is only when varying insights are held in some sense within the unity of the common life of the church that their contact is fruitful of new and rich insights. The attempt to find a basis of Christian unity in a completely articulated theological system is part of the essence of sectarianism.[1] Thus Whichcote tells us that as long as we are agreed on fundamentals, incidentals may be a means to our mutual enrichment.

One of the most striking things about Whichcote's view of Christian tolerance is that it is so modern and fits so neatly into the framework of all constructive thought of the present ecumenical discussion. Yet one wonders what Whichcote would have said if he were faced with all the recognized denominations of our time. His course was clear since he was mainly speaking of tolerance among parties within the Church of England, but he was notoriously intolerant to the nonconformist sects and the Roman Catholics. In a situation in which the Established Church was supreme, his intolerance was quite marked.[2] One asks, what would his attitude have been if he were confronted by any number of independent, organized, ecclesiastical systems? He accepted without question the historic episcopate as essential to the well-being of the Church. In our time, this belief is one of the greatest hindrances to Church union. If Whichcote were faced with a situation where many or even the majority of Protestant denominations were non-episcopal, one wonders if his principles of toleration, as generous as they are, would be ample for our present needs. But allowing for

New York, 1932); D. T. Suzuki, *Mysticism: Christian and Buddhist*, ed. R. N. Anshen (New York, 1957); D. T. Suzuki and Richard De Martino, *Zen Buddhism and Psychoanalysis* (New York, 1960); Fumio Masutani, *A Comparative Study of Buddhism and Christianity* (Tokyo, 1959); Bryan de Kretser, *Man in Buddhism and Christianity* (Calcutta, 1954); W. C. Smith, *The Meaning and End of Religion* (New York, 1963); S. Radhakrishnan, *Eastern Religions and Western Thought* (Oxford, 1939); and, Horst Bürkle, *Dialog mit dem Osten* (Stuttgart, 1965), see especially the discussion on Christology (pp. 121–138) the new ethic (pp. 146–167) and the new approach to missions (pp. 173–180).

[1] Cf. Lesslie Newbigin, *The Reunion of the Church* (London, 1948), pp. 184–186.

[2] According to Leslie Paul, the Cambridge Platonists were strongly opposed to moral relativism – in moral philosophy they were not tolerant. *English Philosophers* (London, 1953), p. 94.

these shortcomings, in which Whichcote is limited by his age, we observe much in his message of reconciliation of permanent worth. His views that we should magnify our agreements and minimize our differences, that we should seek unity in diversity by agreeing to differ on non-essentials, that "all things saving" are clear to all who sincerely seek the truth, that all inter-faith discussions should be reasonable and in the spirit of love according to the Scripture, and that in spite of our differences all true Christians may find sufficient ground for communion, are invaluable for our ecumenical discussion.

The significance of the life and thought of Whichcote cannot be fully estimated. From the available accounts of his influence upon his contemporaries and successors, he was one of the foremost preachers and theologians of seventeenth century England. We have seen that he stands, by virtue of his rational theology and ethical theory, among a noble succession of thinkers, both philosophical and theological, before his time, and that by virtue of his assimilation and transmission of thought by teaching, preaching and personal influence, he lives on in the thought and action of those who have been apostles of freedom in moral and religious thought.

Whichcote and his disciples entered directly into the formation of modern philosophical and theological thought, and thus their influence in an altered form persists to this day. This school, with Whichcote as its leader, forms what Cassirer calls "a sort of connecting link between minds and epochs." Cassirer also conceives this school as being "one of the piers of that bridge linking the Italian Renaissance with German humanism in the eighteenth century."[1] Whether we concede Cassirer his point or not, we would contend, on what I believe to be safer ground, that Whichcote's contribution to British moral and religious thought down to the present is unquestioned. Further, the "sweet temper" of his good-natured personality, his benevolent spirit, his concern for justice and his deep spirituality has an abiding significance.[2]

In spite of all the criticisms of Whichcote's rational theology, it seems fair to conclude that in no period in the history of thought has there been manifest a more perfect alliance between Christianity and Platonism, faith and reason, religion and morality, nature and grace, than in the thought of Whichcote. This meeting of philosophy

[1] E. Cassirer, *The Platonic Renaissance in England,* tr. by Pettegrove (New York, 1953), p. 201.
[2] Whichcote's influence is still evident both at the University of Cambridge and in his former parishes.

and theology was not a shallow synthesis, but a union of truth from all spheres with the best in biblical thought and Christian history as the norm. In Whichcote's thought the God of Creation and Redemption are one, and Jesus Christ is the Saviour for our justification and the Example of our sanctification. Those who have difficulty in reconciling the apparent contradictions above will do well to read Whichcote and find in his writings a philosophy which embraces "all time and all existence" and a religion which permeates the whole life of the total man.

APPENDIX

A CRITICAL EXAMINATION OF WHICHCOTE'S WRITINGS

We are concerned here with an examination of the sources of Which-cote's thought. The fact that all his publications are posthumous and that the authorship of some books attributed to him is doubtful, demands of us a more critical examination than is usually necessary. His writings deserve to be remembered for the teachings which they embody, for their style, and most of all for the revelation which they give of Whichcote's character.[1]

J. B. Mullinger has given a comprehensive list of works attributed to Whichcote. They are: (1) *Select Notions* (1685); (2) *A Treatise Of Devotion* (1697); (3) *Select Sermons*, edited by Shaftesbury (1698); (4) *Several Discourses*, edited by Jeffery (1701); (5) *The Malignity Of Popery* (1717); (6) *The Works* (1751); and (7) *Moral and Religious Aphorisms* (1753).[2] For our convenience we may list the writings of our author under four headings, namely; (1) *Aphorisms*; (2) *Letters*; (3) *Sermons*; (4) *Miscellaneous Works*.

Salter's examination of the *Aphorisms* is invaluable. He tells us that the collector and publisher of Jeffery's works found among them these aphorisms as an anonymous book, but was later informed (Salter does not say by whom) that these aphorisms were composed by Whichcote and that Jeffery had copied them from Whichcote's writings. In this manner Jeffery collected nearly five thousand aphorisms. He published a thousand of them in 1703. In this edition Jeffery prefixed a preface and added a prayer. Salter revised this collection, preserving the best of the former publication. Later he found another collection more emphatic and more fully expressed. He sought to take out the repetitions, by the use of five hundred aphorisms from the new collection

---

[1] E. T. Campagnac, *The Cambridge Platonists*, (Oxford, 1901), p. xi.

[2] D.N.B., XXL, 1–3. The above does not include all publications attributed to Whichcote. Others will come forth in the discussion to follow.

and the best from Jeffery's selection. Thus Salter brought one thousand two hundred of them together for his publication in 1753. He tells us that he "selected only those that stood out as being superb." Jeffery transcribed the aphorisms from his collection but he was not always accurate. As a result there are some twenty or thirty repetitions either in the same words or with slight variations. Salter attempted a more accurate publication of the aphorisms that reminds us of the "tedious-ness of the task of treating more than one thousand independent sentences with exactness and precision." He regrets that our author's original papers are not available; for his appeal to Mr. Benjamin Whichcote, nephew of Dr. Whichcote, who had inherited his uncle's manuscripts and others of the family, had proved fruitless.[1] The *Aphorisms* seem to represent the many favourite notions of Whichcote but as used in various contexts. For instance, they are to be found scattered throughout his sermons. Thus a reader who is anxious to get a brief but representative understanding of his thought might pursue an investigation of this work. According to Inge, this book was popular in the eighteenth century. He asserts that there is no reason why it should not be popular in the present century: "for there are few writers from whom such an anthology of wit and wisdom could be put together." [2]

We turn now to an examination of the *Letters*. There is no question as to the genuineness of these letters which passed between Whichcote and Tuckney. Letters one, three, five and seven were written by Tuckney, while the remainder of the eight letters are by Whichcote.[3] The original transcripts of the letters, in Whichcote's own hand, were part of the collection entrusted to Jeffery. Whichcote's handwriting was poor. Further, he seems to have had "an eagerness and enthusiasm, but always under the command of reason which made him neglect his style in pursuit of an argument." Salter concludes that Whichcote did not always write accurately neither did Jeffery always read "exactly."

The copy of the letters used by Salter was taken by one of Which-cote's brothers and corrected by Jeffery. Salter attempts to be faithful to the copy in hand and to make no unnecessary variations. He merely

---

[1] Salter, *Preface to Aphorisms*, pp. ix-x, xix–xxii, xxvi. The following editions of the *Aphorisms* are available: (1) Jeffery's (1703); (2) Salter's (1753); (3) *Christian Tract Society*, no. XXVII, Vol. III (1821); and (4) Inge's (1930). Salter's edition will be used in this study. The preface to these various editions is a good index to the thought of the *Aphorisms*.

[2] Inge, *Preface to Aphorisms*, p. iii.

[3] While Salter's edition, 1753, will be used primarily in this study, the original Letters are in "Sloane" MS. in (B.M.) 2903–25, pp. 88ff. Similarly, "philosophical and Theological Reflections," the substance of which is contained in the Letters, is in "Sloane" MS 2716–4 (n.p.). See also *Supra*, ch. III.

takes the passages written by the first writers in the margin into the text and "encloses them in brackets." [1]

These letters are valuable to an understanding of Whichcote's thought, especially his reaction to Puritanism. Perhaps most important these letters "teach us by the example of these two learned and good men" how to live in friendship and love in spite of differences.[2]

Next in order is an examination of Whichcote's sermons. These give the most comprehensive statement of his thought. They are nearly all we have to attest to the power of his preaching, as well as to the "novelty and force" with which he preached.[3] According to Salter, Whichcote never wrote his sermons in full and usually preached from short notes of headings, which he filled in while speaking.[4] Because of his great reputation as a preacher, "many persons of varied opinions" transcribed his messages into writing as he delivered them. Thus soon after his death several sermons were "sent forth in his name by persons of different characters for different motives." In 1697 there appeared in his name a *Treatise on Devotion*. This must be the work mentioned by Shaftesbury as being unworthy of Whichcote.[5] This work has disappeared and warrants no further consideration from us.[6] The work *Select Notions* is still available and will receive special consideration later.[7] *The Malignity of Popery* is included in the *Works*.[8] The various publications of Whichcote's sermons are as follows: (1) *Select Sermons* (1698) and *Twelve Sermons*, 2nd ed. of the former (1721), edited by the Third Earl of Shaftesbury, and *Select Sermons* (1742), edited by Principal Wishart; (2) *Several Sermons*, 3 Vols. (1701–3), edited by Jeffery, and a fourth volume (1707), edited by Samuel Clarke; and (3) *The Works*, 4 vols. (1751), by an unknown editor.

According to Salter there is some confusion concerning the preface generally attributed to Shaftesbury. Salter says:

.... In a copy now before me, which was Dr. Jeffery's, that Dr. has written in the title page; that Mr. Wm. Stephens, Rector of Sutton in Surrey, was the publisher. The accounts are easily reconciled; this gentleman did most likely revise the discourses; at the request and under the request of the learned Nobleman.[9]

---

[1] Salter, *Preface to Letters*, pp. xxxvi–xxxvii.

[2] *Ibid.*, pp. xxxix–xl.

[3] Tulloch, *C. R.* (Oct., 1871), p. 318.

[4] See Tuckney's *Second Letter*, ed. by Salter. Cf. Richardson, *Ibid.*, pp. 71, 81–82; Mitchell, *Ibid.*, pp. 30–37.

[5] *Select Sermons*, (1698), p. xvi.

[6] Tulloch, *Ibid.*, p. 323. Cf. *D.N.B.*, *Ibid.*

[7] A copy of this work is in the (B.M.). It is interesting that the following are agreed upon its non-existence; Salter, *Ibid.*, p. xxxiii; Tulloch, *Ibid.*

[8] *Works*, I, 180–182.   [9] Salter, *Ibid.*, p. xv.

It is obvious that Salter had no knowledge of the 1721 edition of the *Twelve Sermons*. Thus he moves at once to a consideration of the 1742 edition published by Wishart. The latter published his edition because the first edition was "out of print and scarce." Wishart remarks that Shaftesbury "providentially met with" the manuscript; and was so impressed that "he revised it, put it to press, and wrote the preface." [1] Shaftesbury claims no such stroke of good fortune, but says that he "searched officiously after" these sermons.[2] We shall never know exactly how Shaftesbury arrived at his collection. It is noteworthy that Jeffery apparently had no knowledge of Shaftesbury's first edition.[3] We may observe that the *Twelve Sermons*, as edited by Shaftesbury and Wishart, were divided into two groups of six each. Six sermons were on the foundations of natural and revealed religion and the proofs of Christianity, while six were on religious and moral subjects. These sermons were later included in the *Works*.

The collections of Whichcote's writings entrusted to Jeffery consisted of many papers in Whichcote's own hand, besides what had been "digested in some form or another." Jeffery had also a number of sermons transcribed from the spoken words of Whichcote by the Smith who said he "lived on Whichcote." Though Jeffery was assured of the genuineness of these sermons, he felt unauthorised to print any of them. Accordingly, he was displeased when Samuel Clarke published a fourth volume in 1707. Salter considered Jeffery too cautious since Clarke was not under the same obligation as himself. Salter confesses to possessing two collections of the sort that Jeffery would perhaps refuse to publish – one containing twenty-four sermons on a passage in Philippians; the other, thirty-six, on a text in Jeremiah. From the former of these, Clarke selected the first thirteen sermons of his volume, from the latter three sermons and the remaining ten sermons from a source unknown to Salter, on a verse or two of the Fifth Psalm. The above facts attest to Jeffery's faithfulness to his trust and explain the difference between his three volumes and whatever else may bear the name of Whichcote.[4] It is valuable that three out of four volumes - included in the *Works* were compiled by one so faithful to his trust and who had at his disposal many of Whichcote's own notes.[5] One can

---

[1] *Ibid.*, pp. xv–xvi. Cf. *Select Sermons*, ed. by Wishart, p. xviii.

[2] *Ibid.*, p. xvi. Cf. *Select Sermons*, ed. by Shaftesbury, p. ii.

[3] *Ibid.*, pp. xvi–xvii.

[4] Salter, *Preface to Aphorisms*, pp. xviii–xvix.

[5] *Ibid.*, pp. xvi–xviii. Jeffery was entrusted with this responsibility to prevent publications which might misrepresent and dishonor the memory of Whichcote. Mr. Benjamin Whichcote, nephew of Dr. Whichcote, who had inherited his uncle's papers, turned them over to Jeffery.

appreciate Jeffery's caution, but when the fourth volume of our author's sermons has been studied, one is grateful for Clarke's addition.

Four volumes of Whichcote's sermons, known as the *Works*, were published in Aberdeen in 1751. This appears to be the most popular and accessible edition of Whichcote's sermons. One wonders if Wishart's introduction of our author's sermons to Scotland in Edinburgh in 1742, to the "ministers and students of divinity," led up to this publication. Unfortunately, the editor's name is unknown. He makes use of Shaftesbury's preface in the 1698 edition and merely adds a brief editor's note. According to the editor of the *Works*, he compared all available publications of Whichcote's sermons with a view to presenting a complete edition.[1] A careful check of all editions of Whichcote's sermons reveals that all of his available (genuine) sermons are included in the *Works*. To this day, there appears to have been no improvement upon this massive publication of the sermons.[2]

Since Whichcote's sermons were published after his death, it is impossible to give an exact date of their composition. However, it is possible to decide approximately whether they were written in his early ministry or during his more mature years by the internal evidence of the thought contained in them. Mitchell estimates that the first edition of Whichcote's sermons published by Shaftesbury were written during Whichcote's London Ministry, when he had learned that citations would no longer be acceptable. However, since they were published posthumously, we have no way of knowing what amount of such quotations would have been restored or inserted had Whichcote published them himself.[3] There are only a few sermons that come to us with definite dates. Two examples are: (1) A sermon preached in the New Chapel, December 7, 1668, and (2) A sermon preached before the House of Commons, February 4, 1673.[4] But for most of his sermons there is insufficient evidence to attempt a definite dating for them.

This was done with the knowledge that Jeffery "had the highest veneration for the deceased author" and every talent necessary to "qualify him to be a diligent, faithful and judicious editor." In the second volume of his edition of Whichcote's *Several Sermons*, Jeffery requested anyone possessing any of Whichcote's writings to turn them over to him. See *Several Sermons* (1702), II, iv. In the first volume, *Ibid.*, I, iii, he confirms his endeavour to be faithful to his trust. Salter regrets that he has failed to find further original sources of Whichcote's writings, but resolves to make full use of the available material. See Salter, *Ibid.*, pp. xxvi–xxvii.

[1] *Works*, III, x–xi. It is noteworthy that Salter reveals no knowledge of this publication in 1751, in his edition of the *Aphorisms* and *Letters* in 1753.

[2] See *Preface* of Shaftesbury, Jeffery and Wishart for critical introduction to Whichcote's sermons.

[3] Mitchell, *English Pulpit Oratory From Andrews To Tillotson* (London, 1932), pp. 285–286.

[4] *Works*, I, 56–58, 119–120.

However, though there is a lack of information concerning the sermons, they attain considerable excellence. It is plain that the notes from which the sermons were printed must have been fairly full, and that their printed form does not radically injure the preacher's style. From them we see that Whichcote's manner was uniform. His plainness and directness may represent the transition from the style of the Puritans to that of the more pictorial and poetical of the Platonists. He appears to have belonged to the tradition of preachers who used a straight forward or malleable prose.[1] Though the material he left to the future is fragmentary and partly confused, it is not difficult to gain a clear view of his opinions from it. His frequent repetitions, his bright epigrams, his earnest simplicity, bring his main thoughts vividly before the reader. When he spoke from the pulpit he appears to have laid aside the technical forms of expressions which on other occasions provoked criticism.[2] His sermons are amongst the "most thoughtfull" in the English language, not only for his own, but for all time.[3]

Finally, it is necessary to deal with a few miscellaneous works ascribed to our author. There are the prayers: (1) The *Prayer* at the end of the *Works*, and (2) *A Prayer for Morning and Evening* at the end of Salter's edition of the *Aphorisms*. Whichcote wrote some Latin verses upon the death of Cromwell in 1658.[4] In this poem Whichcote laments the death of the Lord Protector and rejoices at the succession of Richard. Most of the poem is a forthright denunciation of popery. Though this poem is insufficient evidence to indicate the political views of Whichcote, it is reasonable to assume that he was impressed by Cromwell's "moderate" policy. Finally, we come to the "problem book" of all the extant writings ascribed to our author. The *Select Notions* contains a hundred pages of notes on five texts of Scripture and twenty-eight pages of what the editor calls *Apostolic Apothegms*. It is valuable in that it was published in 1685, only two years after Whichcote's death. Its entire authenticity is however in doubt. The editor who calls himself Philanthropus was according to his own statement a "pupil and particular friend" of Whichcote who had known him at Emmanuel. He desired to publish Whichcote's thoughts during his lifetime, but was refused that privilege. This editor was determined, however, that, if he survived Whichcote, he would "exert what I thought fit of those Instructions and Notions which I received from him." He waited two

---

[1] Mitchell, *Ibid.*, pp. 285–286, 312.
[2] B. F. Westcott, *Religious Thought in the West* (London, 1891), p. 370.
[3] Tulloch, *Rational Theology*, II, 46.
[4] *Works*, I, iii.

years for more "learned persons to publish Whichcote's notions, but saw that no publication was forthcoming. He therefore presented these *Notions* in Whichcote's honor.[1] There appears to be no reason to question the editor's sincerity; but whether he really presents Whichcote's thought is another matter.

Concerning the texts of the discourses, it is found that discourses 1, 2 and 4 of the *Select Notions* are identical with texts of sermons in the *Works* as follows: *Works*, III, LLI; II, XXXIV, XXXV, and XXV. respectively. But though the texts are the same, the treatment is entirely different. In the first discourse on truth, many ideas compare favourably with Whichcote's but the style is found nowhere in his genuine works. Further the development of the notion and the form of argumentation is foreign to their supposed author. The second discourse reveals a noteworthy variation from Whichcote's doctrine of salvation. It is fundamentally Puritan in thought and imagery. Some insights of our author appear scattered here and there.[2] The third discourse is an intermingling of legal and moral righteousness in a style and "temper" unusual for Whichcote. But here appears a possibility of a "stage" in the thought-development of our author. When the writer rises to the level of Wichcote's notions of the "light of God's own candle set up within," he immediately lapses into Puritan dogma.[3] The fourth discourse presents "reasons for error in human judgment," which appear more typical of Whichcote. But the statement of the doctrine of the Fall has no resemblance. Later in the same discourse, he approaches Whichcote's tolerant spirit as he speaks of the mere essentials of Christian communion.[4] The fifth discourse comes closest to the philosophical insight of Whichcote, but even here the language is not typical.[5] Finally, there are the concise and wise statements at the end of the work, which remind us of Whichcote's *Aphorisms*. Some few of these appear to reflect precisely what Whichcote says elsewhere, but there are also many statements "unworthy" of him.[6]

From our examination of *Select Notions*, we arrive at three probable conclusions. First, they may have been the views of Whichcote in early life.[7] This view would explain the confusion of Puritan notions with flashes of the philosophical approach to religion. It would thereby be

1 *Select Notions*, pp. i–iii.
2 *Ibid.*, pp. 28–30.
3 *Ibid.*, pp. 54–56, 62.
4 *Ibid.*, pp. 66–68, 80–82.
5 *Ibid.*, pp. 85–87.
6 *Ibid.*, pp. 83–85.
7 Salter, *Preface to Aphorisms*, p. xii.

assumed that Whichcote, while at Emmanuel, as tutor, uttered the notions, but only as he sought fuller expression and understanding which developed into what we know as his mature thought. That would mean that he had not as yet made a radical break with his Puritan background. We know from Tuckney that this is possible; he says of Whichcote that when he first came to Cambridge, he was "somewhat cloudie and obscure" in his expressions. Later, according to his former tutor, he studied and taught so much philosophy, that ever since he had been cast in "that mould" in words and notions.[1] Yet, even though Whichcote's "open break" with Puritanism did not come until 1651, he confesses that he had held the views for at least seven years.[2] Second, there is the possibility that the editor of *Select Notions* had known Whichcote in his youth and had studied under him, but had not "kept pace" with the developing thought of Whichcote. If his intentions were wholesome, this appears to be a probable explanation. On this basis he would be blameworthy for his misrepresentation of our author. And, third, there is the alternative view that the editor wished to publish his own notions, while making full use of the influence of Whichcote before it waned by the passing of time; hence, this publication just two years after his death. We conclude that the evidence does not admit *Select Notions* as a representation of the best and most mature thought of Whichcote. What is best in our author's thought is said better in his authenticated work.

---

[1] *Letters*, pp. 36–38.
[2] *Supra*, Ch. III.

SELECTED BIBLIOGRAPHY

A. PRIMARY SOURCES [1]

1. Collected Works

Whichcote, Benjamin, *Moral and Religious Aphorisms*, ed. John Jeffery (Norwich, 1703).
— *Aphorisms* (contains also: *Eight Letters*, life of Whichcote, testimonials, introduction to his writings and a prayer), ed. Samuel Salter (London, 1753).
— *Select Aphorisms*, Christian Tract Society, No. XXVIII, Vol. III (London, 1821).
— *Aphorisms*, ed. W. R. Inge (London, 1930).
— *Select Sermons*, ed. The Third Earl of Shaftesbury (London, 1698).
— *Twelve Sermons*, 2nd ed. of Shaftesbury's collection (London, 1721).
— *Select Sermons*, ed. Will Wishart (Edinburgh, 1742).
— *Several Discourses*, ed. John Jeffery, (London 1701–3). Vols. I–III.
— *Several Discourses*, ed. Samuel Clarke, (London 1707), Vol. IV.
— *Works* (Aberdeen, 1751).
— *The Malignity of Popery*, ed. John Jeffery (London, 1717).

2. Manuscripts [2]

(a) Manuscript Writing by Whichcote
   Whichcote, Benjamin, "Eight Letters" (letters 2, 4, 6, 8), "Sloane" MS. 2903, 25.
(b) Manuscripts with Information about Whichcote
   "Cole" MS. 5810, 182 (Milton, Cambs. *Parish Register: Extracts*).
   "Harley" MS. 7034, pp. 229, 332 ("Baker," VI193b–B102).
   "Harley" MS. 7038, pp. 17, 213.
   "Harley" MS. 7045, pp. 473–476 ("Baker," VI90–B98).
(c) Church Records [3]
   St. Anne's Blackfriars, London, *Baptism Register*, 1560–1700.
   St. Anne's Blackfriars, London, *Burial Register*, 1566–1700.

[1] In view of the long descriptive titles of seventeenth century books, we shall use only as much of each title as appears necessary to convey its meaning.
  It seems appropriate to mention, *Select Notions* (London, 1685). We consider this work to be of dubious authorship. Cf. *Supra*, Ch. I, Pt. II.
[2] All manuscripts are included under primary sources because they contribute original biographical information concerning Whichcote. Thomas Baker's miscellaneous collection is for the most part included in the "Harley" MSS. A valuable bibliography of Whichcote is contained in J. E. B. Mayor's, *Cambridge Under Queen Anne*, p. 305. MSS in (B. M.).
[3] In (Gh. L.).

St. Anne's Blackfriars, London, *Marriage Register*, 1562–1726.
St. Lawrence Jewry, London, *Vestry Book*, 1556–1669.
St. Lawrence Jewry, London, *Minutes of Vestry*, 1669–1720.

3. The Writings of Cudworth, More and Smith [1]

Cudworth, Ralph, *A Sermon Preached Before the House of Commons*, March 31,
1647 (reproduced from the original edition), The Facsimile Text Society
(New York, 1930).
— *A Treatise of Free-Will*, ed. Allen (London, 1838).
— *A Treatise Concerning Eternal and Immutable Morality*, ed. Edward Duresme
(London, 1731).
— *Works*, ed. Thomas Birch, First American Edition (Andover, 1837), 2 Vols.
— *The True Intellectual System of the Universe*, 2nd ed. (London, 1743).
More, Henry, *Theological Works*, ed. Joseph Downing (London, 1708).
— *Complete Poems*, ed. A. B. Grosart, Chertsey Worthies' Library (Edinburgh,
1876–78).
— *Philosophical Writings*, ed. F. I. MacKinnon, The Wellesley Semi-Centennial
Series (New York, 1925).
— *Divine Dialogues* (London, 1668).
— *Philosophical Poems*, ed. Geoffrey Bullough (Manchester, 1931).
— *Enchiridion Ethicum* (Eng. tr., 1690, reproduced from 1st ed., 1666), The
Facsimile Text Society, Series III, Philosophy (New York, 1930).
Smith, John, *The Excellency and Nobleness of True Religion* (Glasgow, 1745).
— *Select Discourses*, ed. H. G. Williams, 4th ed. (Cambridge, 1859).

B. SECONDARY SOURCES

Affifi, A. E., "The Rational and Mystical Interpretation of Islam," *Islam – The
Straight Path*, ed. by K. W. Morgan, ed. (New York: Ronald Press, 1958),
pp. 144–179.
Anselm, St., *Cur Deus Homo?* tr. E. S. Prout, Christian Classics Series (London,
n.d.).
— *Proslogium; Monologium; An Appendix in Behalf of the Fool by Gaunilon;
and Cur Deus Homo?*, tr. S. N. Deane (Chicago, 1903).
— *Ante-Nicene Fathers* (Buffalo, 1887). Vol. III.
Anthanasius, *De Incarnatione Verbi Dei*, Intro. by C. S. Lewis (London: A.
R. Mowbray, 1953).
Aquinas, St. Thomas, *Summa Contra Gentiles*, tr. Dominican Fathers (London:
Burns Oates, 1924), Vol. I.
— *Summa Theologia*, tr. A. G. Herbert (London, 1927). Pt. I.
Aristotle, *The Nicomachean Ethics*, tr. H. Rackham, The Loeb Classical Library,
Edited by T. E. Page, E. Capps, W. H. D. Rouse, *et al.* (London: Heinemann,
1926).
— *Metaphysics*, tr. H. Tredennick, Loeb (London: Heinemann, 1933–35), 2 Vols.
— *The Politics*, tr. H. Rackham, Loeb (London: Heinemann, 1932).
— *Rhetoric*, tr. T. Buckley (London: Heinemann, 1906).
Armstrong, A. H., *The Architecture of the Intelligible Universe in the Philosophy
of Plotinus* (Cambridge, Eng.: University Press, 1940).
— Armstrong and Markus, R. A., *Christian Faith and Greek Philosophy*
(London: Darton, Logman & Todd, 1960).

[1] The life and thought of Whichcote's disciples are so closely related to him that we feel
justified in including their writings among the primary sources.

Aspelin, Gunnar, *Ralph Cudworth's Interpretation of Greek Philosophy* (Goteborg: Elanders Boktryckeri, Aktiebolag, 1943).

Aulén, Gustaf, *The Faith of the Christian Church*, tr. by E. H. Whalstrong and G. E. Arden (Philadelphia: Muhlenberg Press, 1948).

— *Christus Victor*, tr. A. G. Herbert (London: S.P.C.K., 1931).

Augustine, St. A., *Works*, ed. Marcus Dods, new translation, Vols. I–II, *City of God* (E.T., 1871); VII, *Trinity* (tr. Hadden, 1873); VI, XIII, *Letters* (tr. Cunningham, 1872–5); XIV, *Confessions*, tr. Pilkington (Edinburgh, 1876).

Austen-Leigh, A., *King's College* (London, 1899).

Austin, E. M., *Ethics of the Cambridge Platonists* (Philadelphia: University of Pennsylvania Press, 1935).

Baciocchi, J. de, *La Vie Sacramentaire De L'Église* (Paris: Les Éditions Du Cerf, 1958)

Bacon, Francis, *Advancement of Learning*, ed. G. W. Kitchin, Everyman's Library (London, n.d.).

Baillie, D. M., *God was in Christ* (London: Faber and Faber, 1948).

Baillie, John, *Our Knowledge of God* (London: Oxford University Press, 1939).

— *The Idea of Revelation in Recent Thought* (London, 1956).

— *The Sense of the Presence of God*, Being the Gifford Lectures at the University of Edinburgh, 1961–62 (New York: Scribner's, 1962).

Barbour, Hugh, *The Quakers In Puritan England* (New Haven: Yale University Press, 1964).

Barker, Arthur, *Milton and the Puritan Dilemma, 1641–1660* (Toronto: University Press, 1942).

Barrett, C. K., *The Gospel According to St. John* (London: S.P.C.K., 1935).

— *The Holy Spirit and the Gospel Tradition* (London: S.P.C.K., 1947).

Barry, Alfred, *Masters in English Theology;* Being the King's College Lectures for 1877 (London, 1877).

Barth, Karl, "Christ and Adam Man and Humanity in Romans 5," tr. by T. A. Smail, *Scottish Journal of Theology Occasional Papers*, no. 5 (Edinburgh: Oliver & Boyd, 1956).

Baxter, Richard, *The Reasons of the Christian Religion* (London, 1667).

— *Autobiography;* Being *The Reliquiae Baxterianae* (abridged from the folio of 1696), ed. J. M. L. Thomas (London: J. M. Dent, 1931).

Beard, Charles, *The Reformation of the Sixteenth century in Relation to Modern Thought*, The Hibbert Lectures, 1883 (London, 1885).

Bennett, J. C., *Social Salvation* (London, 1935).

Berdyaev, N. A., *The End of Our Time*, tr. Donald Atwater (London: Sheed and Ward, 1933).

Bergson, Henri, *Creative Evolution*, tr. Arthur Mitchell (New York: Henry Holt and Co., 1911).

— *Matter and Memory*, tr. N. M. Paul and W. S. Palmer, Library of Philosophy, ed. Muirhead (London: S. Sonnenschein & Co., 1911).

— *Time and Free Will*, tr. F. L. Pogson, Library of Philosophy (London: S. Sonnenschein & Co., 1910).

Bigg, Charles, *The Christian Platonists of Alexandria;* Being the Bampton Lectures of 1886 (Oxford: Clarendon Press, 1913).

Bigge, Sir L. A. Selby, editor, *The British Moralists* (Oxford, 1897), 2 vols.

Birch, Thomas, *The Life of Tillotson*, 2nd ed. (London, 1753).

Bonhoeffer, Dietrich, *Creation and Fall. A Theological Interpretation of Genesis 1–3* (London: SCM, 1962).

Boulger, James D., *Coleridge As Religious Thinker* (New Haven: Yale University Press, 1961).

Bourne, H. R. Fox, *The Life of John Locke* (London, 1876) 2 Vols.
Bradley, W. L., *P. T. Forsyth: The Man and His Work* (London: Independent Press, 1952).
— *The Meaning of Christian Values Today*. Westminister Studies in Christian Communication (Philadelphia: The Westminister, 1964).
Blichler, A., *Studies in Sin and Atonement: In the Rabbinic Literature of the First Century* (London: Oxford University Press, 1928).
Brightman, E. S., *A Philosophy of Religion* (London, 1947).
Brown, John, *The English Puritans* (Cambridge, Eng.: University Press, 1910).
Browne, Sir Thomas, *The Religio Medici*, ed. C. H. Herford, Everyman's Library (London, 1909).
Brunner, Emil, *Revelation and Reason*, tr. O. Wyon, First British Edition (London: Butterworth, 1947).
— *God and Man*, tr. David Cairns (London: S. C. M. 1936).
— *Dogmatics*, tr. Olive Wyon (London: Butterworth, 1949–52), 2 Vols.
— *Man in Revolt*, tr. Olive Wyon (London: Butterworth, 1939).
— *Eternal Hope*, tr. H. Knight (London: Butterworth, 1954).
— *Natural Theology;* Being the controversy between Brunner and Barth on "Nature and Grace," tr. Peter Fraenkel, intro. John Baillie (London: Geoffrey Bles, 1946).
— *The Philosophy of Religion*, tr. A. J. D. Farrer and B. L. Woolf (London: James Clarke, 1937).
— *The Mediator*, tr. Olive Wyon (London: Butterworth, 1934).
— *Justice and the Social Order*, tr. Mary Hottinger (London: Butterworth, 1945).
Bultmann, Rudolf, *Essays Philosophical and Theological*, tr. J. C. G. Greig, Library of Philosophy and Theology (London, 1955).
Bunyan, John, *The Pilgrim's Progress, Holy War, and Grace Abounding*, ed. W. Landels, family ed. (London, 1875).
Burnet, Gilbert, *History of His Own Time*, edited by Dean Swift *et al.*, 2nd ed. (Oxford, 1833), Vol. I.
Burnet, John, *Early Greek Philosophy* (London, 1945).
Burtt, Edwin Arthur, *The Metaphysical Foundations of Modern Sciences*, revised ed. (London: Kegan Paul, Trench, Trubner & Co., 1932).
Bush, Douglas, *Paradise Lost in Our Time;* Being Messenger Lectures at Cornell University in November, 1944 (Ithaca, New York: Cornell University Press, 1945).
— *English Literature in the Earlier Seventeenth Century* (*1600–1660*) (Oxford: Clarendon Press, 1945).
Butler, Joseph, *The Analogy of Religion*, ed. S. Halifax, London, 1812. Also 6th ed. of the same work (Glasgow, 1764).
— *Sermons*, 4th ed. (London, 1749).
— *Works* (Oxford, 1836), Vol. II.
— *Works*, ed. J. H. Bernard, new ed. (London: Macmillan, 1900), Vol. II.
Butterfield, H., *The Origins of Modern Science 1300–1800* (New York: Macmillan, 1959).
Buttrick, G. A., editor, *Interpreter's Bible* (New York: Abingdon, 1954–56), Vols. III–V.
Cairns, David, *The Image of God in Man* (London: S.C.M., 1953).
Calamy, Edmund, *The Nonconformist's Memorial; Being an Account of the Lives, Sufferings, and Printed Works, of the Two Thousand Ministers Ejected from the Church of England, chiefly by the Act of Uniformity, August 24, 1662*, edited by Samuel Palmer, 2nd and abridged ed. (London, 1802) Vol. I.
Calvin, John, *The Institution of Christian Religion*, "written in Latine by M. John

Calvine, translated into English according to the author's last edition; etc. . . . by Thomas Norton" (London, 1611).

Campagnac, E. T., *The Cambridge Platonists* (Oxford: Clarendon Press, 1901).

Campbell, W. C., *Erasmus, Tyndale and More* (London: Eyre and Spottiswoode, 1949).

Candlish, R. S., "Professor Maurice and His Writings," *The London Quarterly Review*, Vol. III, No. VI (Oct. 1854–Jan. 1855), pp. 393–436.

Capps, Walter H., "Two Contrasting Approaches to Christology," *The Heythrop Journal*, Vol. VI, No. 2, April, 1965.

Carré, M. H., *Phases of Thought in England* (Oxford: Clarendon Press, 1949).

Casserley, J. V. L., *The Christian in Philosophy* (London, 1949).

Cassirer, Ernst, *Das Erkenntnisproblem in der Philosophie und Wissenschaft der neueren Zeit*, 3rd ed. (Berlin, 1922), Vol. II.

— *The Platonic Renaissance in England*, tr. J. P. Pettegrove (New York: Nelson, 1953).

— Oskar, P., Randal, J. H., et al., editors, *The Renaissance Philosophy of Man* (Chicago, 1945).

Chadwick, Henry, *The Vindication of Christianity in Westcott's Thought.* The Bishop Westcott Memorial Lecture 1960 (Cambridge: University Press, 1960).

Chillingworth, William, *The Religion of Protestants* (London, 1866). *Christian Century*, Vol. LXXI, No. 38 (Sept. 22, 1954), p. 1137.

Cicero, *De Natura Deorum Academica*, tr. H. Rackham, Loeb (London: Heinemann, 1933).

— *Letters to Atticus*, tr. E. O. Winstedt, Loeb (London: Heinemann, 1912), 3 Vols.

Clark, G. N., *The Seventeenth Century* (Oxford: Clarendon Press, 1929).

Clarke, Samuel, *Discourse on the Being and Attributes of God;* Being the Boyle Lectures 1704–5 (London, 1716), 2 Vols. Also 6th ed. (London, 1725).

Clement, (of Alexandria), *Miscellanies*, tr. Hort-Mayor (London, 1902), Bk. VII.

Coleridge, S. T., *Notes on English Divines*, ed. Derwent Coleridge (London, 1853).

— *Aids to Reflection*, ed. Thomas Fenby, revised (London, n.d.).

Collingwood, R. G., *Philosophical Method* (Oxford: Clarendon, 1933).

— *The Idea of Nature* (Oxford: Clarendon, 1945).

Conger, Yves, *After Nine Hundred Years* (New York: Fordham University, 1959).

Cooper, A. A. (Third Earl of Shaftesbury), *Characteristics*, 3rd. ed., London, 1723, 3 Vols. 5th ed. (London, 1732).

Cooper, C. H., *Annals of Cambridge* (Cambridge, 1845), Vol. III.

Cornford, Francis Macdonald, *Plato's Cosmology* (New York: The Liberal Arts Press, 1957).

Courtines, Leo Pierre, *Bayle's Relations with England and the English* (New York, 1938).

Cragg, G. R., *From Puritanism to the Age of Reason* (Cambridge, Eng.: at the University Press, 1950).

Crozier, J. B., *History of Intellectual Development on the Lines of Modern Evolution* 2nd and revised ed. (London, 1902).

Cullman, Oscar, *Christ and Time*, tr. F. V. Filson (London: S.C.M., 1952).

— *The Christology of the New Testament* tr. S. C. Guthrie and C. A. M. Hall (Philadelphia: Westminister, 1959).

Culverwel, Nathanael, *Of the Light of Nature*, ed. John Brown, based on the 1652 ed. published by the author (Edinburgh, 1857).

Cusa, Nicholas of, *The Vision of God*, tr. E. G. Salter (London: Dent, 1928).

— *Of Learned Ignorance*, tr. D. J. B. Hawkins (London, 1954).

Daniélou, Jean, *Platonisme et Théologie Mystique.* Essai Sur La Doctrine

Spirituelle De Saint Grégoire De Nysse (Paris: Editions Montaigne, 1944).

Davis, Leroy, "Typology in Barth's Doctrine of Scripture," *Anglican Theological Review*, vol. XLVII, no. 1 (January, 1965), pp. 33–49.

De Boer, J. J., *The Theory of Knowledge of the Cambridge Platonists;* Being a published Ph. D. thesis in Philosophy, Columbia University (Madras: Methodist Publishing House, 1931).

De Pauley, W. D., *The Candle of the Lord* (London: S.P.C.K., 1937).

Descartes, René, *Discourse on Method*, 4th ed. (Edinburgh, 1870).

— *The Method, Meditations, and Selections from the Principles*, tr. by John Veitch (Edinburgh: William Blackwood and Sons, 1881).

De Wolf, L. H., *The Religious Revolt Against Reason* (New York: Harper, 1949).

Dillistone, F. W., *The Structure of the Divine Society* (London: Butterworth, 1949).

Dodd, C. H., *The Authority of the Bible* (London: Nisbet, 1955).

Dodds, E. R., *The Greeks and the Irrational* (Berkeley, Cal.: University of California Press, 1956).

Dorner, J. A., *History of the Development of the Doctrine of the Person of Christ*, tr. W. L. Alexander (Edinburgh, 1861), Vol. I.

Dubarle, A. M., *The Biblical Doctrine of Original Sin*, tr. by E. M. Stewart (New York: Herder & Herder, 1964).

Dunlap, Knight, "The Principles of Human Nature," *Religious Education*, Vol. XVIII (1923), pp. 18–19.

Duthie, C. S., *God in His World* (London: Independent, 1954).

Dyer, George, *History of the University and Colleges of Cambridge* (Cambridge, 1814), Vol. II.

Eastwood, D. M., *The Revival of Pascal* (Oxford: Clarendon, 1936).

Egg-Olofsson, Leif, *The Conception of the Inner Light in Robert Barclay's Theology* (Lund: Gleerup, 1954).

Einstein, Lewis, *The Italian Renaissance in England* (New York: Columbia University Press, 1902).

Elsee, Charles, *Neoplatonism in Relation to Christianity* (Cambridge: University Press, 1908).

Elwood, Douglas J., *The Philosophical Theology of Jonathan Edwards* (New York: Columbia University Press, 1960).

Erdman, J. E., *A History of Philosophy*, tr. W. S. Hough, 2nd ed. (London, 1891), Vol. I.

Fairbairn, A. M., *The Philosophy of the Christian Religion* (London: Hodder & Stoughton, 1902).

Farmer, H. H., *The Servant of the Word* (London: Nisbet and Co., 1955).

— *The World and God* (London: Nisbet and Co., 1955).

— *Revelation and Religion;* Being the Gifford Lectures at the University of Glasgow, March, 1950 (London: Nisbet and Co., 1954).

Farner, Oskar, *Zwingli The Reformer* tr. by D. G. Sear (New York: Columbia University Press, 1960).

Farrer, Austin, *The Freedom of the Will*. Being the Gifford Lectures at the University of Edinburgh for 1957 (London: Adam and Charles Black, 1958).

Ferré, Nels, F. S., *The Christian Understanding of God* (London: S.C.M., 1952).

— *Faith and Reason* (London, 1946).

— *Reason in Religion* (Nelson: Edinburgh, 1963).

— *The Finality of Faith* (New York: Harper and Row, 1963).

Festugière, Jean, *La Philosophie de l'Amour de Marsile Ficin et son influence sur la littérature française au XVIe Siècle* (Paris, 1941).

Fisher, G. P., *History of Christian Doctrine* (Edinburgh, 1896).

Fletcher, Joseph, *William Temple: Twentieth–Century Christian* (New York: Seabury Press, 1963).

Flew, R. Newton, *The Idea of Perfection in Christian Theology* (London: Humphrey Milford, 1934).
— *Jesus and His Church* (London: Epworth Press, 1938).
Florovsky, Georges, "Saint Gregory Palamas and the Tradition of The Fathers," *The Greek Orthodox Theological Review*, vol. V, no. 2 (Winter, 1959–1960), pp. 126–127.
Forrester, W. R., *Christian Vocation* (London: Butterworth, 1951).
Fowler, Edward, *A Free Discourse Between Two Intimate Friends*, 2nd ed. (London, 1671).
Fraser, A. C., *Locke* (Edinburgh, 1890).
Fuller, Thomas, *The History of the University of Cambridge*, ed. J. Nichols, new edition (London, 1840).
Galloway, George, *The Philosophy of Religion* (Edinburgh: T. & T. Clark, 1914).
Galton, Arthur, *Our Outlook Towards English Roman Catholics and the Papal Court* (London: Elliot Stock, 1902).
Gardiner, S. R., *The Constitutional Documents of the Puritan Revolution 1625–1660*, 3rd ed. (Oxford: Clarendon Press, 1966).
— *The First Two Stuarts and the Puritan Revolution 1603–1660*, 8th ed. (London: Longmans, Green & Co., 1888).
Gelder, H. A. Enno, Van, *The Two Reformations in the 16th Century: A Study of the Religious Aspects and Consequences of Renaissance and Humanism* (The Hague: Martinus Nijhoff, 1961).
Geoghegan, William D., *Platonism in Recent Religious Thought* (New York: Columbia University Press, 1958).
George, E. A., *Seventeenth Century Men of Latitude* (London: T. Fisher Unwin, 1909).
Gibson, James, *Locke's Theory of Knowledge and its Historical Relations* (Cambridge, Eng.: at the University Press, 1917).
Gilson, Etienne, *History of Christian Philosophy in the Middle Ages* (London: Sheed and Ward, 1955).
— *Reason and Revelation in the Middle Ages* (London, 1939).
Glanvill, Joseph, *Sadducimus Triumphatus*, 4th ed. (London, 1724).
— *The Vanity of Dogmatizing* (London, 1661).
Goodwin, John, *The Redemption Redeemed* (reprinted from the 1651 ed.) (London, 1840).
Gore, Charles, *The Body of Christ*, 2nd ed. (London: J. Murray, 1905).
Grandgeorge, L., *Saint Augustin et Le Néo-Platonisme* (Paris, 1896).
Grierson, H. J. C., *Cross-Currents in English Literature of the XVIIth Century; Being the Messenger Lectures at Cornell University, 1926–27* (London: Chatto and Windus, 1929).
Gwatkin, H. M., *Church and State in England to the Death of Queen Anne* (London: Longmans & Co., 1917).
Gysi, Lydia, *Platonism and Cartesianism in the Philosophy of Ralph Cudworth* (Bern: Herbert Lang, 1962).
Hales, John, "A Tract Concerning Schism and Schismaticks" (1642), in *Several Tracts* (London, 1677).
Haller, William, *The Rise of Puritanism* (New York: Columbia University Press, 1938).
Harrison, A. W., *Arminianism* (London: Duckworth, 1937).
Harrison, J. S., *Platonism in English Poetry of the Sixteenth and Seventeenth Centuries* (New York, 1903).
Hartshorne, Charles, *The Logic of Perfection and Other Essays in Neoclassical Metaphysics* (Lasalle, Ill.: Open Court Publishing Co., 1962).

Hearnshaw, F. J. C., editor, *the Social and Political Ideas of Some of the Great Thinkers of the Sixteenth and Seventeenth Centuries* (London: George G. Harrap & Co., 1926).

Heiler, Friedrich, *Prayer*, ed. by Samuel McComb and J. Edgar Park (New York: Oxford, 1958).

Henson, H. H., *Studies in English Religion in the Seventeenth Century* (London: John Murray, 1903).

Herbermann, C. G., *et al.*, editors, *The Catholic Encyclopaedia* (New York), 1907–11. Vols. I, V, VII, X, XII.

Hertling, G. F. von, *John Locke und die Schule von Cambridge* (Strassburg: Zweignieder lassungen, 1892).

Heywood, James, *The Ancient Laws of the Fifteenth Century for King's College, Cambridge, and the Public School of Eton College* (London, 1850).

— editor and translator, *Collection of Statutes for the University and Colleges of Cambridge* (London, 1840).

Heywood, James, and Wright, Thomas, *Cambridge Transactions (During the Puritan Controversies of the Sixteenth and Seventeenth Centuries)* (London: S.C.M., 1854), Vol. II.

Highams, Florence, *Faith of Our Fathers, The Men and Movements of the Seventeenth Century* (London, 1939).

Hobbes, Thomas, *Leviathan* ed. A. D. Lindsay (London: Everyman's Library, 1914).

Hobhouse, L. T., *The Elements of Social Justice* (London, 1922).

Hocking, W. E., *Human Nature and Its Remaking* (New Haven: Yale, 1918).

Hodgson, Leonard, *The Doctrine of the Trinity* (London: Nisbet & Co., 1944).

Hook, Norman, *The Eucharist in the New Testament* (London: The Epworth Press, 1964).

Hooker, Richard, *Works*, ed. Isaac Walton (Oxford, 1846), 2 Vols.

Hoops, Robert, *Right Reason in the English Renaissance* (Cambridge, Mass.: Harvard University Press, 1962).

Hügel, Baron F. von, *Eternal Life* (Edinburgh, 1912).

Hunt, John, *Religious Thought in England* (London, 1870), Vol. I.

Hutchinson, F. E., *Milton and the English Mind* (London, 1946).

Hutton, W. H., *The English Church From the Accession of Charles I to the Death of Anne* (1625–1714) (London: Macmillan, 1903).

Huxley, Julian, "The Biology of Human Nature," *Yale Review*, Vol. XXII (Dec., 1932), p. 337.

Inge, W. R., *The Philosophy of Plotinus;* Being the Gifford Lectures at the University of St. Andrews, 1917–1918 (London: Longmans, Green and Co., 1918), 2 Vols.

— *Christian Mysticism*, 3rd. ed. (London: Methuen and Col. 1913).

— *The Platonic Tradition in English Religious Thought* (London: Longmans & Co., 1926).

— *Christian Ethics and Modern Problems* (London: Hodder and Stoughton, 1930).

Jaeger, Werner, *Early Christianity and Greek Paideia* (Cambridge, Mass.: Harvard University Press, 1961).

James, William, *A Pluralistic Universe* (London, 1909).

— *The Will to Believe* (New York, 1898).

— *Essays Philosophical and Psychological in Honor of William James* ed. O. Lovejoy (London: Longmans, Green and Co., 1908).

Jayne, Sears, *John Colet and Marsilio Ficino* (London: Oxford University Press, 1963).

Jeremias, Joachim, *The Origins of Infant Baptism*. Studies in Historical Theology tr. by David Cairns (London: S.C.M., 1960).
— *The Eucharistic Words of Jesus*, tr. Arnold Ehrhardt (New York: Macmillan, 1955).
Jones, Rufus, *Spiritual Reformers in the Sixteenth and Seventeenth Centuries* (London: Macmillan, 1914).
Jordan, W. K., *The Development of Religious Toleration in England* (London: George Allen and Unwin, 1939), Vol. IV.
Jowett, J. P. K., *Emil Brunner's Concept of Revelation*, Evangelical Theological Society (London, 1954).
Kant, Immanuel, *The Metaphysic of Ethics*, tr. J. W. Semple (Edinburgh, 1869).
— *Critique of Pure Reason*, tr. with commentary by N. K. Smith (London: Macmillan, 1918).
Kaufman, M., "Latitudinarianism and Pietism," *The Cambridge Modern History* (Cambridge, 1908), Vol V., pp. 742–753.
Kenwood, S. H., *The Emmanuel Platonists* (Giggleswick, 1916).
Kidd, B. J., *The Later Medieval Doctrine of Eucharistic Sacrifice* (London: S.P.C.K., 1958).
Kierkegaard, S., *Concluding Unscientific Postscript*, tr. Swenson-Lowrie (London, 1941).
King, P. L., *The Life and Letters of John Locke*, new ed. (London, 1858).
Kirk, K. E., editor, *The Apostolic Ministry* (London, 1946).
Klibansky, Raymond, *The Continuity of the Platonic Tradition During The Middle Ages* (London: The Warburg Institute, 1939).
Knappen, M. M., *Tudor Puritanism* (Chicago, 1939).
Knudson, A. C., *The Principles of Christian Ethics* (New York, 1943).
Kretser, Bryan de, *Man In Buddhism and Christianity* (Calcutta: Y.M.C.A. Publishing House, 1954).
Kristeller, P. O., *The Philosophy of Marsilio Ficino*, tr. Virginia Conant (New York: Columbia University Press, 1943).
Küng, Hans, *Justification: The Doctrine of Karl Barth and a Catholic Reflection* tr. by Thomas Collins, E. E. Tolk, and David Granskow (New York: Thomas Nelson & Sons, 1964).
Kulandran, Sabapathy, *Grace: A Comparative Study of the Doctrine in Christianity and Hinduism* (London: Butterworth, 1964).
Laird, John, *Hobbes* (London: Ernest Benn, 1934).
Lamprecht, S. P., "Innate Ideas," *Philosophical Review*, Vol. XXXV (1926), pp. 553–573.
La Ramée, Pierre De, *Dialectique* (1555), Édition critique avec introduction, notes et commentaires de Michel Dassonville (Genève: Librairie Droz, 1964).
Lecky, W. E. H., *History of European Morals*, 13th impression (London, 1899), 2 Vols.
Lehmann, Paul L., *Ethics in a Christian Context* (London: S.C.M., 1963).
Leibnitz, G. W., *Essais de Theodicée sur la Bonté de Dieu, la Liberté de l'Homme, et l'Origine du Mal*, seconde édition (Amsterdam, 1712).
Lewis, C. S., *A Preface to Paradise Lost;* Being the Ballard Matthews Lectures at University College, North Wales, 1941, revised ed. (London, 1942).
Lichtenstein, Aharon, *Henry More: The National Theology of a Cambridge Platonist* (Cambridge, Mass.: Harvard University Press, 1962).
Locke, John, *An Essay Concerning Human Understanding*, 31st ed. (London, 1853).
— *Four Letters on Toleration* (London, 1876).
— *The Reasonableness of Christianity* (London, 1695).

— *Works*, 12th ed. (London, 1824), Vol. III.

Lodge, Richard, *The History of England* (London, 1910), Vol. VIII.

Lossky, Vladimir, *The Mystical Theology of the Eastern Church* (London: James Clarke & Co., 1944).

Lowery, C. E., *The Philosophy of Ralph Cudworth* (New York, 1884).

Mace, C. A., ed. *British Philosophy in the Mid-Century* (London: George Allen & Unwin Ltd., 1957).

MacKenzie, J. S., *A Manual of Ethics*, The University Tutorial Series, 4th ed. (London, 1900).

MacKintosh, H. R., *Types of Modern Theology* (London: James Nisbet and Co., 1962).

— *The Doctrine of the Person of Christ* (Edinburgh, 1912).

— *The Christian Experience of Forgiveness* (London, 1927).

Mackintosh, Sir James, *On the Progress of Ethical Philosophy* (Edinburgh, 1872).

MacLachlan, H. J. *Socinianism in Seventeenth-Century England* (Oxford: University Press, 1953).

MacMurray, John, *The Clue to History* (London, 1938).

MacQuarrie, John, *Twentieth-Century Religious Thought* (New York: Harper and Row, 1963).

McGiffert, A. C., *A History of Christian Thought* (London: Scribner's, 1933), 2 Vols.

McIntyre, John, *Anselm and His Critics: A Re-Interpretation of the Cur Deus Homo* (Edinburgh: Oliver and Boyd, 1954).

McKeon, Richard, *Selections from Medieval Philosophers* (London, 1931), Vol. II.

McRae, Robert, "'Idea' as a Philosophical Term in the Seventeenth Century," *Journal of the History of Ideas*, vol. XXVI, no. 2 (April–June, 1965), pp. 175–190.

Maritain, Jacques, *Redeeming the Time* (London, 1946).

Martin, Hugh, *Christian Reunion* (London, 1941).

Martineau, James, *Types of Ethical Theory* (Oxford, 1885), 2 Vols.

Marty, M. E. and Peerman, D. G., ed. *New Theology*, no. 1 (New York: Macmillan 1964).

Mascal, E. L., *Existence and Analogy* (London: Longmans, Green and Co., 1949).

Masson, David, *The Life of John Milton* (London, 1873), Vols. I, III.

Masterman, J. H. B., *The Age of Milton* (London, 1897).

Masutani, Fumio, *A Comparative Study of Buddhism and Christianity* (Tokyo: CIIB Press, 1959).

Maurice, F. D., *Moral and Metaphysical Philosophy*, new ed. (London, 1873), Vol. II.

— *The Kingdom of Christ*, 3rd ed. (London, 1883), 2 Vols.

Mayor, J. E. B., *Cambridge in the Reign of Queen Anne*, The Cambridge Antiquarian Society (Cambridge, 1911).

Mead (or Mede), Joseph, *Works*, ed. John Worthington, 3rd ed. (London, 1672).

Merlan, Philip, *From Platonism is Neoplatonism*, 2nd ed., revised (The Hague: Martinus Nijhoff, 1960).

Metcalfe, W. M., editor, *The Cambridge Platonists*, Introduction by Matthew Arnold (London, 1885).

Meyendorff, John, *The Orthodox Church* (New York: Pantheon Books, 1962).

Miller, Samuel H. and Wright, G. Ernest, eds. *Ecumenical Dialogue at Harvard: The Roman Catholic-Protestant Colloquium* (Cambridge, Mass.: Harvard University Press, 1964).

Miles, Leland, *John Colet and the Platonic Tradition* (Lasalle, Ill.: Open Court, 1961).

Milton, John, *Paradise Lost*, ed. G. M. Davis (London, 1931).
— *De Doctrina Christiana*, tr. Charles Sumner, (Cambridge 1825).
Minear, Paul S., *Images of the Church in the New Testament* (Philadelphia: Westminister, 1960).
Mintz, Samuel I., *The Hunting of Leviathan* (Cambridge, England: at the University Press, 1962).
Mitchell, A. F., *Minutes of the Sessions of the Westminster Assembly of Divines* (London, 1874).
Moffatt, James, editor, *The Golden Book of John Owen* (London, 1904).
— *The Golden Book of Tillotson* (London, 1926).
Montague, F. C., *The History of England* (London, 1907).
Mooney, Christopher F., "Teilhard de Chardin and the Christological Problem," *The Harvard Theological Review*, vol. 58, no. 1 (January, 1965), pp. 91–126.
Moorman, J. R. H., *A History of the Church of England* (London: Adam and Charles Black, 1953).
Mowrer, O. Hobart, *The Crisis in Psychiatry and Religion* (Princeton: D. Van Nostrand, 1961).
Muirhead, J. H., *Coleridge as Philosopher* (London, 1930).
— *The Platonic Tradition in Anglo-Saxon Philosophy* (London: George Allen and Unwin, 1931).
Mullinger, J. Bass, *A History of the University of Cambridge* (London, 1888).
— *The University of Cambridge* (Cambridge at the University Press, 1911), Vol. III.
— *Cambridge Characteristics in the Seventeenth Century* (London, 1867).
Nelson, J. Robert, *The Realm of Redemption* (Greenwich: Seabury Press, 1951).
Newbigin, Lesslie, *The Reunion of the Church* (London, 1948).
Nicolson, Marjorie, "Christ College and the Latitude-Men," *Modern Philology*, Vol. XXVII (1929–30), pp. 35–47.
Niebuhr, H. R., *Christ and Culture*; Being an expanded series of lectures given at Austin Presbyterian Seminary in January, 1949 (London, 1952).
— *The Meaning of Revelation* (New York: Macmillan, 1941).
Niebuhr, Reinhold, *Moral Man and Immoral Society* (London, 1933).
— *The Nature and Destiny of Man;* Being the Gifford Lectures at Edinburgh University in 1939, 2 Series (London, 1941–43).
Niebuhr, Richard R., *Resurrection and Historical Reason* (New York: Scribner's, 1957).
Niesel, Wilhelm, *The Gospel and the Churches*, tr. by David Lewis (Philadelphia: Westminister, 1962).
Nock, A. D., Conversion: *The Old and the New in Religion from Alexander the Great to Augustine of Hippo* (Oxford: Clarendon Press, 1933).
Nussbaum, F. L., *The Triumph of Science and Reason, 1666–1685* (New York: Harper, 1953).
Nuttall, G. F., *Studies in Christian Enthusiasm* (Wallingford, Pa: Pendle H. U., 1948).
Oesterly, W. O. E., *The Book of Proverbs* (London, 1929).
Ogg, David, *Europe in the Seventeenth Century* (London: A. & C. Black, 1925).
Ollard, S. L., Crosse, G., and Bond, M. F., *A Dictionary of English Church History* new edition (London, 1919).
Oman, John, *The Problem of Faith and Freedom in the Last Two Centuries;* Being the Kerr Lectures in the Glasgow Colleges of the United Free Church, 1906 (London: Hodder and Stoughton, 1906).
Origen, *Contra Celsum*, tr. Henry Chadwick (Cambridge, 1953).
— *De Principiis*, tr. G. W. Butterworth (London, 1936).

Otto, Rudolf, *Die Gnadenreligion Indiens Und Das Christentum: Vergleich Und Unterscheidung* (Munich: C. H. Becksche, 1930).
Parker, Samuel, *A Free and Impartial Censure of the Platonic Philosophie*, 2nd ed. (Oxford, 1667).
Pascal, Blaise, *Pensées*, ed. Stewart (New York, 1947).
Passmore, J. A., *Ralph Cudworth: An Interpretation* (Cambridge, 1951).
Passmore, John, *A Hundred Years of Philosophy* (London: Gerald Duckworth & Co., 1957).
Patrick, Simon, "A Brief Account of the New Sect of Latitude Men" (1662), *The Phenix* (London, 1707).
Paul, Leslie, *The English Philosophers* (London, 1953).
Paul, Robert S., *The Atonement and the Sacraments* (New York: Abingdon, 1960).
Pawson, G. P., H., *The Cambridge Platonists and Their Place in Religious Thought* (London: S.P.C.K., 1930).
Pelikan, Jaroslav, "Bonhoeffer's Christologie of 1933," *The Place of Bonhoeffer*, ed. by M. E. Marty (New York: Association Press, 1962).
Phillips, J. B., *Letters to Younger Churches*, Fontana Series (London, 1951).
Pike, Nelson, ed., *Good and Evil* (Englewood Cliffs, N. J.: Prentice-Hall, 1964).
Plato, *Apology, Phaedo and Phaedrus*, tr. W. R. M. Lamb, The Loeb Classical Library (London, 1914).
— *Cratylus*, tr. H. N. Fowler, Loeb (London, 1926).
— *Laws*, tr. R. G. Bury, Loeb (London, 1926), 2 Vols.
— *Theaetetus*, tr. H. N. Fowler, Loeb (London, 1921).
— *Timaeus and Critias*, tr. Bury, Loeb (London, 1929).
— *Republic*, tr. P. Shorey, Loeb (London, 1930–35), 2 Vols.
Plotinus, *Enneads*, tr. Stephen Mackenna (London, 1917–30), 5 Vols.
Plummer, Alfred, *English Church History (1573–1649)* (Edinburgh: T. & T. Clark, 1904).
Powicke, F. J., *A. Dissertation on John Norris of Bermerton* (London, 1895).
— *The Reverend Richard Baxter under the Cross 1662–1691* (London, 1927).
— *The Cambridge Platonists* (London, 1926).
Proclus, *The Elements of Theology*, ed. E. R. Dodds, 2nd ed. (Oxford: at the Clarendon Press, 1963).
Przywara, Erich, *An Augustine Synthesis* (New York: Harper, 1958).
Pseudo-Denys L'Aréopagite, *Oeuvres Complètes*, traduction par Maurice de Gandillac (Paris: Aubier, 1943).
Quick, O. C., *The Christian Sacraments* (London, 1927).
Ramsey, A. M., *Maurice and the Conflicts of Modern Theology* (Cambridge, 1951).
Ramsey, Paul, ed., *Faith and Ethics: The Theology of H. Richard Niebuhr* (New York: Harper, 1957).
Rankin, O. S., *Israel's Wisdom Literature* (Edinburgh, 1936).
Raven, C. E., *Christian Socialism, 1848–1854* (London, 1920).
— *English Naturalists from Neckham to Ray* (Cambridge, 1947).
— *The Theological Basis of Christian Pacifism*, The Fellowship of Reconciliation (London, 1952).
— *Synthetic Philosophy in the Seventeenth Century;* Being The Herbert Spencer Lectures for 1945 (Oxford, 1945).
— *Religion and Science;* Being the L. T. Hobhouse Memorial Trust Lecture No. 16, 1946, at Bedford College (London, 1946).
— *Christianity and Science*, World Christian Books No. 4 (London, 1955).
— *Natural Science and Christian Theology;* Being the Gifford Lectures in the University of Edinburgh, 1951–52, 2 series (Cambridge, 1953).
— *John Ray, Naturalist, His Life and Works* (Cambridge, 1942).

Reid, J. K. S., *The Authority of Scripture: A Study of the Reformation and Post-Reformation Understanding of the Bible* (London: Methuen & Co., 1962).

Rémusat, Charles de, *Histoire de la Philosophie en Angleterre depuis Bacon jusqu'à Locke* (Paris: Librairie Académique, 1875), Vol. II.

Richardson, C. F., *English Preachers and Preaching*, 1640–1670 (London: S.P.C.K., 1928).

Rigg, J. H., *Modern Anglican Theology*, 2nd and revised ed. (London, 1859).

Rigg, W. H., *The Fourth Gospel and Its Message Today* (London, 1952).

Ritschel, Dietrich, *A Theology of the Proclamation* (Richmond, Va: John Knox Press, 1960).

Roberts, David E., *Psychotherapy and a Christian View of Man* (New York: Scribner's Sons, 1950).

Roberts, J. Deotis, *Faith and Reason: A Comparative Study of Pascal, Bergson and James* (Boston: Christopher, 1962).

— "Kierkegaard on Truth and Subjectivity," *Journal of Religious Thought*, Vol. XVIII, no. 1 (Winter-Spring, 1961), pp. 41–55.

— "Christian Conscience and Legal Discrimination," *Journal of Religious Thought*, vol. XIX, no. 2 (1962–63), pp. 157–161.

— "A Theological Conception of the State," *A Journal of Church and State*, vol. IV, no. 1 (May, 1962), pp. 66–75.

— "Bergson As a Metaphysical, Epistemological and Religious Thinker," *Journal of Religious Thought*, vol. XX, no. 2 (1963–1964), pp. 108–109.

— "Majoring in Minors," *The Link*, vol. 20, no. 9 (Sept., 1962), pp. 5–8.

Roberts, J. D., "The Problem of Faith and Reason as Treated in the Writings of Pascal, Bergson and James" (Unpublished S.T.M. thesis, Hartford Theological Seminary, 1952).

Robinson, C. K., "Philosophical Biblicism: The Teaching of the Westminister Confession Concerning God, The Natural Man, and Revelation and Authority," *Scottish Journal of Theology*, vol. 18, no. 1 (March, 1965), pp. 23–39.

Robinson, J. A., T., *The Body*, Studies in Biblical Theology, No. 5 (London, 1955).

Robinson, J. M., Cobb, J. B., eds. *New Frontiers in Theology*, vol. II, "The New Hermeneutic" (New York: Harper & Row, 1964).

Robinson, Matthew, *Autobiography*, ed. J. E. B. Mayor (Cambridge, 1856).

Rogers, A. K., "Art and Conscience," *International Journal of Ethics* (Jan., 1931), p. 146.

Ross, F. H., "Personalism and the Problem of Evil, A Study in the Personalism of Browne, Knudson, and Brightman," *Yale Studies in Religion*, No. 11 (New Haven, 1940).

Ross, W. D., *Aristotle* (London: Methuen & Co., 1923).

Sanders, C. R., *Coleridge and the Broad Church Movement* (Durham, North Carolina, 1942).

Santayana, George, *Platonism and the Spiritual Life* (New York: Scribner's, 1927).

St. Francis de Sales, *On the Preacher and Preaching*, tr. by J. K. Ryan (New York: Henry Regnery, 1964).

Schweitzer, Albert, "The Decay and Restoration of Civilization," tr. C. T. Campion, and "Civilization and Ethics," tr. John Naish, *The Philosophy of Civilization*, Pts. I, II; Being the Yale Memorial Lectures, 1922 (London, 1923).

Scott, W. R., *An Introduction to Cudworth's Treatise Concerning Eternal and Immutable Morality with the Life of Cudworth and Critical Notes* (London, 1891).

Selwyn, E. G., *The First Epistle of St. Peter* (London, 1946).

Seneca, *Ad Lucilium Epistulae Morales*, tr. R. M. Gummere, Loeb (London, 1917–25), 3 Vols.

Seth, James, *English Philosophers and Schools of Philosophy* (London: J. M. Dent, 1912).

Sewell, Arthur, *A Study in Milton's Christian Doctrine* (London, 1939).

Sherman, John, *A Greek in the Temple* (Cambridge, 1641).

Shuchburgh, E. S., *Emmanuel College* (London: F. E. Robinson & Co., 1904).

Smith, Preserved, *A History of Modern Culture* (New York: George Routledge and Sons, 1930), Vol. I.

Smyth, Charles, *The Art of Preaching*, 1749–1939 (London: S.P.C.K., 1940).

Sorley, W. R., *A History of English Philosophy* (Cambridge: at the University Press, 1920).

Stendahl, Krister, ed., *Immortality and Resurrection* (New York: Macmillan, 1965).

Stephen, Leslie, *History of English Thought in the Eighteenth Century* (London, 1876), 2 Vols.

— and Lee, Sidney, editors, *Dictionary of National Biography* (London: Elder & Co., 1908–09), Vols. IV, V, XIII, XVIII, XXI.

Sternbeck, Alfred, *Shaftesbury über Natur, Gott und Religion* (Berlin: Buch-druckerei, 1904).

Stewart, J. A., "Cambridge Platonists," *Encyclopaedia of Religion and Ethics*, ed. James Hastings (Edinburgh: T. & T. Clark, 1910), Vol. III, pp. 167–173.

Stillingfleet, Edward, *Origines Sacrae*, 3rd ed. (London, 1666).

— *Irenicum* (London, 1681).

Stoughton, John, *History of Religion in England*, new and revised ed. (London, 1881), Vols. I, II, IV.

Suzuki, D. T., *Mysticism: Christian and Buddhist*. ed. R. N. Anshen, World Perspectives vol. 12 (New York: Harper, 1957).

— Erich Fromm, and Richard De Martino. *Zen Buddhism and Psychoanalysis* (New York: Harper & Brothers, 1960).

Sykes, Norman, *The English Religious Tradition* (London: S.C.M., 1953).

— *Old Priest and New Presbyter* (Cambridge, 1956).

Tacitus, *The Annals*, tr. John Jackson, Loeb (London, 1937), Vol. III.

Tallack, William, "Quakers and Cambridge Platonists," *The Friends' Quarterly Examiner*, Nos. LXXXIX–XCII, Vol. XXIII (1889), pp. 187–196.

Talon, Henri A., *John Bunyan* (London, 1956).

Taylor, A. E., *Socrates* (Boston: Beacon Press, 1951).

— *Plato, The Man and His Work* (London, 1926).

Taylor, Jeremy, *A Discourse of the Liberty of Prophesying*, The Sacred Classics, (eds. Cattermole-Stebbing) (London, 1834).

Taylor, Thomas, *Selected Works of Plotinus*, tr. G .R. S. Mead (London, 1895).

Taylor, Vincent, *Forgiveness and Reconciliation* (London: Macmillan, 1948).

Temple, William, *Plato and Christianity* (London, 1916).

— *Nature, Man and God*; Being the Gifford Lectures delivered in the University of Glasgow in the academical years 1932–1933 and 1933–1934 (London, 1934).

Tennant, F. R., *The Nature of Belief*, The Christian Challenge Series (London, 1963).

— *The Sources of the Doctrine of the Fall and Original Sin* (Cambridge, 1903).

— *The Origin and Propagation of Sin;* Being the Hulsean Lectures at the University of Cambridge, 1901–2 Cambridge, 1902).

— *The Concept of Sin* (Cambridge, 1912).

The Encyclopaedia Britannica, Edited by Hugh Chisholm, Eleventh Edition (Cambridge, 1910), Vol. IX.

Tertullian, "The Prescription Against Heretics," *The Ante-Nicene Fathers*, ed. by Alexander Roberts and James Donaldson, revised by A. C. Coxe (New York, 1896), pp. 343–265.

Theologia Germanica: The Way to a Sinless Life, ed. T. S. Kepler (Cleveland: World Publishing Co., 1952).

Thompson, A. N., *Cambridge and Its College* (London: Methuen & Co., 1968).

Tillich, Paul, *Love, Power, and Justice* (London: Oxford, 1954).

— *The Courage to Be* (New Haven: Yale University Press, 1953).

— *Systematic Theology* (London, 1953), Vol. I.

Thomas, Owen C., *William Temple's Philosophy of Religion* (London: S.P.C.K., 1961).

Thomson, D. F. S., and Porter, H. C. eds. *Erasmus and Cambridge* (Toronto: University of Toronto Press, 1963).

Thornton, L. S., *The Incarnate Lord* (New York: Longmans, Green & Co., 1928).

Tillotson, John, *A Sermon Preached at the Funeral of . . . Dr. Benjamin Which-cote. . . ., May 24th, 1683* (London, 1683).

— *Works* (London, 1757), Vols. I–III.

Tillyard, E. M. W., *Milton* (London, 1916).

Titus, H. H., *Ethics for Today* (New York, 1936).

Toland, John, *Christianity not Mysterious* (London, 1696).

Torrance, T. F., *Calvin's Doctrine of Man* (London, 1945).

Trevelyan, G. M., *English Social History* (New York, 1942).

— *History of England* (London, 1945).

Trueblood, D. E., *Philosophy of Religion* (New York: Harper, 1957).

Tuckney, Anthony, *None But Christ; Being a Sermon Preached at St. Maries in Cambridge on the Commencement Sabbath, July 4, 1652* (Cambridge, 1654).

Tulloch, John, *English Puritanism and Its Leaders* (London, 1861).

— *Rational Theology and Christian Philosophy in England in the Seventeenth Century* (Edinburgh, 1872), 2 Vols.

— "Benjamin Whichcote," *Contemporary Review*, Vol. XVIII (August to November, 1871), pp. 297–333.

Ueberweg, Friedrich, *A History of Philosophy*, tr. G. S. Morris, 2nd ed. (London, 1875), Vol. I.

Venn, John and Venn, J. A., editors, *Alumni Cantabrigienses* (Cambridge: at the University Press, 1927), Pt. I, Vol. IV.

Von Rad, Gerhard, *Genesis: A Commentary*, tr. by John H. Marks (Philadelphia: Westminister, 1959).

Ward, A. W., Prothero, G. W., *et al.* editors, *The Cambridge Modern History* (Cambridge, Eng.: at the University Press, 1906–1908), Vols. IV, V.

— Waller, A. R., editors, *The Cambridge History of English Literature* (Cambridge, Eng.: at the University Press, 1912), Vol. VIII.

Ward, Richard, *The Life. . . . of Henry More, To Which is Annexed Divers Philosophical Poems and Hymns*, The Theosophical Publishing Society (London, 1911).

Watt, W. Montgomery, *Free Will and Predestination in Early Islam* (London: Luzac & Co., 1948).

Webb, C. C. J., *Problems in the Relations of God and Man* (London, 1915).

— *God and Personality;* Being the first course of Gifford Lectures, University of Aberdeen, 1918 (London, 1918).

— *Studies in the History of Natural Theology;* Being the Wilde Lectures in the University of Oxford, 1911–1913 (Oxford, 1915).

Weiss, Roberto, *Humanism in England During the Fifteenth Century* (Oxford: Basil Blackwell, 1941).

Westcott, B. F., *Essays in the History of Religious Thought in the West* (London, 1891).
— *The Gospel According to John* (London, 1882).
Westfall, Richard J., *Science and Religion in Seventeenth-Century England* (New Haven: Yale University Press, 1958).
Whale, J. S., *Christian Doctrine* (Cambridge, 1956).
Whewell, William, *Lectures on the History of Moral Philosophy in England*, new edition (Cambridge, 1862).
Whitehead, A. N., *Science and the Modern World* (Cambridge: at the University Press, 1926).
— *The Function of Reason* (Princeton, 1929).
Whiting, C. E., *Studies in English Puritanism from the Restoration to the Revolution, 1660–1688* (London, 1931).
Whitley, W. T., ed. *The Doctrine of Grace* (London: S.C.M., 1942).
Whittaker, Thomas, *The Neo-Platonists* (Cambridge, 1918).
Wild, John, *George Berkeley: A Study of His Life and Philosophy* (New York: Russell & Russell, 1962).
Wilkins, John, *The Principles and Duties of Natural Religion*, 5th. ed. (London, 1704).
Willey, Basil, *The Seventeenth Century Background* (London: Chatto & Windus, 1934).
— *The Eighteenth Century Background* (London, 1940).
— *Nineteenth Century Studies* (London, 1949).
Williams, G. H., *Anselm: Communion and Atonement* (St. Louis, Missouri: Concordia Publishing House, 1960).
Windelband, Wilhelm, *History of Ancient Philosophy*, tr. H. E. Cushman (London: Sampson Low, Marston, 1900).
— *A History of Philosophy*, tr. James H. Tufts (New York: Macmillan, 1893).
Wingren, Gustaf, *Gospel and Church*, tr. Ross MacKenzie (Edinburg: Oliver & Boyd, 1964).
Wolfson, Harry Austryn, *The Philosophy of the Church Fathers*, vol. I, Second Edition, Revised (Cambridge, Mass.: Harvard University Press, 1964).
— *Philo* (Cambridge, Mass.: Harvard University Press, 1947).
Worthington, John, *Diary and Correspondence*, ed. James Crossley, Chetham Society Publications (Manchester, 1847), Vol. I. Also Vol. II, ed. R. C. Christie (Manchester, 1886).
Zernov, Nicolas, *Eastern Christendom* (New York: G. P. Putnam's Sons, 1961).

INDEX

A

absolute 134
Act of Uniformity 10
Adam 123, 129
adoption 143
Agape 134, 164
Age of Reason 230, 238f., 240, 250, 260
Alberti 27
Alexandria 21
Alexandrian mysticism 221
American Idealists 250
Anaxagoras 18
angels 96, 160
animals 160
Anselm 24
Apostles Creed 32
apostolic succession 175
Aquinas 30, 75
Aristotle 18, 19, 30, 75, 100, 106, 134, 172, 206, 251
Arminianism 34, 35, 37, 57
articles (thirty-nine) 179
atheism 72, 73, 249
atonement 136, 137, 138
Augustine 24, 99, 116, 123, 125–126, 259
Austin, E. M. 236
Author of Nature 133, 202
authority 56

B

Bacon, Francis 38, 39, 235f.
Baillie, John 80, 116, 118, 125, 126, 133
baptism 183, 187
Baptists 134
Barclay, William 231
Barth, Karl 125, 260
Baxter, Richard 37
beautiful 242
beauty 70
Being 19
belief 142

believe 75
benevolence 108, 242, 245
Bennett, J. C. 132
Berdyaev, Nicolas 73
Bergson, Henri 80, 160, 260
Berkeley, George 240
Bessarion 27
biblical literature 82, 86
biblical revelation 261
Bigg, Charles 254
blessedness 144
body 86, 87, 169 (spiritual), 169
Bohemists 37
Bradley, F. H. 250
Brightman, Edgar 80
British philosophy 235
Broad Church 230
Brunner, Emil 104, 106, 116, 125, 126, 132, 134, 138
Bultmann, Rudolf 82
Burnet, Gilbert 13, 16, 201, 204f., 227f.
Butler, Joseph 151, 163, 164, 240, 241, 243f., 245

C

Cabbalism 221
Calvin 34, 52, 54, 124, 206
Calvinism 34, 36, 37, 44–46, 52, 102, 215
Calvinists 207
Cambridge Platonism 178, 219f., 252ff., 254
Cambridge Platonists 15, 22, 30, 34, 49, 74, 202, 203, 205f., 208–10, 220–22, 226, 228, 230–32, 234–38, 247, 252, 254
Candle of the Lord 66, 76, 83f., 116, 223, 232, 254, 259, 261
Cassirer, Ernst 265
Cavaliers 43
ceremonies 179f.
Charles I 43
Charles II 9
Chillingworth 34, 39, 57, 178, 191, 208,

228, 233, 246
Christ 70f., 106, 128, 133–37, 142–50, 155, 161, 165–168, 170, 179–83, 185, 187–94, 229, 231f., 254, 262
Christ College 207–209, 218, 220
Christendom 193
Christian doctrine 230
Christian dogma 258
Christian life 161
Christian love 193
Christian morality 148, 150
Christian morals 147f., 151f., 156, 170
Christian philosophy 239
Christian Platonists 210, 223f., 217, 223
Christian Principles 170
Christian Socialism 251
Christian theology 132
Christian tolerance 171, 189, 194, 198, 258, 264f.
Christian union 189
Christian virtue 151
Christianity 229
Christians 189
Christology 123
Church, 135, 173ff., 181, 189, 190–92, 198, 201, 237, 251
Church (Christian) 176, 190, 193
Church (of England) 171, 177–79, 181, 191, 194, 199
Church (of God) 194
Church (Reformed) 177, 179, 197
Church (of Rome) 174f., 207
Church (universal) 171, 198
Church Fathers 223
Cicero (or Tully) 20, 204
citizen 107
Clarke, Samuel 240, 241, 244
Clement 22, 221
Coleridge, S. T. 248–50
Colet, John 30, 32, 33
Collingwood, R. G. 99
Collins, Samuel 3, 6, 19, 213
Colucci 27
combativeness 94
common notions 68
communication 109
communion 87, 89, 183–87, 193, 197, 224
compassion 134, 138, 245
congregation 179
connatural 68, 98
conscience 95f., 103, 124, 127, 129f., 146, 164, 245, 250
contemplation 86, 114
conversion 143, 144
cosmological proof 75
councils 177
Covenant 4, 43, 44
creation 76, 79, 81–83, 97, 133, 139, 144, 152, 245, 262
Creator 19, 29, 81, 181, 190, 259

creaturehood 189
creatures 81
crisis theology 260
Cromwell, Oliver 6
cross 137
Cudworth ,Ralph 69, 72, 91, 103, 132, 198, 203, 209f., 213–19, 223, 227, 233, 247, 260
Cullmann, Oscar 161
Cusa, Nicolas 24

D

death 8, 136f., 144, 166ff., 168f.
De Boer, J. J. 205f., 209
dei-form 84, 113
deity 134f., 181
Deists 239f., 241
demonic 131
De Pauly, W. C. 116, 206
Descartes, 14, 38f., 73f., 223, 240
determinism 224, 249
Dionysius the Areopagite 221
Dissenters 178, 247
divine grace 139
divine nature 132, 148
divine perfection 76
divine revelation 123
divine truth 71, 117
divine wisdom 119
Doget, John 21

E

earthly life 152, 212, 251f., 253, 262
Ecclesiastes 205
ecclestical hierarchy 191
ecumenics 264–66
education 112
eighteenth century 246, 249
élan vital 161
Eleatics 18
emanation 118
Emmanuel College 2, 49, 209, 213, 218
emotionalism 229
English Humanism 33
English Renaissance 30
English theology 238
enjoyment of God 88
enthusiasm 215f., 227, 236, 238
equality 101
equity 79, 101
equivocation 173
Episcopius 233
epistemology 70, 99, 234, 258
Erasmus 30–33, 99, 209
Erigena 24, 30
eschatology 262
essences 69
estranged 114

eternal 68, 161, 165
eternal death 167
eternal life 119
eternity 76, 112, 156f., 161
Eternal Mind 69, 75
ethical monotheism 99
ethics 246, 261
Eton 208, 209, 218
Eucharist 207
evangelical righteousness 212
Evanston 161, 199
evil 82, 84, 85, 97, 113, 127, 168, 177, 261
existence of God 70, 72–75

F

faith 51, 74, 117, 120, 139, 142, 144, 146, 149, 177, 191f., 195, 198, 222, 230, 248, 250, 254, 258ff.
faithfulness 77
Fall 93, 94, 123–25, 129
fallible 101
family 104f.
fanaticism 227
Farmer, H. H. 80, 82, 122, 179, 185, 258
Fathers 177
Feast 186f.
fellowship 197
Ferré, Nels, F. S. 80, 81
Ficino, Marsilio 27, 28, 29, 31, 221
fidelity 120, 248, 250
filial affection 245
finite 189
First Cause 87
Fleetwood, James 7–10
flesh 133
forgive 103, 136
forgiveness 79, 141
Fowler, Edward 178, 183
Fox, George 230
Frank, S. L. 83
Fraser, A. C. 233
free moral agent 141
freedom 123, 141, 194, 217, 224
free-will 217
friends 230f.
friendship 245
fruition 89
future life 88

G

Galloway, George 79
generosity 94
Genesis 123, 205
German Idealism 249
Giver of Grace 133, 139, 202
Glanvill, Joseph 228
glorification 143

God 27f., 66–69, 71, 74–77, 81, 87, 91–92, 97–102, 113f., 117f., 129f., 134f., 137, 139, 142–144, 145f., 148, 150f., 155, 160, 162–166, 170–75, 179, 180f., 184, 188f., 193–97, 214, 224, 227, 234, 239, 244f., 248f., 253, 259, 262; creation 166, 170; freedom 78; goodness 133, 138f., 142, 144, 163; giver of grace 166, 170; governor 81, 162; judgement 165; justice 165; knowledge 67, 74, 259; laws 231; personality 79, 80; providence 74, 76, 81–83, 88, 107, 154, 166, 215; revelation 244, 253; sovereignty 79, 154; voice 67; will 78
God-man 136
Golden Rule 151
good 18f., 77, 81, 84, 94, 98, 151, 177, 242
good (and evil) 92f.
good life 81, 151, 154, 229
good-nature 154
goodness 28, 77, 79, 92, 103, 134, 148, 155
good-will 109f.
Gospel 135, 139–42, 145–50, 167, 182f., 199, 211, 231
gospel-revelation 135
government 107, 179, 193f.
grace 124, 139, 140, 142, 144, 146, 149, 151, 155, 188, 198, 229, 244, 262
Greek 26, 30, 207, 209, 220, 223
Guildhall 11

H

Hales, John 34, 39, 178, 208
happiness 89, 92, 114, 154, 167, 242
Hartshorne, Charles 83
heaven 158f., 160, 189
Hebrew 258
Hebrew Scripture 219
hell 159, 164, 167
Hertling, G. F. von 236
High Church 233
High Priest 135
history 80
Hobbes, Thomas 38f., 102, 108, 235, 242, 249
holiness 77, 79, 137, 145, 152f., 155, 177, 179
Holland 233
holy 179
holy life 153
Holy Spirit 67, 146, 156, 196
Hooker, Richard 34–36, 208
House of Commons 131
human freedom 80, 84f.
human knowledge 234
human nature 73, 93, 98, 108, 126, 133, 245
humanitarianism 262
humanity 224

Hume, David 235
humility 151
hypocracy 127, 181

I

Ideas 18f., 23, 25, 69, 234
idolatry 181
Ignatius 254
ignorance 174
illumination 76, 111, 144, 149, 155
image of God 83
image-worship 174
imago dei 123–26
imitation of God 110f., 113
immanent 83
immaterial 86
immoral freedom 102f.
immortality 71, 88, 166f., 168, 170, 227, 251
immortal soul 157f.
immutable 68
impersonalism 80
implicit faith 120
Incarnation 24, 132f., 170, 231f., 251
indulgence 174
Inge, W. R. 147, 170, 201, 252–57, 261
innate ideas 230, 234
inner peace 89
instinct 93
intellect 116
intellectualism 260
intention 94
intercession 145
inward man 151
Inward Teacher 231
Inward Voice 230f.
irrationality 71f., 135
Islam 71, 85
Isocrates 17
Italian Humanism 33
Italian Renaissance 26f., 31, 52

J

James I of England (James VI of Scotland) 42
James, William 99, 260
jealously 94
Jesus 153, 170, 172, 180
Jesus College 248
Jewish 21, 135
Jews 134f.
Job 163, 205
Johannine 21, 161, 170, 205, 251ff., 254, 262
Judaism 71, 137
justice 99, 138, 152
justification 138f., 143f., 167, 175

K

Kant, Immanuel 214, 235, 248, 250
Kierkegaard, Søren 68, 87, 260
Kingdom (of Christ) 152f. (of God) 158
King's College 8, 251
Knowledge (and morality) 92, 94, 95 (and obedience) 95 (and virtue) 95, 111 (of God) 113f., 119, 250
Knudson, Albert 151

L

Latin 26, 207
Latitudinarians 37, 178, 226ff., 230, 232f.
Lauderdale (Lord) 8
Laudians 179, 198, 207, 243, 251
law 101, 102
lawgiver 101
law of creation 199
learned ignorance 120
Leibnitz, G. W. 240
light 114 (of creation) 66, 97, 122, 194, 227, 261 (within) 230
Limborch, Phillip von 233
liturgy 179, 193f.
Locke, John 13, 232–39, 258
Logos 25, 106
London 251
Lord Herbert of Cherbury 34
Lord's Supper 185, 187
Lord's Table 187
Luther, Martin 34, 99, 209
love 73, 140, 151, 195; of enemies 152; of God 110, 119, 162, 193, 231; of neighbor 92, 110f., 151
Love, Richard 8
Lowery, C. E. 236

M

Mackintosh, H. R. 146
magistrate 107
man 73, 83, 87, 123–126, 129f., 133f., 143f., 224, 259
Manchester, Earl of 3, 5
Martyr, Justin 22
Masham, Lady 233f.
master-servant 105
materialism 249
Matthew, Bishop of Ely 10
Maurice, F. D. 232, 242, 250f.
Mead, Joseph 178, 206f., 209, 218, 220
means of grace 185
medians 220
mediation 88, 114, 119, 134–136, 177
Mediator 134–136
Meno 26
mental devotion 109f.; faculties 227
mercy 140, 145, 152

merit 174
metaphysics 23, 24, 113
Millenarians 37
Milton, John 10f., 97, 112, 197
mind 68, 86, 113
ministers 179, 182
Mirandola, Pico della 27
missionary work 189
modesty 99
Mohammed 71
monotheism 21
moral, 180–84; absolutism 91; agent 84, 94–98; decision 93, 95, 111; depravity 124; duties 92; evil 96, 127; ends and means 94; faculties 94; freedom 102f.; order, 91f.; perfection 151; principles 111, 149, 262; psychology 215f.; relativity 91, theory 94, 96, 98f.; virtue 110
moralism 230
morality 71, 114, 149, 243, 258, 262
morals 118

N

natural 67; appetite 99; ethics 99; evil 96; goodness 94f.; knowledge 117, 121, 142; morality 148, 227; order 81; principles 92; religion 66, 111, 199, 227f.; revelation 159; science 203; theology 80, 113, 116; natural truth 116f.
naturalism 258
naturalist 134
nature 133, 244, 246
Neo-Orthodox 257f.
Neo-Platonists 20, 26, 38, 83, 134, 211, 214, 221, 223, 251
new birth 144
New Israel 180
new science 161
New Testament 99, 176
Niebuhr, Reinhold 126, 127, 129, 132
non-Christian religions 70f.
non-Conformist 228
non-moral freedom 102f.
non-violence 94
Norris, John 247f.
North Cadbury 213
Nous 25, 106
Numenius 29
Nygren, Anders 140, 164

O

Ockham, William 30
obedience 138, 142, 146, 175f.
Old Israel 180
Old Testament 21, 163, 180; prophets 99, 132
oppression 104–107
optimism 108, 109

orders of creation 107
Origen 22, 164, 202, 221
Oxford University 233

P

panentheism 82
papists 178f., 247; pope 172–76, 207; popery 38
pardon 146, 174, 184
Parliament 43
participation 19, 113, 149
Pascal, Blaise 83, 99, 140, 239
passion 86
Passmore, John 215
Passover 186
Paul 105, 107
Pauline 21, 159, 161, 205
perfection 81
perfectionism 153
Pelagian 37
personalism 80
Petrarch 26f.
Phaedo 26
philanthropy 230
Philemon 105
Philipp ans 205
Phillips, J. B. 188
Philo 21, 221
Philosophy 172
physics 24
piety 99
Pilgrims 159
Plato 17–19, 27, 29, 31, 33, 77, 106, 148, 166, 169f., 201f., 205f., 209, 211, 221, 247–50, 253
platonic 19, 86, 134, 158f., 161, 211f., 223, 248, 257, 259
Platonic Academy of Florence 26
platonism 26, 38, 113, 201ff., 212f., 214, 248f.
platonists 210f., 224, 226–28, 232, 234
Pletho 27
Plotinus 19, 23f., 31, 77, 204f., 221
politics 104, 107f.
Pope, Alexander 243
Poverty 153f., 175
power 104
Powicke, F. J. 205, 226, 233
Powritans 220
practical reason 248
prayer 114, 177, 181, 184f.
preacher 231
preaching 182f.
Predestination 46, 65, 81
Presbyterians 43
pride 126f.
priesthood 135
Prime Mover 75
probability 173, 244
probation-state of man 96

professional knowledge 111f.
Protestant 177
Proverbs 205
Provost 5, 7–9, 49
prudence 120
Psalms 205
psychology
punishment 79, 101, 103, 141, 145, 163
Purgatory 174
Puritan 7, 10, 15, 41–46, 97, 178f., 198, 206, 213, 216, 251, 262
Puritanism 65, 209, 218, 220, 227f., 230–233
purity 152
Pythagoras 221
Pythagoreans 18, 29

Q

Quakerism 230–32, 251
Quakers 37

R

rational 180; theologians 117, 256
rationalism 230, 246, 258, 260
rationalists 227, 236, 238
Raven, C. E., 201ff., 205, 207, 210, 251, 256, 257f.
Ray, John 201
reason 51, 59, 66f., 81–84, 95, 101–102, 111, 116–19, 121, 127f., 130, 146, 149, 155, 178, 194, 197f., 222, 227, 229f., 236f., 241, 247–50, 258–61
reason in things 102, 105, 131
Reconciler 136
reconciliation 60–64, 137f., 143f., 157, 190
Redeemer 106, 190, 259
redemption 143, 145, 152, 182, 199
Reformation 30–33, 52, 59, 150, 178, 209
Reformed Faith 178, 184
Reformers 145
regeneration 143f., 160
relation of things 91
religion 67, 181, 193, 196, 224, 229, 236, 243, 245, 249
religion of after-revelation 261
religion of creation 197, 199
religion of first-inscription 66
religious consciousness 79
religious experience 221, 224
religious knowledge 144
religious liberty 191, 237
religious tolerance 247
Renaissance 83, 213, 221, 223, 261
repentance 79, 103, 141f., 165
Restoration 6f., 40, 213, 226
resurrection 169f.
revealed religion 66, 228
revealed theology 116

revealed truth 116f.
revelation 70f., 116–18, 121f., 125, 155, 188, 227, 238, 240f., 261
reverence for life 105
rightousness 77, 79, 138, 145–47
rites 180
ritualism 181
Robinson, J. A. T. 169
Roman Catholic 145
Romanists 35, 37, 41, 153, 171f., 174, 176, 226
Romans 205
Rousseau, Jean-Jacques 93
Royalist 7
Royce, Josiah 250

S

sacrafice 137
Sacraments 179, 181, 183, 185f., 192, 198f.
st. Anne 11
st. Lawrence Jewry 11f., 227, 233
st. Thomas 206
Salonika, Isidore of 27
Salvation 81, 120, 122, 140f., 143, 160, 164, 189, 193, 241, 251–53, 262
Sanctification 143, 145
satisfaction 136–38, 145
save 134
saving knowledge 121f., 140, 142, 146, 148, 196, 229
saving truth 193f.
Savior 132f., 137, 139, 160, 177, 186
scepticism 33
Scholastics 206
Schoomen 20
Schweitzer 105
science 219
Scotus, Duns 30
Scripture 22, 32, 46f., 49–53, 58f., 65, 71, 81, 84, 99, 118f., 135, 143, 145, 148, 155, 165, 176–78, 180f., 185–17, 192–95, 197f., 219, 222, 228f., 231f., 237, 244, 246
Second Adam 137
second causes 87, 96
sectarian 179, 198, 227
Sectaries 216, 251, 262
Seekers 37
self 158f.
self-concern 153
self-condemnation 129f., 164
self-control 151
self-denial 150
self-enjoyment 88
self-evident 72
self-giving 164
self-humiliation 137
self-interest 151
selfishness 94

self-love 151, 245
self-surrender 150, 160
sense 84, 248
sensuality 126f.
sermon 228, 240–42
servant 150
Shaftesbury, Third Earl of 13, 241–45, 256
Sherman, John 206, 207
sin 79, 81, 85, 123, 125–32, 137, 142, 145–48, 151, 162, 164, 168, 184
sinner 81, 123, 130, 134, 141
Slater, Samuel 2
Smith, John 2, 112f., 180, 188, 203, 210–13, 223, 247, 252
sobriety 99, 104
sociability 94
social consciousness 262; justice 99, 104; order 109; responsibility 102; sins 131f.
society 108
Socinian 34, 228
Socrates 12, 17, 18, 29, 166, 190, 209, 216
Son of God 137
Sophists 18
Soteriology 132
soul 17, 19, 29, 68, 86–88, 113, 162, 211, 214
speech 109f.
Spinoza, Benedict 240
spirit 120f., 151, 155f., 180f., 229–32; spiritual 67; spiritual life 211f.
state 237, 251
Stephens, Leslie 239f.
Stillingfleet, Edward 12, 40, 191, 227f.
Stoicism 20, 106
Stuarts 36
substances 69
Summum Bonum 28, 113
supernatural 67, 179
super-rational 135
superstition 227
Sykes, Norman 232
sympathy 94

T

Taylor, A. E. 17
Taylor, Jeremy 40, 178, 191
temperance 99
Temple, William 253
Tennant, F. R. 128
Theologia Platonica 29
theurgy 221
Tillich, Paul 58, 83, 131
Tillotson, John 11f., 14, 196, 226–29, 232f., 238
Timaeus 23, 26
time 156f.
Titus, Harold 93
Toland, John 239
tolerance 221

toleration 230, 237
Torrance, T. F. 124
total depravity 258
tradition 177
transcendent 83
Transubstantiation 173
Traversagni, Lorenzo 31
treasure of grace 175
Trinity Church 236
Trismegistus 23, 221
Truth 68, 77, 92, 95, 110, 177, 196
truthfulness 137
truth of after-revelation 117, 229
truth of first-inscription 68, 70, 117, 229
Tuckney, Anthony 15, 35, 43–47, 49, 55–57, 60–64, 161, 201, 246, 258
Tulloch, John 16, 211
Tyndale, William 32, 33

U

understanding 95, 248f.
union 89
unity 28
unity-in-diversity 195f.
universal acceptance 70; acknowledgement 70f.
University of Cambridge 209
University Preacher 221
unnatural 99
unrighteousness 148
utilitarianism 249

V

Valla, Lorenzo 33
Vanists 37
vicarius suffering 138
vice 124f.
Vice-Chancellor 49 **
virtue 97f., 151, 167, 242
vocation 143

W

War 94
wealth 153
Webb, C. C. J. 80, 117
Westcott, B. F. 252f., 262f.
Westminster Confession 45f., 48, 53, 213
Whale, J. S. 125f., 131, 138, 179
Whichcote, Benjamin 1, 8–10, 15, 20, 30, 34, 39, 46, 49, 60–65, 72, 99, 105–107, 110, 112, 129–135, 138, 143, 146, 148, 150, 157, 161, 172, 188f., 194, 198f., 208f., 210–212, 214, 218f., 222f., 241f., 243f., 247, 254, 256f., 260; Writings in Appendix 267–273
Whichcote, Christopher 1
Whichcote, Jeremy 13

Wilkins, Bishop of Chester 11, 228
will 95, 102, 141, 249f.
wisdom 144
Wisdom Literature 205
Wisdom of Solomon 205
Word 155

worship 79, 113, 177ff., 180f., 184, 190
Worthington, John 2, 210

                    X

Xenophon 17

DATE DUE

NO 2 8 72			
FE 1 2'81			
GAYLORD			PRINTED IN U.S.A.